MR CHURCHILL'S PRO...

PETER CLARKE was formerly a professor of m... ...
and Master of Trinity Hall at Cambridge. His ma.., ..ooks
include *Keynes: The Twentieth Century's Most Influential Economist*,
The Last Thousand Days of the British Empire, *The Keynesian
Revolution in the Making, 1924–1936*, and the acclaimed final
volume of the Penguin History of Britain, *Hope and Glory:
Britain 1900–2000*. He lives with his wife, the Canadian writer
Maria Tippett, in Cambridge, England, and Pender Island,
British Columbia.

MR CHURCHILL'S PROFESSION

Statesman, Orator, Writer

Peter Clarke

B L O O M S B U R Y
LONDON · NEW DELHI · NEW YORK · SYDNEY

First published in Great Britain 2012
This paperback edition published 2013

Copyright © 2012 by Peter Clarke

Extracts from the works of William Churchill are reproduced with
the permission of Curtis Brown, London, on behalf of the Estate of
Sir William Churchill. Copyright © William S. Churchill

The moral right of the author has been asserted

No part of this book may be used or reproduced in any manner whatsoever
without written permission from the Publisher except in the case
of brief quotations embodied in critical articles or reviews

Every reasonable effort has been made to trace copyright holders of material
reproduced in this book, but if any have been inadvertently overlooked
the publishers would be glad to hear from them. For legal purposes the
acknowledgements on page 333 constitutes an extension of the copyright page

Bloomsbury Publishing Plc
50 Bedford Square
London
WC1B 3DP

www.bloomsbury.com

Bloomsbury Publishing, London, New Delhi, New York and Sydney

A CIP catalogue record for this book is available from the British Library

ISBN 978 1 4088 3123 6

10 9 8 7 6 5 4 3 2 1

Typeset by Hewer Text UK Ltd, Edinburgh
Printed and bound in Great Britain by CPI Group (UK) Ltd, Croydon CR0 4YY

For Mark and Michael, fifty years on …

Contents

Prologue   IX

PART I
The Two Careers of Winston S. Churchill

1   Father's Boy: Heritage, 1874–97   3
2   Mother's Boy: The Author of his Fortune, 1898–1921   34

PART II
The Author of his Reputation

Entr'acte   73
3   The English-Speaking Peoples Before Churchill   81
4   One Author, Two Contracts, 1922–32   116
5   The Struggle on Two Fronts, 1933–38   152
6   The Historian as Prophet, 1938–39   195
7   The Author of Victory, 1940–45   232
8   The Author as Celebrity, 1945–65   268

Epilogue   290

Appendix: Churchill and the British Tax System   297
Notes   301
Bibliography   317
Acknowledgements   333
Index   337

Prologue

The Nobel Prize for Literature is the world's greatest accolade for an author. The roll call of recipients salutes many of the literary giants of the twentieth century and in turn makes it likely that more will be written about them as authors – books about books, often piling up by the score or by the hundred. There is one notable exception. Rarely can an author's writings have received less attention than those of the winner of the Nobel Prize for Literature in 1953. This particular Nobel laureate's literary achievements have generally received only passing acknowledgement, even though he liked to remind everyone that he had always earned his living by writing. We could call Winston S. Churchill the most famous unknown author of the twentieth century.

This is not because his books were suddenly forgotten after his death in 1965. It is surely because they have long been eclipsed by the author's fame in politics, above all as Britain's wartime prime minister and, alongside Roosevelt and Stalin, as one of the Big Three who reshaped our world in the mid-twentieth century. Churchill's literary career, by contrast, consumed much of his prodigious energy during the four decades before he and Roosevelt met face to face as leaders of their respective countries in August 1941.

In fact, this was not their first meeting. For Franklin D. Roosevelt, who had visited Britain while serving as Assistant Secretary of the Navy (under President Woodrow Wilson) in World War I, certainly remembered meeting Churchill in 1918. It was at a banquet at Gray's Inn, where London barristers meet to dine in the ancient hall; and it is claimed that FDR recollected in later years that he found Churchill 'a stinker' and felt that the British Minister of Munitions was 'lording it all over us'.[1] And what did Churchill recollect? Nothing at all, apparently, as became embarrassingly obvious when the two men next met twenty-three years later, though Churchill made amends in his later volume of memoirs, *The Gathering Storm*, with the brazen claim that, back in 1918, 'I had been struck by his magnificent presence in all his youth and strength.'[2] Thus an embarrassing political lapse was retrospectively amended by the author's well-practised literary artifice.

The name Churchill, it might seem, was simply better known at the time of World War I, whereas the name Roosevelt then usually meant not Franklin but his cousin Theodore, the former president, who died in 1919. The possibilities of confusion, though, are not all on one side. There is an intriguing remark in one of FDR's letters in July 1917: 'I am just back from lunch with Winston Churchill. He saw the President yesterday and apparently had a very satisfactory talk.'[3] No, there had not been an earlier meeting that both men had somehow forgotten. The reference was actually to the American author Winston Churchill: no relation, but, born in 1871, only three years senior to his English namesake. He was to live until 1947. Some of his novels, in their original editions, can still be found in second-hand bookstores, especially in North America – often shelved inadvertently in the history and war section. He did not win the Nobel Prize; this book is not about him; it is a salutary tale of the evanescence of fame.

Part One of this book, 'The Two Careers of Winston S. Churchill', comprises two mainly biographical chapters on his early life. He was first known simply as the son of the late Lord Randolph Churchill, whose brilliant but erratic career as a Tory politician had been cut short, first by his own unforced errors and then by his physical collapse and early death in 1895. Here is the largely political perspective in which his aristocratic heritage is examined in Chapter 1, 'Father's Boy'. Winston's biography of his father (1906), a monument to filial piety, identified the author as the keeper of the Churchill flame – for better or worse. 'I dislike the father and dislike the son' was the reaction of Theodore Roosevelt when he read the book, needlessly adding, 'so I may be prejudiced.'⁴ Perhaps the elder Roosevelt and the younger Churchill, so similar in many superficial ways, were simply too competitive, for public attention and literary recognition alike, to admire each other.

Still in his early twenties, the young Winston had already begun his own literary career. Why and how he did so is the theme of Chapter 2, 'Mother's Boy'. In becoming the author of his fortune, Winston was positively encouraged and supported by his American mother, and even the negative impact upon him of her own financial improvidence worked to the same effect, in spurring him on. He was tireless in capitalising on his family connections and his high profile as a controversial war correspondent, determined to get and keep his name before the public. Two books based on his newspaper assignments were published by the time of the author's twenty-fifth birthday (30 November 1899). Moreover, a third was currently appearing in serial form – a novel entitled *Savrola* – published in *Macmillan's Magazine* between May and December 1899.

This made for a remarkable literary debut. He wrote later in his memoir *My Early Life* (titled *A Roving Commission* in the United States): 'In the Spring of 1899 I became conscious of the fact that there was another Winston Churchill who also wrote books; apparently he wrote novels, and very good novels too, which achieved an enormous circulation in the United States. I received from many quarters congratulations on my skill as a writer of fiction. I thought at first that these were due to a belated appreciation of the merits of *Savrola*.'⁵

Hence the tongue-in-cheek formality of the transatlantic correspondence that ensued: 'Mr Winston Churchill presents his compliments to Mr Winston Churchill, and begs to draw his attention to a matter which concerns them both' – namely that the English Churchill proposed to adopt a formal convention: 'In future, to avoid mistakes as far as possible, Mr Winston Churchill has decided to sign all published articles, stories, or other work, "Winston Spencer Churchill", and not "Winston Churchill" as formerly.' This was all very amicably agreed. It was another good gimmick for publicity. When the two men met in Boston in the following year, it made front-page news in the *Boston Herald*: 'Namesakes Meet: Winston Churchills Fast Friends.'[6] The story is that they were duly introduced by a mutual friend – 'Mr Churchill. Mr Churchill' – and took a walk together on Boston Common, in the course of which the English Winston said to the American Winston: 'Why don't you go into politics? I mean to be Prime Minister of England: it would be a great lark if you were President of the United States at the same time.'[7]

The English Churchill duly fulfilled his ambitions as a statesman – after some delay. Moreover, throughout his literary career the name that graced his long list of publications was either Winston Spencer Churchill or simply Winston S. Churchill. 'The initial S. is added,' his secretary was still routinely explaining in the 1930s, 'because this is Mr Churchill's distinction from the American author of the same name, whose books appear in England.'[8] It would be agreeable to suppose that the American novelist, whenever he happened to see any new volumes in later years, checked that the middle name or initial had duly appeared, in fulfilment of their youthful contract, thus implicitly acknowledging that *he* was the real Winston Churchill.

Like so much Churchilliana, however, this story seems to have been improved in the telling. A glance at the original editions of his early books will confirm that the English author's name is already given on the title page as Winston Spencer Churchill. Legally, indeed, his family surname was Spencer-Churchill, and had been for over half a century before his own birth. This is the name he answered to at school; he complained unavailingly about his low position in the alphabetical roll call, under 'S' rather than 'C'. Even *Liberalism and the Social Problem* (1909) – the first of many volumes of political speeches – carries on the title page the full name Winston Spencer Churchill. Possibly he later opted for his middle initial rather than the full form to avoid any impression that he was adopting a hyphenated name in his political career: the more so since his father had made a famous gibe against upstarts who used double-barrelled names. For in politics Winston was never known as anything but simply Churchill – like his father before him.

It is this career, treading in his father's footsteps in politics, for which Winston S. Churchill is remembered. Not only did he eventually become prime minister but he did so at the most critical moment in his country's history, charged with resisting the relentless Nazi surge through Europe. Thus in May 1940 he faced nothing less than a crisis of national survival. It was, however, one for which he sensed himself peculiarly prepared, as shown implicitly by his demeanour at the time and explicitly by what he later wrote in *The Gathering Storm*: 'I felt as if I were walking with destiny, and that all my past life had been but a preparation for this hour and for this trial.'[9]

These well-known words have usually been interpreted solely with reference to his political career. True, he already had long and varied political experience: entry to the House of Commons at the age of twenty-five, cabinet minister in a Liberal government by the time he was thirty-three, recall to the Lloyd George coalition as Minister of Munitions, five years as Chancellor of the Exchequer in a Conservative government when he was in his early fifties, a return to office at the outbreak of war in 1939 in the same office (First Lord of the Admiralty) that he had held at the outbreak of war in 1914. Hence the sense of inevitability and the legendary message sent to the ships of the Royal Navy: 'Winston is back.' Moreover, the vicissitudes of Churchill's political career, which had seemed terminally blighted in the 1930s, supplied him with a wartime alibi – a clean record of opposition to the policies that had resulted in Hitler's string of triumphs by 1940. The shaping of Churchill's political career indeed seemed providential in retrospect. What is less appreciated is that Churchill's life saw him walking with destiny in another sense, in his parallel career.

*   *   *

Mr Churchill's profession was as an author. This is a story that needs telling with sufficient focus to do it justice. Hence the more detailed narrative in Part Two, 'The Author of his Reputation', which, for the first time, fully explores his commitment to writing and his financial dependence on it – something that Churchill himself always acknowledged. 'After all, I am a member of your profession,' he assured one editor in 1945. 'I've never had any money except what my pen has brought me.'[10]

Admittedly, many politicians write their memoirs, not least for money. Churchill did so more than once. His memoirs of World War I, published under the title *The World Crisis*, ran to five volumes. The book was tellingly described by Arthur Balfour, a colleague who knew him well, as 'Winston's brilliant Autobiography, disguised as a history of the universe'.[11] Churchill's later set of war memoirs, *The Second World War*, was to run to six volumes with a similarly expansive ambit: at once an extraordinary achievement in making sense of the course of the hostilities, on all fronts worldwide, while all the time providing a highly personal viewpoint – and, of course, vindication. He remained confident of the verdict of history, as he is recorded as saying at the time, 'because he intends to be one of the historians'.[12] Between the wars he had published *My Early Life* (London, 1930) with well-deserved acclaim for its evocative qualities and its nicely distanced irony in exposition. It crossed the Atlantic as *A Roving Commission* (New York, 1930), though its publisher, Charles Scribner, felt disappointed that, until 1939 at least, it failed to achieve the American sales that it merited.

But Churchill's literary output went far beyond this, in range and scope and quality alike. The authorised edition of his Collected Works runs to thirty-four volumes. The oeuvre is formidable even if we discount a dozen volumes of memoirs, and also his false start as a novelist, and likewise books essentially republishing his journalism. The eight volumes of his great speeches from 1936 to 1945 stand in a unique position, as we shall see later. Memoirs, speeches and journalism aside, Churchill was the author of two major biographies: the double-volume work of his youth, *Lord Randolph Churchill* (1906), and the four volumes – six in Scribner's original American edition – on the first Duke of Marlborough (1933–38). Churchill ultimately became more widely known as the author of *A History of the English-Speaking Peoples*, published in four volumes in 1956–58, with enormous success on both sides of the Atlantic. It is a book with a special position in his oeuvre, but its authorship has been little studied.

Why Churchill chose to write on the English-speaking peoples came to seem blatantly obvious, not least to himself. Indeed in 1963 he was to become an honorary citizen of the United States of America. Everyone saw it as fitting that a man already laden with so many tributes should nonetheless have received from President Kennedy this particular recognition. Churchill was now too infirm to attend the ceremony at the White House, but an appropriate message was sent: 'Mr President, your action illuminates the theme of unity of the English-speaking peoples to which I have devoted a large part of my life.'[13]

Yet, in a literal sense, this was only a half-truth. Churchill at nearly ninety could certainly have looked back over half his lifetime – to an auspicious occasion, forty-five years earlier, on American Independence Day, 4 July 1918. It was then that he gave a widely reported speech to an Anglo-American rally at the Albert Hall in London. 'The Declaration of Independence is not only an American document,' Churchill declared. 'It follows on the Magna Charta [*sic*] and the Bill of Rights as the third great title-deed on which the liberties of the English-speaking people are founded.' This was the key passage in his speech, reported as such in *The New York Times* the next day.

This public meeting in 1918 marked the public launch of the English-Speaking Union, of which Churchill was to serve a term as president a few years later. It was not the only Anglo-American organisation active in this era but it quickly became the most prominent, with branches proliferating in both countries. Franklin D. Roosevelt seems to have been an early member. The ESU absorbed a previous body called the Atlantic Union, founded in 1899, at the time of the Spanish-American War, supporting American claims over Cuba. The Pilgrims Society, founded in 1902, late in the South African War, correspondingly offered support of the British side. This was essentially a dining club hosting distinguished Anglo-American visitors, initially sponsored by prominent members of the military in both countries.

The South African connection was significant, for it was the hub of British imperialist activity at the turn of the century. It was there that Lord Milner had occupied a pro-consular role, recruiting a talented group of disciples as his 'Kindergarten' in pursuit of a common vision of Empire; and it was there that the plan for the Rhodes scholarships at Oxford University had originated. These recruited able students from the United States as well as the British Empire, many of them going on to prestigious careers on their return home. The scholarships thus fulfilled the vision of Cecil Rhodes, who had died in 1902, leaving the terms of his extraordinary last will and testament to fuel 'the union of the English-speaking peoples throughout the world'.[14] Lord Rosebery, a former prime minister and family friend of the Churchills, chaired the Rhodes Trust for its first fifteen years, to be succeeded in 1917 by its real helmsman, Milner, by this time a cabinet colleague of Winston Churchill.

Because institutional and personal ties of this kind are easy to sketch out, a pattern of elite manipulation has sometimes been alleged. Some people point, with intermingled disdain and suspicion, to the emergence of an 'Anglo-American establishment'. Undeniably, there remains a reasonable and widespread assumption that the concept of the English-speaking peoples originated in socially privileged, politically conservative and generally establishment-minded circles; and that it subsequently achieved its peak of influence in the Churchill-Roosevelt era spanning World War II.

But how much of this is actually true? Part Two poses this question in Chapter 3, which documents a rather different pedigree for the concept of the English-speaking peoples. The fact that it emerged from the political left rather than the right, and did so much earlier than we might suppose, may come as a surprise but is surely significant. Moreover, there was a long-standing tension between professed Anglo-American ideals of democratic self-government and the maintenance of the British Empire. To many Americans, these were irreconcilable commitments; yet Churchill claimed to be committed to both. The senses in which he was, and was not, an imperialist need more scrutiny in this context, linking themes that were central to his career from the 1890s to the 1940s.

Churchill had many talents and many interests. Thus he called painting a pastime: one that he enjoyed, working hard to perfect his technique, but without any illusion about his lack of professional status or about the intrinsic value of his own paintings, which he would proudly exhibit and sometimes donate to favoured individuals and institutions, but not offer for sale in the art market. Writing, by contrast, was his profession. Already in the 1920s, while he was in cabinet office more often than not, the pursuit of literary contracts was necessary to support his family and their country house at Chartwell, Kent, in the style that an aristocrat thought fitting. We remember Churchill as a world statesman but sometimes also need to remember how the bills were paid at home. The result was to create an overload in his commitments, on which Chapter 4, 'One Author, Two Contracts', uses Churchill's own archive to throw some revealing light.

The pattern of his life changed after 1929 because he was excluded from government office until 1939. During these 'wilderness years', he retreated more often to Chartwell, partly through choice but also through necessity, since it became his 'word factory'. At this time, his parliamentary salary – his earnings as a professional politician – accounted for about 2.5 per cent of his income, compared with literary earnings no less than thirty times greater. Moreoever, it is not just an accountant's view that Churchill's profession was as an author. He regarded himself as a professional writer, and was simultaneously engaged in juggling the competing claims of his literary projects, especially the two big books he had taken on: his biography, *Marlborough*, and his *History of the English-Speaking Peoples*. This is why Chapter 5 is called 'The Struggle on Two Fronts'.

It is closely interconnected with Chapter 6, 'The Historian as Prophet', which examines the making of the *History* as a feat of authorship. The fact that the publication of this work was delayed by almost two decades, and that it later underwent a process of revision by other hands, has masked two crucial facts: that Churchill composed almost all of the original text himself, and that he did so in 1938–39. It is not just hindsight to perceive that these were years that foreshadowed the coming war. Churchill talked as early as 1936 of a 'gathering storm', a phrase later appropriated as the title of the first volume of *The Second World War*. The pages of the *History* are infused with a sense of an impending conflict in which the common destiny of the English-speaking peoples would be put to the test.

Churchill had to put the *History* aside for the duration of World War II, despite all his pre-war efforts to finish it. 'I knew the war was coming,' he subsequently explained to one of his research assistants in 1947, 'and I knew that I should be called to high office, but I also knew that I could only lead the people of our country if I understood how they felt and behaved, so I determined to steep myself in their history.'[15] This claim, like his political claim to have been walking with destiny, cries out for critical scrutiny. But if not the literal truth, it may embody a sort of literary truth, as Chapter 7, 'The Author of Victory', will suggest in examining Churchill's wartime leadership and oratory in the context of his other career.

When this *History* finally appeared, in four substantial volumes (1956–58), it met with enormous success on both sides of the Atlantic, for reasons explored in Chapter 8, 'The Author as Celebrity'. And clearly politics is an inescapable part of the explanation. For Churchill's concept of the English-speaking peoples has a resonance beyond the writing of two thousand years of history. It has also informed the making of history throughout the second half of the twentieth century. The idea was influentially developed in the post-war period in Churchill's famous speech at Fulton, Missouri, in March 1946, when he talked of a 'special relationship' between the United States and Great Britain. Moreover, far from disappearing when Churchill made his own political exit in 1955, the 'special relationship', for which he had pleaded, continued to carry significant political freight through subsequent decades, under Harold Macmillan and Dwight Eisenhower, Margaret Thatcher and Ronald Reagan – right down to the era of Tony Blair and George W. Bush, and beyond.

Churchill has been dead for nearly half a century, during which time his name and his words have often been invoked for rhetorical effect, without paying much attention to context. The origin of the concept of the English-speaking peoples is itself an instructive story, warning us not to assume too much about the provenance of ideas that were only later put to very different ideological uses. The year 1940 indeed remains his great historical moment – a moment when Churchill's two careers opportunely converged, each providing its own kind of 'preparation for this hour and for this trial'.

PART I

The Two Careers of Winston S. Churchill

Father's Boy: Heritage, 1874–97

'He has a great talent for show off exaggeration and make believe.'
Lord Randolph Churchill on his son Winston, 1893.

It is impossible to understand the political career of Winston Churchill without giving attention to his father. The latter was styled Lord Randolph Churchill, a courtesy title since he was the younger son of a duke. But this aristocratic lineage was no impediment to his seeking a political career in the House of Commons – quite the reverse, for the father as for the son in due course. In Winston's own account, the Churchills, though often wracked by family quarrels, placed great emphasis upon close relations between fathers and sons – 'both Lord Randolph and his elder brother, throughout lives strongly marked by an attitude of challenge towards men and things, preserved at all times an old-world reverence for their father'.[1] Winston himself duly perpetuated the old-world reverence but got nothing back, craving a kind of supportive intimacy and mutual understanding that his father was unable or unwilling to give.

Lord Randolph, always more of a taker than a giver, had been luckier. He evidently received paternal indulgence of his own transgressions, whether being impertinent to his schoolteachers or breaking other people's windows; and for Lord Randolph this was simply the beginning of a lifelong habit. At fourteen he was writing from school at Eton to tell his father of how he and other boys had 'knocked down' the policemen who were seeking to protect the newly wed Prince and Princess of Wales in nearby Windsor: 'There was a chain put across the road, but we broke that; several old *genteel* ladies tried to stop me, but I snapped my fingers in their face and cried "Hurrah!" and "What larks!"' Indeed he was described by a fellow Etonian as 'very fond of collisions with "cads"'. Winston is our source for such anecdotes, and also for a comment that is all too revealing: 'Nothing will change him much. Lord Randolph's letters as a boy are his letters as a man.'[2]

Winston's letters as a boy tell their own story. As a neglected pupil, sent away just before his eighth birthday to an appalling boarding school at Ascot, he writes home (perhaps under supervision): 'My dear Papa, I am very happy at school.' Only after two school years have passed do the parents notice that something is amiss and Winston is sent to a relatively more humane establishment in Brighton, where he languishes unvisited. To 'darling Mama' he has to point out that if she gives priority to her dinner party in London, she will obviously have to default on attendance at a school play, for which Winston pleads in vain. And to 'dear Papa' there is the bleak reproach: 'You never came to see me on Sunday when you were in Brighton.'[3] Winston's devoted nanny, Mrs Everest, watched the boy growing up, apparently with a warmer concern for furthering his prospects than in protecting her own interests from the Churchill family's shabby treatment that she was to receive at the end of her life.

Instead of resenting the callous neglect of his hedonistic parents, Winston idolised them, his father especially. Winston had been eleven years old when Lord Randolph reached the peak of his political career. In August 1886, aged only thirty-seven, he ascended to the post of Chancellor of the Exchequer, the office in which his great Liberal opponent Gladstone had made his own reputation thirty years previously by turning the Treasury into the powerhouse of British government. But whereas Gladstone had seized his chance, fashioning a series of famous budgets, establishing canons of sound public finance that became hallowed throughout the British Empire and beyond, and duly rising to become prime minister four times, Lord Randolph muffed it. By the time of Winston's twelfth birthday at the end of November, his father was already restive in the new Conservative cabinet and before the end of the year he had resigned, before even presenting his first budget.

He never came back. The meteoric career was over. By 1895 he was dead. The ceremonial Chancellor's robes – 'those imposing and expensive robes which seem to assert the opulence which should result from thrift, rather than thrift itself', as Winston described them – were worn on only one formal occasion and subsequently 'kept in tissue paper and camphor' by Lady Randolph until her own death in 1921, when they passed to her son.[4] Thus in 1924 Winston had the satisfaction of bringing the opulent robes out of storage when he fulfilled the ambition of himself becoming Chancellor. He stayed to present five budgets; he did not resign; he served more than twice as long as any of the seven Chancellors who preceded him; the tissue paper was at last thrown away and the smell of camphor was left to evaporate.

There is, of course, no problem in explaining why any of the Churchills went into politics. It was the family business. Winston was born in 1874 at Blenheim Palace, the truly palatial home of the Dukes of Marlborough. His grandfather, John Winston Spencer-Churchill, was the 7th Duke, and had sat in the House of Commons as Marquis of Blandford, the courtesy title of the heir to the dukedom. In the *Oxford Dictionary of National Biography* he is categorised as 'politician', as is the 6th Duke, the 5th Duke, the 4th Duke and the 3rd Duke (there was no 2nd Duke). To describe the 1st Duke of Marlborough, John Churchill (1650–1722), as 'politician and army officer' risks understatement. He was renowned throughout Europe, on a scale later termed Napoleonic, as the victor of the Battles of Ramillies, Oudenarde, Malplaquet and, of course, Blenheim, which saved Vienna from the French and the Bavarians in 1704 and gave its name to the vast stately home erected in rural Oxfordshire. This was provided to the victorious hero under an Act of Parliament of 1706, at public expense, along with a perpetual pension of £5,000 per annum.

The father of the first Duke had borne the name Sir Winston Churchill (*c.* 1620–1688). This was a source of family pride to his namesake, who later wrote about him at some length in the first volume of his *Marlborough* and even gave him a walk-on part towards the end of the second volume of *A History of the English-Speaking*

Peoples, quoting with approval the seventeenth-century Sir Winston's prescient vision of Britain's horizons 'extending to those far-distant regions, now become a part of us and growing apace to be the bigger part, in the sunburnt America'.[5] The first Sir Winston's own attempt at authorship, in a work 'still widely extant and universally unread', is treated with evident sympathy, as is his genealogical reconstruction of the Churchill family tree, apparently later cited with respect by Sir Francis Galton whose name became notorious, in the light of twentieth-century adaptations of his doctrines, as the founder of 'eugenics'.[6] Winston Spencer Churchill plainly liked to cultivate the sense that, as the bearer of a famous name, he strode into the twentieth century as the representative of an unbroken line of Churchills.

This is not strictly true. The reasons are implicit in his own full name and due to the fact that there was no 2nd Duke of Marlborough. John Churchill and his Duchess, the redoubtable Sarah, had no surviving male heirs, and special provision was made for the title (and the perpetual pension) to pass through their daughters. Thus on Duke John's death in 1722, his daughter Henrietta, Lady Godolphin, succeeded to the Marlborough title, though estranged from her mother Sarah who sat out much of her twenty-two-year widowhood at Blenheim, completing its construction. Moreover, since Henrietta's son predeceased her, the title passed to a son of a younger daughter of the Marlboroughs, who had married into the Spencers, Earls of Sunderland. (The Spencers are the ancestors of the late twentieth-century Lady Diana and hence of Prince William, the present Duke of Cambridge, who is thus also a direct descendant of Duke John.) The result was that it was one branch of the Spencers who took the Marlborough title and Blenheim Palace – not forgetting the pension.

During most of the century and a half that separates the death of the most famous Duke of Marlborough from the birth of his most famous descendant, the heirs to Blenheim were not called Churchill at all. They had naturally used the family name Spencer and their eldest sons had taken, as their courtesy title, the style Earl of

Sunderland. Only in 1817 was the Churchill connection reinvented. The family name was changed by Royal Licence to Spencer-Churchill and the courtesy title Marquis of Blandford was likewise revived. Thus the Churchill blood coursing through their veins was duly legitimated and the ancient pride of the family in its great ancestor was reaffirmed. Or so the story goes.

Genealogy, of course, is roughly one part 'genes' to ten parts 'alogy'. Those who attach great significance to it, among whom many members of the Churchill family can be numbered, might reflect that a lot depends on the forceful impression made by the convention that nomenclature follows the male line. Hence the Spencers' initial opportunity; hence too, perhaps, their later opportunism in 1817. For in an era when reformers were casting a sceptical eye upon the survival of the 'dead hand' in determining property rights and calling the civil list of government expenditure 'Old Corruption', a perpetual pension, as big as the prime minister's salary, which had now passed into a family called Spencer, might seem anomalous and potentially vulnerable. It is likewise possible that, but for this Royal Licence, the British Empire would have faced its finest hour led by a Mr Spencer. Conversely, Galton or no Galton, the genetic endowment that the later war leader shared with his notable predecessor, spanning some eight generations, would be well under 1 per cent – and at such trace levels Prince William too has some claim to Churchill blood.

But this is not how the author of *Marlborough* looked at the matter, nor the author of *Lord Randolph Churchill*. In two of his most solidly constructed works, drawing in a thoroughly professional way upon original historical documents, and taking him years to complete, Winston Spencer Churchill was painstakingly asserting his family's pedigree and claiming his heritage.

He was patently a child of his own aristocratic upbringing. This showed even in his radical moments. He told his mother as early as 1897 that he was in favour of the payment of MPs. 'Payment of members (on request)' was how he put it.[7] The implication was that no gentleman would actually make such a request. Payment of parliamentary salaries to MPs was to be introduced in 1911, under pressure from the Labour Party, by a Liberal government in which Winston was currently Home Secretary. The new salary of £400 a year was princely by working-class standards, niggardly by the standards of Winston's own class, hardly likely to alter his lifestyle either way; but he was in any case disqualified from receiving it while holding cabinet office. His ministerial salary of £5,000 a year was another matter. As Lord Randolph had told his wife, when pondering the prospect of a cabinet post in 1886: 'It seems to me we want the 5000 *l.* a year badly.'[8] Politics was an expensive profession to enter in those days and his lifelong problem, as his son Winston well appreciated, was shortage of cash.

At first it seemed that Lord Randolph had solved the problem with his brilliant marriage to Jennie Jerome in April 1874. She was just twenty, the daughter of Leonard Jerome of New York, who had made a fortune on Wall Street. She was no stranger to Europe. Her father had served briefly as American consul in Trieste. At thirteen Jennie went to live in Paris with her mother, initially leaving her errant father in New York, though he rejoined his family later. It was while living in Paris that Jennie met Randolph, at the fashionable Cowes Royal Regatta. She was subsequently to recruit English husbands for her two surviving sisters, whose own families grew up alongside her own two boys, Winston and Jack.

The anglicised, expatriate Jennie was by birth American, if not quite as American as Winston sometimes found it useful to make out. When he accepted the invitation to address a joint session of Congress on 26 December 1941, less than three weeks after Pearl Harbor brought the United States into the war, his opening remarks seem preordained. 'The fact that my American forebears have for so many generations played their part in the life of the United States,' he duly began, 'and that here I am, an Englishman, welcomed in your midst, makes the experience one of the most moving and thrilling in my life, which is already long and has not been entirely uneventful.' Then the elevated wish, that his mother ('whose memory I cherish across the vale of years') could have lived to see it, was deployed nicely to set up a characteristic Churchillian descent from straight-faced piety to streetwise wisecrack: 'if my father had been American and my mother British, instead of the other way round, I might have got here on my own'. But Churchill's Anglo-American parentage explains only so much. It may help explain why he first visited the United States (very briefly, in transit to Cuba) just before his twenty-first birthday in 1895 – 'This is a very great country my dear Jack,' he assured his younger brother.[9] It may be one part of the explanation for why he did so again five years later, but hardly the main reason. For on leaving the United Sates on 1 February 1901, having pocketed the dollars he came to earn by public lectures, Churchill then steered clear of America throughout nearly three decades, great country and dear mother's memory notwithstanding.

Dollars were much prized by the Churchills. Lord Randolph was admittedly the son of a duke, but only a younger son. And Disraeli's suspicion that the 7th Duke of Marlborough was 'not rich for a Duke' had been confirmed by the sale of the Marlborough gems in 1875. Then the great library was sold, and also the Blenheim enamels. Moreover, the 8th Duke, Lord Randolph's elder brother, on succeeding to the title in 1883, was promptly back in the market offering the best of the Blenheim pictures, Raphaels and Van Dycks alike; and then in 1888 he too married an American heiress ('Duchess Lily'). Like his brother, he was fated to die young, succeeded as 9th Duke in 1892 by his son (and Winston's cousin), called 'Sunny' as a diminutive of his subsidiary title as Earl of Sunderland. Three years later Sunny duly married another New York heiress, Consuelo Vanderbilt. The birth of their own son in 1897 meant that he rather than Winston would later become the 10th Duke of Marlborough.

The love match between Winston's parents needs to be seen in this context. A great name and a great heritage generated expectations rather than income for the cadet branch of the family. Little wonder that the 7th Duke, on hearing of Randolph's plans, took such a keen interest in the proposed marriage settlement. Leonard Jerome's speciality in investments was selling short – high risk but immensely profitable while it worked. He liked to talk about how many thousands of dollars he had made on a good day; but not every day on Wall Street was a good day, of course. He had been reunited with his family in Paris after 1870 mainly because he needed to keep one step ahead of a market that had suddenly turned sour on him. But although his investments popped down at just the time that Lord Randolph popped up, Leonard settled £2,000 a year on Jennie – say a hundred and fifty thousand at today's values – at a time when the exchange rate was nearly five dollars to a pound.

A good income, then? Not in the hands of the happy couple, for the extravagance of the new Lady Randolph Churchill even exceeded that of Lord Randolph himself. She was a social asset to him, a political asset in his meteoric career, but a financial liability in her own right. Winston's parents first lived in what he describes as a small house in Curzon Street, Mayfair, where even small houses do not come cheap, and they moved a few months later to a larger house, with an imposing entrance and a grand staircase, in nearby Charles Street, 'where they continued their gay life on a somewhat more generous scale than their income warranted'.[10] After a brief Irish exile, they had another fashionable house in St James's Place, off Piccadilly, and then one in Connaught Place, overlooking Hyde Park. Here they stayed for nearly ten years, before having to move in, for reasons of economy, with Lord Randolph's widowed mother, 'Duchess Fanny' in Grosvenor Square, Mayfair.

They were thus a glamorous couple. Even Lord Randolph's apprehensions that his life would be short only led him to increase rather than diminish the pace. He latterly became one of the country's leading owners of racehorses, and was lucky with one horse, which, having won ten thousand pounds in prize money, was sold for seven thousand guineas in 1891. But its owner's luck was running out. Trapped in a wild spiral of self-destruction, he became increasingly reckless not only in his politics but in his personal investments.

The new money, American or otherwise, was needed to prop up all the old pretensions; but it was never enough. Lord Randolph's father had, in the 1870s, sold off land to a branch of the Rothschild family, with their vast resources generated in banking. Nathaniel Rothschild, created first Lord Rothschild in 1885, became a close friend of Lord Randolph and an adviser during his brief Chancellorship. 'Natty' Rothschild had financial interests in Burma, which, given the annexation of Upper Burma by Lord Randolph as Secretary of State for India, raised some eyebrows; and Natty was certainly accommodating about his friend's own heady plunge into speculative investments. In fact Lord Randolph's holdings in South African goldfields, at the time of his death in January 1895, were worth about £70,000 (several millions in today's values). It would be naive, however, to conclude that Lord Randolph's will left his widow well provided; the snag was that the overdraft that he had been allowed by Natty to run up at Rothschilds now stood at nearly £67,000.[11]

Such was Winston's inheritance. But he also inherited a great name and, in particular, a great slogan, as he showed himself keenly aware. 'Lord Randolph did not think of himself as a man, but rather as the responsible trustee and agent of Tory Democracy,' was his noble claim when he came to write his father's biography.[12] What did Tory Democracy mean? What did it mean for Winston as biographer? And what substance did it have as Winston's political heritage?

At the gates of Blenheim lay the small borough of Woodstock, which retained its ancient right to its own representation in the House of Commons. Its total population was about seven thousand in 1881, compared with a population at that date in Oldham (the Lancashire cotton town that was to be Winston's first parliamentary constituency) of over 150,000, albeit with two MPs. In Birmingham a population of over 400,000 currently elected three Members, notably including Joseph Chamberlain – the undisputed boss of Birmingham politics, whether he was fighting for the Gladstonian Liberal Party or later against it. The MP for Woodstock from 1874 until the parliamentary borough was abolished in the Reform Act of 1885, which introduced criteria of broadly equal representation by population, was Lord Randolph Churchill.

How had the trustee of Tory Democracy fashioned his own career? It might be supposed that a politician committed to the rule of democracy would have seen the obvious case for giving equal weight to the votes cast in Oldham or Birmingham and would have conceded, with whatever nostalgic sentiments, that little Woodstock was a quaint survival from another era; in short, recognised that in the last quarter of the nineteenth century the game was up. Not so Lord Randolph. His set-piece spats across the floor of the 1874 parliament with the Radical MP, Sir Charles Dilke (with whom he was in evident collusion), were to give each of them a high profile, with Woodstock as the shuttlecock. In attacking Chamberlain's proposals to take local government out of the hands of the squirearchy, Lord Randolph made a point of insulting Birmingham – 'Brummagem trash' – while offering 'opposition to this most Radical and democratic measure, this crowning desertion of Tory principles . . .'[13] Lord Randolph thus championed the Woodstock system against the cads with an adroit combination of rhetorical excess and reactionary zeal. What larks!

His son obviously knew better than to resist the claims of democracy. His biography of his father makes no bones about exposing the electoral situation: 'after the delivery of the Manor of New Woodstock to John, first Duke of Marlborough, and the building of Blenheim, the seat practically became the property of the Churchills and its representatives were uniformly the nominees of the reigning Duke'.[14] Woodstock had been nothing more than the family's pocket borough. During the nineteenth century, the main changes in its representation came when one or other of the junior Churchills fell out with his brother or his father. Otherwise the principle was that, while the Duke of Marlborough sat in the House of Lords representing the landed interest, his eldest son would sit as Lord Blandford in the House of Commons as MP for Woodstock, representing the interests of the people.

One episode remains particularly instructive. In the era after Waterloo when electoral reform came to the fore, eventually bringing the 1832 Reform Act, the Marquis of Blandford had been, true to form, simultaneously the MP for Woodstock and the heir to the 5th Duke. At this moment of political crisis, he had successfully persuaded his Tory allies to embarrass the Whig sponsors of reform, not only by resisting their modest proposals to extend the franchise but also – counter-intuitively – by supporting a bigger extension of the county franchise. The stratagem worked; the Whigs were caught out; the vote was granted to tenant farmers on short leases, as well as to freeholders. Moreover, as everyone well knew, these farmers were in practice likely to follow their landlords in a deferential manner, especially since there was to be no secret ballot for another forty years. In short, the future 6th Duke showed how a Tory demagogue could dish the Whigs by a selective adoption of some of the rhetoric of populism and trust in the people. He was Lord Randolph's grandfather, not least in a tactical sense.

In 1874 Lord Randolph's claims to the seat were preferred to those of his elder brother, the current Lord Blandford. Their father and their uncle had quarrelled, in the usual way, about the representation of Woodstock. Their father had prevailed in 1865, being the 7th Duke, and had ousted his own brother, instead putting in a Marlborough stooge called Barnett, rightly confident that the electors of Woodstock would truckle, as they did, and were to do again in the election of 1868. Winston's account of the next act, as a further General Election loomed in 1874, is ironically conveyed in *Lord Randolph Churchill*, without serious pretence about the process: 'Mr Barnett now, as it turned out, very conveniently, expressed an earnest wish to relinquish the toils and responsibilities of public life; and the ancient borough, with an imperturbable solemnity and a conservative reverence for the form in which things should be done, was prompt in sending a regular requisition for Lord Randolph's services.'[15]

The author spares us any cant about democracy here. As it happened, Lord Randolph was at that point more interested in getting married – he had fallen for Jennie at Cowes – than in going through the rigma- role of a parliamentary election. But his father held all the cards; his wishes were decisive as to both engagements; and Woodstock served as a stepping-stone to the altar – two perfect matches for the price of one. Randolph happily told Jennie of the enthusiasm for his candida- ture among the farmers – 'They all go as one man.' Little wonder; a landed estate usually voted en bloc. The new factor that threatened to spoil the situation, thanks to Gladstone's Liberal government, was the effect of the Ballot Act. 'People that I think know better than anybody, tell me that it will be very close,' the apprehensive candidate reported to his beloved. 'You see, with the ballot one can tell nothing – one can only trust to promises, and I have no doubt a good many will be broken.'[16] But that was politics all over, as Lord Randolph quickly learned, and in the event his anxieties were allayed by a solid result, to be repeated in subsequent elections in 1880 and 1885. Such, then, was his apprenticeship as a democratic statesman.

'It seems incredible that a man of such uncertain education should have risen to such heights.' This is not a comment on Lord Randolph but on Winston as prime minister, as seen by a perceptive admirer, Margot Asquith, whose husband gave the essentially self-taught prodigy his first cabinet position in 1908. She had first known Winston in the days when, so she said, he had never heard of Robert Louis Stevenson and had thought Blake was an admiral.[17] This cannot be the exact truth; in *My Early Life* there is an appreciative reference to the nine-year-old Winston's relish in reading *Treasure Island*. But he also makes clear his relative lack of achievement at school, somewhat exag- gerating it in retrospect and, above all, avoiding any reproach to Lord

Randolph for lack of encouragement. Yet father and son differed less in native intelligence than in the advantages they were given to develop it early in life. The father was pampered; the son left to remedy his embarrassing ignorance by later becoming an heroically accomplished autodidact.

Lord Randolph's academic education had ended in disappointment, entirely his own fault. The lazy, insouciant Etonian became a lazy, insouciant undergraduate at Oxford. He evidently regarded the place less as a great seat of learning than as a handy outpost for continuing to hunt with the Blenheim Harriers, though at least this made him popular with the farmers among his future constituents. On the basis of this experience, Lord Randolph was to deny his own eldest son – equally wayward, perhaps, but surely equally gifted – the possibility of an (expensive) education at Oxford or Cambridge and to direct him instead into the army class at Harrow School. 'For years I thought my father with his experience and flair had discerned in me the qualities of military genius,' so Winston wrote, with tongue in cheek, in *My Early Life*. 'But I was told later that he had only come to the conclusion that I was not clever enough to go to the Bar.'[18] Not all sons would have been so magnanimous.

Despite himself, Lord Randolph had clearly benefited from his Oxford education. Although he had done little work for his history and law examinations until too late, he revealed an intellectual potential that might otherwise have secured the First Class Honours that he just missed. In particular, he had impressed Mandell Creighton, then his tutor at Merton College, and also Edward Augustus Freeman, one of his examiners: both of them eminent historians in their day. Creighton was a churchman, later a bishop, of conservative temperament, perhaps amenable to the charm of a duke's son; but Freeman was notorious as a democrat and a Gladstonian (as will be seen in Chapter 3), and it was certainly an achievement to win his good opinion. It was Creighton who recognised Lord Randolph's 'marked ability for practical politics early in his career' in that 'he chose his ground of attack, and then took every pains about the form of expression'.[19]

A good memory had been trained by his own reading, choosing for himself what he would read. If Lord Randolph chose the Bible, it was not because he shared the conventional Tory reverence for the Church of England – he was 'indifferent about the Church,' claimed his Oxford friend, Lord Rosebery.[20] But Scripture was to provide an adaptable source of sonorous quotation for the platform. It is hardly surprising that R.S. Surtees's comic character, in *Jorrocks, Jaunts and Jollies*, the hero of the hunting field, should have solaced Lord Randolph; and Edward Gibbon's *The Decline and Fall of the Roman Empire*, though doubtless quoted less often than Jorrocks to the Blenheim Harriers, was to prove as instructive in cynical historical insight as in its 'easy though majestic writing'. Winston was impressed that his father 'could recite in an extraordinary manner whole pages at a time'.[21] Winston followed this example faithfully when he later came to educate himself as an army officer in India, getting his mother to send out the books he needed. 'Fifty pages of Macaulay and twenty-five of Gibbon every day' was how Winston recorded progress. 'There are only 100 of the latter's 4,000 odd left now.' That would make about 160 solid days' reading in all. As he candidly told Lady Randolph, he felt that his remedial efforts were necessary because 'my mind has never received that polish which for instance Oxford or Cambridge gives'.[22]

Plenty of the MPs recruited from Lord Randolph Churchill's privileged class had less aptitude for politics in those undemanding days. In 1874 the new Member for Woodstock joined a House of Commons where there was a majority Conservative government for the first time in nearly thirty years. Disraeli, who had waited so long, was finally prime minister at seventy; Gladstone resigned the Liberal leadership, apparently now retired at the age of sixty-five. But for an ambitious young aristocrat of twenty-six, the anticipated joys of sitting on the government backbenches soon palled – much as Winston was to discover for himself in the 1900 parliament, while writing *Lord Randolph Churchill.* 'The Whips do not want speeches, but votes,' he comments, with fellow feeling. 'The Ministers regard an oration in their praise or defence as only one degree less tiresome than an attack. The earnest party man becomes a silent drudge, tramping at intervals through lobbies to record his vote and wondering why he came to Westminster at all.'[23]

Lord Randolph, however, was not so much an earnest party man as an untamed party animal. He had just married a glamorous heiress; the wedding had been on 15 April 1874; their first child was born on 30 November. Some thought the interval rather short; the family story was that Winston had simply made a precocious entrance into the world. He later offered a candid view of his parents' extravagant and frivolous lifestyle. 'Little else was thought of but enjoyment,' he admits; 'and though the member for Woodstock liked discussing politics and took an intelligent interest in affairs, his attendances at the House were fitful and fleeting.'[24] This was actually very different from Winston's subsequent assiduity in his political ambitions from the moment he entered Parliament: the difference between an amateur who never sustained a proper career and a professional who successfully pursued two.

Democratic commitments are less evident than the social commitments of the aristocratic season. Lord and Lady Randolph were members of a fashionable 'fast set' at the very top of London society. It included Lord Randolph's elder brother, Lord Blandford, and Edward, Prince of Wales. They were known as the Marlborough House set, not because of a direct connection to the Churchills but because Marlborough House, on the Mall, had become a royal residence, currently occupied by the heir to the throne. 'Bertie' (as he was known) was notorious for his sexual liaisons, which had initially dismayed his wife, the Danish beauty Alexandra, Princess of Wales; her own increasing deafness and her selective social blindness helped distance her from embarrassment. They were all very close. It is not clear how close Bertie got to Lady Randolph at this stage. Country-house weekends permitted considerable latitude to all parties, so long as discretion was observed among the clique, and so long as a male heir had been duly delivered. When the prince went off on a visit to India in 1875, with what he regarded as inadequate provision from the public purse, Lord Randolph jumped to support his claim for more money with an alacrity that already cast a shadow over his rising reputation in the eyes of Disraeli, who detected signs of a Marlborough House conspiracy. It was not very clever of Lord Randolph to upset the prime minister; but this was only the beginning of the story.

Like many an opera, the plot is complex, with much of the action behind the scenes. Bertie's companion in India was another mutual friend, Lord Aylesford, who also left his wife behind, and subsequently announced that he intended to sue for divorce because of her conduct in his absence. Here was the Churchill family connection. Lady Aylesford was one of their set; in fact she was currently the mistress of Blandford, who was named by the absent Aylesford as co-respondent; and Blandford wanted to marry her; but since he was already married, he too would need to go to the divorce court – which his father, the Duke of Marlborough (offstage), was determined should not happen to his elder son. So the younger son stepped in to save the situation.

Lord Randolph's ill-managed intervention was the real disaster. He well knew that Lady Aylesford had had a previous affair with Bertie himself. Moreover, Lord Randolph had the letters to prove it. None of this came as news to Alexandra; she was shocked, however, when Lord Randolph came to her with a threat that the letters would be used in court unless the Aylesford divorce case was dropped. It was. Lord Aylesford was induced to back off; Lady Aylesford's good name was saved (at least, for the moment); and Lord Blandford was duly thwarted in his plan to marry her, so there was likewise to be no divorce hearing to besmirch the good name of the Churchills (again, at least for the moment). Lord Randolph's actions have often been represented as a chivalrous, albeit imprudent, defence of his brother;

but actually his lovelorn brother was far from pleased. More important, the prince, lingering on his travels, was livid. Not only did he personally drop Lord and Lady Randolph from his circle; on his return, he took steps to shut them out of London society. Scorned and excluded, they now sat friendless in a smart Mayfair house that they could not really afford.

From this fate they were snatched away to find solace in Ireland. Winston tells of 'a little, long, low, white house with a green verandah and a tiny lawn and garden' where he himself grew up for over three years as a child in Dublin.[25] The one person whom Lord Randolph had pleased in 1876 was his own father; and the duke correspondingly saved the situation by agreeing, albeit reluctantly, to go to troubled Ireland as Lord Lieutenant or Viceroy, with an official residence in the Viceregal Lodge in Dublin. Crucially, he took Lord Randolph with him to Ireland, in effect as his secretary. Goodbye, Piccadilly; farewell, Berkeley Square.

Lord Randolph, always a quick learner, naturally developed a better appreciation of the dynamics of Irish politics. It was exactly the period when the Nationalist challenge was being refocused under the leadership of Charles Stewart Parnell, himself a member of the Protestant elite but imposing himself as the imperious leader of his plebeian Catholic followers. He adopted the slogan of a New Departure, linking agitation in the country with ruthless tactics of parliamentary obstruction to insist on his objective, Irish Home Rule. 'Parnell was a squire,' Winston's *Lord Randolph Churchill* notes admiringly, 'reared upon the land, with all those qualities of pride, mettle and strength which often spring from the hereditary ownership of land.' Here is a clear enough suggestion that his own class possessed leadership qualities that could be projected in a democratic context. It gives an insight into Winston's own overarching interpretation of Lord Randolph's politics and explains a comment on the enforced Irish interlude: 'Without it he might have wasted a dozen years in the frivolous and expensive pursuits of the silly world of fashion; without it he would probably never have developed popular sympathies or the courage to champion democratic causes.'[26]

True, in his years of exile from Mayfair, Lord Randolph picked up some useful notions for his own new departure. He showed his ability to reinvent himself as a populist politician, ready to use the methods that had served Gladstone so well (and were currently ensuring his return to the Liberal leadership). But Lord Randolph would exploit popular politics as a Tory, for Conservative ends. It was not so much the substance or content of his politics that changed as the tactics – extenuating parliamentary obstruction, for example (much to his father's disapproval). And it was, above all, the rhetoric.

All this served him well on re-entering Westminster politics. After 1880, Gladstone was back in politics; the Conservatives were back in opposition; the Duke of Marlborough was back from Ireland. The member for Woodstock, back in his place in the Commons, found new room for manoeuvre, in loose alliance with three other back-benchers in the so-called Fourth Party (the Liberals and Conservatives were already facing a third party in Parnell's Irish Nationalists). The Fourth Party was not, of course, actually a party; the label was simply a parliamentary gibe at the degree of tactical independence that Randolph Churchill and three other Tory backbenchers claimed in their dissatisfaction over the ineffectiveness of the official Leader of the Opposition, Sir Stafford Northcote.

The Bradlaugh case, as everyone acknowledged, was the making of the Fourth Party. Charles Bradlaugh was a radical Liberal, elected for the borough of Northampton – about eight times the size of Wood-stock – in the General Election of 1880, and again in successive by-elections in 1881, 1882 and 1884, made necessary by his repeated ejection from the House. The problem was that, as an atheist, he could not conscientiously subscribe to the religious form of the parliamentary oath and initially wished to make a secular affirmation instead. Gladstone, a High-Church Anglican himself, gave one of his greatest speeches upholding what he saw as an issue of civil and religious liberty as against an outmoded requirement that offered a demoralising incentive for cynical conformity.

When Gladstone sat down, it was Lord Randolph's opportunity. It was he rather than the hapless Northcote who took up the challenge. From the bench where the Fourth Party sat, he called the supporters of atheism 'the residuum, the rabble and the scum of the population; the bulk of them are persons to whom all restraint – religious, moral, or legal – is odious and intolerable'.[27] This served to get Bradlaugh ejected (and then re-elected, and re-ejected, and so on). Winston's *Lord Randolph Churchill* quotes several pages of the speech in the same vein, without, of course, endorsing old Tory sentiments that, after Bradlaugh's ultimate triumph in seeing the House adopt the option of affirmation, had manifestly been discredited by the time his book was published in 1906. But what he never mentions is the Marlborough perpetual pension.

For Bradlaugh had been no single-issue crusader and never gratuitously paraded his atheism on the public platform. Instead he was a republican and secularist: a populist Gladstonian who made financial retrenchment a key issue, with a consequent attack on the survival of antique sinecures and aristocratic handouts. He had therefore produced a pamphlet on the perpetual pensions charged to the civil list, seizing on the fact that the present Duke of Marlborough, with his ample landed estate, was still receiving, after tax, £4,000 a year from the public purse (say, £300,000 in today's terms). Lord Randolph, as ever, had sprung to the defence of his family. 'I shall next Session direct my arguments to his sensitive part,' Bradlaugh promised in 1880. 'I shall menace his pocket.'[28] But, of course, he was much inhibited in doing so when the House, inflamed by Randolph Churchill's pious appeal to the moral majority, refused even to seat the Member for Northampton. This shut him up nicely and made the ongoing Bradlaugh case a means of harassing and embarrassing the Liberal government. But, like father, like son: the family name had to be protected, one way or another, by different methods. Winston often did so by silence and suppression in writing the biography. Aristocratic vested interests, by contrast, were never defended with such noisy populist panache as Lord Randolph displayed in his Fourth Party days.

'The working classes must have leaders,' so a friend told Lord Randolph at a moment when his spirits needed reviving. 'Yes,' was the reply, 'but they will not want aristocrats.'[29] Lord Randolph, though self-consciously an aristocrat, was no run-of-the-mill aristocrat. His son was not wrong to see something special in him, and to think that he could himself learn from his father's example. But filial piety blinded him to crucial limitations. For though Lord Randolph had enough insight to see that the old game was up, he had little idea how to change the game itself. He was undoubtedly quick and clever, with a gift for the right riposte, the cutting remark and the memorable catch-phrase. He stepped outside his aristocratic milieu mainly to exploit the sort of tactics that he saw politicians like Chamberlain and Parnell using with apparent success. Each of them, however, had a clear agenda or programme, to be achieved through legislation.

This Lord Randolph lacked. His real model, in mobilising the idiom of democracy, was really Gladstone himself – forty years older – who had been hailed as 'the People's William' once he had emerged as a popular tribune in the 1860s. Public opinion was to be aroused through great oratory, in pursuit of noble ends, of course: a politics of emotion that did not depend on appeals to material self-interest. Gladstone's strategic aims – ultimately Irish Home Rule – may have had a moral dimension, often infused with a strong respect for nationality. What impressed Lord Randolph more was his tactical and rhetorical mastery.

Hence by the early 1880s, in the Grand Old Man's heyday, Lord Randolph seized his own opportunity. He cultivated the newspapers, notably *The Times*, which he would tip off about political secrets; and would brief it with advance copy for his platform speeches, to be printed verbatim. Whereas the Liberal Gladstone had done the same, the Conservative Disraeli had scarcely made any platform speeches; here was the novelty. Winston, of course, in an era when such practices had become common, was likewise to make sure that his great oratorical efforts were never wasted.

He obviously envied his father's gift for publicity, emulated it too. With his jaunty air and his protruding eyes, 'Randy' became a cartoonist's dream: his waxed moustache as much his insignia as his son's cigar became later. Winston's relish for the sheer theatre and effrontery of his father's career is obvious. Several of the cartoons printed in *Lord Randolph Churchill*, with the simplification inherent in the art, give a devastatingly clear-sighted view of what his father was up to; and Winston, always unabashed in puncturing pomp with a stab of vulgar insight, must surely have appreciated this. One cartoon from *Punch* in 1883 shows Randolph (labelled 'an aggravating Boy') rowing his own boat right into the course of the two rival, disciplined crews that are approaching. He says: 'In the way again! 'ooray!!'[30]

Through sheer effrontery Lord Randolph made himself into a larger-than-life figure who could not be ignored. He did so, moreover, by publicly squaring up to Gladstone himself, as he had first done over the Bradlaugh case; and did so increasingly in a way that drew blood. 'Gentlemen, we live in an age of advertisement, the age of Holloway's pills, of Colman's mustard, and of Horniman's pure tea,' Lord Randolph told a big meeting at Blackpool in 1884, speaking in a brash seaside resort built on similar insights; 'and the policy of lavish advertisement has been so successful in commerce that the Liberal party, with its usual enterprise, has adapted it to politics. The Prime Minister is the greatest living master of the art of personal political advertisement.'[31] This stung Gladstone – because it was true. And it was likewise true that the GOM now faced a brand-name war with a Tory rival.

Lord Randolph became a master of the sound bite *avant la lettre*. 'Ulster will fight, and Ulster will be right', once uttered, defined the struggle over Irish Home Rule. Gladstone found his intervention in Egypt all too memorably characterised as 'a bondholders' war'; and his continued efforts over Home Rule damned as those of 'an old man in a hurry'. Lord Randolph's own slogans, in his son's admiring phrase, 'spread with spirit-speed all over the country'.[32] The point about a sound bite is that it makes its impact without requiring anything so tedious as explanation. Lord Randolph was ready to steal Gladstone's thunder – Lincoln's thunder too – when he told his Blackpool audience that 'this Tory party of today' had a simple motto: 'Of the people, for the people, by the people'.[33]

Late in a short life, he stepped out of the Woodstock system, which he had defended so passionately. Under the impact of the electoral reforms of the mid-1880s, he had the courage to stand as a Conservative candidate in Chamberlain's stronghold, Birmingham. It was here that he was to unleash some of his most memorable rhetoric, speaking to vast crowds, in a way that no other front-line Tory politician could. Thus in 1884:

> 'Trust the people' – I have long tried to make that my motto; but I know, and will not conceal, that there are still a few in our party who have that lesson yet to learn and who have yet to understand that the Tory party of to-day is no longer identified with that small and narrow class which is connected with the ownership of land but that its great strength can be found, and must be developed, in our large towns as well as in our country districts. Yes, trust the people.[34]

Also in Birmingham, some four years later, and by then in the political wilderness, Lord Randolph made a further plea for 'the dream of Tory Democracy'. As so often before, he then provided little elaboration about what he meant by the term, in a way that can be termed either tantalising or prudent. 'What is Tory Democracy? Tory democracy is a democracy which supports the Tory party' was virtually all that he left his Birmingham supporters to ponder.[35] This was not a program; it was simply a good election cry.

It was because of his grassroots following among Conservatives in the country that Lord Randolph imposed his claims on his party leaders. In 1885 Conservative electoral gains in the boroughs were often attributed to the apostle of Tory Democracy. So Lord Randolph was now in a strong position, which he exploited by refusing cabinet office unless the hapless Northcote was displaced as Leader of the House of Commons. Meanwhile Lord Salisbury, in the House of Lords, now headed a Conservative government in search of a majority. Lord Randolph thus became Secretary of State for India for a few months, during which he added Upper Burma to the Empire. On his last, doomed voyage around the world in 1894, his ambition to see Burma ('which I annexed') was to be achieved just when his health finally collapsed. Historically, this was to prove one annexation too many for the British Raj, which it weakened rather than strengthened, as Lord Randolph's son was to become sullenly aware some sixty years later.

The Home Rule crisis of 1885–86 finally put Lord Randolph in a position to ask for more or less anything he wanted. He did so, he got it, then he threw everything away. Winston's biography was to spend page after page in unveiling and admiring the proposals of the abortive 1887 Budget – without, however, offering any convincing explanation as to why the Chancellor suddenly threw in his hand, and, consulting virtually nobody, just went one night with his resignation letter to *The Times* (through which Lady Randolph, when she read the paper next morning, first learned of her husband's action).

The resignation was baffling at the time, and remains so in Winston's later account. It is clear that Lord Randolph was fighting over the defence estimates, looking for economies that were unlikely to be forthcoming from an imperial-minded government. Beyond this, however, he was also plainly looking to broaden his challenge to the way that the government itself was run, inevitably bringing him into a direct personal conflict with Lord Salisbury as prime minister. Much of this was unfocused in terms of specific issues; rather it was symptomatic of a power struggle at the top. In his biography, Winston still seems unable to decide whether to endorse his father's claim 'that it is only the sacrifice of a Chancellor of the Exchequer upon the altar of thrift and economy which can rouse the people to take stock of their leaders, their position and their future'. It was actually a very small – and varyingly defined – issue for which this alleged martyrdom beckoned; and Winston also undercuts this sacrificial claim with the comment: 'Undoubtedly he expected to prevail.'[36]

Almost in spite of itself, Winston's *Lord Randolph Churchill* provides compelling evidence about the real breach between the prime minister, already master of his cabinet, and his unruly Chancellor. 'I am afraid that it is an idle schoolboy's dream to suppose that Tories can legislate – as I did, stupidly,' Lord Randolph writes, with all the authority of a minister who never legislated in his life. His son then prints at length Lord Salisbury's magisterial reply; and even a few prosaic, unillusioned sentences convey the tone. 'I think the "classes and the dependents of class" are the strongest ingredients in our composition, but we have so to conduct our legislation that we shall give some satisfaction to both classes and masses', the prime minister lectures the impatient young demagogue. 'This is especially difficult with the classes – because all legislation is rather unwelcome to them, as tending to disturb a state of things with which they are satisfied. It is evident, therefore, that we must work at less speed and at a lower temperature than our opponents.'[37]

Evident, yes indeed, at least to Lord Salisbury. It may help explain why he was to be so successful in rallying the forces of conservatism for most of the next two decades. It was obviously not evident to Lord Randolph, whose alternative strategy was to outbid the Radicals at their own game in the name of Tory Democracy. Yet it was this failed project that initially captivated the imagination of his loyal son and heir.

*   *   *

Syphilis: this is a distasteful suggestion for a son to introduce into a discussion of the early death of his father. The word does not appear in Winston's *Lord Randolph Churchill*. Admittedly, some warning premonitions are given that all is not well. 'How long will your leadership last,' Lord Rosebery is quoted as asking the newly appointed cabinet minister, aged only thirty-seven, in 1886. 'Six months' is the riposte given ('gaily') by Lord Randolph. 'And after that?' 'Westminster Abbey!'[38] The author simply quotes this exchange, as he likewise quotes solicitous comments from cabinet colleagues later in the year. 'Little did they know how short was the span, or at what cost in life and strength the immense exertions of the struggle had been made,' Winston comments, more than halfway through his second volume. 'That frail body, driven forward by its nervous energies, had all these last five years been at the utmost strain.' It would take an alert reader to remember, a mere five hundred pages previously, the passing mention of 'a long and painful illness' in 1882, which confines Lord Randolph to his bed for no less than five months. Given these sparse remarks, uninformative where they are not inconsequential, it might come as a surprise, only twenty pages from the end of the biography, to learn of the sudden onset of 'a very rare and ghastly disease'.[39]

The first allegation in print that it was syphilis came, twenty years after Winston's biography, from Frank Harris. Now Harris was in a position to know; seven years younger than Lord Randolph, he was a well-connected journalist who had moved in the same demi-monde; and he was later useful to young Winston in getting the author a large advance for his *Lord Randolph Churchill*. Harris was in the know; he knew a good story when he heard it on good authority; and, failing that, he would resort to the well-tried journalistic tradition of making it up or at least embellishing the detail. His autobiography, *My Life and Loves* (first published in Paris in 1926), is thus both a revealing and an unreliable source, and its much-quoted anecdote of Lord Randolph contracting syphilis from a prostitute is as unlikely to be true as the rival version that it was from a maidservant at Blenheim. In both cases, the lower classes are conveniently blamed for an affliction just as likely to have come from Lord Randolph's promiscuous contacts with women of his own class – as his wife well knew.

Their own sexual relations seem to have ceased in the early 1880s. There was even a rumour that Winston's younger brother Jack, born in 1880, was not his father's child. Certainly the couple were barely together by the mid-1880s, and Lady Randolph's long-running affair with her husband's friend, the diplomat Count Kinsky, was talked about as 'the Austrian alliance'. Lord Randolph meanwhile was apparently living at the Carlton Club. He was receiving mercury treatment from two doctors, Dr Robson Roose and Dr Thomas Buzzard, who specialised in the treatment of syphilis.[40] So, although we now know more about other causes of neurological disorders, like multiple sclerosis, the presumption seems clear.

As regards the potential impact, less turns on retrospective diagnosis than on what everyone supposed at the time. As Lord Randolph lay dying, the Prince of Wales wanted to know why, not unnaturally. Professional confidentiality disregarded, Dr Buzzard was prevailed upon to supply 'such information about Lord Randolph Churchill's condition as I think may be communicated without indiscretion'. He termed it General Paralysis of the Brain. Winston's biography embroiders this form of words, saying that 'the numbing fingers of paralysis laid that weary brain to rest'.[41] Whether he knew much more at the time is unclear. In 1966, following his death, his official biographer (his own son, also named Randolph) says of his grandfather that 'the older members of the family knew that he was suffering from a severe mental disease'; but he also prints a letter from Winston to his mother saying that 'I asked Dr Roose and he told me everything and showed me the medical reports.'[42] This loyal family biography of Winston, however, does not allude in the text to another, and rather significant, letter from Lady Randolph.

Jennie had become publicly reconciled with her sick husband. Possibly the revelation of his condition had helped. Certainly in Lord

Randolph's years of decline, she stood by him, lived with him, travelled with him. And during her protracted vigil at his deathbed, we find her writing to her sister Leonie with confidential comments that seem fairly conclusive. She simultaneously explains that she and Kinsky have finally parted, on good terms, and then, without a break, admits that 'Randolph's condition and my precarious future worries me much more.' This is written three weeks before his death on 24 January 1895, six months after she had set out with him on a final, nightmarish cruise around the world. 'Up to now,' she explains to her sister, currently out of town, 'the General Public and even Society does not know the real truth & after *all* my sacrifices and the misery of these 6 months, it would be hard if it got out. It would do incalculable harm to his political reputation & memory & is a dreadful thing for all of us.'[43]

As with Henry James's Maisie, what Winston knew has to be inferred from the situation. Whatever Dr Roose had told him in 1894, however little his mother had let slip after the death, it is hardly conceivable that Winston remained in the dark at the time he wrote the biography. He had, after all, spent several years in the army, most of them east of Suez, where we have Kipling's assurance that the best is like the worst and there ain't no Ten Commandments, with regimental medical officers under equally little illusion about the prevalence of sexually transmitted diseases. Even if Winston is supposed to have been cocooned in naivety, what did the other well-connected chaps in the mess, when they were in their cups, hint in their society gossip about his controversial father, who had, in Rosebery's phrase, 'died by inches in public'?[44]

Such was Winston's inheritance in January 1895. Jennie had hit upon the essential point: the need for care and dissimulation in protecting the political reputation and memory of Lord Randolph. He had retained to the end his low estimate of his son's abilities, dismissing any claims 'to cleverness, to knowledge or any capacity for settled work', as he put it forthrightly to Duchess Fanny, who had a higher opinion of her grandson. 'He has a great talent for show off exaggeration and make believe,' Lord Randolph conceded, projecting his own failings onto his son with the bitterness of a disappointed man facing his own imminent death.[45]

Winston was not yet twenty-one, seeking to make his way in the world as a soldier. It was a vocation wished upon him by his father but for which he also showed temperamental affinity. Lord Randolph may have thought the army a relatively cheap alternative to Oxford or Cambridge, but in his last years had become obsessive about the £200 a year that Winston's wish to join the cavalry would cost. Even in Lord Randolph's lifetime, Winston had turned to his mother for a kind of support that his father never gave. 'I never can do anything right,' he wrote to Lady Randolph from the military college at Sandhurst in late 1893.[46] Some sixteen months later, the two of them, now bereaved, were left with each other; and Lord Randolph dead was less of a liability than he had latterly become while still living.

The legacy of Tory Democracy was not really an unfulfilled legislative project. But since it was just about the only legacy that Winston inherited from his prodigal father, he had to make the best of it. In 1897, only two years after Lord Randolph's death, we find his son unburdening himself in a letter to his mother. He wrote as an opinionated army lieutenant of twenty-two stationed in India – 'My views excite the pious horror of the Mess' – with a forthright declaration of his own political position. 'Reform at home' is to be balanced with 'Imperialism abroad' in Winston's early manifesto. 'Were it not for Home Rule – to which I shall never consent – I would enter Parliament as a Liberal,' he confides. 'As it is – Tory Democracy will have to be the standard under which I shall range myself.'[47] Here indeed is his characteristic tone and bravura, already on display. But his declaration needs some unpacking to be understood in context.

Ever since the Home Rule crisis of 1885–86, the defence of the Union between Great Britain and Ireland had been the Conservatives' passport to power. Crucially, the issue brought them into alliance with Liberal Unionists, notably Chamberlain, who had been unable to accept Gladstone's proposals for devolution. This split in the Liberal ranks shifted the balance of political power in a fundamental way. For Lord Randolph Churchill's son and heir, the issue had a double salience: first its general connection with imperialism, and second its particular connection, through the Ulster question, with his father.

Home Rule was perceived and portrayed by Unionists as the imperial problem nearest home. In their view, nothing less than the preservation of the British Empire was at stake, threatened with a process of disintegration that might begin in Ireland but would extend throughout the Empire. Irish Nationalist hostility to imperialism helped confirm the Conservatives' claim that they alone could be trusted – if only to wrap themselves in the flag. Moreover, the historic cry of the Protestant Ulstermen or Orangemen in Northern Ireland, 'No Surrender', served to make the link between defence of the Empire and opposition to Home Rule. This was what the stolid Lord Salisbury meant by saying that, in raising the issue of Home Rule, Gladstone 'awakened the slumbering genius of Imperialism'. Winston was to quote this in *Lord Randolph Churchill*, with the approving gloss: 'Beneath the threshold of domestic politics during the long years of Liberal prosperity the modern conception of Britain as a world-power, the heart of an Empire, the inheritor and guardian of a thousand years of sacrifice and valour, had lived and grown.'[48] Here are sentiments and phrases that could well have been growled out in 1940 – the authentic Churchillian heritage, we might suppose, thoroughly imbued with 'imperialism abroad'.

Winston certainly saw the significance of his father's action in identifying the Conservatives with the Ulster cause in 1886. 'Ulster will fight, and Ulster will be right' was the sound bite that long outlived Lord Randolph's use of it, in overtly sectarian terms, first in a letter, amplified by a notable speech in Belfast. This was inflammatory stuff, which helped stoke resentments that persisted in Northern Ireland for a century or more. The issue became one in which there was no longer any room for political compromise between the overwhelmingly Catholic south and the substantially Protestant north. Was it nonetheless justified, then, by invoking the heart-of-the-Empire rhetoric? Not in Winston's eyes, at least by the time he wrote his father's biography: 'Although Lord Randolph Churchill was never what is nowadays called an Imperialist and always looked at home rather than abroad, his followers in the Tory Democracy were already alive with the new idea.'[49] It is almost as though, with reference to imperialism, his father had had to accept the axiom: I am their leader, therefore I must follow them.

What needs to be remembered is that imperialism is a contested concept. There is no single, prescriptive meaning, and, like his father before him, Winston chose to embrace some forms of imperialism while keeping his distance from others. What Winston had told his mother in 1897 was that he could 'never consent' to Irish Home Rule. Yet, when Winston indeed became a Liberal in 1904, he was called upon to support Irish Home Rule himself, albeit in some post-Gladstonian form yet to be devised, and only step-by-step, later rather than sooner. He thus came to reject the principled case against Irish Home Rule (that it necessarily meant the disintegration of the British Empire).

Winston Churchill did not thereby cease to be an imperialist – certainly not in his own mind, nor in the perception of many of his contemporaries. Again, within a few years, he undoubtedly changed his mind about what imperialism entailed. He tells his mother in 1897 that the colonies must be federated and implies that tariffs might also be used to that effect – key proposals in imperial policy, advocated by major politicians of the day. Here too he was to change his mind. When the young subaltern sketches commitments in social policy, heralding labour regulation, progressive direct taxation and payment of MPs, he indicates measures that he certainly came to support himself, once he became a Liberal. But here the question is not so much Winston's own consistency as whether this programme can really be derived from Lord Randolph's example. Lord Rosebery knew both the Churchills well, father and son alike. He knew them better than they knew each other. Winston later described Rosebery as 'the friend and patron of my youth, and my father's friend before me'.[50] Although Rosebery readily acknowledged that 'Tory Democracy was a good catch-word', he felt that any interpretation of Lord Randolph's career needed to face the fact that 'he left behind him no great measure' and failed to 'found a school or inaugurate a policy'.[51] The rhetoric, in short, may impress us but it should not deceive us into inferring some more substantial agenda. Rosebery had his own axe to grind; but he had been at the very top of British politics, as Liberal prime minister; and he was shrewd enough in judging others. 'No one reads old speeches any more than old sermons,' he wrote, calling them 'as flat as decanted champagne'.[52]

Winston Churchill certainly had a taste for champagne, as he had a taste for oratory, preferably with lots of fizz. He was the one person who did read, along with his Gibbon and his Macaulay, many of Lord Randolph's old speeches, if only in search of his elusive father. And it was as an orator himself that Winston made his own career in politics, appealing to sentiment in a democratic idiom to rally the people of the Empire. As with the father's appeal to Tory Democracy, so with the son's commitment to imperialism: the emotive rhetoric was not the codeword for a consistent economic or political programme, for which we look in vain. Amid many disappointments over his patrimony, what Winston surely inherited was a high conception of the role of rhetoric itself in politics.

Mother's Boy: The Author of his Fortune, 1898–1921

'This literary sphere of action may enable me in a few years to
largely supplement my income.'

Winston to his mother, 1898.

Winston Churchill did have family advantages, of course, and was
determined to capitalise upon them. His parents' connections gave him
immediate access to everyone who counted in the hierarchical society of
the day. He had become a second lieutenant in the 4th Hussars in
February 1895. But even in this lowly rank, he associated with the Prince
of Wales, the Aylesbury scandal now forgotten. Winston also knew the
prime minister – this was now Lord Rosebery, who would later invite
the young politician to stay at one or other of his country houses. And
Winston's mother, the vivacious Lady Randolph, seemed to know
everyone. The young man only had to ask and the introductions were
forthcoming. He instantly moved into the top social circles at a time
when high society and high politics were still coterminous. 'Introduction – connections – powerful friends – a name – good advice well
followed – all these things count,' he acknowledged to his mother,
'– but they lead only to a certain point.'[1]

Lady Randolph, who had neglected him almost as much as his
father had, played a more important part in her son's life after 1895.
Count Kinsky was now gone, the Austrian alliance ended, but Lady
Randolph, at forty, was astonishingly attractive still. One of her lovers,
George Cornwallis-West, almost exactly the same age as Winston, was
to become her second husband in 1900 – obviously a somewhat difficult situation for a son to handle. But Winston remained close to his
mother throughout and, especially in the late-1890s, could rely on the

fact that she was still there to pull the strings – except the purse strings, which the merry widow was as incapable as ever of tightening.

Money remained the problem. Winston, now serving with the 4th Hussars in India, was forced to tackle his mother direct. 'Speaking quite frankly on the subject – there is no doubt that we are both you & I equally thoughtless – spendthrift and extravagant,' he wrote home in January 1898. 'We both know what is good – and we both like to have it. Arrangements for paying are left to the future.' The situation was already desperate and still deteriorating. 'The pinch of the whole matter,' as Winston concluded, 'is we are damned poor.' Now poverty is a relative concept; but Winston was right to note that their own relatives were so much richer than himself and his cash-strapped mother.

Moreover, he was faced with a situation where his own interests were now very directly compromised by Lady Randolph's behaviour. She was currently trying to manoeuvre him into signing away a large slice of his inheritance under his father's will, under which he had been led to suppose that he could expect £1,000 a year (say £80,000 today), which would put him at least on the threshold of social viability in the circles in which he moved. But Lady Randolph was seeking to default on such expectations, in order to manage her desperate short-term loans. Winston reluctantly agreed to much of what she proposed, but only after stipulating pious, and largely ineffectual, conditions to prevent repetition. Hence his tone to his beloved mother:

I need not say – how painful it is for me to have to write in so formal a strain or to take such precautions. But I am bound to protect myself in the future – as I do not wish to be left – should I survive you – in poverty. In three years from my father's death you have spent a quarter of our entire fortune in the world. I have also been extravagant: but my extravagances are a very small matter besides yours.[2]

The position seems to have been much as he describes it. Lady Randolph was obviously out of her depth, reduced to exploiting what assets she could lay hands on, and with bafflingly mixed motives in her subsequent move to marry George Cornwallis-West, who cleared her debts and found that he was himself broke as a result.

For Winston, with his career yet to make, with the tragic circumstances of his father's demise to surmount, and with all his own aspirations for redeeming the Churchill name, the predicament was acute. The residual benefit under Lord Randolph's will seems to have dwindled to a few hundred pounds a year. As a young subaltern stationed in India, he sat in his bungalow, pondering how Gibbon and Macaulay – and other favourite authors like Edmund Burke and Samuel Johnson – could help him in meeting the situation. 'I envy Jack – the liberal education of an University,' he told his mother, now that his younger brother had finished school at Harrow, and added: 'What a strange inversion of fortune – that I should be a soldier & Jack at college . . .'[3] In fact, Jack never went to college either but was told to go into the City of London as his part in redeeming the family's finances.

Winston's army pay was £300 a year. How on earth to live on that? As he later put it in *My Early Life*, it was 'better in a cavalry regiment in those days to supplement the generous rewards of the Queen Empress by an allowance from home three or four times as great'. Hence the need for a thousand a year. But, what with Lady Randolph's system of housekeeping, he was lucky to get half that. It is revealing to see how he puts his difficulty in *My Early Life*: 'all the rest had to be borrowed at usurious rates of interest from the all-too-accommodating native bankers. Every officer was warned against these gentlemen. I found them most agreeable: very fat, very urbane, quite honest and mercilessly rapacious.'[4]

Churchill was to publish this account in 1930. He did so as a former Chancellor of the Exchequer, but one who was by then notorious not for thrift but for bucking financial probity when he balanced his budgets only by raiding the sinking fund on the national debt. He remained the aristocrat, generally unabashed in talking about money. In *My Early Life* he does omit mentioning that, in army days, he had also resorted to even less reputable means of paying for his indispensable polo horses – by passing cheques that he had been warned would not be honoured by Cox's, his fashionable London bankers in Pall Mall. Clearly he was taking a chance that the bank would stick with him on the strength of either his name, his influence or his prospects – which it did. Cox's, later taken over by Lloyds, continued as his bankers, and were drawn into many of his later schemes for making money and, failing that, bailing him out as best they could.

One thing is consistent in Winston's lifelong financial strategy – if it can be called that. This was to seek any means of boosting current income rather than to effect significant cuts in expenditure. And here his mother really did help him – belatedly, improbably, spasmodically, but, on the whole, effectively. She helped her son in fashioning a career that paralleled and supported his political ambitions; a profession that paid the bills; a profession that by most ordinary tests became his primary occupation and source of income; not so much a subsidiary career as one in which he was to achieve professional recognition and satisfaction as well as financial reward, not least in Jennie's faraway native land, the United States. In this other career, Winston was mother's boy.

It was Lady Randolph who paved the way for the writing of the first book published by Winston Spencer Churchill. She was well aware that he had already written newspaper articles, during a period of army leave in 1895, about the confrontation between the Spanish forces and the nationalist guerrillas, when he briefly visited Cuba. These five articles in a paper as undistinguished as the *Daily Graphic* were never likely to make his reputation; but the cheque for twenty-five guineas had helped defray the costs of that expedition. It had given him the taste for more, much more. And since, from September

1896 to March 1899 he was (with intermissions) based in India, he knew that he needed representation in London. Hence his appeals to his mother, 'with all the influential friends you possess and all those who would do something for me for my father's sake', to go into action on his behalf.[5] She was both more and less than his first literary agent.

After Cuba, what he needed next was a bigger war and a better newspaper. Waiting impatiently in Bangalore in April 1897, with a spell of leave to come, the young subaltern thought he had found the right opportunity in Turkey's declaration of war on Greece. 'If you can get me good letters to the Turks – to the Turks I will go,' he wrote to his mother. 'If to the Greeks – to the Greeks.' The point was to go, exploiting useful family contacts, no matter on which side he ended up. How very little this mattered is shown by the contrast between what Winston told his mother at the time – 'all my sympathies are entirely with the Greeks' – and what he later wrote in *My Early Life*: 'Having been brought up a Tory, I was for the Turks.' He simply wanted to go, and go as a special correspondent. 'Of course nearly every paper has one there already, but I have no doubt that you will find one to avail themselves of my services,' he continued to his mother. As for remuneration, it should be ten or fifteen pounds an article – 'Lord Rothschild would be the person to arrange this for me as he knows everyone.'[6] The whole plan seemed set to fall into place; fame and fortune beckoned; but by the time that Winston's ship reached the Mediterranean, peace had broken out, the war was off, and the career of the special correspondent blighted.

But not for long. Having got as far as Italy on his way to his abortive assignment, Winston went on to England in the early summer of 1897, his ear cocked for any other wars in the offing. The British Empire, in its prime, produced plenty of frontier wars, especially on the legendary North-West Frontier of the British Raj, where the great game against a potential Russian threat was a cliché of imperial geopolitical strategy. Indeed, when the young Churchill had, a year previously, met the magnificently named General Sir Bindon Blood – which he had done (inevitably) at a country-house party, hosted (almost as inevitably) by one of the various widows who could still style herself Duchess of Marlborough – Winston had seized his chance. Sir Bindon was the hero of the previous Malakand expedition in 1895. Would he – so the fresh-faced, well-connected lieutenant had asked – agree to take Winston himself along on the next? By all means, my boy! And now, in August 1897, came news of trouble again on the frontier, with a new Malakand expedition to be duly mounted, once more with Sir Bindon Blood in command. Churchill immediately dashed for the next train and got himself on the first boat, without waiting for any of Blood's written excuses about his lightly given, half-forgotten, unwary words.

In the end, then, a special correspondent he became. Churchill took leave from the 4th Hussars and made haste to the area of operations, in territory that has become well enough known in recent years: the Swat Valley, north-east of Peshawar, on the borders of what is now Pakistan and Afghanistan. Meanwhile, back in London, it was Lady Randolph who had the task of approaching the editors of the leading London newspapers. Lord Randolph had had a notably close connection with G. E. Buckle, in his day a famous editor of *The Times*. But in 1897 Buckle told Lady Randolph of his regret that he could not oblige, since he had already appointed a correspondent. So instead she secured terms with the *Daily Telegraph* for Winston's series of dispatches as a war correspondent: three hundred words a day at five pounds a time.

Fifteen dispatches were published. They started in the *Daily Telegraph* of 6 October 1897, under the heading: 'Indian Frontier – by a young officer'. True, as Blood was all along aware, this particular young officer's position was delicate, nominally serving with the 4th Hussars, but himself now embedded with the Malakand Field Force. Anonymity may have suited the army but it was not what Winston had craved in composing these articles. 'I had written them with the design, a design which took form as the correspondence advanced, of bringing my personality before the electorate,' he told his mother. 'I had hoped that some political advantage might have accrued.'[7]

This is an unsurprising avowal. He had made his first political speech while in England that summer and, with his mission to revive Tory Democracy, was pretty obviously on the lookout for a promising constituency to fight. Many army officers had followed a similar route into politics. Though Winston took great pains over the style and composition of his dispatches, and was acutely mindful of the impact that he hoped they would make, they were hardly the product of purely literary ambition but driven by essentially political motives. This was why he needed to get his name before the public.

Moreover, his extraordinary idea of writing a novel while out in camp at Inayat Kila had much the same origin. 'In my novel,' he tells his mother, 'I develop the idea that a "politician" very often possesses mere physical courage. Military opinion is of course contrary.' So there was a daredevil logic in his own deliberately conspicuous acts in exposing himself to danger. He cold-bloodedly recounted how he had ridden his pony along the skirmish line, exposed to sniper fire, to attract attention while everyone else took cover. 'Foolish perhaps but I play for high stakes and given an audience there is no act too daring or too noble,' he privately explained to her. 'Without the gallery things are different.'[8] Moreover, it turned out that, on this occasion, the gallery contained no senior officer to notice; so Lieutenant Churchill rode out again a few days afterwards, again without being noticed; and had to do it a third time, another week later, before (on other grounds) he was finally cited in dispatches. Many people remarked upon his obvious pursuit of a medal; it would nicely embellish the record of a potential parliamentary candidate.

One way or another, Churchill achieved his objectives. He succeeded less through the original newspaper articles than through the book that was made out of them: *The Story of the Malakand Field Force*, published in April 1898. This is not a work of mature reflection – there was no time for that, either in its original composition or in its subsequent hasty publication, proofreading errors and all. The book shows an ability to develop a story with admirable economy and move the action forward with a compelling immediacy. What is circumspectly claimed in the preface is a non-partisan stance by a correspondent who simply wants to report what he has seen for himself. But a reading of the full text, with its references to the British forces having crossed a Rubicon, show it was committed, willy-nilly, to supporting a forward policy – as Winston admitted privately to his mother and as reviewers were well able to detect at the time.[9]

The author's name itself immediately commanded recognition. One especially pleasing review made the comment: 'Lieut Winston Spencer Churchill, named if we mistake not, after the father of the first Duke of Marlborough, omits, indeed, the family hyphen from his name, but has evidently much of the genius of his uncle, of his father, and of their best known progenitor.'[10] When Churchill read such comments, after weeks stuck in Peshawar, it came as little short of a transformation of his prospects, as he later explained in *My Early Life*. 'The reader must remember I had never been praised before. The only comments which had ever been made upon my work at school had been "Indifferent", "Untidy", "Slovenly", "Bad", "Very bad", etc.'[11] What is edited out of this account, of course, is the fact that such comments had mainly come from Lord Randolph. But the book was an undoubted success. Even the Prince of Wales claimed to have read it, and wrote to say so.

The impact upon Churchill's career was doubly satisfactory. The book brought him just the sort of publicity he craved; and it paid. Whereas he had been somewhat disgruntled over the terms he had received from the *Daily Telegraph*, he was better pleased with the deal that Lady Randolph had secured, through an agent, with the publishers Longmans. There was an immediate advance of £50 and the book proceeded to earn £600 in all, with royalties set in Britain at 15 per cent on the first three thousand copies and 20 per cent thereafter; at 10 per cent for the first thousand of the American edition and 15 per cent thereafter. His first book thus netted twice his annual salary as an officer. 'This literary sphere of action may enable me in a few years to largely supplement my income,' he wrote to his mother in April 1898, with the book only just out. 'Indeed I look forward to becoming sooner or later independent. I have in my eye a long series of volumes which I am convinced I can write well'[12] His mind was already jumping ahead to further projects – a life of Garibaldi, perhaps, or a history of the American Civil War – that might sustain a literary career. From this time onward, Churchill took to quoting Samuel Johnson: 'No man but a blockhead ever wrote except for money.'

What next? *Malakand* was not conceived as a book, of course, but made into one with scissors and paste from the day-to-day journalism. Winston later exaggerated to his mother how little time this process had taken – only five weeks, he boasted – but his alternative boast at the time had been that for 'two months I have worked not less than 5 hours a day', which seems more likely. Either way, he fully appreciated the difference between this sort of adaptation and the writing of a biography, whether of Garibaldi or any other historical figure, with a need for proper documentation. The word 'research' was alien to Churchill, though not the concept, since he always had a respect for consulting original sources. Already approached by publishers with the idea of writing a life of the first Duke of Marlborough, or even of Lord Randolph, Winston showed himself wary. It seemed too soon to write about his father, little more than three years dead, 'and if ever I attempted it I should make it a labour of years'.[13]

Instead, Churchill decided to repeat the formula that had made *Malakand* a success. First, the useful contact with a senior officer: in this case, Colonel Ian Hamilton with whom he purposefully struck up a friendship in India. And if Hamilton were to lead a brigade to Egypt, as was rumoured, would he take Churchill? By all means, my boy! Hamilton was another father-figure; he was over twenty years older than Churchill, with an honourable wound from the battle of Majuba

Hill in 1881 that he carried for the rest of his long life (he died in 1947, having witnessed his protégé's greatest achievements). A literate soldier, Hamilton had the measure of his man, telling Churchill in April 1898: 'You have in you the raw material for several successful careers.' But there was now a need for Churchill to choose: either concentrate seriously as a soldier or quit the army to go into politics, sooner rather than later. Maybe Hamilton's forceful advice affected Churchill's decision on priorities. 'I am determined to go to Egypt,' he told his mother in the following month, 'and if I cannot get employment or at least sufficient leave, I will not remain in the army.' The point about Egypt, the British base for operations to control the Nile Valley, was that it would be an adventure in itself 'and profitable as far as finance goes as I shall write a book about it – easily and without the blunders which disfigure my first attempt'.[14]

This was hardly the voice of a real soldier. Sir Herbert Kitchener, as Sirdar or commander of the Egyptian Army, evidently suspected as much and tried to block the appointment of this all too versatile volunteer to his forthcoming expedition to the Sudan. Churchill's response was characteristic. And luck favoured him. This time the key figure was no less than the prime minister, Lord Salisbury, who had read *Malakand* with interest, as his private secretary opportunely disclosed in a highly welcome letter, received out of the blue while Churchill was on leave in London. Might it be convenient for the young subaltern to call at the Foreign Office for a discussion? *My Early Life* makes the most of the story: 'I replied, as the reader will readily surmise, "Will a duck swim?" or words to that effect.' They met; they talked about the difficulties in the Swat Valley; Churchill followed up with a letter about his own ambitions to serve next in the Sudan. 'My mother has exerted what influence she can for two years,' he wrote to Salisbury. 'Even HRH has allowed his name to be used as a recommendation.' Was it possible that the prime minister himself could intervene?[15] The outcome was Churchill's grudging appointment as a supernumerary lieutenant in the 21st Lancers, at his own expense – provided that the Indian Army could spare him. And since he immediately made his own way to Egypt by a route that rendered him incommunicado to the Indian authorities, he got away with it.

Again, this does not look like the path to a military career. Before leaving England, Churchill tested the political waters once more, this time with a speech in July 1898 in the industrial city of Bradford, where Lord Randolph's name still counted. Winston had been worried that his own slight lisp, a distinctive slurring of some consonants that was lifelong, might make him ineffective as a public speaker. 'My impediment is no hindrance,' he reported happily to his mother, conscious of his need to communicate to large audiences if he were to run for Parliament, and concluded: 'At any rate my decision to resign my commission is definite.'[16]

This was the secret that he took with him in his service in Kitchener's expedition to Khartoum. He also accepted a contract with the *Morning Post* to write dispatches at £15 a column. The campaign was at once an awesome spectacle and highly predictable in its outcome. It was to be a one-sided encounter in which the mechanised Anglo-Egyptian forces were crucially aided by a new railway, which gave them a key advantage in mobility and supply. By contrast, their Islamic opponents, the Mahdists (or Dervishes in contemporary parlance), equipped only for highly traditional warfare, made a defiant, doomed stand against the might of imperialism. The slaughter at the battle of Omdurman in early September 1898 both thrilled and shocked Churchill; the treatment of the wounded Dervishes appalled him, as he made clear in his reports. Such criticisms of the campaign were resented not only by Kitchener but by many of the readers of the Tory *Morning Post*, including the Prince of Wales, though this did not prevent the offending correspondent from dining with His Royal Highness at Marlborough House on his return to London in October. Churchill's priority was not campaigning journalism of this kind but the task of again producing the book that he had envisaged all along. This time it spilled into two volumes, published in November 1899, as *The River War*.

Meanwhile, however, Winston's novel *Savrola* had also commanded his attention. Begun during the Malakand campaign, work on it was resumed after his first book's publication, during 1898, and then again interrupted, this time by the author's disappearance up the Nile. *Savrola* is saturated in politics: not British politics, however, but those of a vaguely Hispanic Lauranian republic, where the idealistic hero finds his liberal dreams frustrated. This is, like Anthony Hope's Ruritania, tempered by democracy. It lacks the specific, concrete details of Westminster that might have given its political theme verisimilitude, thus remaining trapped within the conventions imposed by the artificial context. It is frankly nowhere near as good as *The Prisoner of Zenda*, with which Anthony Hope (Hawkins), ten years older than Churchill, had made his name and his fortune a few years previously. And as a romantic tale, *Savrola* simultaneously lacks romance.

Winston sent a draft of the novel to his grandmother, Duchess Fanny, always his redoubtable supporter. She immediately saw its flaws, especially the deficient portrayal of women, but urged him to follow up on the possibility of publication. 'It cannot injure your reputation in a literary Point of View,' she told him on the eve of his twenty-fourth birthday, 'for the faults are those of youth and inexperience and not Want of Ability, 250£ is not to be despised and to my mind you have earned it.'[17]

By the time she wrote this in November 1898, the old duchess was well aware that his reports in the *Morning Post* had created a stir. Moreover, they had apparently upset the Prince of Wales; and, haunted by echoes of the Aylesford scandal and her family's subsequent years of exile in Dublin, she regretted Winston's outspokenness as ill-advised. This time around, however, a little notoriety proved happier in its consequences. The fact that the critic of the mighty Kitchener had now turned novelist surely helped produce the offer of an advance as high as £250 – nearly a year's army pay. In fact, by January 1899 Churchill had received an additional offer of £100 from *Macmillan's Magazine* for the serial rights to the novel.

Savrola was thus scrambled into print without delay. Currently enmeshed in the making of *The River War*, the author had no time for possible revisions, whether to enhance the love interest or otherwise. In 1908, when Churchill became a cabinet minister, a reprint of this early novel, riding its curiosity value, brought him a useful £225 (say £17,000 at today's prices). Looking back, while he noted with satisfaction that the book had netted about seven hundred pounds altogether, he did not choose to defend its literary merits – 'I have consistently urged my friends to abstain from reading it.'[18] He proved as good as his word. When, in the summer of 1940, the publishers Chapman and Hall wrote to Downing Street to ask for permission to republish *Savrola*, the prime minister simply instructed his secretary, in one of his terse but effective marginal annotations: 'civil discourage.'[19] This stands as a rare example of Winston Churchill refusing to maximise the earning power of his literary estate. It is not unfair, then, to set *Savrola* aside as an apprentice work, and in a trade that the author did not pursue further. Winston Spencer Churchill thereafter quit the field and left his American namesake in sole possession of the fiction shelf.

There was one other abortive episode. At just the moment in 1898–99 when Winston was considering his options – the sword or the pen – his mother too became persuaded that financial salvation was to be found in the world of letters. As she blithely writes in her memoirs: 'I determined to do something, and cogitating for some time over what it should be, decided finally to start a Review.'[20] Like everything else about Lady Randolph, this was a brilliant rather than a cogent idea, since temperament, upbringing and circumstance had all conspired to leave her with no experience of business, no spare capital, no capacity for sustained effort and, of course, no literary training. Winston nonetheless evinced enthusiasm, writing on New Year's day, 1899: 'You will have an occupation and an interest in life which will make up for all the silly social amusements' – as though Lady Randolph's role as editor (which is what she intended) would simply keep her too busy for shopping and parties. 'It is wise & philosophic,' he continued, even more implausibly. 'It may also be profitable. If you could make £1000 a year out of it, I think that would be a little lift in the dark clouds.'[21]

Buoyed up in his optimism, real or affected, he momentarily contemplated collaboration with his mother. But he was actually more than fully occupied otherwise. The first number of the *Anglo-Saxon Review* appeared in June 1899, at the very high price of a guinea, or five dollars at the time. It was aimed at a niche market on both sides of the Atlantic, with Lady Randolph's contacts important in recruiting both contributors and subscribers, as satirists were not slow to point out:

> Have you heard of the wonderful magazine
> Lady Randolph's to edit, with help from the Queen?
> It's a guinea a number, too little by half,
> For the Crowned Heads of Europe are all on the staff.[22]

Churchill had not liked the proposed title. Its implications about a transatlantic commitment to imperialism rang false to him; and he thought it hit the wrong note for sales. 'People don't pay a guinea for such stuff,' he warned. 'And besides there is a falling market as regards Imperialism now.'[23] The political comment here is perhaps surprising, coming from him; and he swallowed his qualms for the moment when he tried to collaborate with his mother on the preface for the first number, which duly quoted Dr Johnson on blockheads. But he had been right to sense difficulties, especially across the Atlantic, over both the title and the cost. The New York *World* had acumen as well as obvious self-interest in saying: 'You pay five dollars for this magazine. It may be good, but you can buy the *World* for a cent.'[24] Sure enough, the tenth and last issue was to appear in September 1901. Everyone had quickly lost interest in the *Anglo-Saxon Review*: the readers in high society who declined to subsidise Lady Randolph on an indefinite

basis; the editor and publisher herself who quickly tired of the tedi-
ously menial tasks that she was expected to undertake; and the editor's
supportive son, increasingly able to support himself by other means.
In this context, he displayed little concern for promoting the unity of
the English-speaking peoples.

Back in India since the end of 1898, Churchill had pressed on with
his own substantial task. He was following up on the success of his
first military-campaign book with his new two-volume work, *The
River War,* having got his novel finished in the interstices. 'Please send
without delay the Annual Registers for 1884, 1885 & 1886,' he asked his
mother. 'I want them.'[25] These useful volumes, replete with digests of
political events and extracts from parliamentary speeches, were wanted
at this juncture because *The River War*, rather than plunging into the
campaign of 1898, contains a discursive historical account of Britain's
previous entanglement with the Sudan, when Gladstone's government
had been held responsible in 1885 for the death of the ill-fated General
Gordon. Indeed Churchill's first-hand war reporting, so much the
staple of his other early publications, does not begin until, more than
halfway through the book, an allusion to the 21st Lancers elicits the
footnote: 'The author led a troop in this regiment during the final
advance to Omdurman: and it is from this standpoint that the ensuing
chapters are to some extent conceived.'[26] Though the first part of his
book was relatively less well received by the critics, it remains significant as the author's first sustained effort in a new genre: as historian
rather than war correspondent.

Churchill was thus both ambitious and industrious. Through toil
and application, as well as natural gifts, he had achieved a literary style
that was to stand him in good stead throughout his life. Though he
was sometimes compared with the young Disraeli, his avowed mentors
were chiefly Gibbon, Johnson, Burke and Macaulay, and it was their
Augustan grand manner that he wilfully appropriated and faithfully
acknowledged. The influence was stylistic rather than intellectual.
Churchill made few substantial references to Gibbon's historical

interpretation of the decline of the Roman Empire, though this theme had fascinated many of his elders and contemporaries, and fed their current anxieties about the fate of the British Empire. But in the author's only attempt at fiction, in the very final sentence of *Savrola*, it is anticipated that the reader 'will remember the splendid sentences of Gibbon, that history is "little more than the register of the crimes, follies, and misfortunes of mankind"; and he will rejoice that, after many troubles, peace and prosperity came back to the Republic of Laurania.'

Gibbon's influence thankfully proved more fruitful in the writing of non-fiction. Churchill, however, did not develop an Augustan fondness for classical allusions, still less in the original Latin, though in Lord Randolph's day this had been common in parliamentary oratory. By contrast, Winston was more playful, ready like Kipling (whom he much admired) to descend into demotic speech to make a point. He applied himself consciously to achieving his desired effects, early or late, throughout his career. Like wine, Churchill's distinctive style matured, and sometimes went over the top, but it was in the early books that he laid down some vintages that he would revisit with satisfaction in later years, as evidenced by his thrifty reblending of some favourite selections. In his old age, his early campaign histories were to be republished in an abridged edition, *Frontiers and Wars* (1962), still readable today for its lucid and bold exposition, and still capable of surprising a modern reader by some of its mordant asides about, for example, the intractable nature of the resistance to Western dominance in Afghanistan.

In India in 1898–99, Lieutenant Churchill worked hard, played hard. The 4th Hussars won the inter-regimental polo tournament and, despite playing with his shoulder strapped, he claimed credit for three of the four goals they scored in the final. His fellow officers regarded him with puzzlement tinged with admiration, sometimes grudgingly given. He was a peculiarly well-formed round peg in a square hole; but one who now had the means of getting out of the hole he was in. There was by this time no great surprise over the import of a letter that he sent from Suez to Duchess Fanny, on his way home in March 1899:

> I am about to leave the army, and have already forwarded my papers to the Horse Guards. I fear that you will not commend my decision, but I have thought a great deal about it and although it is possible I may live to regret it, I don't think I shall ever regard it as unreasonable. On one point I am clear – the time had come when it was necessary to choose definitely. Had the army been a source of income to me instead of a channel of expenditure – I might have felt compelled to stick to it. But I can live cheaper & earn more as a writer, special correspondent or journalist: and this work is moreover more congenial and more likely to assist me in pursuing the larger ends of life.[27]

* * *

Ends and means, yes. There is little doubt that Churchill opted for a career as a writer as a means of forwarding another career in politics. Bradford came to nothing, but he had better luck in another industrial constituency, this time in Lancashire rather than Yorkshire: the cotton town of Oldham. By June 1899, now a civilian, he had been adopted as Conservative candidate in a by-election to be held in the following month. The contest was peculiar in several ways. Oldham returned two Members of Parliament; one of the previous Conservative MPs had died, the other now retired; so there were two vacancies. In their place, the aristocratic Churchill was paired with the leader of the cotton spinners' union – an almost unique instance of a prominent trade unionist fighting in Conservative colours. Churchill duly seized on this to spill some rhetoric about Tory Democracy but mainly talked imperialism, at a time when the South African situation made a war against the Boer republics seem possible. Oldham had gone Tory at the last election; but the result had been close; the Unionist government of Lord Salisbury was now in the doldrums, so the two seats were vulnerable to capture by the Liberals.

Did Churchill really expect to win? He blamed government efforts to give financial assistance to the Church of England for blighting his chances; but in turn risked blotting his own record as a party loyalist by vainly trying to repudiate the measure. In short, his inexperience showed. In defeat, he blamed the system. 'Altogether,' he wrote privately, 'I return with less admiration for democracy than when I went.'[28] But when the votes were counted on 6 July 1899, giving narrow Liberal victories in both seats, this result was actually ideal from his own point of view. He had spoken well; he had been prominently reported, not just locally but in the London press; and the close vote meant that there was no personal discredit. Moreover, if the hostilities against the Boers had begun earlier, war fever might have swept him into Parliament before he had amassed the resources necessary to sustain him; whereas the fact that the South African situation continued to threaten throughout that summer made the prospects for an increasingly famous war correspondent all the more promising. And Oldham could wait – as it did.

In an era when MPs, like cavalry officers, were expected to be men of means, they had to cover their own expenses. True, Winston's cousin Sunny, now a wealthy man after his Vanderbilt marriage, gave material assistance, much needed. But a parliamentary candidate required an independent source of income. This Churchill now proceeded to secure.

Churchill went as special correspondent to cover the South African war in September 1899 for the *Morning Post*. For this he got £1,000 for the first four months, then £200 a month. And when, as anticipated, the newspaper columns were reworked as his next book, *London to Ladysmith*, he set his mother to get him an advance of £2,000. Again, a little notoriety helped. The fact that Winston had been captured by the Boers in late 1899, and had made a well-reported escape, was a key point in strengthening the case for getting more than had originally been agreed. Lady Randolph had meanwhile attracted much publicity in raising funds from her American friends to support a hospital ship, the *Maine*, in which she herself briefly sailed to South Africa, arriving in Cape Town in time for a short reunion with her two sons in early 1900. Jack, serving in the field, was wounded and became an early patient on the *Maine*. Winston, riding alongside his brother, made another escape – from injury, yet again – and indomitably seemed to be making his own luck, all of it duly reported in the press. His new book, culminating in the relief of Ladysmith from the Boer siege (February 1900), was happily published in May 1900 – five days before the relief of Mafeking, the occasion for widespread public jubilation in Britain. No fewer than fourteen thousand copies of this, Churchill's fourth book, were sold.

But that did not exhaust the resources of the back files of the *Morning Post*. Its busy war correspondent had meanwhile kept his promise to his readers, 'if I am not interrupted by the accidents of war, to continue the series of letters'.[29] General Ian Hamilton (as he had now become) was given the command of one of the British columns marching on Pretoria, the capital of the Transvaal. He was happy enough to allow Churchill, along with his helpful cousin, the Duke of Marlborough, to join the expedition; and when Hamilton captured Pretoria in June, the war seemed to be over (though actually it was simply entering its long, inglorious guerrilla phase).

Churchill promptly decided to leave for England, splicing his later dispatches into book form on the passage home. Like *London to Lady-smith* this sequel was described as a 'collection of letters', with each one dated and republished virtually as originally sent. Since each of the books was to be published within a few weeks of the events described, the spontaneity of the reporting is part of the appeal. More-over, the deliberate impression of a personal narrative is reinforced by Churchill's use of passages of dialogue, often casual conversations with ordinary soldiers or civilians rather than formal interviews, which also allows him to smuggle in a non-official viewpoint while keeping his own distance.

Ian Hamilton's March was the title he gave to his fifth book. It was likewise formally dedicated to his old friend, 'with whose military achievements it is largely concerned'. While not achieving the same sales as its predecessor, this celebratory volume sold a very creditable eight thousand copies. War and politics were by now closely intertwined. By the time *Ian Hamilton's March* was published in October 1900, Churchill was one of two Conservative MPs for Oldham, newly elected in the General Election of October 1900, the so-called 'Khaki Election', which marked the high tide of popular imperialism.

Few candidates were more khaki than Churchill. As war correspondent and escaped prisoner of war – how could he be both? – his precise status may have been inconsistent but his exploits were well reported, not least by himself. Once the votes were counted, the victor of Oldham, now a 'star turn', as he later put it, immediately cashed in on his fame. While still on the boat back from South Africa, he had asked his mother to investigate whether his political career would be compromised by giving paid lectures in major towns. Bookings were already in hand by the time the General Election intervened. Immediately afterwards, in one intensive month of public lectures on the war throughout Britain, some chaired by leading politicians like Joseph Chamberlain in Birmingham or Lord Rosebery in Edinburgh, Churchill made nearly four thousand pounds. Then, hopping across the Atlantic, exploiting his American family connections, he sought to repeat his success. Again he had big-name support. Mark Twain, despite his own strong stand against current exercises in imperialist expansion, whether British or American, took the chair for Churchill in New York. And in Boston, of course, the chairman for Winston Spencer Churchill's lecture was none other than the American Winston Churchill.

Half-American or not, Churchill was unsentimental about his reception in the United States. His subject proved more acutely politicised than he had naively anticipated, with pro-Boer sentiment strong among Dutch and Irish communities alike; and his celebrity drawing-power was naturally far less than in Britain. His own prior assumptions had been rather patronising. 'Five thousand pounds is not too much for making oneself so cheap,' so he had told his mother. Expectations on this scale, never very realistic, were to be dashed by his actual experience on the road, though he also received much kind hospitality, both in New England and in Canada. 'But sometimes it is very unpleasant work,' he was to report later, seizing in particular on the example of one American town where he found that his agent 'had not arranged any public lecture but that I was hired out for £40 to perform at an evening party in a private house – like a conjuror'.

The old soldier simply soldiered on, night after night, even in virtually empty theatres, totting up the receipts all the while. But the fact that it was not easy, and sometimes, demeaning for a duke's grandson, makes his achievement in earning his $8,000 the more creditable. He wrote to Mrs Cornwallis-West (as his mother had now become) towards the end of his North American visit: 'I am very proud of the fact that there is not one person in a million who at my age could have earned £10,000 without any capital in less than two years.' True, this would be about three-quarters of a million pounds in today's money; and it was split fairly equally between the total lecture fees and the total proceeds of the five books. Having netted the proceeds, he also wrote another letter, no doubt equally welcome:

> My dearest Mamma, I enclose a cheque for £300. In a certain sense it belongs to you; for I would never have earned it had you not transmitted to me the wit and energy which are necessary.

Moreover, before the year 1901 was out, he renounced his allowance from her of £500 a year, he defrayed the expenses of the loan that had been necessary to bail out his mother four years previously, and he waived any further claims on what was admittedly a bankrupt inheritance. This was a tangible reinforcement of the sentiments conveyed in a covering letter to Mrs Cornwallis-West from the busy new MP, now increasingly absorbed in his career and living in his new Mayfair flat, provided by Sunny Marlborough: 'No my dear, I do not forget you.'[30]

The parliament elected in 1900 sat for over five years, during which Unionist fortunes declined dramatically. The next General Election in January 1906 brought a Liberal landslide. Churchill's own fortunes meanwhile prospered, in politics and literature alike. The fact that he had now joined a very select league of financially successful authors was shown by the terms of the contract for his two-volume biography, *Lord Randolph Churchill* (1906). Even a quarter of a century later, in negotiations over advances, Winston still cited the fact that 'for the *Life of Lord Randolph Churchill* I received £8,000 in days when money was worth much more than now'.[31]

It was a good moment for an aspiring young author to capitalise on promise and potential. In the Victorian period, it had been normal for publishers to pay a lump sum for outright purchase of the copyright, not only of novels but of biographical works, which might occasionally hit the jackpot with unexpectedly high sales, as Canon F. W. Farrar's *Life of Christ* had done in 1873, leaving Farrar fuming while his publisher reaped all the subsequent rewards. Winston Churchill, who would have fully shared the canon's sense of authorial outrage without any clerical inhibition in expressing it, was spared any such fate by the fact that, during the last two decades of the nineteenth century, the American system of paying the author by a percentage royalty on sales was imported, combined with a part payment in advance. The rise of the professional literary agent, hard-nosed enough to negotiate terms that an unworldly or gentlemanly author might be unable or unwilling to extract, was a further development in this new literary marketplace.[32]

It was appropriate that, in marketing his biography of his father, Winston put himself in the hands of his father's flamboyant associate, Frank Harris. Harris's ebullience proved infectious, generating confidence that he could improve on the £4,000 advance already offered by Longmans, previously Churchill's publishers. Harris solicited interest from many of the biggest London publishing houses – Heinemann, Methuen, Cassell, Hutchinson, John Murray – before securing an offer at the end of October 1905 from Macmillans: £1,000 on signing, £1,000 on correction of the proofs, £6,000 on publication. Once Macmillans had themselves made £4,000 profit, it was stipulated that further profits in London would be divided with the author; and in New York there would be a royalty of 20 per cent on sales. Harris himself got £400, being 10 per cent of the value he had added to the Longmans offer. 'I think he has earned it well,' Churchill told his mother. 'I could certainly never have made such a bargain for myself.'[33]

This was undoubtedly true. Longmans had made a good offer; they were disappointed but not disgruntled over the outcome. Macmillans may have sensed more opportunity in the American market, but only £500 of the advance actually came from New York. The sale of 2,300 copies in the first week seemed impressive in London, linked to the fact that the book was published amid the political excitement of the General Election campaign itself – a high-risk strategy that paid off, though the subsequent rate of sales then fell away sharply. The book's high profile proved to be more to the benefit of the author than of his publishers who had, in today's money, parted with about six hundred thousand pounds for a book with sales still short of six thousand after four months on the market. Churchill declared a net payment of £7,400 for income-tax purposes, spread over the three fiscal years 1906–09. Thus, before he first enjoyed a full cabinet salary on becoming Home Secretary in February 1910, his literary earnings made it possible for him not only to accept ministerial office but also to consider marriage, without curtailing the extravagant lifestyle to which he was habituated.[34]

The book had cashed in on expectations as much as achievement. Such a biography was bound to attract attention, on Lord Randolph's name alone; the fact that it was to be written by the 'astonishing young man' already hailed by reviewers of *The River War* was a further enticement. But could he pull it off? As a son, he faced one challenge in handling the filial relationship with a kind of tact with which he was not generally credited. As a writer, he faced a different challenge in going beyond the sort of reportage that had made a success of his war books. As a biographer, moreover, he faced a further challenge for which his readings in the Annual Register had only been an apprenticeship. Could he handle unwieldy archival and other sources with the necessary historical skills?

The author had begun work in 1902. He first had to face the executors who had been charged with safeguarding the archive under the terms of his father's will, and he quickly browbeat them into giving him a free hand. 'Lord Randolph Churchill made a regular practice of preserving every letter he received,' the author was to explain; and not until Winston had first looked through the eighteen formidable 'Tin boxes and Drawers', during his first archival foray at Blenheim, did he fully realise the scale of the task, with 'six times as many papers as those I have looked through' confronting him.[35] But he realised too that he needed to sift all the available evidence before he began writing, and again had good reason to be grateful for the further hospitality of the Duke of Marlborough. The other side of any important correspondence also needed to be located; permission to use it sought, whether from touchy widows, competitively filial children, forgetful old statesmen or – most delicate of all – those among Lord Randolph's colleagues and rivals who were still active in politics, with their own reputations at stake. For the politics of the mid-1880s presented many issues still alive, like many of the protagonists themselves, in the political world of the early 1900s.

Lord Randolph, born in 1849, had had two significant near-contemporaries at Eton who both went into politics, like himself. They became his friends, his rivals, his benchmarks. One was Lord Rosebery, two years older, who knew him best from Oxford days. He had become Liberal prime minister in 1894 at the age of forty-six and lived on until 1929. The other, less than a year older than Lord Randolph, was Arthur Balfour. He became Conservative prime minister in 1902, just short of his fifty-fourth birthday, and lived on until 1930. Winston came to know both statesmen well, and naturally turned to them for help in writing the biography. But Balfour purported to have lost the letters that he had first promised. Then Rosebery, after volunteering early cooperation, eventually published a (much shorter) book of his own, pretending all the while that it was an advertisement for the one by Winston. The young man, however, was inured to receiving rebuffs from his elders.

Writing *Lord Randolph Churchill* was, by any standards, a massive undertaking for an ambitious MP. He plainly had other ambitions as well as authorship. His two volumes certainly show Churchill's assiduity and aptitude in his literary career, but they also disclose a clear political mission in retrieving his father's reputation. It is hardly plausible today to accept this version as an objective historical account of Lord Randolph's own career. In this respect Winston's work has been definitively superseded by modern scholarship. But his two volumes remain indispensable for us in reconstructing his own sense of how Lord Randolph's political career shaped his own.

When the author began the biography in August 1902 he was sitting in the House of Commons as a Conservative, just like his father. The long and successful leadership of Robert Cecil, 3rd Marquis of Salisbury – who had been so relieved to get rid of Lord Randolph back in 1886 – had just ended. Salisbury, master of British politics for so long, had been able to keep the premiership in the family on his retirement by passing it on to his sister's son, Arthur Balfour. The Cecils were a close-knit family, about whom the expression 'Bob's your uncle' was coined, pointing to a cosy state of aristocratic nepotism in government. Balfour, who had deserted the Fourth Party for Uncle Bob, knew how to look after himself.

It was not Balfour who fascinated the young Winston so much as the older man who sat next to him on the government front bench. Joseph Chamberlain was a pivotal figure in the political careers of both Churchills, father and son alike. Winston later offered a revealing retrospective comment in his *Great Contemporaries* (1937), conceding that he watched while 'wise, cautious, polished, comprehending, airily fearless, Arthur Balfour led the House of Commons. But "Joe" was the one who made the weather.' He was the man who had thwarted Gladstone in 1886 over Home Rule, thereby transforming British politics. Despite the gap in age and seniority, Winston discovered not only an invaluable source for the biography but a confidant. A rueful aside – 'I must have had a great many more real talks with him than I ever had with my own father' – has its own poignancy. By 1904 Winston was recording his appreciation of 'five or six hours most pleasant and interesting conversation with Joe', evidently ranging over current and past politics alike. 'He is, of course, tremendously partisan in his views both on men and things,' Winston reported to his mother, 'but it was quite clear to me that we understood each other on lots of questions . . .'[36] This is remarkable, coming at just the time when Churchill turned against Chamberlain's current policy and instead joined the Liberals.

Across the generational divide they found a bond of affinity. Just as Churchill now broke with the Conservatives, so in his time Chamberlain had broken with the Liberals. Both had experienced a sort of change (as Winston observed in *Lord Randolph Churchill*), 'counting more in political warfare than any change of principles, however sudden or sweeping: they had changed sides.'[37] Such a simple point, of course; but one on which the author wrote with some feeling.

And why did Churchill himself change sides? Because, for a second time, Joe decided to make the weather in a way that realigned the party system. In 1903 Chamberlain signalled a dramatic turn in Unionist policy by broaching novel proposals for imperial preference, which would mean abandoning Britain's historic policy of Free Trade. In 1900 'Joe's war' in South Africa had been the imperial issue of the day, appealing to sentiments of loyalty that Winston had readily evinced. But for many imperialists at the turn of the twentieth century, 'sentiment' and 'loyalty', however admirable in themselves, needed more solid material reinforcement, in particular from economic self-interest. This was certainly Chamberlain's view. Imperialism was his great cause; and since for him politics was always a matter of seeking a specified end, then hammering out relevant policies to reach it by enlisting a self-interested constituency, the rest followed. In his programmatic view of politics, if the unity of the Empire could not be sustained by political means (federation), it would have to be sustained by economic means (preference). Hence his Tariff Reform campaign. His declared aim was 'to consolidate an Empire which can only be maintained by relations of interest as well as by relations of sentiment'.[38]

For all his personal awe of the formidable Joe, the young Winston now rebelled. It was a decision of fundamental importance, in terms of policy, ideology and, not least, his own career. He rejected imperial preference and declared himself a Free Trader, citing his experience 'in peace and war of the frontiers of our Empire' to argue that it was not founded on the material basis that the Tariff Reformers now claimed as essential: 'The strength and splendour of our authority is derived not from physical forces, but from moral ascendancy, liberty, justice, English tolerance, and English honesty.'[39] The economic orthodoxy of the day no doubt reinforced his attachment to Free Trade; but just as important was his sense that sentiment rather than economics was the true motive force in imperial policy. Having made this stand, it was only a matter of time before he walked across the floor of the House of Commons in May 1904 to sit as a Liberal.

A principled stand? Not everyone thought so. At the General Election of January 1906 there was to be a huge swing to the Liberals and their new allies in the Labour Party. Churchill, elected as a Conservative with the flowing tide in 1900, was now elected as a Liberal with the flowing tide in 1906. This was certainly opportune, some said opportunistic.

Here is the highly charged political context in which the publication of *Lord Randolph Churchill* needs to be understood. Its author was the son of a man generally dismissed by political friends and foes alike as a gifted but unstable opportunist, not to be trusted for long by anyone. Those who had been shocked by the political expediency of Lord Randolph were naturally disposed to see young Winston as a chip off the old block. The book thus had to serve not only as an explicit defence of Lord Randolph's career in loyally sticking with the Conservative Party in the 1880s but also as an implicit apologia for Winston's action in abandoning it twenty years later.

Winston's defence of Lord Randolph is generally robust. The biography does not deny that he was a brilliant tactical player of the party game; but it is much concerned to show that he played fair, offering a painstaking exoneration of its hero from a string of petty personal charges that he had broken or bent the rules. Sometimes this is done simply by assertion, sometimes by suppression. The cryptic references to Lord Randolph's fatal illness must have teased Frank Harris, who read the final proofs for the busy author. Likewise, in the Bradlaugh case, the failure to mention the Marlborough perpetual pension at any point must have been deliberate. This has the effect of elevating the terms of debate here, making Lord Randolph's protestations of religion and morality much more plausible. By then Winston himself had personally rejected 'the Christian or any other form of religious belief'; but, in writing of his father, he was still ready to make unsupported comments on the 'strong religious strain in his nature' and assert that he was 'always a devout man'.[40]

Of course the author laboured under obvious inhibitions in writing about people still alive. Chamberlain, having been notably helpful, was also notable in not exacting any price for his cooperation. By contrast, Rosebery, who saw the early proofs, is himself virtually omitted from the story; but, when he read the biography, he relished one particular reference to Balfour. This was in a letter of 1891, when Balfour was appointed Leader of the House of Commons, a position briefly occupied by Lord Randolph five years previously, provoking the latter's mordant comment: 'So Arthur Balfour is really leader – and Tory Democracy, the genuine article, at an end!'[41] The fact that Winston's biography prints this letter says much. By 1906 the author did not need to conceal his own coolness towards the leader of a party that he had now left.

Then there was the great Aylesford scandal of 1876, affecting the royal house. Lord and Lady Aylesford were both now dead, as was Lord Randolph's brother, the 8th Duke of Marlborough, formerly Lord Blandford; but his son, Sunny, was at once Winston's cousin, his friend, his host at Blenheim and a source of political subsidies. There was even more at stake than family considerations. The scandal had all the makings of a good story, like something out of Somerset Maugham, another young writer of almost exactly the same age as Winston; but it was certainly not a story that it was advisable for an author of non-fiction to tell in good King Edward's reign. In *Lord Randolph Churchill* the account of the scandal could easily be missed altogether by a careless reader since it is hidden away in the middle of a paragraph. 'Engaging in his brother's quarrels with fierce and reckless partisanship,' it tells us, hinting obscurely at a chivalrous defence of Blandford, 'Lord Randolph incurred the deep displeasure of a great personage. The fashionable world no longer smiled.'[42] And that is more or less all that the innocent reader learns. The next thing is that the family abruptly absconds to Ireland. But at least the son, when he published in 1906, learning from his father's mistake, perhaps also remembering Duchess Fanny's admonitions, did not lay himself open to the social retribution meted out thirty years previously.

Winston's own current interests are also protected in other ways. A key episode is obviously the Home Rule crisis of 1885–86. In particular, the idea that Lord Randolph was playing a tactical game to unseat the Liberal government of the Grand Old Man is only explored by the author in a perfunctory way, for reasons that are highly understandable. By 1906, after all, as a newly minted Liberal, he was himself under pressure to support Home Rule. This is perhaps the single most embarrassing political dilemma that the biography has to confront. Either the father was sincere in regarding Orange Ulster as a conscientious impediment to granting Home Rule – in which case, what was his son doing in acknowledging the same policy as a claim of justice for nationalist Ireland? Or was Lord Randolph simply up to his usual tricks? But this was exactly the impression of him that it was the general aim of the biography to contest and refute.

Lord Randolph's great friend in Ireland had been the distinguished Protestant judge, Gerald FitzGibbon, to whom he wrote with great candour and freedom of expression. Winston had the letters; they are now lost. If he had so wished, he could well have chosen to lose them himself before publication; Balfour had shown how easy it was; and FitzGibbon was hardly likely to have objected to suppression. To his credit, the author chose instead to print many of Lord Randolph's letters to FitzGibbon – indeed, the only version of them that we have – but he also chose, very often, to refrain from overt comment of his own. In particular we owe the following to Winston's *Lord Randolph Churchill*:

'I decided some time ago,' he wrote bluntly to FitzGibbon, on February 16, 1886, 'that if the G.O.M. went for Home Rule, the Orange card would be the one to play. Please God it may turn out the ace of trumps and not the two.'[43]

There is seldom a smoking gun in politics. Lord Randolph's friends knew that he was often not to be taken literally, and that he was temperamentally out to shock respectable opinion. Nonetheless, this comment about the 'Orange card' has often been quoted from *Lord Randolph Churchill* as a devastatingly candid acknowledgment of its subject's motives and methods alike. But Winston's hands are clean. Like a fastidious defence counsel, privately unconvinced of his client's innocence, he duly presents the case for his father while leaving the evidence to speak for itself. In the process, it should be noted, the young Liberal politician has not made opposition to Home Rule into a core principle, still less has he countenanced Ulster intransigence.

Perhaps it was the soldier in Winston that itched to move from defence to offence, especially in the second volume of *Lord Randolph Churchill*. His father was to emerge, after a thousand pages, as a consistent and far-seeing statesman with principled convictions. 'There is an England which stretches far beyond the well-drilled masses who are assembled by party machinery,' begins the peroration on the penultimate page. It is, we are told, 'an England of wise men', an England 'of brave and earnest men' and 'of "poor men" who increasingly doubt the sincerity of party philanthropy. It is to that England that Lord Randolph Churchill appealed: it was that England he so nearly won; it is by that England he will be justly judged.'[44] This passage is certainly faithful to its subject in inflating its rhetoric far above any substantive political claims that can be made. It supplies the frame for a picture that was never actually painted: a fitting tribute to a politician who failed as Chancellor of the Exchequer even to bring forward a budget, proved an impossible cabinet colleague, and disappeared in a puff of smoke, which soon cleared, with a lingering memory sustained only by evocative phrases.

One obvious moral of the biography is that there are higher ends in politics than mere party loyalty. The great causes that Lord Randolph had vainly championed might yet be won, in another era, and perhaps under another banner. Winston was asserting a view of politics that put great national and imperial causes at the centre of the story, that elevated bold, visionary prophets above party wirepullers, while acknowledging the immense, immovable weight of partisan interests that made it so difficult to effect change. He persuaded himself, at the time he was writing *Lord Randolph Churchill*, that he was justified in rejecting the Tories, by waking up from the 'idle schoolboy's dream' that had deluded his father. If Lord Randolph had once eulogised the recently deceased Disraeli as a great imperial statesman, asking pointedly on whom 'the mantle of Elijah' should now fall, the son left his own contemporaries in little doubt as to the mantle he was in turn now claiming. Winston had, like Hamlet, appeased his father's ghost; but he was quite unlike Hamlet in his determination to seize his own moment in politics.

Lord Randolph Churchill remains a significant book in considering Winston Churchill's career, whether as politician or as author. It also marks a watershed. It was written while Churchill was a Member of the House of Commons, sitting as a backbencher, unsalaried and unsupported by office staff. He wrote the book himself, literally, in his fluent longhand, from which the book was typeset, with several proofs to be amended later; and he had himself worked through the mass of original documents on which the book is largely based, with some assistance initially from his brother Jack. All this was a highly professional way for an author to write a book.

Then Churchill's career trajectory changed. Balfour's Unionist government had resigned in December 1905; so Sir Henry Campbell-Bannerman's Liberal government was formed shortly before the inevitable General Election that followed a month later. Churchill joined the new government, in the Colonial Office, which suited his current interests and his expertise, especially on South Africa. He served as a junior minister, albeit one clearly marked for higher office. It was when Campbell-Bannerman, near to death, was succeeded by Herbert Henry Asquith in April 1908 that Churchill entered the cabinet as President of the Board of Trade, with the status, though initially not the full salary, of a Secretary of State.

He was only thirty-three, the youngest member of Asquith's cabinet. But Churchill was very quickly accepted as one of its key figures, alongside men a decade or more older, notably the new Chancellor of the Exchequer, David Lloyd George. His relationship with Lloyd George was to be formative and long-lasting, despite many subsequent political divergences. 'It was Lloyd George,' Churchill was to tell the House of Commons on 28 March 1945 in a memorial tribute, 'who launched the Liberal and Radical forces of this country effectively into the broad stream of social betterment and social security along which all modern parties now steer. There was no man so gifted, so eloquent, so forceful, who knew the life of the people so well.' This extraordinary Welshman was like Churchill in having no university education: unlike him in background in every other way, with his deep-seated resentments against the English aristocracy channeled into reinventing the Liberal Party as a vehicle for social reform.

The young President of the Board of Trade signed up to this agenda. Asquith's introduction of old-age pensions in 1908, Lloyd George's raid on Bismarckian precedents to institute health insurance in 1911, Churchill's own pioneering scheme for unemployment insurance, likewise part of the 1911 National Insurance Act – these measures became building blocks of this New Liberalism. Learning fast, Churchill emerged as its prominent and coherent public spokesman, as his volumes of collected speeches testify: *Liberalism and the Social Problem* (1909) and *The People's Rights* (1910). In a sense, he had discovered the legislative project that had always eluded Lord Randolph. Or maybe he should be seen as devising for himself the sort of nuts-and-bolts programme that inspired a Chamberlainite view of politics; certainly in the 1920s he was to work (in a Conservative government) with Neville Chamberlain, son of the great Joe, in extending the British system of National Insurance. But for the moment, what with Lloyd George's 1909 Budget, controversially characterised as 'Peers versus People', Winston's visits to his cousin Sunny at Blenheim Palace had a certain piquancy.

All this was integral to the switchback course of Churchill's political career. Like Whitman, he was large, he contained multitudes. Successively as Liberal, Coalitionist and finally Conservative again, he was to hold cabinet-level office, with a few short gaps, until June 1929. He was appointed by three different prime ministers in turn as President of the Board of Trade (1908–10), Home Secretary (1910–11),

First Lord of the Admiralty (1911–15), Chancellor of the Duchy of Lancaster (1915), Minister of Munitions (1917–19), Secretary for War and Air (1919–21), Secretary for Air and Colonies (1921), Colonial Secretary (1921–22) and Chancellor of the Exchequer (1924–29). For most of that time his ministerial salary was £5,000 a year, which before World War I would have been worth up to four hundred thousand pounds in today's money (though only half that in the early 1920s). Most cabinet ministers could live well on this.

Even with Churchill's tastes, the salary went a long way. Since his literary earnings from *Lord Randolph Churchill* were nominally spread over three tax years, at £2,466 per annum, this sum was several times greater than his official salary as a junior minister; and even when he became President of the Board of Trade in April 1908, the salary was, for historic reasons, still fixed at less than that of his cabinet colleagues, only £2,000 per annum. By contrast, what with the final tranche from *Lord Randolph*, and the first tranche from the proceeds of his book *My African Journey* (1908), compiled during an official visit to the colonies, and also the reprint of *Savrola*, Churchill reported literary earnings of over three thousand pounds in 1908–09 – half as much again as his government salary.[45]

Still, ministerial office not only gratified political ambition but provided financial security: all the more important when he contemplated marriage. To his credit, at least morally, in 1908 Winston broke with the current Marlborough habit of marrying money. Clementine Hozier had less than he did. She was, however, not only beautiful, but also resourceful and, as it turned out, resiliently adaptable. Clementine's mother, from aristocratic lineage, had married Henry Hozier, a London financier, himself already once divorced and no more successful in his second marriage than in his first. He was almost certainly not the father of Clementine, born in 1885.

Clementine's mother was, all too like Lady Randolph, notorious for having a string of lovers, both before and after the breakdown of her marriage in 1891. Thereafter, ill-provided by Hozier until his death in 1907, the family often lived, for reasons of economy, in Dieppe; when in London with her mother, Clementine gave French lessons for half a crown an hour. To translate this into 12.5 new pence, of course, misses the point; rather, eight lessons would produce one pound, at a time when this was the basic weekly wage of an unskilled labourer. Clementine Hozier was not without her own skills but, like her future husband, proved ready to turn her hand to the problem of remedying a lack of assured family money. No more than Winston was she making a financially prudent marriage, but it was to prove more stable and long-lasting than that of most of their relatives. Perhaps each was seeking reassurance, given their own parents' marital instability.

The newly-weds needed a home suitable for a cabinet minister, within easy reach of government offices in Whitehall as well as the House of Commons. They first lived in Eccleston Square, near Victoria Station, in a modest-sized house, at least by the standards of a fashionable London square, since it could be managed with only five servants. On Winston's appointment as First Lord of the Admiralty in 1911, Admiralty House, next to Horse Guards Parade and with a colonnaded entrance in Whitehall, was on offer as the imposing official residence – requiring, however, a much bigger staff to maintain it, as Clementine quickly perceived. For the time being she was able to prevail upon Winston to decline the offer and stay put; but in 1913 he got his way, with the minor concession of sealing off the grand suite on the first floor, thus cutting the number of servants required from a dozen to a mere nine.

At Admiralty House, Churchill lived in the style of his ancestors. It was prized as a perquisite of his post, but as such had to be unwillingly surrendered along with the Admiralty itself in 1915. The Gallipoli crisis in the Dardanelles brought Churchill down after the controversial failure of his plan to knock out Turkey, Germany's ally. Feeling the financial strain, what with a cut in official salary too, his family eventually moved in with that of his brother Jack in the Cromwell Road in Kensington. In London, several borrowed and rented houses followed during wartime, while Churchill's career went through its vicissitudes, not least his own six months of military service in the trenches in 1915–16: a quixotic decision on his part that threw further stress upon the long-suffering Clementine.

Meanwhile Winston's mother naturally played less of a role in his life, both before and after her divorce from George Cornwallis-West in 1913. Her subsequent third marriage to the handsome and obliging Montagu Porch, three years younger than Winston, came in 1918. 'She could have married young men until she was a hundred,' one of her nephews remarked later, intending a compliment to her enduring good looks. Her prospects of longevity seemed excellent – as good as those actually fulfilled by her elder son – and her third marriage was perhaps her best, though also her shortest. For in June 1921, full of grace and vigour, literally tripping down the stairs in a new pair of shoes on a country-house visit, Jennie had an awkward fall. The fracture led to a gangrene infection and to amputation of her leg. By the end of the month she was dead. Winston reflected that 'she suffers no more; nor will she ever know old age, decrepitude, loneliness'.[46] At sixty-seven she seemed in many ways younger than he himself did at forty-six, already with over a dozen years of experience as a cabinet minister behind him and, in the other career on which she had helped launch him, with his most intensive period of authorship now unfolding.

PART II

The Author of his Reputation

Entr'acte

As a cabinet minister, Churchill was successively faced with new responsibilities and new briefs to master. His literary career lay virtually dormant, at least until the end of World War I. But he also now had staff at his command. His first private secretary, going back to his time at the Colonial Office in 1906–08, was Edward Marsh, who became a lifelong friend, involved in many later literary projects. Marsh prided himself on his literary style, making a speciality of his mastery of punctuation, with his doctrine on the use of the hyphen a set-piece that he was always ready to rehearse at the slightest provocation. He developed a remarkable reputation as a proofreader for writers as diverse as Walter de la Mare, whose poetry he admired and promoted; for Dorothy L. Sayers, the chronicler of Lord Peter Wimsey's forensic triumphs; for A. A. Milne, the rhapsodist of Winnie the Pooh; and for Somerset Maugham, not only a novelist but the most successful playwright of his era. Disciplining the prose of Winston S. Churchill into a form acceptable to the printer was all in a day's work for Marsh, whether in the office or out of it.

As a minister, Churchill no longer had to push his own pen. He dictated letters as a way of transacting government business; and he transferred the habit into his subsequent literary life. Whether working on books or newspaper articles, he latterly did much of the hard work late at night, pacing up and down as weary secretaries took down the ceaseless flow of words. 'I lived in fact from mouth to hand', was how he liked to put it.[1]

The series of volumes that he later published about both World

Wars represent a sort of hybrid. They were built around official papers that were themselves dictated, and then fashioned into a coherent text through the same medium. He relied upon others to ferret out the documents as needed. The collaboration of assistants in the production of writings published under Churchill's name became a standard feature of his subsequent career. No later book was simply his, at least not in the same sense that *Lord Randolph Churchill* had been. In one respect, however, it had blazed the way ahead. Frank Harris's negotiations may have left Macmillans waiting for many years to recoup on their investment; as late as 1939 Harold Macmillan told Churchill that they still had ten years' stock of the cheap edition on their hands.[2] But the author naturally had a more favourable perspective on a contract that had propelled him into the big league. In particular, the tangible impact of receiving a lump sum of several thousand pounds in advance of sales shaped Churchill's future thinking about how he might resume his literary career.

While still in cabinet office in Lloyd George's post-war Coalition (1918–22), Churchill's literary ambitions twitched into life, with a motivation common in writers of political memoirs. There were, by then, political reasons why he should have wished to write about his time in office, since the fate of the Gallipoli expedition in 1915 had led to his leaving the Admiralty under a cloud that blighted his political career. He wanted to set the record straight, like many politicians when they leave office; and, like them, he was not unaware that publishers would pay good money for the beans to be spilled. What was distinctive in Churchill's case was that he set about writing these memoirs while still in office. During the winter of 1919–20 he began mobilising the resources that lay to hand in seeking out documents, dictating drafts and revising typescript and proofs alike.

Given the circumstances of its composition, *The World Crisis* (1923–29) is an extraordinary achievement. Throughout its five volumes it shows a sweep in its historical vision of World War I that sets it far above the ordinary set of war memoirs. This is necessary in the early volumes since Churchill needs to indicate a glowing potential for success in forcing the Dardanelles by naval power in 1915 and for subsequently achieving the promised military victory on the Gallipoli peninsula. He thus presents this attack on the Germans' Turkish ally as an outflanking strategy that could, with better luck and more perseverance, have turned the course of the war without prolonging the deadly carnage of the Western Front. Much of the crucial second volume of *The World Crisis* is devoted to this issue; and in turn, much of the text consists of documents printed in order to sustain the case.

The verdict of the most thorough modern appraisal of this work is severe but well justified: 'The reader is never sure that the version given by Churchill is complete, or if material damaging to the case Churchill is building up has been omitted, or if any deletions have been made in the text.'[3] As with *Lord Randolph Churchill*, the author resorts both to outright suppression and to selective deletion, likewise unacknowledged, in the documents chosen; so he is appealing for vindication to a record that is itself incomplete and partial, too often relying on prolixity to stun the weary reader into submission. He has his favourites among the commanders involved, normally dashing and debonair figures like his old friend General Sir Ian Hamilton, who comes off lightly from his abortive efforts at Gallipoli. The work's composition was a formidable exercise in narrative, boldly accomplished, sometimes successful but invariably geared to retrieving the credentials of an active politician.

It was geared also to putting Churchill's post-war finances on a better footing. By this time, Winston and Clementine had four children to be looked after and provided for. They had a daughter, Diana, born in 1909; a son in 1911, inevitably named Randolph; then Sarah in 1914; in 1918, Marigold, who was to die aged three; and, just over a year after this loss, perhaps in compensation, Mary was born in 1922. Family expenditure naturally increased; school fees now had to be met. Churchill was determined that his son should have chances denied to himself; Randolph's wild schooldays at Eton were to be followed by a brief but extravagant undergraduate foray at Oxford. Moreover, Winston held to the conventional ambition of aristocratic fathers that each daughter should be provided with her own trust fund and marriage settlement to secure her future, though no means for making such provision lay readily to hand, as things stood up to 1920.

By November of that year, however, Churchill had enough of the war memoirs written to seek an advance. He already knew what he wanted: at least £20,000. The well-known London literary agents, Curtis Brown, agreed to accept this stipulation. The London publisher Thornton Butterworth quickly came up with an offer of £9,000 – worth less in post-war terms than the advance for *Lord Randolph Churchill* thirteen years before, but still up to three hundred thousand pounds in today's money. This was a good start, especially since the agents also had a further American advance of £2,500. On 21 December Churchill got an early Christmas present: *The Times* would pay £5,000 for serialisation in London. A month later Curtis Brown kept up the flow of good news, with an offer of £8,000 for American serialisation plus a better offer for book rights in New York – £5,000 from the well-respected house of Scribners. All of this was to be cash; all of it outright and non-returnable, whatever sales were achieved. So already Churchill knew that he would get no less than £27,000.[4] True, the British inflationary spike of 1920 made these pounds worth appreciably less than pre-war; still, by the time the bulk of the money came in, it must have been worth at least three-quarters of a million pounds in today's terms. In any case, by then much of it had already been spent.

Instead of new income covering existing commitments, it fed new needs. Churchill had a propensity to expand his ambitions in line with any increase in his resources. This was certainly true of the family legacy that Churchill received in 1921. He came into possession of an Irish property, Garron Towers, inherited indirectly (after a cousin's death) from the estate of his beloved grandmother, Duchess Fanny, whose father, with his princely income as Marquis of Londonderry,

had been able to set up his daughter in style. Winston had long entertained expectations that the Garron Towers estate would pass to him.
When it did so, the prospect it offered was an income of at least four
thousand pounds a year, so if Winston were content to pocket this, he
would now have the means of maintaining his own family, with
adequate comfort and security, at their current level of expenditure.

Of course this did not happen. The new ambition was for Winston
to set up his family with their own substantial country property.
Winston and Clementine had bought a farmhouse called Lullenden,
in rural Kent, during the latter part of the war, sometimes described as
a cottage, though one with eleven bedrooms. It had hidden problems,
not hidden for long from Winston but apparently concealed from Sir
Ian Hamilton when the old soldier and his wife fell in love with the
place on visiting the Churchills in 1919. The Hamiltons were induced
to pay nearly ten thousand pounds; and the Churchills put the
proceeds towards a London house, in Sussex Gardens, just north of
Hyde Park. But the itch for a country home remained. What with the
unexpected legacy, Winston now became intent on acquiring not only
a country house but one with farmland attached.

Clementine, with more first-hand experience of what was entailed,
heard the alarm bells ringing. 'Darling let us beware of risking our
newly come fortune in operations which we do not understand &
have not the time to learn & to practise when learnt,' she wrote in July
1921. 'Politics are absolutely engrossing to you really, or *should* be,
& now you have Painting for your Leisure & Polo for excitement &
danger.'[5] But her hopes that a country home would be simply 'a rest
and joy' were predictably brushed aside once Winston, almost immediately, fell for Chartwell Manor, also in Kent. He committed himself
to purchasing it behind Clementine's back: the most serious offence
that he caused her in over half a century of marriage.

Chartwell was to be his real home for the rest of his life. Everything
was now on a far grander scale than before. It had twenty-two
bedrooms, twice as many as Lullenden. Winston was right to see a fine

aspect with a stupendous view, on a clear day looking far over the
Weald from high on the escarpment of the North Downs. And Clementine was likewise right to see huge, expensive problems in the
conversion and reconstruction of a rather ugly Victorian mansion, its
red-brick face towards the road belying the amenities within, including a large and handsome drawing room largely of her own creation.
A mortgage on the trust funds left under Lord Randolph Churchill's
will was needed; and the Garron Towers legacy, which might have
provided substantial steady income, was also raided for new capital –
not just for Chartwell but to set up the Children's Trust.

The financial arrangements into which Winston entered are
complex, and they were to be modified over time, but the essence is
simple. He used both Garron Towers and Chartwell as security for
various mortgages that he took out, partly to finance his children's
trust funds, which would provide marriage settlements for his daughters in due course.[6] In doing this in the inflationary conditions of
1920, when the Bank of England discount rate was 7 per cent, he was
not only locking himself into servicing these mortgages indefinitely,
but doing so at rates that were bound to prove onerous if interest rates
declined. Maybe he could not have been expected to foresee that the
Bank rate would fall as low as 2 per cent throughout the years 1931–39;
but the risk was always there. Whatever the moral merits of this enterprise in assuming such burdens, the financial implications were
inescapable, in radically reducing the net annual return from the
Garron Towers estate while imposing obligations that Churchill could
only meet by increasing his other sources of income. Either he would
have to generate such income by writing more – or he would have to
face the fact that he could not really afford Chartwell at all.

It is little wonder that Clementine's initial enthusiasm for Chartwell
was soon dimmed by such considerations. She remained understandably
worried and Winston's line in reassurance left her more so. 'Chartwell is
to be our *home*,' he argued, developing his case with curious economics.
'It will have cost us £20,000 and will be worth at least £15,000 apart from

a fancy price.' And Garron Towers? 'The estate at this moment is at least as large as it was when I succeeded, but part is invested in Chartwell instead of in shares,' he told Clementine in September 1923. 'You must think of it in this light,' he explained to her.[7] He naturally harped on his expectations, and paid lip-service to the need to economise, but within a household budget of £10,000 a year. Ultimately, a London flat in Morpeth Mansions, near Victoria Station, was to be acquired in place of the family house in Sussex Gardens. But the ongoing commitments, hinging on the maintenance of Chartwell in a style that Winston considered appropriate, were henceforth on a dizzying new scale of expense.

How on earth was it all to be done? At the time he was writing these letters to Clementine, Winston was not only out of office but also temporarily out of Parliament, having lost his seat as a Coalition-ist Liberal – yet contemplating living at twice the rate of a cabinet minister's total salary. True, he now had the Garron Towers legacy; but the brunt fell on *The World Crisis*. At least, so it might be supposed, the backbenches now promised him ample time for writing. But, having rejoined the Conservatives, he was unexpectedly offered the post of Chancellor of the Exchequer at the end of 1924. His solution was to pocket the salary (still set at £5,000 a year) while, in the other pocket, continuing to count on the proceeds of *The World Crisis*.

It is an extraordinary fact that most of this work, which eventually ran to five volumes, was completed in his spare time as a cabinet minister. Admittedly, this showed in the later volumes, which have less of the cogency that gave his apologia for Gallipoli its own fascina-tion. 'For authorship is a whole-time job; and so is the Chancellorship of the Exchequer,' wrote the economist John Maynard Keynes in an otherwise kind review in 1929.[8] It remains remarkable that, in the spare time from his spare time, the Chancellor had dictated much of *My Early Life* (1930), which surely ought in the circumstances to have been a mere potboiler. Yet it managed to challenge Keynes's concept of what constitutes a full-time job by turning out to be one of Church-ill's most graceful literary achievements.

Churchill was a prodigy; but was he still really an author? After all, one could argue that his frenetic activity was nothing but an exceptionally elaborate spin-off from his political career, early or late, in an era that saw the beginnings of the modern memoir industry. The real test came after 1929, when his political luck ran out. After his long spell of ministerial office, in one party or another, in one government or another, in one department or another, he now endured exclusion from power until the outbreak of war in September 1939. But these were not simply wilderness years. He relished spending more time at Chartwell. It was now, through choice or necessity, that he had his most productive years as an author. In this Churchill was unlike, say, Lloyd George, whose war memoirs were on a similar scale to his own and fetched even more in the publishing market – a now familiar kind of one-off retirement project for superannuated statesmen.

What Churchill was doing was surely qualitatively different. His literary commitments were on a substantial scale, requiring scholarly preparation, and much time and effort to complete. They culminated, of course, in his authorship of *A History of the English-Speaking Peoples*. This is such a familiar fact that it may seem unnecessary even to wonder why he chose to write on this theme, so fully did he later claim it as his own. But to understand why he chose this subject, we first need to understand what the concept signified, not just to Churchill and his contemporaries, but to the surprising number of his predecessors who had, in one way or another, anticipated him.

The English-Speaking Peoples Before Churchill

'We therefore seek to draw from the past history of our race inspiration and comfort to cheer our hearts and fortify and purify our resolution and our comradeship.'

Churchill on American Independence Day, 1918

How much interest had the young Winston, half-American as he was, actually shown in the English-speaking peoples? He certainly did not pluck the term out of thin air on 4 July 1918 when he made his widely reported speech in the Albert Hall, London, at the inaugural meeting of the English-Speaking Union. The expression already had long currency on both sides of the Atlantic, as I discovered from a digital search of the databases of leading newspapers. In the archive edition of *The New York Times*, from its foundation in 1851 to 1980, the phrase appears 1,250 times – about ten times a year on average. In *The Times*, the London equivalent, there are over a thousand references from the same period. Given all the differences in scale and coverage in these two leading newspapers, and the fact that there were seven issues a week in New York but only six in London, this is impressive testimony to the extent to which both were participating in a common dialogue.

The term does not appear at all in *The New York Times* until 1871, and only in the 1890s did it really catch on. World War I saw a further boost in usage; and by the peak in the 1920s it was being used two or three times every month. Thereafter the number of references to the 'English-speaking peoples' declined, despite World War II, and fell again in the 1950s, when Churchill's *History of the English-Speaking Peoples* was finally published – which was itself responsible for generating a number of these. By the 1970s the term had almost dropped out of sight.

But perhaps the British experience was rather different? It might seem plausible to suppose that the British, whose post-war leaders often invoked a 'special relationship' which seemed more special in ex-imperial London than in newly empowered Washington, likewise continued through the twentieth century to hug the notion of the English-speaking peoples – like a security blanket, perhaps, as a sort of latter-day surrogate for their declining international status. But the fact is that usage of the term 'English-speaking peoples' was much the same in London as in New York, following a closely similar chronology. *The Times* gives it only one mention before 1870; then the same upward slope as across the Atlantic and the same peak in the 1920s, and a similar decline in the 1930s. Only at this juncture does a significant difference appear. Whereas *The New York Times* did its bit for the war effort by printing over two hundred allusions to the 'English-speaking peoples' in the 1940s, in London the comparable figure reached barely more than half (admittedly in British wartime newsprint that was appreciably less than half that available in the United States).

Thus the historical pattern of newspaper references to the English-speaking peoples was much the same in London as in New York. Moreover, much the same is true if we look in other American newspapers, whether in the *Chicago Tribune*, the trumpet of midwest isolationism, or in the *Los Angeles Times* or *The Washington Post*. In Britain, likewise, if *The Times* (more conservative) is compared with the *Manchester Guardian* (plainly liberal), the story is the same.

'The worthy, pious, and substantial citizen hurriedly turning over the pages of his *Times* or still more respectable *Morning Post* and folding it to his convenience,' is how Winston Churchill visualised the newspaper-reading habits of a typical member of his privileged class in the 1880s.[1] And this stereotypical reader was plainly already becoming habituated to reading about the English-speaking peoples: as were American citizens, no less worthy, pious or substantial. In understanding the origins of the concept, we need to look as far back as the 1860s and 1870s; and in charting its growing prevalence, to look back to the 1880s and 1890s. The idea of the English-speaking peoples was already in currency well before the commencement of Winston Churchill's political career, albeit in contexts largely ignored by his younger self; and in 1918 he was opportunely appropriating it just as it was coming into high fashion through the past efforts of others.

Many early public uses of the expression – and these were picked up on both sides of the Atlantic – were in the speeches of William Edward Forster. He is usually remembered in Britain (if at all) simply as Forster of the Education Act: the minister responsible in 1870 for the first great measure providing for mandatory elementary education. Public schooling, free of religious control, as reformers had long argued, was a field where England conspicuously lagged behind provision in the United States. But Forster's horizons were wider and his contemporary prominence greater.

Forster was recognised as Gladstone's chief lieutenant during the Liberal government of 1868–74; many saw him as the party's future leader. Forster's father, a Quaker, had been a philanthropist with strong connections to the United States, where he was buried, having died on a visit in 1854. His son had a long-standing wish to visit the grave; he shared the abolitionist zeal of his father and his favourite uncle; he gave hospitality at his Yorkshire home, near his textile mill, to many American visitors; he became a trusted friend of Charles Francis Adams, the patrician American minister to London during the Civil War. It is thus no surprise to find Adams reading a report of one of Forster's speeches in 1869 and assuring him, from temporary retirement in Massachusetts, that 'I shall try to get it inserted in some of the papers here.' Such networking manifestly bore fruit, as Forster discovered for himself on his own visit to the United States in 1874, after the fall of the Liberal government set him free; though he protested that General William Sherman was flattering him in telling Forster, 'You are as well known in America as in England.'[2]

Here is a significant cue to the provenance of this new catchphrase, 'English-speaking peoples'. It was a means of refighting the American Civil War by other means: not by marching through Georgia, like Sherman, but by beating swords into ploughshares. Forster and Adams were so close because they had the common cause of international conciliation at heart. They were appalled that their respective countries had displayed, during the war, a degree of mutual incomprehension and bellicosity that belied their shared English-speaking heritage. It could only be overcome, they believed, by reaching out to the peoples themselves over the heads of their out-of-touch governments, their legalistic diplomats and their chauvinistic politicians. Grievances over the wartime depredations of the British-built Confederate warship, the *Alabama*, fed on lingering American resentment over hostility to the North among the British political class.

It was in this context that Forster stood out, alongside the famous Radical leaders, John Bright and Richard Cobden. Indeed it was Adams's private opinion that 'Mr Forster has been our firmest and most judicious friend' – 'we owe to his tact and talent even more than we do to the more showy interference of Messrs Cobden and Bright.' They were seen as the saving remnant that had kept the newly coalescing forces of popular Liberalism clear of sin. For it was not just the Tories who had failed to support the North: the Liberal leaders of the British government that was in office during the American hostilities – Palmerston, Russell and Gladstone alike – had sadly strayed in giving countenance to the pretensions of the South. John Stuart Mill, the epitome of intellectual Liberalism, was appalled at 'the rush of nearly the whole upper and middle classes of my own country, even those who passed for Liberals, into a furious Southern partisanship . . .'[3]

As Forster liked to put it, the root of the trouble was to be found in 'fashionable drawing rooms'. He was ready to use the platform in great public meetings to give voice to a different view and thus redress the balance. The way that aristocrats advocated the pro-Southern cause sometimes told its own story. One of them, Lord Wharncliffe, in a meeting at Manchester, made the basis of their support obligingly explicit: 'They knew the affection which was entertained by the negro population towards their young masters and mistresses, a sentiment much akin to that which prevailed largely in England between the owners of an estate and those resident among them who were treated kindly, justly and generously.'[4] This was the Woodstock system writ large. With slavery and wage slavery so easily assimilated, the Civil War had much of the resonance of a class war too.

The noble populist myth was thus established: that the English-speaking peoples – as distinct from the British ruling class to which the Churchills belonged – had shown themselves in this hour of trial to be upright, true and moral. America had long been celebrated as 'the beacon of freedom' for many British working men from the era of Tom Paine, often politely ignored as an American founding father but always celebrated as a totemic figure by British radicals. For them, Abraham Lincoln hit the same chord, especially after his Emancipation Proclamation on 1 January 1863, which cleared away ambiguity over whether the North in fact condoned slavery. The Gettysburg Address in November 1863 was in this sense a simple reaffirmation of Painite common sense: from the self-evident truth asserted in the Declaration of Independence, that 'all men are created equal', to the logical conclusion that 'government of the people, by the people, for the people, shall not perish from the earth'. 'I should hope that this question is now so plain that most Englishmen must understand it,' Bright had declaimed; 'and least of all do I expect that the six millions of men in the United Kingdom who are not enfranchised can have any doubt upon it.'[5]

These are bold simplifications, of course. The impressive point remains the high degree of popular support shown in Britain for the North. This helped to Americanise British politics, with a significant legacy for Anglo-American relations. The abolitionist fervour of a previous generation of evangelical Anglicans and Quakers had long sustained transatlantic pressure-group activity. Such people had always identified slavery rather than states' rights as the root cause of the Civil

War. Bright and Forster, both from a Quaker background, were simultaneously the key figures in rallying support for the federal side and for making electoral reform the key issue in Britain. Democracy was seen as the great issue; Lincoln seen as its exemplar, as its eloquent champion and ultimately as its martyr. In death as in life, 'honest Abe, the rail-splitter' helped usher in the reign of democracy in Britain as well as in America.[6]

This struggle for electoral reform in Britain resulted in the 1867 Reform Act, which brought household suffrage to the towns that were parliamentary boroughs. Though it was imperfect by modern democratic standards – it excluded all women and almost all younger and unmarried men – contemporaries were not wrong to think of this as a democratic franchise. Household suffrage was extended to the rural areas by Gladstone's second government in the mid-1880s. It was the way that the Gladstonians made this into a great populist cause that prompted, in response, Lord Randolph's rhetoric about Tory Democracy. The outcome was an electoral system, open to mass party organisation, that increasingly approximated to an American model. The language of populism, moreover, rather than that of class, captures contemporary perceptions of politics on both sides of the Atlantic.

One American visitor expatiated in this vein while on a well-publicised visit to Britain in 1877. 'I entertain views of the progress to be made in the future by the union and friendship of the great English-speaking people,' he told a large assembly of working men in Newcastle-upon-Tyne, 'for I believe that it will result in the spread of our language, our civilization, and our industry, and be for the benefit of mankind generally.'[7] This was Ulysses S. Grant, beginning a world tour after serving two terms as president, in effect speaking as Lincoln's heir.

It was during Grant's presidency that the scars of the war in diplomatic relations had been healed. It came as no surprise that the victorious Republic was claiming compensation for the damage caused by the *Alabama*, and also pressing for settlement of outstanding disputes over the international border with Canada. A subtext was the possible annexation of Canada. What had ramped up these claims in 1869 was the intervention of Senator Charles Sumner, powerful as chairman of the Senate Foreign Relations Committee. He was a leading abolitionist and another of Forster's former house guests in England. Sumner now demanded reparations from Britain for the indirect costs of the war. Instead of a possible settlement of a few million dollars for the *Alabama* itself, this suddenly suggested a far higher figure. On this basis, the Americans might well demand $2,500,000,000 (nobody thought in billions in those days) – or, of course, Canada, as Grant himself sometimes hinted.

As Mill put it, there was 'reason to be thankful that a few, if only a few known writers and speakers, standing firmly by the Americans in the time of their greatest difficulty, effected a partial diversion of these bitter feelings, and made Great Britain not altogether odious to the Americans'.[8] Thus the various champions of the English-speaking peoples snatched a further moral victory, adding international arbitration to their common principles. Private correspondence between Sumner and Forster, by then in Gladstone's cabinet, was maintained despite their public disagreement. The decision of the Liberal government to allow the American claims to go to arbitration at Geneva was both a diplomatic milestone and an intensely partisan issue in Britain. It was Gladstone who ultimately got Liberal cheers over a tolerable result for Britain, a politically affordable $15.5 million; but it was his colleague Forster who had done more in holding the negotiations together. At critical junctures, Forster was busy on the backstairs with like-minded Americans, notably with Adams, recalled to diplomatic duty in the arbitration. Grant helped, at a critical moment, by replacing J. L. Motley as US minister in London with the more personable General R. C. Schenk. It should be said that Motley, the great historian of the Dutch Republic, was actually no enemy of England, but he was certainly a friend of Sumner, whom Grant was determined to oust from the negotiations.

The *Alabama*, in short, left a complex mess of flotsam and jetsam churning in its wake. The key development, however, was the conclusion of the Treaty of Washington in 1871. Indeed it was 'The Great Event of the Age', according to an editorial in *The New York Times*: 'Henceforth the two great English-speaking peoples of the world – the leaders in Protestantism and free government – will in all probability pursue their careers without ill-feeling, and with increased harmony and friendship.' This heady moment fuelled further aspirational rhetoric. Schenk's reported readiness to contemplate Anglo-American union (like his boss) prompted one Washington paper to enthuse that this 'would enable the English-speaking peoples to give law to the world, and at the same time be the means of increasing and strengthening the people everywhere who are struggling to secure for themselves, and for their children, the inestimable blessing which we now enjoy – the God-given right of self-government.' All of this was very close to what Gladstone was to call 'Forsterism', with its moralistic interventionism fortified by democratic Protestant zeal.[9]

What impression did such stirring testaments make upon the young Winston Churchill? He seems to have been oblivious. His father is not on record as talking about the English-speaking peoples, perhaps spurning any slogan that he had not invented himself, and this particular one tainted with too many radical connotations. In *Lord Randolph Churchill* there is an intriguing aside that Forster 'may be described as the first of the Liberal Imperialists'.[10] At the time of writing, in the early years of the twentieth century, this was a political position with which Winston Churchill had much sympathy; but he did not explain or elaborate his point. Still less did the author, at any point in these two volumes, employ the phrase 'English-speaking peoples', seemingly unaware of its significance in the era of which he was then writing. Young Winston was naturally more habituated to what was said *in* the fashionable drawing rooms of the West End of London than in what was said *of* them in the street.

*   *   *

In late Victorian Britain, references to the English-speaking peoples had sometimes vied with the use of another term, 'Greater Britain'. This was the title that the Liberal politician Charles Dilke, Lord Randolph's parliamentary sparring partner, had used for a widely read record of his travels, first published in 1868. Greater Britain was sometimes a synonym for the British Empire; sometimes only for the colonies of white settlement – Canada, Australia, New Zealand and South Africa. More problematically, it sometimes included the United States. The term 'Greater Britain' was deployed with wide resonance by the historian J. R. Seeley, as a variant of his own trademark phrase, used as the title of his book, *The Expansion of England* (1883). This captured the sense that, through emigration and settlement, likeminded communities had been established overseas, through 'the diffusion of our race and the expansion of our state' – albeit 'in a fit of absence of mind', as Seeley's famous and sardonic phrase had it.[11] 'Greater Britain', however, was not terminology that appealed to either Lord Randolph Churchill, Colonial Secretary in 1885, or to his son, who was to serve in the Colonial Office in 1905–08 as Under-Secretary and again, as Secretary of State for the Colonies, in 1921–22.

Enthusiasts for Greater Britain were rarely interested in India, despite its vast population, continental scale, strategic significance and economic importance to Britain. Theirs was clearly not Disraeli's exotic vision of Empire – Winston Churchill's atavistic vision too, in many ways – with an Empress to reign over it and Viceroys to rule in her name. Imperialists who exalted India often disparaged the settlement colonies, and vice versa. Thus in the parliamentary debate on the Royal Titles Act of 1876, granting Queen Victoria the title of Empress of India, Forster criticised Disraeli, who had sponsored the bill, for describing colonists as 'nugget finders and fortune hunters who merely went out to come back', and instead asserted that they were 'founders of a Commonwealth'. He later reiterated the expression, asserting of the British Empire in 1885 that 'at the present time it is one commonwealth'. Rosebery, too, eyes fixed on the free association of the English-speaking colonies of settlement, was toying with the expression 'commonwealth of nations' by the mid-1880s.[12]

This line of thinking often led to proposals for some kind of imperial federation. The victory of the American North, as well as being a triumph for democracy, had offered a vindication of federalism as a constitutional model, which might be applied to Britain's imperial problems. It was a cause of which Forster, Rosebery, Joseph Chamberlain and Seeley, though not Dilke, became advocates. To Forster, federation was the essential means of preventing the growth of colonial self-government from bringing the disintegration of the British Empire, for which he felt strong affection. 'But it will be said that this is mere sentiment,' Forster conceded in 1885, a year before his death. 'Well, sentiment has ruled the world since the world began . . .' The point was to channel this sentimental force into federalism, thereby capturing its energy. Lord Randolph, by contrast, had brusquely declared that 'all the present talk, by the way, about Imperial federation is mere moonshine'.[13]

Winston was to take the same dismissive view of federation. He did not pursue it as a practicable imperial strategy, any more than he advocated preferential tariffs within the Empire. Instead, he cultivated imperialist sentiment in itself, as a motivating force in its own right, without any need to institutionalise it. It is true that the Imperial Federation League was itself the victim of disintegration – or moonshine perhaps. Its collapse in 1893 came precisely because of its failure to agree on specific proposals that would simultaneously please the British government, in its quest for sharing the defence costs of the Empire, and satisfy each of the self-governing colonies, with their own specific interests at stake and their own separate proto-nationalist identities.

The career of Goldwin Smith nicely illustrates some of these tensions. Smith had once been Regius Professor of Modern History at Oxford in the 1860s; then he became an eager emigrant to the United States; and ended as a forty-year resident of Canada. Always a restless figure, his ideas are equally difficult to pin down. A prominent champion of the North in the Civil War, he had been equally prominent in making the case for electoral reform in Britain. It was the link between these two causes that motivated him, as it did other Oxford colleagues who accepted his leadership. As the young James Bryce put it in 1863, 'the prospects of anything being done for ourselves in England seem so much connected with the progress of more democratic republicanism against oligarchy that we feel less disposed to acquiesce in secession'.[14]

Only five years later, for personal reasons, Goldwin Smith left England for the United States, in body if not in spirit. 'Being in America, I am in England,' he proclaimed at one point, and at another: 'I am a loyal and even ardent citizen of the Greater Britain, and most sincerely wish to see all the children of England, including the people of the United States, linked to their parent by the bond of the heart.' His book, *Commonwealth or Empire* (1902), affirmed his Forsterian distinction between Britain's export of self-government to the English-speaking peoples (laudable) and British imperial domination (deplorable). With his habitual scorn for the petty prejudices of others, Smith became notorious in Toronto for saying that he looked forward to Canada's annexation to the United States, or, as he put it in his history of the United States, published in 1893, the 'voluntary reunion of the American branches of the race within its pale'.[15] In this, Smith was in tune with those British radicals who professed 'to look to the Great Republic for their precedents, and not to the corrupt and snobbish Dominion'.[16]

'English-speaking peoples', in its North American context, was thus a fraught expression. It was treated with suspicion north of the 49th parallel, as little more than a codeword for the annexation of Canada by the United States. This is surely why Canadians were egregious in avoiding the term altogether, at least while 'the Canada question' remained a live issue. The presence of a prominent francophone community cannot be the sole reason. The incorrigibly anglophone *Globe and Mail* in Toronto, which was the nearest equivalent to *The Times* in London or to *The New York Times*, either avoided the expression or else pointedly referred to 'the two English-speaking peoples', thus excluding Canada.[17] Admittedly this Toronto sense of the term, as applying solely to the British and American nations, seems to have been common also in Melbourne, where the *Argus* was similarly hesitant to claim that Australians too were among the English-speaking peoples; but Australian newspapers were not otherwise inhibited in using the expression, with benign if distant interest, especially in the 1890s and 1920s.

Like a word-game out of *Alice in Wonderland*, competitive catch-phrases chase each other around these late-Victorian debates. Imperialism, we must have imperialism, young Winston is told. Yes, plus federation, of course, some of his elders add. Moonshine, scoffs Lord Randolph. Just Greater Britain, Dilke keeps interjecting. Expansion of England rather, mutters Professor Seeley. A commonwealth, suggest Forster and Rosebery and Goldwin Smith from time to time. And failing federation, Chamberlain sums up, Tariff Reform and imperial preference! Little wonder, one might suppose, that an impressionable young politician, with an hereditary weakness for rhetoric and sentiment rather than a programmatic agenda, might prefer to talk about the English-speaking peoples. But, as a child bred in a privileged Tory household, this was not his native idiom.

Instead, it was a populist, radical, plebeian language, pitched against the values of aristocratic England. The United States, though supposedly peopled by Seeley's absent-minded race, had deliberately cast off its colonial fetters. For Victorian radicals, there was simply no difficulty in understanding this exemplary assertion of their own values. Joseph Cowen, for example, a Liberal MP and a wealthy manufacturer like Forster, took his role as 'tribune of the plebs' to the extent of dressing in miner's Sunday clothes and speaking in a strong Northumberland accent that may have been incomprehensible in London drawing rooms. But it had served well enough to welcome Ulysses Grant to Newcastle in 1877. 'We sprang from the same race, spoke the same language, were moved by the same prejudices, animated by the same hopes,' Cowen declared on that occasion; 'we sang the same songs, cherished the same liberal political principles, and we were imbued with the conviction that we had a common destiny to fulfill among the children of men.'[18]

True, Anglo-American allusions often did not require much decoding. Despite the fact that the United States did not recognise the Berne Convention on copyright until 1891, there was a mass transatlantic readership for some contemporary authors, whether in pirated editions or not. Sometimes the reasons were as much ideological as literary; British sales of *Uncle Tom's Cabin* (1852), Harriet Beecher Stowe's abolitionist tour de force, were even higher than in the United States. Conversely, Charles Dickens had a huge American following; though the novel that draws most explicitly on his own impressions of the United States, *Martin Chuzzlewit* (1843–44), hardly presents a flattering image of Americans, who routinely confirm every stereotype of boorishness and braggadocio, spiced with ignorance and insularity. Mark Twain was to be celebrated with similar transatlantic acclaim; and Tennyson, Longfellow and Whitman were contemporary poets who could likewise be quoted with the confidence of recognition on either shore.

The appeal *in* a common language to the ties created *by* a common language was self-reinforcing. English was the language of the King James Bible in an age when this was read, marked, learned and freely cited. One contemporary expression of the sentiment that 'Shakespeare is a bond of union between all English-speaking peoples' can stand for dozens. Lincoln, educating himself when growing up on the Indiana frontier, had read impressively widely. He certainly found it prudent to make allusions to Scripture, sometimes with a humour that reached out to his rank-and-file supporters. His own literary devotion, however, was reserved for Shakespeare, Burns and Byron, whose works he would carry with him on his long horseback journeys to newly settled townships where such volumes might not readily have come to hand.[19]

Little wonder, then, that 'Honest Abe' became a populist hero. Gladstone, though likewise hailed as 'the People's William', had been luckier in his own educational opportunities. The great charismatic spokesman of Victorian Liberalism certainly found that the phrase 'English-speaking peoples' rolled nicely off his well-exercised tongue, as an appeal in emotional rather than material terms. This was entirely consistent with Gladstone's vision of politics. Public opinion was to be aroused through great oratory in pursuit of noble ends, always with a moral dimension but often infused with a strong respect for nationality. The number of American streets and even towns bearing his name tells its own story about an influence projected well below the intellectual level of an academic admirer like Professor Woodrow Wilson of Princeton. Nations rightly struggle to be free – here is the paradigm for many of Gladstone's political crusades (indeed, his premature identification of the Southern Confederacy in these nation-building terms had been a temporary embarrassment during the American Civil War).

In this realm of populist rhetorical uplift, visceral moral intensity brooked no equivocation. The classic expression of Gladstonianism was the campaign denouncing the Bulgarian atrocities, which Gladstone himself adroitly joined at a late stage in 1876 after some effective orchestration of popular protest, notably by the journalist W. T. Stead, at the time editor of the radical Darlington paper *The Northern Echo*, and the historian E. A. Freeman, Lord Randolph's old examiner. Each of these Gladstonians, in very different ways, was to play an important part in disseminating the idea that the English-speaking peoples had a common identity based on shared values, and a singular destiny based on a single origin.

In Stead's case the moralistic dimension is particularly blatant. After moving to London and becoming editor of the Gladstonian *Pall Mall Gazette*, he instituted a series of high-profile journalistic campaigns, often exposing sexual lapses in high places. The political career of Sir Charles Dilke, scorchingly reproached as an adulterer, was to be one casualty. Stead himself went to jail for three months, as he afterwards proudly proclaimed in his entry in *Who's Who*, following his eye-catching campaign against prostitution in 1885, denounced as 'The Maiden Tribute of Modern Babylon'. By contrast, the nineteen-year-old son of Lord Randolph Churchill, while still an army cadet, helped mount a protest against a municipal campaign to restrict the activities of the prostitutes in Leicester Square, which he denounced as 'the prowling of the prudes'.[20] It is a small but telling indication of the fact that Winston Churchill's early life, which he later described with wit and insight, had been spent in wholly different circles, with wholly different values, from those of a man like Stead.

Yet it was Stead who was an early champion of the English-speaking peoples. In the 1890s he happily accepted subventions from Cecil Rhodes, who confided in him his own plans 'to promote the unity and extend the influence of the English-speaking race'.[21] With Rhodes's support, Stead took his methods of campaigning journalism to the United States, and was to lead a crusade for civic reform in Chicago; though his later opposition to the South African War led to his being removed as a trustee of Rhodes's will. Stead's own final testament to the cause of the English-speaking peoples came when he accepted an invitation to speak on world peace in New York in April 1912, booking his last voyage on the *SS Titanic*.

Stead, in one sense, was half-American as much as Churchill was in a more literal sense. The overt and unembarrassed exaltation by Americans of their democracy, their populism, their moralism, too, struck chords of mutual sympathy at non-elite levels of British society. Thus Stead, steeped in the plebeian culture of Congregationalism, with all its moralistic petty prurience, could reach out sympathetically to the democratic values that he saw embodied in American life – no landlords, no state Church, no established social hierarchy to deny the Lincolns and Grants their due place. There remained strong links not only between British and American Quakers, but also between Congregationalists, Baptists, Methodists and other denominations that spanned the Atlantic in an era of evangelical revivalism. They were almost literally singing from the same hymn-sheet. This was an important part of a common context that had many secular manifestations, still emotive in the early twentieth century.

Lloyd George, speaking in 1904, knew his audience when he threw back Chamberlain's references to the English-speaking peoples of the world. 'A fine idea,' Lloyd George snorted. 'But there is only one way in which you can put yourselves at their head. It is by going ahead of them. [Loud cheers] They have got free education; they have liberated religion from State control; they have no great landlord system. [Cheers]' Little wonder that Winston Churchill found the Welsh radical so stimulating as a cabinet colleague, in opening new windows for him. In late 1917 Arthur Mee, whose widely read *Children's Encyclopedia* was only one of his many evangelising enterprises, was still in this register: 'Is it really a vain dream that the United Kingdom may yet line up with the younger English-speaking races?'[22] He meant by adopting Prohibition. That was never Churchill's cup of tea.

In origin, references to the English-speaking peoples can claim an honourable provenance, steeped in democratic aspirations. But the increasing prominence of the term by the end of the nineteenth century may appear tainted in our eyes by its links with the vogue for Anglo-Saxonism. Though such ideas were developed at different levels of sophistication, the cruder narratives idealised Anglo-Saxon characteristics as a superior racial stereotype.

Anglo-Saxonism was much celebrated in Victorian Britain, not least by the historian Edward Augustus Freeman. Lord Randolph Churchill may have found him a sympathetic examiner at Oxford; but he was far from the modern stereotype of an Oxford professor who writes as an academic for academics. Freeman was never noted for his caution, scholarly or otherwise, nor for his reticence in passing judgement. On touring the United States in 1881–82, where he was gratified to find many academic admirers, he readily extenuated Russian pogroms and Californian anti-Chinese riots alike, as 'only the natural instinct of any decent nation to get rid of filthy strangers'.[23] This was the same Freeman who had, some five years previously, actively enlisted in the great humanitarian agitation over the Bulgarian horrors – better described for him, perhaps, as a crusade against 'the unspeakable Turk' (originally Carlyle's term) or even as a way to get rid of 'the Dirty Jew', as Freeman himself privately called Disraeli.

Freeman was egregious in his Anglo-Saxon prejudices. But he had been joined in the Bulgarian agitation by an impressive roll call of fellow historians. These numbered not only Seeley and James Bryce, who were seldom averse to bringing their scholarship on relevant modern themes into the public arena, but also specialists on much earlier periods who could reasonably have pleaded that Bulgaria was a faraway country of which they knew little. These included Freeman's mentor and predecessor as Regius Professor of Modern History at Oxford, William Stubbs, whose edition of medieval English charters long remained magisterial; J. A. Froude, whose twelve volumes on the history of England concluded in celebration of the defeat of the Spanish Armada in 1588; and J. R. Green, whose *Short History of the English People* (1874) was dedicated to 'my masters in the study of English history', Freeman and Stubbs.

What had his masters taught him? They shared a vision that is usually identified as a 'Whig' interpretation of history, of which Lord Macaulay, in the previous generation, had been the great exemplar. Macaulay's *History of England* was a classic text; eight volumes of his collected works, in an edition of 1879, survive in Winston Churchill's own library, books that he had read in India at the age of twenty-two. Macaulay himself may have been a British Whig, at the end of an era when Whigs and Tories had dominated parliamentary politics; but the 'Whig interpretation' did not depend upon a narrow sense of political partisanship. It was not a common party allegiance that brought the Tory Stubbs, the imperialist Froude, the democrat Freeman and the social radical Green into support for the Bulgarian campaign; rather, it was the emotional pull of their moralism, exerted upon a defining national issue. Freeman's apophthegm was notoriously: 'History is past politics and politics present history.'

Here we can surely see a link with the kind of history that they wrote. It was not only 'Whig' in its celebration of the unbroken continuity of national institutions and the growth of liberty, it was also 'whig history' (lower case) in a more general sense. This has been succinctly defined as 'a story written from hindsight and by taking sides, whose sense of what is relevant is determined by a future end to which the story is advancing, probably represented by the historian's own time'.[24] Whig history is judgemental history. It assumes that we take sides, as historians, just as we do as citizens. As citizens we do so – in supporting Mr Gladstone, perhaps – because we know right from wrong. As historians, we do so because we know the end of the story, which itself discloses who was right and who was wrong. Winston Churchill, when he came to write history, was often whiggish; he later disagreed with Macaulay about the exact words but hummed the same tune.

It is a perspective on the past from the superior vantage-point of the present. Hence historians who celebrated the achievements of the English-speaking peoples in the late nineteenth century were naturally tempted to perceive – and celebrate – the comfortingly familiar origins of their own beliefs in the lives of their common ancestors. Freeman was able to detect that 'something very like the distinction of Whig and Tory can be traced as far back as the eleventh century'.[25] With bold anachronism, he developed his partisan history of freedom as a sort of relay, with its good guys successively identified through many generations and across more than one sea.

Green's *Short History* became a transatlantic best-seller (even though the sense of 'short' is shown by the fact that the popular edition published in New York runs to five volumes). It was a favourite of Winston Churchill; he still browsed in his copy of the original 1874 edition in the 1950s – competitively by that time. 'I am comforted by reading it,' he told his doctor. 'My account is clearer, simpler.'[26]

Green begins, nominally in the year 449 AD, with the pregnant words: 'For the fatherland of the English race we must look far away from England itself.' He means, of course, that we must look to Germany, for origins that are described as Teutonic, and by extension, Anglo-Saxon. These Teutonic origins are inescapable, whether historiographically or ideologically. The common story may have been told with more scholarly restraint in Stubbs, with more partisan abandon in Freeman, with more nationalist fervour in Froude, and with more populist commitment in Green. But, in this respect, it was always the same story, of Teutonic origins as the foundation of Anglo-Saxon superiority and an Anglo-Saxon mission. Here was one template for writing the history of the English-speaking peoples; but not, for various reasons, quite the template that Churchill was ultimately to adopt.

How far was Anglo-Saxonism a racial doctrine? It has long been recognised that this terminology was often linked with a wider ideology of Social Darwinism. This was actually more strongly rooted in late-nineteenth century thought in the United States, where Anglo-Saxonism enjoyed a popular surge, associated with American stirrings towards Empire. Kipling's call for Americans to 'take up the white man's burden' in 1899 is probably the best-known expression of the notion that Britons might now look to their kith and kin for mutual support in a civilising mission.

In the United States, the idea of 'manifest destiny' had long legitimated conquest within North America (and sometimes threatened Canada). Theodore Roosevelt, when he first published *The Winning of the West* in 1889, happily entitled Part I 'The Spread of the English-Speaking Peoples', and here his story outlined 'the spread of the English-speaking peoples over the world's waste spaces' covering three centuries. This line of thinking was congruent with that of a British imperial prophet like Seeley. But would two rival imperial projects, driven by great-power imperatives, inevitably clash in the dawning era of American international self-assertion? When the dispute over the boundary between British Guiana and Venezuela prompted President Cleveland to assert that this fell under the Monroe Doctrine in 1895, Roosevelt's bellicosity – 'this country needs a war' – was no secret, nor that his war aims would have included Canada.[27] Since a northern annexation represented the traditional fulfilment of manifest destiny, this may seem unsurprising.

The alternative scenario, however, was that of sharing the white man's burden. Thus the diversion of American energies overseas might simultaneously take the historic 'Canada question' off the agenda and, elsewhere in the world, bring partnership. The world, after all, surely had plenty of waste spaces, albeit populated by plenty of backward peoples, who needed ruling.

The waste spaces of the oceans were wider yet. Nobody drew attention to sea power as the root cause of British ascendancy more successfully than Captain Alfred Thayer Mahan, whose magnum opus on this theme was published in 1890. Yet Mahan, despite an obvious career interest in building up the American fleet, found many supporters in Britain for 'breaking down the barriers of estrangement which have too long separated men of the same blood'. On a visit to London in 1894, he was feted at a great public banquet in London, draped with a banner: 'Blood is thicker than water.'[28] It was a catchphrase at the time. The assumption that Americans were simply cousins was, of course, literally true in some of the aristocratic families that had recently wooed brides from across the Atlantic. Young Winston Churchill had several American cousins.

In diplomatic terms, rivalry was now constrained by a sense of cultural affinity among the Anglo-American elite. In the midst of the Venezuelan crisis, President Cleveland duly used Shakespeare's supposed birthday to appeal to 'the relations that should exist, bound close by the strongest ties, between English-speaking peoples'.[29] Sir Julian Pauncefote, the long-serving British ambassador in Washington (1889–1902), duly helped to facilitate an adroit accommodation of successive American demands over the Bering Sea, Venezuela, Cuba, the Philippines, Alaska and Panama. Serving Lord Salisbury's Unionist government in Britain for most of his tenure, Pauncefote was able to rely on public support for his project of reconciling the English-speaking peoples from each of Salisbury's likely successors, Arthur Balfour and Joseph Chamberlain.

It was Chamberlain who went furthest, becoming an embarrassment to the traditionalist prime minister (still doubling up as his own Foreign Secretary) in December 1899. Chamberlain's offence was to use his old methods of public agitation rather than discreet diplomacy to call for 'a new triple alliance between the Teutonic race and the two great branches of the Anglo-Saxon race'. At the time, the British were embroiled in trying to subdue the Boer republics – 'Joe's war' – and the Americans in trying to subdue the Philippines. Albert J. Beveridge was making congruent noises in the US Senate: 'God has not been preparing the English-speaking and Teutonic peoples for a thousand years for nothing but vain and idle self-admiration. No! He has made us the master-organizers of the world to establish system where chaos reigns.'[30]

This kind of public rhetoric certainly gave Anglo-Saxonism more resonance. It was plainly no longer just an academic phenomenon, adopted by an earlier generation of American constitutional historians who had read their Freeman. Admittedly, Freeman himself had been unabashed in declaring his typically Victorian enthusiasm for an Aryan heritage, of which the Teutonic manifestation happily provided the most elevated examples. If triumphalist Aryanism pointed to an unfolding historical destiny for the Teutonic race, this inevitably seems rather sinister in the light of twentieth-century experience. Yet it would be wrong to jump to conclusions.

It is not difficult to find references to race; the real difficulty is to decide what is meant by them in any particular context. Winston Churchill can certainly be found employing such vocabulary not just in his 1918 speech but later during World War II. In his classic oratory of the summer of 1940, there are indeed appeals to the British people to show 'the finest qualities of their race' (18 June), to 'the British race in every part of the world' (14 July) and to 'our famous Island race' (11 September). On 21 March 1943 Churchill tells the House of Commons that 'my faith in the vigour, ingenuity, and resilience of the British race is invincible'. On reading further, however, this is hardly some reactionary lurch into Social Darwinism but part of his longest wartime speech in favour of state-sponsored social security 'for all classes for all purposes from the cradle to the grave'. At the conclusion of the war in Europe, Churchill likewise tells President Truman on 10 May 1945: 'At no time has the principle of alliance between noble races been carried and maintained at so high a pitch.'

Churchill, a child of his time, admittedly harboured some racial prejudices that jar on modern sensibilities. His language about Indians, in particular, reveals prejudices that he held into the 1930s and 1940s. Yet he was never an Anglo-Saxon racialist in the genetic sense. For Churchill, 'race' remained, in the elevated diction of his oratory, a synonym for 'nation' or 'people', with little further force as a systematic means of explanation. Nor was this a later sanitisation of his thinking. Indeed if we go back to 1898–99 we can make sense of his reaction to Lady Randolph's short-lived literary project, with its pregnant title, the *Anglo-Saxon Review*. It is surely pertinent that Winston Churchill, though loyally supporting his mother, had never liked its title, and was particularly scathing about its motto, 'Blood is thicker than water'. His own concept of the English-speaking peoples was not to depend on such appeals.

The son of Lord Randolph Churchill proved more than ready to 'play the American card' at key moments in two world wars when Anglo-American cooperation was salient; and he always hoped that it would turn out to be the ace of trumps and not the two. The course of world politics demanded a new rhetoric and helped shape a new interpretation of history. By 1914, Britain was at war with Germany and its chief ally was France. This was simply a different world from that in which

Freeman had argued passionately in 1871 for the 'restoration' of what he always called 'Elsass' (Alsace) to Germany; or had written: 'The Norman was a Dane who, in his sojourn in Gaul, had put on a slight French varnish, and who came into England to be washed clean again.'[31] By the time the United States entered World War I, a major shift in perspectives and sympathies among Anglo-American historians was apparent.

Constitutional history remained the flagship of the profession. What changed was the way that the whig interpretation, celebrating a common ancestry for both British and American systems of government, ceased to be a strictly Anglo-Saxon narrative. Freeman, despite his own lapses into crude stereotypes, provides a clue as to how this reorientation was possible. 'We have our part in the great deliverance by the wood of Teutoberg,' he had proclaimed; 'Arminius, "liberator Germainiae", is but the first of a roll call which goes on to Hampden and to Washington.'[32] His roll call did not read out the names of kings and queens, least of all those of unwashed Norman usurpers, but instead honoured the unexpectedly long pedigree of a free people with liberties already established by custom, though regrettably poorly documented, long before 1066 brought a French intrusion into the Teutonic idyll.

Even in Freeman's version, however, there were no insuperable racial barriers. After 1066, the Normans were subsequently assimilated by the English, their French varnish scrubbed away. Thus the Anglo-Saxons, who had peopled England, remained ready to people North America later – or so the story goes. The baton of liberty, first carried by Arminius in the German woods, was passed, via the Saxon Harold in the eleventh century, to Hampden in the English conflicts of the seventeenth century, and transported in the eighteenth century to George Washington, the founder of a new republic in America, with an implicit selection problem over whether Lincoln should be preferred to Gladstone in running the last lap.

But how had Lincoln, in the wilds of Indiana or Illinois, received this torch? The *origin* of political liberty might (or might not) be ascribed to the village communities of northern Germany; but the dynamic force in its *growth* relied on a process of emigration – perhaps a notion with particular appeal for Americans. Thus J. L. Motley, in the days before he presented London with a bill for two and half billion dollars as a diplomat, had written as the historian of the Dutch Republic: 'To all who speak the English language, the history of the great agony through which the Republic of Holland was ushered into life must have peculiar interest, for it is a portion of the records of the Anglo-Saxon race – essentially the same, whether in Friesland, England, or Massachusetts.'[33]

With emigration, moreover, went cultural adaptation. Thus in Freeman's own version – whenever he stopped to think it through – there were no barriers that can properly be called racial. As he reiterated himself, race was 'an artificial doctrine, a learned doctrine', hence his readiness to see an extension of the learning experience across the Atlantic: 'Men of various nationalities are on American ground changed into good Americans.'[34]

In repudiating the racial mystique of Anglo-Saxonism, constitutional historians were far from alone. In social thought, an unforgiving model of genetic Darwinism was less appropriate than a more expansive kind of cultural Lamarckism, which relied on social adaptation. Anglo-Saxonism, of course, had often been linked with the fears of elite Americans about the perils of immigration. Racial Anglo-Saxonists saw huddled masses who might be yearning to breathe free but were supposed to have all too little genetic ability to do so. It may have been comforting to think of the English, the Dutch, the Germans, all as distant kin, as Motley had; but the Celtic Irish had often given trouble, as the impulsive Freeman had been rather too quick to spot in suggesting that the best remedy for American social problems 'would be if every Irishman should kill a negro and be hanged for it'.[35] And how could new waves of Mediterranean Europeans and Slavs be accommodated?

But there was now an alternative scenario available. Modern research suggested that the English were actually mainly Celts who had acquired some Anglo-Saxon characteristics, which were in turn acquired by Normans. If so, how much more was a melting-pot metaphor necessary to comprehend American experience! Attention shifted from the fixed categories of blood and descent, supposedly Anglo-Saxon, to an ongoing assimilation of American immigrants into a common culture. 'Statistics', as even Churchill's reactionary comrade-in-arms, F. E. Smith, acknowledged by 1924, 'make it plain how obsolete is the talk that blood is thicker than water.' It was a point obvious to the New York publisher, Charles Scribner, who told Churchill in 1930 that 'unfortunately enough, from my point of view, the American people are becoming less and less of an Anglo-Saxon race, and the Nordic tradition with England as the mother country of the USA is less popular in this country than one might expect'.[36]

In the twentieth century, the supposed racial underpinning had become an anachronistic embarrassment for any sophisticated person. Claims about blood were watered down, their inherent implausibility now conclusively dismissed by scientists, and spurned in the twentieth century as embarrassing by politicians and diplomats. 'Some people call it Anglo-Saxon feeling. But it is not really that as between us and you,' Sir Edward Grey, Foreign Secretary in the new Liberal government, told President Theodore Roosevelt in 1906. 'Your continent is making a new race and a new type, drawn from many sources, just as in old times the race of these Islands was evolved from many sources. So I do not dwell upon race feeling. But common language helps to draw us together, and religion also.'[37]

Language, understood as the bearer of customs and culture, made the concept of the English-speaking peoples deeper than simply a linguistic category. Crucially, it also made the concept wider in its ability to assimilate across a supposedly fixed racial line. For historians, likewise, the story of liberty, though still whiggish in applauding its Hampdens and Washingtons, did not need to appeal to an ethnic

Anglo-Saxon identity; it could be satisfactorily told in terms of the institutions and laws that were seen as crucial in shaping a community. This focus, moreover, made it easier to think in terms that were genuinely common to American and British practice.

Though the Anglo-Saxon terminology was still used in the twentieth century, its use was often merely habitual or residual. It was a concept that had now been hollowed out. 'The civilization of the United States is essentially Anglo-Saxon,' explained George Burton Adams, co-founder of the *American Historical Review*, in 1917, 'for civilization and "race" are matters of institutions, not of mere blood.' Furthermore, Adams added the significant rider: 'So far as general institutions are concerned, English constitutional history begins with the Norman Conquest.'[38] For Adams was one of the 'Normanisers' who now disparaged Anglo-Saxon precedents, supposedly derived from the German woods. Instead, the Normanisers were creating a narrative more amenable to those of a more conservative temperament. They escaped from Anglo-Saxonism by appealing to evidence that was more firmly grounded on post-Conquest documents, of feudal and French provenance. And of these documents, the most famous was obviously Magna Carta – the first great title deed on which the liberties of the English-speaking people were founded. By July 1918, when Churchill spoke in this vein, the concept of the English-speaking peoples had been defined, or redefined, in ways that helped make it more usable from his own perspective.

By the time the United States entered World War I in April 1917, it was, if nothing else, a tactical mistake to retain the Anglo-Saxonist idiom in preaching Anglo-American reconciliation. For example, when George Louis Beer, an American imperial historian from a Jewish background, published his collected essays in 1917, he did so under the title, *The English-Speaking Peoples*. This signalled an explicit break with the Mahan era, when the relative viscosity of blood and water had bulked large. Beer's perspective was that immigrants to the United States (Caucasians at any rate), through their steeping in the

English language itself, acquired 'a common mind, and this does not differ in essentials from that of the other English-speaking peoples'. He prefaced his analysis by invoking Milton's *Areopagitica*, 'that inalienable heritage of all English-speaking people, whatever be their physical race or geographical origin'. Beer did not actually quote its famous call: 'Let not England forget her precedence of teaching nations how to live.' Perhaps it would have been otiose. His own current concerns were centred on making a reality of proposals for a League of Nations. His efforts as an adviser to the US delegation on colonial policy at the Paris peace conference – he introduced the idea of 'mandates' – was to evoke the subsequent tribute from Lord Milner, who, as Lloyd George's Colonial Secretary had worked with him in Paris, that Beer 'appreciated the spirit in which we were trying to carry "the white man's burden" '.[39]

The mission of the 'English-speaking peoples', now used in this more inclusive way, was conceived by true believers as a common endeavour in which the historic breach between the United States and the British Empire was to be healed. The new twist was to translate their own countries' recently declared commitment to principles of conciliation and arbitration into more universal terms, in an era when plans for a League of Nations were taking shape. One impulse behind this predated World War I. The centenary of the Treaty of Ghent was to be celebrated in 1914 as marking a century of peace between the United States and Britain. The Treaty's actual centenary on Christmas Eve, in the midst of war on the Western Front, was not front-page news; but there were high-minded appeals for the lesson of international peace between the English-speaking peoples to be universalised. 'An Object-Lesson for the World' was the *Manchester Guardian* headline. This was, of course, faithful to the original Liberal conception of the English-speaking peoples as united in their wish for peace, whatever the posture of their governments. It is no surprise, then, to find that supporters of the various plans for a League of Nations, as subsequently canvassed on both sides of the Atlantic, numbered so many figures who were already prominent champions of the English-speaking peoples. James Bryce, a viscount since 1912 and well on his way to accumulating over thirty honorary degrees, was as active as ever in this stage army of the good.

It is also evident that, by the time the United States entered the war, the concept of the English-speaking peoples had experienced some upward social migration. It was now that it became a buzzword in fashionable drawing rooms, which had once excited the derision of the plebeian moral populists who had first given the expression currency. Balfour, who had employed the rhetoric of the English-speaking peoples since the 1890s, could now do so with wider impact, speaking as Foreign Secretary in Lloyd George's Coalition government. At the conclusion of a visit to North America in 1917, he stated that he discerned 'the true realities which lie at the base of our race, the basic feelings of our Empire, out of which spring our institutions, which I verily believe are going to make the English-speaking peoples of the world the great foundation of the future liberties of the human race'.[40] This can be called the stepping-stone theory: from 'race' in its heroic sense, via Empire in a Greater Britain sense, to the common institutions of the English-speaking peoples, to the universalisation of such aspirations, implicitly in a League of Nations. It was a theory that had more British adherents than American.

The name of John Evelyn Wrench deserves mention at this point. A journalist from an Anglo-Irish family, he had been shown, while on a visit to Canada, a copy of Rhodes's last will and testament. Wrench's foundation of the Over-Seas Club in 1910 (now the Royal Over-Seas League) — 'Grown-up Boy Scouts' was his own view of the membership — proved to be an institutional stepping stone, once the United States joined the war, in much the same trajectory as Balfour's remarks. Wrench was thus ready by 1918 to launch his new project: the English-Speaking Union. He secured the agreement of Balfour to take the chair. The public inauguration was to follow a few days later, on 4 July; it was to be a great demonstration for which the Albert Hall was booked as London's largest public venue. Almost inevitably, one of the speakers at such a meeting would be the octogenarian Lord Bryce, the intellectually eminent former ambassador to Washington, the author of a classic work on American governance, and a champion of the English-speaking peoples for more than half a century. An invitation also went out, as an agreeable courtesy, to Balfour's half-American government colleague, Winston Churchill.

Churchill's only previous recorded references to the English-speaking peoples had come in the winter of 1911–12. The crisis over the Irish Home Rule Bill provided the context. The Liberals had, since Gladstone's time, been unable to implement any Home Rule proposal because it could be vetoed by the Tory House of Lords; but in 1911 the Liberal government had passed the Parliament Act, removing this veto, so Home Rule became a real possibility. Protestant Ulster's opposition was the problem, as it had been since Lord Randolph's day, and his son, filial but troubled, was currently toying with a possible compromise via 'Home Rule All Round'. This chimed in with the contemporary extension of ideas about imperial federalism that were being developed at this time by the Round Table group, an inter-party imperial think-tank, itself largely recruited from Milner's former South African 'Kindergarten'. Churchill framed the question in geopolitical terms, with 'four consolidations of the human family', actual or latent – 'the Russian power, the Yellow races, the Teutonic alliance, and the English-speaking peoples'. In further improving relations with the United States, on 'the road to the unity of the English-speaking races', the reconciliation of the English and Irish peoples would prove 'the first milestone'.

Churchill was obviously right to identify Ireland as a key problem in Anglo-American relations. It was one that would be exacerbated so long as ardent Anglo-Saxonists purported to discern deep racial divisions between themselves and the alien Celts. Yet if there were ever two peoples divided by a common language it was surely the British and the Irish, at least in the era of Oscar Wilde and Bernard Shaw, to either of whom the epigram is alternatively attributed. Whether the Irish were included within the English-speaking peoples was often a matter of opinion and ideology. Churchill included them, Irish-Americans not least. Hence his appeal, in a fraught and famous speech in Belfast early in 1912, for reconciliation over Ireland. Thus, in a strategy 'far wider even than the unity of the British Empire, the great dream could be dreamed of good relations and ultimate unity with the English-speaking peoples all over the world'.[41] The federal dimension of Churchill's analysis on this occasion was characteristically subordinated to an appeal to sentiment, 'the great dream'.

Of this, however, no more was heard from Churchill until six years later. On 4 July 1918 he again reached for this rhetoric in expounding the foreign policy of his cabinet colleague Balfour for the benefit of a new generation of Anglo-American boy scouts, opportunely recruited by Evelyn Wrench. He spoke at a moment when American participation in World War I had finally brought Allied victory into sight, and he duly added his voice in celebration of the fact that they all now met as 'brothers-in-arms'. He continued in this vein: 'We therefore seek to draw from the past history of our race inspiration and comfort to cheer our hearts and fortify and purify our resolution and our comradeship.' No one can accuse Churchill on this occasion of not being transparent about his agenda, ready to raid 'the past history of our race' for exemplary lessons.

Naturally a celebration on the Fourth of July was freighted with historical significance. But if the occasion was, for Americans, a patriotic celebration that the right side had won its battle against the redcoats, there was an awkward corner for a British orator to negotiate. The way that Churchill's speech fulfilled its rhetorical task was worthy of his skills as author and politician alike: 'A great harmony exists between the spirit and language of the Declaration of Independence and all we are fighting for now,' he claimed. 'A similar harmony exists between the principles of that Declaration and all that the British people have wished to stand for, and have in fact achieved at last both here at home and in the self-governing Dominions of the Crown. [Cheers]' Hence the claim that the Declaration was 'the third great title-deed', following Magna Carta and the English Bill of Rights of 1689.

The notion of history as 'a repository of title deeds' was admittedly already rather old-fashioned. Macaulay, writing his *History of England* some seventy years previously, had criticised it for encouraging a highly selective ransacking of the past for precedents that served partisan ends in the present. But even if Churchill had remembered that point from his reading of the great Whig historian, he plainly saw that the concept still had some purchase for Anglo-American audiences in the early twentieth century.

It is significant that Churchill's whole style of argument on 4 July 1918 had a particular appeal for liberals. He spoke at this time as a British Liberal himself, having learnt the language of liberalism, slightly self-consciously, in the Edwardian period; and the *Manchester Guardian*, the bellwether of progressive liberalism in Britain, carried enthusiastic reports of the occasion. Its editor, C. P. Scott, a strong ally of Churchill during his pre-war campaigns for the New Liberalism, had published a supportive leading article on the morning of 'The Historic Fourth', as the headline termed it. Its line of argument is broadly the same as Churchill's, though it is given one further twist.

This is seen in its more explicit appeal to an ideological understanding of Anglo-American relations. Thus the *Manchester Guardian* baldly asserts that 'for generations it has been freely recognized in this country that, though the division of the English-speaking peoples was a tragedy, it would have been a still greater tragedy if George III had defeated the American colonists'. Scott's paper does not blench from saying that such lessons have yet to be applied to British rule in Ireland and also in India. In short, 'the folly of 18th-century Imperialism' is the essential problem; and the essential solution is that proclaimed by President Wilson, 'to make the world a safe place for democracy'. Not just Woodrow Wilson, however: the name of Abraham Lincoln is duly invoked. 'We discovered in 1914 that Europe could not continue to exist half-enslaved and half-free,' the argument runs. 'Americans discovered in 1917 that the same thing was true of the entire world.' All of this was faithful to the roots of the concept of the English-speaking peoples.

Liberal British rhetoric in this vein was also supportive of a League of Nations. Likewise, there was increasing talk of the Empire as a commonwealth of nations: another posthumous triumph for the long-forgotten Forster. It was the Balfour Definition of 1926, enshrined five years later in the Statute of Westminster, that constitutionally established the British Commonwealth. The reanimation of this concept was closely associated with the Round Table group, comprising not just Milnerite Tories but also Liberals. Among the latter, one significant figure in the story of the English-speaking peoples needs to be identified at this point – Ramsay Muir. Nowadays largely forgotten, his name was well known at the time as both imperial historian and charismatic Liberal publicist, celebrated in the Liberal Summer Schools of the 1920s:[42]

> My pamphlets wring the souls of men,
> My lectures grip them sure;
> My words are as the words of ten,
> Because I'm Ramsay Muir.

It came as a great disappointment to many stepping-stone internationalists in Britain that the United States finally played no part in the League of Nations. As the *Manchester Guardian* commented, when the isolationist tenor of debates in the US Senate was first becoming apparent, American abstention would 'destroy the co-operation of the English-speaking peoples, which has been counted on as the cornerstone of the League of Nations'.[43]

Yet in the United States, things looked different. The Republicans were swept to office in the 1920 elections in a backlash, fed by highly charged perceptions of Wilsonian internationalism. This had divisive ethnic connotations at a time when 'hyphenated Americans' were still suspect (and often voted Democrat). The public commendation of the English-speaking peoples by Warren Harding, as President-elect, in January 1921 spoke to such fears. 'Destiny has made it a historical fact that the English-speaking peoples have been the instrument through which civilization has been flung to the far corners of the globe,' declared Harding. But the crucial caveat was that only 'when the wisdom of America is summoned to assist the world in building a workable, as distinguished from a bungling agreement or association for the prevention of war', could the United States be expected to participate.[44] That meant, in effect, no League.

The final stepping stone in the British scenario was thus removed. In an imperfect world, this limited rhetorical commitment became one tolerable American alternative to an institutional commitment to a League that had fallen out of electoral favour along with Wilson. It reminds us that, rather than simply being isolationists, the Republicans in power looked for more elastic, less prescriptive means of engaging with the world outside. It was in this spirit, and with this constraint, that American readiness to embrace the idiom of 'the English-speaking peoples' reached its recorded peak – not under Franklin Roosevelt but under Warren Harding, whose repeated readiness to reach for the phrase at this point might otherwise appear surprising. Compared with Britain, there was thus some difference in the American constituency in use of the phrase.

As for Churchill, his attention was soon diverted. He supported the League of Nations but was not an enthusiast in the 1920s. He preferred to talk of the British Empire rather than the Commonwealth. He made a few references to the English-speaking peoples in advocating acceptance of the Irish Treaty of 1921, reiterating the point that he had made in 1911–12 about the American dimension. Linked with this, he agreed readily enough to assume the honorific office of President of the English-Speaking Union for the year 1921. But he played little role in the organisation and said equally little about the English-speaking peoples throughout the rest of the decade.

Churchill's career turned in other directions. First he was a busy minister until the collapse of Lloyd George's Coalition government in 1922. Then he lost his seat in the House of Commons: temporarily, as it turned out. And he returned to the Conservative Party in 1924: permanently, as it turned out. As some doors closed, others soon opened. Churchill's career as a writer was blossoming as never before; once *The World Crisis* was finished, he was to write substantial historical works.

A history of the English-speaking peoples was clearly an attractive project and it duly found its historian. The work was to run to no fewer than 1,638 printed pages in all. As the introduction to the American edition made explicit, the book 'was as much the history of America as of the British Empire'. It began with the physical disruption of Britain from continental Europe, and continued in narrative mode, with an ample literary confidence that belied the fact that this historian was no specialist in such distant periods but had his attention explicitly fixed on the growth of 'institutions of political freedom'. The themes are familiar, and may well seem distinctively Churchillian. But this book was actually by Ramsay Muir: his two-volume *History of the British Commonwealth*, published in London and New York in 1922–23.

It was to be another ten years before Churchill signed his own contract for *A History of the English-Speaking Peoples*. Even then, he enjoyed no monopoly on the idea – nor deserved it. Forced to put his work aside in 1940, Churchill was beaten to publication when a work of over five hundred pages appeared under the same title in 1943. This was written by the prolific British historian R. B. Mowat and finished, after Mowat's wartime death in an air crash, by his American collaborator, Preston Slosson. Mowat was already the biographer of former ambassador Lord Pauncefote, who had used the leverage of the Washington embassy to defuse a whole string of formerly troublesome

Anglo-American disputes; and Mowat was also the author of a string of admonitory books on the importance of Anglo-American relations. Both Muir and Mowat were respected historians in their day; both had long-standing credentials as authorities on the English-speaking peoples; both wrote their histories with real commitment, allied with professional zeal and literary facility. But today their books, so long unread, have largely disappeared from the shelves and are rarely recalled from the stacks of university libraries – a story of authorship quite unlike that of Winston Spencer Churchill.

One Author, Two Contracts, 1922–32

'I have to keep this rate up continuously, if we are to finish by
October 31; and I do not conceal from you that it is a task.'

Winston to Clementine, 1928

Churchill served as Chancellor of the Exchequer from 1924 to 1929. He
and his family moved into the official residence, 11 Downing Street, next
door to the Conservative prime minister, Stanley Baldwin, using
Chartwell as their weekend home. His Chancellorship was at once the
fulfilment of Winston's ambition as the son of Lord Randolph and an
educational process in itself. 'It has been accepted generally until quite
recent times,' Churchill said shortly after leaving this office, 'that the best
way of governing states is by talking.'[1] That was the premise of his own
political career, of course, and he found plenty to talk about at the Treasury. Even when he put Britain back on the international Gold Standard
in 1925, which he later came to acknowledge as his biggest blunder, it was
his own decision, thrashed out in long hours of argument before he was
himself persuaded. In office at the Treasury, then, he proved not only a
good talker but a quick learner, unawed by the sheer professional authority of his advisers but ready to benefit from their expertise, curious to
discover more about monetary and fiscal policy alike.

What the Chancellor learned about taxation spoke to his own
experience as an author. As a cabinet minister earning £5,000 a year,
he had been accustomed to the deduction of income tax from his
salary, in much the same way as happens to people in regular employment today. But the tax system in those days was both more arcane
and more archaic in its provisions; and, unless these are understood,
Churchill's dilemmas as an author cannot be understood either.

In Churchill's profession as author, taxable receipts were especially irregular, depending on whether he was in cabinet office at the time and whether he had just negotiated a large lump sum as an advance. The Inland Revenue's rules allowed for such fluctuations by levying the tax, not on receipts in the current year of assessment but on the average for the preceding three years. This is why Churchill had paid tax on the lump sum from *Lord Randolph Churchill*, not in the fiscal year 1905–06 when payment was actually received, but by equal instalments over the three following years. This procedure was intended to smooth out variable profits, making the tax liability more even and predictable, so that the system would avoid creating sudden crises for a taxpayer if anomalously large sums became due for payment in one particular year. Such, at any rate, was the theory.

Churchill's personal finances, however, constituted one long crisis. His methods for dealing with it were various and versatile; but they all had the common theme of immediate crisis-management, with resort to expedients that could only be justified by unfailingly optimistic assumptions that the future would provide for itself. His normal strategy was to tackle the persistent gap between net income and net expenditure by a combination of lip-service to the possibilities for domestic economies together with a desperate search for increased income from his professional literary activities. Moreover, building on the example of his big advance for *Lord Randolph*, it was obvious to him that the best way for an author to maximise immediate income in the present was to sign a publisher's contract that would provide money up-front for work that would be completed in future years. Thus the magnificent advance secured from the publisher Thornton Butterworth (and supplemented by Curtis Brown's efforts) for *The World Crisis* in 1921 provided for a total sum of £27,000 (about three-quarters of a million pounds at today's values), much of it paid over the next two years even though the first volume was not to be published until April 1923 and other volumes were not to be written until years later.

Churchill's system depended on mortgaging the future to provide cash flow in the present. He spent freely; but he also intermittently amassed large sums in this way for investment. Thus *The World Crisis* provided most of his means of acquiring Chartwell at a point when he could have raised the capital sum required in no other way (though Garron Towers also helped). Churchill had to pay his taxes, of course; but the way that the tax system worked served to compound the problems that he was storing up for the future.

Though incorrigibly optimistic, Churchill was not wholly oblivious of the implications of what he was doing. Thus he appreciated the future pattern of tax liabilities incurred by his literary receipts from *The World Crisis*. There was, of course, no deduction at source on such payments. So Churchill could always bank the full amounts as received from his publishers or agents. And, since such receipts were not assessed for income tax in the current year, it was only in the following tax year that an assessment was made, based on an average of the previous three years. So the final tax assessment on the final part of his advance would be pushed forward into the fiscal year 1927–28 – with the net result that in January 1929 Churchill would be paying a tax bill on a sum agreed with his publishers no less than eight years previously. This is what Churchill was warned would happen. He was aware of the liabilities that might pile up. In negotiating the hazards – and temptations – of the fiscal regime, he was little different from any other successful author of his day.

But he was simultaneously one of the half-dozen leading politicians in Britain. This had several implications, both public and private. It is evident that, as a private individual, he was already engaging in a sort of tax planning that is today commonplace, so as to manipulate his income in the most tax-efficient way. In this he was both helped and hindered by his abruptly varying political fortunes. As it turned out, 1923–24 was to be his last full fiscal year out of cabinet office before he was appointed Chancellor in November 1924. In the fiscal year 1923–24 he actually received the bulk of the advance for *The World Crisis*; but none of this became immediately assessable for tax, because income tax would only become due in subsequent years, on the basis of the retrospective three-year rolling average. This was only to be expected.

How, then, was Churchill's position affected by his unexpected return to office? In the eyes of the Inland Revenue, about halfway through the fiscal year 1924–25, a former professional writer had become a public servant with his salary subject to deduction at source. Could it be argued that Churchill had ceased at that point to pursue his profession as an author? If that were the case, as his tax advisers made clear to him, his receipts from his literary activities might be treated in a wholly different way by the Inland Revenue.

The important issue was to clarify his tax status. It was a cardinal principle of the British tax system in those days that capital gains were not taxable; and, once a writer retired, literary receipts could arguably be regarded as capital windfalls rather than current earnings. Churchill was evidently exploring the option of declaring that he had now quit his profession as author, and consequently need pay no further tax on his literary receipts. Thus the slate would be wiped clean and any payments in the pipeline for work already done would be treated as capital gains rather than taxable income. It was a stratagem that he was to keep in mind; when he took office again during World War II he was treated as having retired from authorship. And the advantage of receiving a lump sum as a capital payment rather than as earned income was not lost upon him, as will be seen later.

But as Chancellor of the Exchequer he did not pursue the point. It is not clear exactly what decided him, but two considerations seem obvious. One is that an unseemly wrangle with Inland Revenue officials, who were responsible to him as Chancellor, might have had political repercussions, just when Churchill was rehabilitating himself as a respectable Conservative statesman. Even more compelling is the fact that ceasing authorship, in a manner that would prove convincing to the Inland Revenue, was not really an option for Churchill. Keynes might criticise the literary defects of later volumes of *The World Crisis*, written in office, on the grounds that authorship was a full-time job and so was the Chancellorship; but Churchill took a different view.

Brimful of energy and confidence, he thought that he could do both at once. Needful of the continued income, he could not jump off his literary treadmill without scaling back his lifestyle in a way that he never seriously contemplated. Ceasing authorship would have meant living on a cabinet minister's salary, which Churchill calculated as £3,300 after tax, compared with his current disposable income some three or four times higher. An author he remained. As Winston told Clementine in 1928: 'Butterworth has sent the extra £1,500 advance on *The Aftermath*; & I have sent my first 2 articles (£1,000) to America – so that we can jog along.'[2]

World War I was the real fiscal watershed, for Britain and Churchill alike. Estimates suggest that a married man with children, in roughly his own circumstances, would have paid well under 10 per cent of his total income in taxes, both direct and indirect, before 1914; but by 1919 he would be paying around 40 per cent. The incidence of taxes thus took on a new salience, especially for someone on Churchill's high income.

Part of the reason was the imposition of a form of higher-rate 'super-tax'. Super-tax was regarded by the purists at the Inland Revenue as different in conception from the historic income tax. It was assessed, not only on a separate scale, but also on an even more extended timetable. Thus the same income, assessed for income tax on the basis of receipts up to four years previously, was then assessed for super-tax a further year later. Super-tax had a graduated scale, with a top rate of 25 percent, which Churchill had to pay on net income above £8,000 a year; and since he would already have paid income tax on the same income in the previous year – and at the same rate – he was thus facing marginal rates of taxation of 50 per cent on his income in the mid-1920s.

Because of the deferred basis of assessment, however, in any particular year there was little correlation between Churchill's tax bill and his income. It is often difficult to make sense of his own calculations, though many jottings in his own hand survive in his archive, mixing up tax years and calendar years, gross and net receipts, income and capital. In particular, Churchill deploys the term net income in a way that defies the principles of accountancy but expresses his own priority: cash in hand. The paradox in these years was that his tax bills increased whereas his total income decreased, sharply accentuating the decline in his disposable income after tax: £17,000 in 1923–24 but projected as less than £10,000 three years later.

Confronting this system, the Chancellor found his reforming impulses inflamed by his own experience as a taxpayer. He succeeded in reducing income tax, first from 25 per cent to 22.5 per cent, then to 20 per cent by 1926, which was in line with Conservative policy. He met more difficulty in implementing his ambitious plans to tackle the incidence of super-tax. In 1928 he achieved partial success; the super-tax was renamed surtax and was now amalgamated with the income tax on a single graduated scale. Churchill thus struggled to impose his 'Sovereign Principle' upon the recalcitrant Inland Revenue: 'to get the money, as near as possible to the moment when it was received by the taxpayer'.[3] He was pointing, somewhat wistfully, to an ideal that he was unable to implement, either in public policy or private life.

As Chancellor, then, Churchill had several different perspectives on the British tax system. His own personal finances inhabited a universe that observed dislocated chronologics. In the present, the author signed contracts for books that he promised to write several years in the future; he pocketed the gross proceeds and added them to his net salary, calling this sum his income in the present year; and out of income in future years he paid such taxes as belatedly came due on income that he had received (and spent) during years in the distant past. He knew that, if the music stopped, he would be insolvent. Meanwhile he looked to Lloyds Bank, at the fashionable Cox's and King's branch in Pall Mall, which had long handled his account, to support him through rolling over his (tax-efficient) loans. By the 1920s and 1930s he was also using them to make his tax returns as necessary, leaving Eddie Marsh free for more proofreading – and sparing an irreproachable civil servant, who had faithfully followed his master to the Treasury, of a possible conflict of interest. And then Churchill trusted to luck, always confident that the next big advance would somehow do the trick but also always conscious that he could not get off the treadmill.

The Conservative government, elected in 1924, was in power for a full parliament with a secure majority. As prime minister, Stanley Baldwin was happy enough to have Churchill at the Treasury, where he himself had recently served; though the new Chancellor's decision to put Britain back on the Gold Standard in 1925, by over-pricing British exports in world markets and thus aggravating unemployment, weighed against the government's chances of re-election. Baldwin, a cousin of Rudyard Kipling and a man with his own acute literary sensibilities, was seven years older than Churchill, whose rhetorical gifts he admired but whose political judgement he mistrusted, especially over imperial issues. Indeed, when Baldwin read *My Early Life* in proof, it struck him as a wonderful period piece but reinforced his sense that the former lieutenant of the 4th Hussars was an unreliable authority on political trends in modern India. The direction of British policy in the Indian Empire, however, was not a salient issue – at least, not for the moment. And in the meantime, for nearly five years, the two men worked amicably together. There was no reason to suppose that Churchill would be ejected from the cabinet.

In the General Election held on 30 May 1929, however, the government lost its majority and Churchill lost his office as Chancellor accordingly. He was notably disgruntled while watching the results come in on the ticker tape and obviously upset to see that the Labour Party, under Ramsay MacDonald's leadership, would be able to form a government with Liberal support. Churchill was evidently unprepared for such a political reverse. Only a few days previously he had agreed contracts with publishers in New York and London to write a major new book, to be completed within five years. This was the normal span of a parliament, so he was now making an immediate commitment when, if he had waited only a week or so, he would have known the election result. As it was, and given his misplaced confidence that the Conservatives would be returned, he must have expected to write this new book while in cabinet office, whether at the Treasury or elsewhere. This may seem a surprising decision for him to have made at such a moment. But the money was needed anyway. Moreover, since he had written large parts of *The World Crisis* and *My Early Life* (both published by Butterworth) while in office, with Baldwin's connivance and encouragement, Churchill was confident of his ability to perform a similar feat again, remarkable as it may seem.

The least surprising aspect of the whole business was the new book's subject, which seemed to many people predictable and virtually predestined. We can certainly find moving speeches in the 1920s about the values 'underlying everything in the English-speaking peoples', formed as they had been by a common English culture, especially the King James Bible, which had 'penetrated the life and thought of the people' in both the British Empire and the United States.[4] But these are the words of Baldwin, not Churchill, who, as Chancellor of the Exchequer, found the United States tiresome in expecting Britain to repay the debts contracted in wartime. One weekend visitor to Chartwell recorded Churchill's after-dinner views on the Americans in 1928: 'He thinks they are arrogant, fundamentally hostile to us, and that they wish to dominate world politics.' He argued in Baldwin's cabinet against further efforts at appeasement in dealing with such unreasonable people – 'it only shows how little advantage is to be gained by making such efforts to conciliate American opinion'. Little wonder that Clementine had qualms about what might happen if Winston moved to the Foreign Office, suggesting privately in November 1928 that 'your own known hostility to America might stand in the way'.[5] The fact is that Churchill had shown little interest in the English-speaking peoples since the

Anglo-Irish Treaty of 1921 and was not proposing to write their history in May 1929.

Instead, his new project was a biography of John Churchill, first Duke of Marlborough. There had been talk of his writing such a biography ever since young Winston had first established his literary reputation at the turn of the century. His own striking aptitude for military history, from *The Malakand Field Force* to *The World Crisis*, attested to his professional qualifications for the task. Perversely, his main inhibition arose from his family connection. While Marlborough's military genius was widely acknowledged, his political reputation had languished, not least through his depiction by Macaulay, whose barbed tribute to 'that decorum which he never failed to preserve in the midst of guilt and dishonour' exemplifies the general tone.[6] To a generation brought up on Macaulay's *History of England*, this view of an unscrupulous opportunist, ready to betray king and country alike in serving his own career, had become conventional, hardly even controversial. For example, an early and favourable review of Winston's first book in 1898, while hoping that its author might 'become as great a soldier' as his great ancestor, naturally added 'and a straighter politician!'[7] Having imbibed Macaulay himself, Churchill felt uneasy about a possible conflict: either letting the family down or defending the indefensible.

It was Lord Rosebery who had revealed the way forward. In the preface to his *Marlborough*, Churchill singles out two men for thanks in encouraging the work, both of them contemporaries of Lord Randolph but both outliving him by more than thirty years. One was Balfour, remarkable in still serving as a cabinet minister alongside Winston until 1929. The other was Rosebery. In the preface, Churchill recalls having lunch in August 1924 with the former Liberal prime minister, who prided himself on his own historical learning and had a fine working library at The Durdans, one of his several country houses. The aged statesman had risen from the table and made his way to the shelf containing a neglected work of critical scholarship, John Paget's

Examen, first published in 1861, and had put the out-of-print volume into Churchill's hand as his 'answer to Macaulay'.[8]

This was the turning point. Churchill, newly impressed by the way that the case for the defence of 'Duke John' could be marshalled, came to feel that, in principle, he could write his ancestor's biography with a clear conscience, setting the record straight while vindicating the family honour. As he immediately told Clementine, he was consequently warming to 'the great literary project which so many people are inclined to saddle me with'. Sunny, the current Duke of Marlborough, who held the archives at Blenheim, was encouraging. 'Although the labour will be hard and long, the task is inspiring,' Winston wrote to his ducal cousin in 1926. 'To recall from the past this majestic shade and invest it with life and colour for the eyes of the twentieth century, would be a splendid achievement and is even, in a certain sense, a duty.'[9]

Consequently, by the winter of 1928–29, the Marlborough biography was on the market. The fifth volume of *The World Crisis*, supposedly the last, was in the press, published in London by Thornton Butterworth, and in New York by the larger firm of Scribners. But, from an early point, there were other expressions of interest in the biography, notably an offer by George Harrap, by then in his sixties, a financially successful publisher of textbooks and dictionaries but one with few established literary credentials. He did not appear in *Who's Who* until after he had published *Marlborough*, whereupon his entry proclaimed: 'Left school at the age of fourteen with a love of reading.' The two autodidacts, author and publisher, got along well. Churchill was impressed by Harrap's readiness to offer £10,000 for the British Empire rights, with £4,000 to be paid as an advance on signature of the contract.

The American rights were crucial. It is clear that Butterworth, in offering £15,000 overall, was relying on his link with Scribners in New York to find most of the money. Sixteen years junior to Churchill, Charles Scribner, with his flair for drawing, had been headed off from his early wish to become a painter. Instead, Charlie (as he was known, since the line of Scribners all bore the name Charles) had entered the family firm under his dictatorial father ('the czar'). After war service in France in 1917–18, Charlie commuted to Manhattan from his property in Far Hills, New Jersey, where he had his stables. Little wonder that Churchill warmed to him; and Charlie, having long fought his father to insist on publishing Scott Fitzgerald, was hardly likely to worry about his authors drinking too much.

Though initially recruited as the American publisher of *The World Crisis* through Butterworth and the agent Curtis Brown, Charlie Scribner now took matters into his own hands. He made his own bid direct to Churchill on 20 May 1929, offering $25,000 for the American rights. Given that Churchill had put sterling back on the Gold Standard at the historic exchange rate of $4.86, this sum was currently worth about five thousand pounds. So, with a similar offer of five thousand pounds from the *Daily Telegraph* for the serial rights, plus ten thousand already in the bag from Harrap, Churchill was assured of twenty thousand pounds in all (nearly a million pounds at today's values). 'It is a wonderful thing to have all these contracts satisfactorily settled,' he wrote to Clementine from a liner steaming up the St Lawrence River in August 1929, 'and to feel that two or three years agreeable work is mapped out and, if completed, will certainly be rewarded.'[10] After a couple of months of travel in North America, he planned to meet Scribner personally in New York.

Churchill had envisaged *Marlborough* as a five-year project, to be written in his spare time as a cabinet minister. Suddenly out of office in 1929, with more time to devote to authorship, he now thought that he could do the job in about half the period specified in the contracts. This was partly a reflection of his usual over-sanguine expectations, but partly also because he now planned to pay for expert assistance. Winston's son Randolph was currently (and briefly) an undergraduate at Christ Church, Oxford, where his tutor was the historian Keith Feiling, author of a well-regarded book on the Tory Party in the age of

Marlborough. By the end of June 1929, on Feiling's recommendation, Churchill engaged the services of Maurice Ashley, a twenty-one-year-old graduate with First Class Honours in History, who would remain in Oxford as a half-time research assistant on *Marlborough*, for £300 a year. Feiling was also given an honorarium of £100 for his occasional advice; the equivalent today would be a consultation fee of five thousand pounds (which almost any professor of history would gladly accept as fair recompense). These arrangements meant that preliminary work on the project could begin at once, buying books and exploring the Marlborough archives at Blenheim, to which Churchill's cousin Sunny obligingly granted exclusive access.

This work now progressed in the author's absence. On 3 August 1929 'the Churchill Troupe', as Winston called it, left for North America. The troupe comprised Winston and his brother Jack, and their respective sons, Randolph and Johnny; Clementine, recovering from a tonsils operation, was disappointed not to join them. It was to be a holiday, especially for Winston after busy years at the Treasury, with an itinerary that took him first across Canada, and thence down to California, all in great luxury, with private railcars and hospitable accommodation made freely available. Churchill got the full celebrity treatment, not only as a leading British politician but as an author whose name was now increasingly well known in the United States. He had planned to continue working on *Marlborough*, but little actually got done.

This was his first visit to the United States for twenty-nine years. He had made little effort to get back there in the meantime but his current enthusiasm made up for it. He responded warmly on meeting kindred spirits, especially when they footed the bill for the troupe. 'A vast income always overspent,' he gushed in a letter to Clementine after meeting William Randolph Hearst, proprietor of supposedly anglophobic newspapers. Yet Hearst entertained them all at his spectacular home, San Simeon, overlooking the Pacific (a grandiose setting, later evoked in Orson Welles's film, *Citizen Kane*). To his American stockbroker, Van Antwerp, Churchill wrote of Hearst: 'He seems very much set upon the idea of closer and more intimate relations between the English-speaking peoples, – a cause, which, as you know, is very near my heart.'[11]

Not only was his heart full but also his pocket. Churchill was now using the hotel facilities put at his disposal to speculate in stocks, advised in the background by Van Antwerp. Winston told Clementine that he had already made £1,000 pounds in this way and was giving Van Antwerp another £3,000 to keep up the good work. This was all in addition to the speculative gains that Churchill had netted earlier in the trip. Before leaving he had arranged with Lloyds Bank to increase his borrowing limit to £9,000, thus anticipating his advances from *Marlborough*. This was his speculation fund. His letters home give an impression of a pyramid of wealth, conjured up by increasing his stakes in the bull market of which he saw so many amazing signs in the United States. At this rate, loss of a mere ministerial salary was of little account. Winston, in his usual fashion, totted up every kind of gain, capital and income alike, actual and prospective, and assured his wife that 'there is money enough to make us comfortable & well-mounted in London this autumn & you shd be able to do the nursery wing all right'.[12] Thus not only living expenses but further investment in Chartwell could easily be financed.

His luck held, temporarily. When Churchill arrived in New York in early October, he made a speech to a group of Anglo-American businessmen for which he was sent a cheque for $12,500; the covering letter spoke of furthering 'a great relationship between your Country and ours'.[13] The American card seemed to be turning up trumps. Still buoyed up by good news, a few days later Winston reported to Clementine that he had obtained a contract to write no fewer than twenty-two magazine articles on his return, at rates that had secured his immediate assent to this diversion of his literary labours.

In fact, the speculative bubble was already close to bursting, for Wall Street and Winston alike. After an intervening visit to Washington and Virginia, to see Civil War battlefields, he returned to New

York in time to witness 'Black Thursday', 24 October 1929, when the Great Crash finally overtook the Stock Exchange, bringing many over-confident investors to their knees, Churchill among them. Returning home at the beginning of November, he made no attempt to disguise the seriousness of this financial setback.

Churchill went at once to see the manager at Lloyds Bank in Pall Mall, trying to buy time. On 13 November, with authorisation for his loan of £9,000 set to expire within days, he was pointedly reminded that 'when permission was given it was on the assumption that certain sums you promised would be paid in by the end of October', which had evidently not happened; and he was asked to make 'a substantial reduction' accordingly.[14] His American investments had collapsed; since many of them had been acquired on credit, he owed the money to the bank; now this line of credit was to be cut; and meanwhile, as the bank had already advised him, his tax bill in January, hanging over from more prosperous days, would be over four thousand pounds.

Churchill was nothing if not resilient. Though he often battled with what he called 'the black dog', he rarely succumbed to inert despondency. Instead, his characteristic response to adversity was to throw himself into vigorous activity, which became self-sustaining in a kind of bipolar cycle (though hardly manic-depressive in any clinical sense). In late 1929 he was down, but not out. At least his time was his own, with many fewer duties on the opposition benches than would be the case today. Like Walter Scott before him, Churchill knew that there was only one way out of his predicament. He set about maximising his literary income, following up every promising lead, with a more exacting writing schedule than his contract for *Marlborough* had ever envisaged.

Churchill had long wanted to spend more time at Chartwell. He had happily put in a great deal of his own labour on ambitious plans, not only building walls and a cottage but also hiring men to dam streams, create lakes and form a swimming pool. He looked on these projects as improving the estate; Clementine saw them as consuming their stretched income by putting extra workers onto an already large payroll. Winston particularly enjoyed laying bricks himself, sometimes while dictating his literary works to his secretaries. As he told Baldwin in September 1928, when beginning *My Early Life*: 'I have had a delightful month – building a cottage & dictating a book: 200 bricks & 2000 words per day.' Yes, it was a fine accomplishment; but a few weeks earlier, while actually on the job, he had told Clementine: 'Nearly 3000 words in the last two days! I have to keep this rate up continuously, if we are to finish by October 31; and I do not conceal from you that it is a task.'[15]

Chartwell was not only his much-loved home but also his word-factory, serving simultaneously as the site of enormous production and of conspicuous consumption. For it was undoubtedly an expensive house to run. Clementine thriftily made do without a trained cook; but in the 1920s there were two servants in the kitchen, preparing hospitable dinners, especially at weekends, and another two in the pantry; and there were two housemaids, making up rooms for house guests. Clementine similarly tried to instill her daughters with an ethic of self-help. 'I am *quite* comfortable without a maid,' she wrote to Winston from Venice in 1927, '& I am teaching Diana (gradually) how to keep her room tidy & how to darn her stockings & generally to keep herself neat & like a lady without having to be waited on.'[16] At Chartwell, however, there was a personal maid for Clementine, a nursery maid for their youngest daughter Mary, and an 'odd man' to cope with boots and boilers and dustbins. Nine wages to be paid in the house itself, then; though most of these payments went to women, who would have earned well under two pounds a week in the interwar period, so the weekly bill for all of them may have been under fifteen pounds. But in addition there was Mary's nanny or governess, and, of course, a couple of secretaries; and outdoors, there was a chauffeur, three gardeners and a groom for the polo ponies (not counting a bailiff for the nascent farm). These employees would have been more highly paid: not only the secretaries but also at least two pounds a week for most of the men – we know from tax returns that the chauffeur was the only one to earn over £125 a year – so up to twenty pounds a week in all. In total, then, the wages bill must have approached two thousand pounds a year.

The secretaries played a key role in the Chartwell workforce. They directly helped the boss generate the firm's income stream. In all literary work, Winston relied from 1929 on Violet Pearman, who was allowed great discretion in acting for him, covering for his absences, making plausible excuses, accompanying him on exotic working visits (whether to the Riviera or Marrakesh) and generally delivering the goods. Grace Hamblin was in a hybrid position, fondly remembered by Mary as a local girl first recruited to help out. She blossomed not only as an assistant to Mrs Pearman, taking dictation on literary work, but also increasingly as the general administrator of Chartwell (which indeed she was to become when it was finally handed over to the National Trust).

Churchill later presented an idyllic picture of his life at Chartwell in the early 1930s. He had always liked the passage from *Ecclesiasticus* that begins, in the King James Bible, 'Let us now praise famous men'; and especially its benign reference to 'Rich men furnished with ability, living peaceably in their habitations'. In *The Gathering Storm* he was to apply these words to himself, modestly omitting to state exactly how rich or how well furnished with ability: 'Thus I never had a dull or idle moment from morning till midnight, and with my happy family around me dwelt at peace within my habitation.'[17] In the winter of 1929–30, however, the picture was rather different, following the Great Crash. The cottage that he had recently completed, intended for a butler, was instead taken over for the family, accommodating Mary and her governess. Clementine stayed mainly in London; but Winston would come down regularly, certainly at weekends. The big house was closed up, the only room not under dust sheets being Winston's own study. Mary learned from an early age that this was 'holy ground', though she writes that she 'did not understand till later – when my mother impressed it upon me – that my father earned his living, indeed our family's living, by his pen, and that our domestic economy at certain periods survived precariously from article to article and book to book'.[18]

One wholly new book was inserted into this already packed schedule. In the course of writing a couple of his magazine articles, covering the Russian Front in World War I, Churchill was seized with the idea of expanding this treatment to add a sixth volume to his five on *The World Crisis*. He sold the idea of *The Eastern Front* to Thornton Butterworth, his London publisher for the original volumes, and likewise to Scribners in New York, where it was published as *The Unknown War*. The work was supposed to be completed within the year, admittedly with paid help from military historians, engaged on similar terms to those for Maurice Ashley, who meanwhile continued the research for *Marlborough*.

When Churchill went back to Charles Scribner with yet another proposal in June 1930, he encountered understandable hesitation. He had been dictating his memoirs of his early life since 1928 and now wanted to hasten their publication during 1930. Scribner tactfully suggested that 'although your name is as well known here as that of any public character outside of America, there is not the same prompt of curiosity to induce an American to purchase your book'. This was not the only problem. Churchill was also gently reminded that 'with actual advances and obligations, we have already committed ourselves to about $33,000 advance royalty to be earned on your books, which is a considerable amount against any one author.'[19] In the end Scribner agreed to accelerate payment of royalties in lieu of an advance for the book, and since its initial American sales exceeded expectations, Churchill got his money quickly after all. On his own suggestion, the book was to be entitled *A Roving Commission* in New York, though Butterworth opted for *My Early Life* as the main title in London.

All this was well in hand by the summer of 1930. When Harold Nicolson and his wife Vita Sackville-West, both writers themselves, encountered the Churchills at a house party in the country, the atmosphere seemed relaxed and benign on a rare weekend off. 'He is writing three books: one a last volume of *The World Crisis*; one a life of the Duke of Marlborough; one of reminiscences of his own,' Nicolson noted with due professional admiration. 'He is in gentle and intelligent form. He goes on a long walk with Vita and tells her his troubles and hopes.'[20] He was currently well supplied with both, of course. At the end of September, with *My Early Life* already serialised in the Liberal newspaper, the *News Chronicle*, Churchill told Baldwin: 'I am already hopeful that the book will do more than it was originally written to do, namely to pay the Tax Collector. There may even be a small surplus to nourish the author and his family.' Three months later he estimated his worldwide earnings from the book at £3,375, and within a year or so it had sold eleven thousand copies in London.[21] In a more buoyant mood, the Churchills reoccupied their Chartwell home and resumed their opulent lifestyle.

Many exaggerated stories of Churchill's income have been put into circulation. Some of these are derived from his own compulsively optimistic private notes – they can hardly be called accounts – listing diverse expectations, which were often disappointed and seldom fully realised. Thus even the standard biographies recycle claims that his income at this time was thirty-five thousand pounds, or even higher, and that his magazine articles alone were worth forty thousand pounds. Yet such sums are totally inconsistent with Churchill's tax returns, even if we allow for the fact that tax was assessed on his net income, after the payment of expenses, which were increasingly heavy with the provision for paid research assistance. As Ashley recalled, 'Churchill himself was wont to say airily about his expenses in writing history books that he got half of them back from the Inland Revenue.'[22]

It is likely that Lloyds Bank, from long experience, had the best grip on the state of Churchill's unruly finances. In 1937 the Bank produced a clear summary of his tax returns, covering eight years.[23] What these tables show is that his assessed income totalled £10,495 in 1929–30, his first year out of cabinet office. In 1930–31, which included much of the magazine work he had contracted in the United States, as well as his assessment on the first tranche of the advance on *Marlborough*, his income certainly increased, though it did not triple or anything like it. The actual figure for Churchill's assessed income in 1930–31 was £12,883, which was a very satisfactory sum in itself, and almost exactly in line with the average of £12,738 for the eight years 1929–37.

All exaggeration apart, this was a high income, whether by the standards of his day or ours. In today's values, his net annual income was certainly over six hundred thousand pounds, with tax taking about a third of this. By comparison, the best-known British professional historian of the post-war period, A. J. P. Taylor, who had earnings from television as well as print media, had a freelance income in his heyday, from the mid-1950s to the mid-1970s, that was impressively into six figures (sterling) at today's prices, but only in rare years even a quarter of what Churchill had been making in the 1930s.[24] It is doubtful whether any living historians, even in the age of media celebrity and television tie-ins, can supplement their academic salaries with literary profits that would support a Chartwell, even though they may receive more income from their day jobs than this hard-pressed statesman was able to rely upon from politics.

Churchill was thus in a different league. If we compare him with a spectacularly successful writer, Somerset Maugham, almost an exact contemporary, it is obvious that Maugham's earnings were much higher, with income from the theatre able to generate enormous returns in that era. A play on Broadway could bring him $2,000 a week, and he often had several running simultaneously in New York and in London, sometimes for months at a time. The fact that Maugham lived on the French Riviera enabled him to escape not only British legal restraints on homosexuality but also the British tax regime. Chartwell was a modest establishment compared with the lavish arrangements at the Villa Mauresque on Cap Ferrat. A photograph of Maugham entertaining two other successful writers on the villa's terrace gives a glimpse into this world: Maugham seated companionably on one side of the low table with H. G. Wells on the other; and standing between them, Winston Churchill.[25]

Churchill does not look out of place in this company. Why should he? When Wells dedicated his book *Star-Begotten* to Churchill in 1937, the latter responded: 'It gives me great pleasure to feel that my early admiration of thirty-five years ago for yr wonderful books should have come to nest in our later lives in a harbour of personal friendship.'[26] Churchill was, like them, a successful professional author. It is difficult to give an exact figure for the proportion of his income that came from literary earnings, but it was at least three-quarters in the 1930s. By contrast, his parliamentary salary as a backbencher, after the 10 per cent cut imposed as an exemplary economy measure in the crisis year of 1931, was £360 per annum, which was less than 3 per cent of his average income. Indeed, it was appreciably less than Churchill's wine bill.

It is as common to exaggerate how much Churchill was drinking as how much he was earning. But in each respect, it was still impressive, as the surviving accounts in his archive demonstrate. Churchill had his account with the wine merchants Raymond Payne (later Hatch, Mansfield and Co.), barely a step away in Pall Mall from Lloyds Bank; so the money almost literally went in one door and out of the other. In 1935 Churchill's bills show four hundred pounds for wines and spirits supplied to Chartwell and just over one hundred for Morpeth Mansions, the Churchills' London flat. The total was thus £515, or ten pounds a week – about three times the earnings of a male manual worker at the time, or enough to employ half a dozen female domestic servants at Chartwell. This expenditure is in real terms about double what Churchill had been spending on wine before World War I; it represents about 6 per cent of his average disposable income after tax in the 1930s; or, in today's money, about five hundred pounds a week. Whether we consider this a high figure is, of course, a matter of taste.

As is Churchill's actual selection of what he chose to consume. About 10 per cent of his account was for port and sherry, especially the former, in accordance with the British liking for fortified wines in that era; conversely, only about 6 per cent went on claret, white wine and hock, which would seem a surprisingly low proportion today. Over 30 per cent of the total was for spirits, notably about eighty bottles of brandy and ninety of whisky – in total over three bottles a week.

There is one significant difference in the accounts for spirits in 1936. The explanation is to be found in a letter that Winston had written to his wife two days before the New Year from the Hotel Mamounia in Marrakesh – a luxurious haunt that he was just discovering, in Lloyd George's company, while Clementine preferred to go off skiing in the Alps. The newspaper proprietor Lord Rothermere was at the Mamounia too, and offered to bet Churchill no less than £2,000 if he could stay teetotal in 1936. 'I refused as I think life would not be worth living,' Winston explained to Clementine, 'but 2,000 free of tax is nearly 3,500 & then the saving of liquor, 500 = 4,000. It was a fine offer.' Thus Winston fully appreciated what was at stake – a sum sufficient to finance Chartwell for a year; but at a personal cost that he simply could not countenance. So he settled instead for Rothermere's alternative bet: £600 'not to drink any brandy or undiluted spirits in 1936'.[27] Since he drank whisky diluted with soda water, it escaped this stricture. The brandy order for the coming year was duly cut back to twenty bottles – suggesting that sixty had been for Winston himself – while the whisky order remained unchanged at ninety.

And the rest of the bill? Predictably, given everything we know about Churchill's pattern of consumption, over 50 per cent was spent on champagne. Here he upheld the preferences of Edwardian high society, believing that there are times when only champagne will do, and that these times come around at least once daily. Not just any champagne, however; all of it was vintage. In 1935 he was still buying Vin d'Ay Sec 1906, and in large quantities: a rosé champagne of a kind that makes it almost a period piece today. In addition, in 1936 the labels ordered include Krug, Goulet, Perrier Jouet, Clicquot and Lanson. But Churchill's true love was reserved for Pol Roger. The 1921 vintage formed most of his purchases at this time, available at about £9 a case, or 15 shillings a bottle (say, forty pounds a bottle at today's values). Churchill bought about a hundred bottles in 1935. In those days champagne often came alternatively in pint bottles, about four-fifths the size of a 75-centilitre bottle. Churchill also bought about 240 pints of the Pol Roger 1921 – and ten magnums too.

This was all a great luxury, of course, but the quality is more impressive than the sheer quantity. All told, the annual supply of champagne that Churchill laid in averaged about a bottle a day – not just for himself, of course, but for the household at Chartwell, with most consumption at weekends, often including guests. Conversely, during the week in London, Churchill himself was usually dining out, with alcoholic beverages that are excluded from these accounts.

His own habits, however, obviously determined what he ordered. The crates of champagne were dispatched regularly from Pall Mall by train to the local station at Westerham and thence to Chartwell, where a cellar book catalogued consumption, bottle by bottle. We also know from diverse anecdotal reports that Churchill sometimes enjoyed beef and beer as a working lunch when writing; we know too that he liked his whisky and soda from the late afternoons onward, when the more conventional British preference was for a nice cup of tea; we know that he served champagne during dinner; and we know that he insisted on brandy, for himself and for even reluctant guests, after both lunch and dinner. This was all part of the Chartwell regime, at once very relaxed and highly disciplined. Churchill needed lubrication to keep the wheels turning in his workshop, in which he sat late into the night, repairing his fortunes.

*   *   *

The big job in hand was the biography of Marlborough. The contract had specified a work in two volumes, of at least 90,000 words each and probably running to 250,000 words in all. This was much like Winston's *Lord Randolph Churchill*, which he had written himself in longhand. But a quarter of a century later, this was no longer his mode of composition; dictation made for prolixity; and professional research assistance, while relieving the author's immediate burden, revealed the sheer volume of archival evidence which Churchill had simply not contemplated. For two years Maurice Ashley beavered away at Blenheim, with the guidance only of some windy rhetoric about the great duke, derived mainly from Churchill's memory of what he had read in Macaulay in his days in India – on which he was currently writing, of course, in completing *My Early Life* for publication.

Progress on *Marlborough* stalled. The mere fact that the research was incomplete did not inhibit Churchill, whose method as an author was to plunge into the construction of a text as quickly as possible. He decided to start in the middle. This was on the grounds that it was not Marlborough's rather dubious early career that mattered but his years of military glory – 'the years 1702 to 1711 are the great period and must form the corpus of the book,' Churchill instructed Ashley. Thus a couple of possible chapters were quickly compiled, with the notion of then working backwards, so that Churchill immediately proposed 'The Protestant Wind' as his next draft chapter, covering the English constitutional crisis of 1688 and the advent of William of Orange, with his ambitions of securing the throne for himself. Churchill started here because he regarded it as 'the most awkward part of the story', in view of Marlborough's betrayal of King James II in favour of William. Now this chapter (much revised) eventually appeared as Chapter 16 – about halfway through Volume One of *Marlborough* in the London edition and towards the end of the first volume in New York (where the sheer bulk of this first instalment eventually caused it to be split into two for publication). If young Ashley, straight from Oxford, thought this an odd way to begin, he was to be even more amazed that the manifestly under-rehearsed author was sending his text straight to the printer, on the principle that 'it is always a good thing to get into "cold lead"'.[28]

This is where things stood by January 1931. Only two chapters were actually in good enough shape to be shown to the London publisher, George Harrap, who was then warned that Churchill would have to switch his efforts to writing *The Eastern Front* – not only another book but one for another publisher (Butterworth). And surely nobody believed that this survey of the entire Russian war effort could be completed in just a couple of months, as Churchill had breezily assured Harrap. Instead, though *The Eastern Front* was written extraordinarily quickly, even given the assistance of military historians, it was not until September 1931 that it could be declared finished. This would permit the imminent resumption of work on *Marlborough* – at least that is what the author told his publisher – and still he added with cheery confidence that the first volume of the biography would be ready for publication in 1933. Churchill's contract for *Marlborough*, then, which had been agreed in May 1929 with Harrap in London and Scribner in New York, had resulted in all too little real progress more than two years later.

Churchill was proud of his ability to fulfil the terms of a contract. But this one, far from being the author's main task, had meanwhile become ensnared by the other commitments that he had taken on. His response was extraordinary, even by his standards. Rather than clearing the decks for a single-minded assault on a project that he now knew was even more formidable than he had at first realised, the author was already, in a rather clandestine way, deep into negotiations for a second big book contract. This was to be for a more popular work: *A History of the English-Speaking Peoples*.

Why not? He was acting as an author in search of a saleable book title, and in an already well-proven field. Ramsay Muir's more academic volumes were no competition. Churchill knew that some of the standard Victorian histories of England, notably those by Macaulay and J. R. Green (both of whom he often quoted), had been best sellers in their day. Indeed Green's work still held the field right in to the 1920s, when it was effectively superseded by G. M. Trevelyan's *History of England* (1926) which was currently enjoying an astonishing success (with ongoing sales that were to reach 200,000 by 1949). Trevelyan went on to become Regius Professor of Modern History at Cambridge, but, as Macaulay's great-nephew and a member of a prominent landed and political family in Northumbria, he had made his reputation essentially as a literary man, with a combination of useful connections and sheer hard work not so different from Churchill's experience.

Churchill saw himself as a professional author whose stock in trade was to turn his hand to popular history if he so chose. This is what Victorian and Edwardian men of letters had long done. For there were also histories of England on the shelves by Charles Dickens and later (for children) by Rudyard Kipling; likewise by Churchill's own contemporaries, G. K. Chesterton and Hilaire Belloc, both writing from an embattled Catholic viewpoint. H. G. Wells felt that he was taking a chance with his ambitious *Outline of History* in 1920, originally published in parts. But in his *Autobiography*, written in the early 1930s, he explained how his own amateur approach to the subject – 'properly "vetted" by one or two more specialized helpers' – succeeded in catching a public response that resulted in sales of over two million, which he publicly admitted 'earned me a considerable sum of money'.[29] When he was at Somerset Maugham's Villa Mauresque, only a short drive from his own villa in Provence, hobnobbing with Churchill amid every luxury that top literary earnings could supply, what did they talk about privately?

Churchill was well placed to supply a transatlantic twist to his own proposal in this sector of the market. He records being impressed when Americans in the book trade told him 'that I had not yet reached the public which was at my disposal in the United States'.[30] In particular, when he had been in New York in October 1929, he was taken by Charles Scribner to watch a football game, during the course of which

Churchill came up with the specific idea for the new project: 'a history of the English speaking race' in two large volumes. Scribner was not hostile to the general idea. He certainly wanted to cash in on Churchill's increasingly high profile in the United States, especially since this was partly the result of his firm's investment in promoting *The World Crisis*. Scribner had initially countered Churchill's proposal with the suggestion of a history of the British Empire, which went nowhere. Above all, Scribner did not see any reason for hurry. Since he successively agreed to publish not only *Marlborough* but also *The Eastern Front* (as *The Unknown War*) and *My Early Life* (as *A Roving Commission*), yet another contract hardly seemed a pressing concern – at least not until the summer of 1931, when Scribner in New York was indirectly approached about a proposal that, so he gathered, was now before the London publishers, Eyre and Spottiswoode.

This was the doing of Brendan Bracken. At the age of thirty, Bracken had emerged as Churchill's most faithful follower in the House of Commons. His bright red hair made him distinctive; his carefully concealed origins (Irish via Australia) made him suspect in London society; but his own self-educated dynamism made him a fortune in financial publishing, stemming from an association in the 1920s with Eyre and Spottiswoode, who specialised in this field. Together with the financier Sir Henry Strakosch (whose similar devotion to Churchill was later crucial in saving Chartwell), Bracken now controlled *The Economist*, which was to become an internationally prestigious publication under his proprietorship. With a finger in every pie, he was ready, willing and able to act as Churchill's man of business, now and later. It was Bracken who acted as agent in putting the proposal for *A History of the English-Speaking Peoples* to a subsidiary of Eyre and Spottiswoode and securing an expression of interest from them in June 1931, with a figure of £20,000 initially suggested for world rights.

Clearly, a lot hinged on the potential American market. Churchill was in fact planning to visit the United States again in October 1931 (despite all his promises to concentrate on *Marlborough*) in an explicit quest for ready cash, just like his tour thirty years earlier. Forty lectures were now planned, with the theme of the unity of the English-speaking peoples to the fore, for a guaranteed fee of £10,000, with almost as much again for newspaper articles in the *Daily Mail*, the latter negotiated by Bracken. As he told Churchill: 'As you are going on this hateful American journey you will have time to dictate a number of articles on American and other topics which will give you but little labour and will swell your income.'[31] Meanwhile the negotiations over *A History of the English-Speaking Peoples* had naturally prompted Eyre and Spottiswoode to make an approach to Scribners, as Churchill's established New York publisher, about the American rights.

The trouble was that Charles Scribner knew too much. As well as recently publishing *A Roving Commission*, he also had Churchill under contract for *The Unknown War*, not yet delivered, and, above all, for *Marlborough*. Yet Eyre and Spottiswoode were now talking about a further substantial work by the same author. How on earth could that too be envisaged? 'I was surprised at the fact that it was to be published in 1933, as between finishing the *Marlborough*, lecturing in America, and all of the other calls on your time, this would scarcely seem possible,' Scribner wrote on 19 June 1931, in the course of 'the longest letter of my business career' – civil in tone but with an underlying sense of reproach. Here he was, some twenty months after the football game at which this bright idea had first been broached, now learning at second hand that his star author was talking to other publishers behind his back – and before completing existing contracts. 'I therefore have not mentioned it to you,' Scribner continued, 'as I hoped we might have the two forthcoming books published, or at least practically finished, before taking it up.'[32] Worse still, Scribner had learned that Churchill was also simultaneously toying with a further proposal for a short history of World War I – in addition to his agreed abridgement of *The World Crisis*, on which Scribners had been counting to recoup their considerable outlay in promoting Churchill's work in the United States.

At this shaky moment in his relationship with Scribner, Churchill too wrote at length in his reply on 30 June. He wriggled out of responsibility for initiating the short-history proposal, making light of it – 'having all the facts at my fingers' ends the task would not be a very hard one' – and pretending that it might help Scribners' sales. (Nothing was to come of this particular proposal.) Unabashed, Churchill retailed to Scribner an edited version of Bracken's dealings with Eyre and Spottiswoode, explaining how the publishers' plan for a History of England had been superseded by 'my idea which I had imparted to you for a work of a wider character'. It was for a two-volume history, 250,000 words in all, 'popularly written, telling the whole story of the origin, quarrels and re-association of the English-speaking peoples'. Though mentioning 'our common civilization in all parts of the globe', Churchill evinced no interest in the Commonwealth and actually meant that the work would be 'about half-and-half British and American history'.

So much for the grand, airy conception of the work. But how did Churchill conceive the sheer practicability of this second major book proposal, especially in the light of his contract for *Marlborough*? Having piously expressed the hope that Scribner might take the new book, Churchill added the warning: 'But I could not make a great financial sacrifice and I am sure you would not wish it.' As for *The Eastern Front* (or *The Unknown War*), it was almost finished, so Churchill claimed, though in fact several months' work remained. And as for *Marlborough*, in which Scribner had invested so much, it was said to be 'steadily progressing', which was certainly a creative way of describing stasis. Hence Churchill's continued assurance that 'I hope to publish in the Spring, or at latest, in the autumn of 1933.' This was ambiguous; he could only have meant the first volume of *Marlborough*; yet unless the whole biography were finished, he was in no position to suggest, as he did, that his *History of the English-Speaking Peoples* could be completed by 1935. Admittedly this was on condition that the author could 'set experts to work assembling material under my directions and in accordance with my general design'.[33]

The lack of realism in this schedule could hardly have induced confidence. Scribners quietly dropped out of the bidding on this new contract. This was certainly understandable, given their financial exposure on *Marlborough*, but it was a business decision, not a personal breach. For over ten years Churchill had had links with both Butterworth in London and Scribners in New York. Both had published all six volumes of the extended *World Crisis*, which had certainly sold well – by 1933 Butterworth reported total sales of 58,334 plus 5,844 for the abridged edition. Both continued to publish other books by Churchill. In 1930 Butterworth's *My Early Life* had been Scribner's *A Roving Commission*, and its success prompted thoughts of a sequel. Butterworth was more attracted by the idea of a volume of short biographies (what eventually became *Great Contemporaries*) but, since Scribner insisted that at least one of the subjects must be American, Churchill deferred this idea in favour of a largely recycled volume. Published by Butterworth as *Thoughts and Adventures* in December 1932, it quickly achieved unexpectedly high sales, which caused printers and binders to work overtime to meet demand. The publisher found himself 'truly delighted at this success which confounds the Jonahs of the Bookselling trade' and was 'in the nature of a minor triumph'.[34] Scribner, still waiting for a major triumph with *Marlborough*, was less fulsome. He issued his edition of this interim offering from his wayward author under the title *Amid These Storms*.

The summer of 1931 was certainly stormy. It was hardly the best time to negotiate an international book deal, especially not for an author whose career supported his political ambitions. The Great Crash of 1929 was the prelude to the Great Depression, which progressively engulfed the world economy. In Britain financial uncertainty provoked a crisis of confidence in the minority Labour government. It was replaced in August 1931 – without an election at that stage – by a so-called National government led by the former Labour prime minister, Ramsay MacDonald, who broke with his party to form a coalition with the Conservatives under Baldwin. A number of prominent Liberals were also appointed as ministers.

Prostate surgery provided a sufficient reason to exclude Lloyd George at this crucial juncture. There were several reasons to freeze out Churchill too, not least the fact that he had a reputation, especially after the General Strike of 1926, for intransigent opposition to the Labour Movement – not good credentials for coalition and conciliation. But his exclusion also followed from his break with Baldwin's leadership over the issue of India. There was a political consensus at the top that moves towards Indian self-government were overdue; opposition came mainly from the Conservative right wing, stronger at the grassroots than in the parliamentary party. Churchill had found time in 1930–31 to champion the cause of the diehards (though it might have been better for everyone if his already excessive commitments as an author had kept him quiet). He was noisy enough to provoke the hostility of the Conservative leadership while failing to mount a serious threat to Baldwin's leadership. Churchill thus lost former friends while making new enemies. The net result was that the National government was formed without him in August 1931. It was to weather Britain's abrupt departure from the ill-fated Gold Standard in September; and it was to achieve a sweeping electoral victory in October, which heralded a long period in power, successively under three prime ministers. Ramsay MacDonald (1931–35), Stanley Baldwin (1935–37) and Neville Chamberlain (1937–40) had one thing in common: distrust of Churchill and determination to keep him out of the cabinet.

It took time for Churchill to realise that his political career was now in long-term eclipse. Through the weeks of crisis in the summer of 1931 – all the while finishing his writing of *The Eastern Front* – he remained active also in his pursuit of a contract for the *History of the English-Speaking Peoples*. He told Bracken at the end of July that if

Eyre and Spottiswoode now wanted three volumes, totalling 450,000 words, he would certainly need at least five thousand pounds per volume for the English rights alone, and at least four thousand as an immediate advance, as on *Marlborough*, so as to employ research assistants. Sticking to his optimism about finishing *Marlborough* in 1933, he envisaged that work on the *History* might overlap with it, with a first volume of the *History* ready for publication in 1934, a second in 1935 and a possible third in 1936. The proposed shape and scale of the book was now settled in these terms.

Yet no contract was agreed in 1931. The national situation was highly unstable, what with the collapse of confidence in the markets, the change of government, drastic budget cuts, a sterling crisis and a likely General Election. At the end of September, Churchill was told that Eyre and Spottiswoode were unable, in present circumstances, to make the kind of offer he expected.

Because of the financial and political crisis, Churchill's American visit had been postponed. He obviously had to stay in England to fight the General Election, if not as a minister then at least as a back-bencher. On 27 October 1931 he was re-elected as Conservative MP for the Epping division of Essex (today in the encroaching suburbs of north-east London), for which he had sat in the House of Commons since 1924. In 1929 he had polled 48.5 per cent, 10 per cent ahead of the Liberal in second place and with Labour a poor third. In 1931, with the collapse of both opposition parties, Churchill got over 60 per cent of the vote (and was to get just under 60 per cent at the next General Election in 1935).

Epping was thus an impregnably safe seat. It was to be the least of his worries. Moreover, not only did the political outcome of the 1931 crisis, by excluding him from office, leave Churchill free to go to the United States: the economic outcome also made it even more financially advantageous for him to do so. Once the pound sterling had gone off the Gold Standard, it was no longer worth the canonical $4.86 at which it had been set since 1925, but a rate that fluctuated around

$3.60 in 1931–32. Churchill's dollar earnings were suddenly worth about one-third more to him in sterling. When he finally arrived in New York in December 1931, he had reason to thank his luck.

There was, however, another great crash. This time it was strictly personal: Churchill got out of a taxi on Fifth Avenue, looked the wrong way, and was hit by a car, with serious injury. As usual, he found a bright side. From his hospital bed he filed his copy for Lord Rothermere's *Daily Mail*, day by day, with an increased fee for the human interest generated by his narrow escape from death. He was hit on his forehead and cracked two ribs; he developed pleurisy; he continued for a long time to get pains in his arms and shoulders. 'Last night he was very sad,' reported Clementine from the Bahamas, where they went for recuperation, 'and said that he had now in the last 2 years had 3 very heavy blows. First the loss of all that money in the crash, then the loss of his political position in the Conservative Party and now this terrible physical injury.'[35]

He did not give in. The lectures were not cancelled – he could not afford that – but again postponed, this time allowing him more time for preparation. Though often in pain, he went across the country, preaching the theme of the unity of the English-speaking peoples. His lectures were delivered with varying responses (especially when the sensitive topic of British war debts to the United States was raised) but with unvarying ebullience. *The Washington Post*, for example, declared it strange 'for a debtor to offer a partnership to his creditor'.[36] The comment showed some lack of insight into Churchill's peculiar financial conceptions.

Churchill continued to explore every promising avenue. In New York he had an account at the National City Bank. On the day that he sailed for home, 11 March 1932, he instructed them to cable Lloyds Bank in London the sterling equivalent of $10,000. At a rate of $3.64, he netted £2,747. Under the Gold Standard, he would only have got just over two thousand pounds. This might be thought highly satisfactory from the point of view of housekeeping at Chartwell. But the exchange rate, of course, was now set by the market, making for significant fluctuations, up and down.

Churchill's accounts show that, as well as remitting income, he was also using his account for fairly large-scale currency speculation. He had bought sterling forward: £13,000 in all at various dates and rates, costing him at the time of purchase $46,410. His stake was thus a year's income. When he decided to close out at the end of April 1932, the dollar had meanwhile depreciated against the pound, so Churchill got back $49,010 – a net profit of $2,600. This was not just a one-off transaction, seeking the most efficient way of remitting his current American earnings. He established a system for telegraphing the National City Bank from England, using the codeword WINCH. For example, on 8 October 1932 he sent a cable: 'Winch. Please buy me twenty thousand dollars between 345 and 346 for January.'[37] This was pure speculation, some of it very short-term indeed, in and out within days. Churchill speculated heavily against the dollar in the early part of 1932; then, with impressive Anglo-American impartiality, he speculated against sterling later in the year.

Although he did not sustain his early winning streak, what he gained was pure profit. The same was true of the investments he made on Wall Street. The fact that capital gains were not liable to tax in Britain carried its own lesson, with implications for the author's next contract. Churchill had a clear incentive to find more tax-efficient ways of maintaining his net income, in order to continue living as a rich man, peaceably in his habitation.

Since his own reforms as Chancellor, the assessment of income tax and surtax had become more consistent, given the single scale of assessment that he had introduced. Churchill was paying roughly equal amounts of each, with his liability for surtax obviously more volatile, depending on whether he happened to enjoy a fat or a lean year in his lumpy literary receipts. The year 1931–32 was a fat one. This clearly reflected his current American earnings, rather than the capital value of his investments, which did not affect his current income in the eyes of the taxman. Thus in 1931–32 Churchill's taxable income increased to £15,240, and the amount due in income and surtax (£5,976) climbed to a peak of 39 per cent of his income.

As it happened, Churchill suffered prolonged bouts of ill health at this time. This was partly as a result of his New York traffic accident in December 1931 but also because he contracted paratyphoid fever in September 1932, requiring sanatorium treatment in Bavaria and subsequent convalescence at Chartwell. 'I am quite well though somewhat weakened,' he reported to one of his advisers on military history when he got home, 'but in ten days or so I hope to be okay. Meanwhile I can do a great deal of work.'[38] He had already paid out up to two thousand pounds, in a quite reputable way, for tax-deductible professional research assistance, both to finish off *The Eastern Front* in 1930–31 and to hold the line on the *Marlborough* front.

Maybe it was an indication of his weakened state that he now went further down the road of subcontracting his literary work. His friend Lord Riddell owned the *News of the World*, with an enormous circulation as a pruriently salacious Sunday newspaper, more likely to be read below stairs at Chartwell than by the master of the house. Riddell had already tried to commission Churchill to produce an unlikely series of articles, 'Great Bible Stories Retold', for serialisation in the *News of the World*. Failing that, another series, 'Great Stories of the World Retold', with plot summaries of famous novels, was now in progress from his sickbed in 1932: six articles for a fee of £2,000. Churchill was thus getting £333 per article – but was also getting his loyal friend, Eddie Marsh, still a senior civil servant at the time, to write them, for an honorarium of £25 each. Syndication in the *Chicago Tribune* for a further £1,800 made the arrangement even more profitable. There was accordingly a second series; in his cryptic private forecast of income for 1933, Churchill noted '6 Riddells – 2500'.[39]

Churchill was ready to stoop to such devices in search of ready money. 'I am not particularly keen on them myself from an artistic point of view,' he admitted, 'though they have been very satisfactory as journalism.'[40] But he thought differently about his big books, his flagship literary enterprises, in which his pride as an author was invested. He had returned from the United States intent on maximising his dollar income and firmly believing that his own commitment to finishing *Marlborough* could profitably be followed up by reaching out to a transatlantic readership for a popular history book that would be as much American as British. It was only a matter of time before his quest for a second major contract, thwarted in 1931, came to fruition.

Churchill was aware that Butterworth was neither ready nor able to commit the large sum demanded for his proposed *History of the English-Speaking Peoples*. Nor were Harraps, where the directors were already fretting at the delays to *Marlborough* and intimated that they were losing enough money already. The Scribners board likewise declined to go further with an idea of which Charlie Scribner himself had certainly had longer notice than anyone, and which he now had the pleasure of consigning instead to the London publishers Cassells (though there is also some suggestion that the agents Curtis Brown were responsible for making this approach). At any rate, by September 1932 Churchill was himself handling detailed negotiations with the proprietor of Cassells, Newman Flower. Since much of the groundwork had been done by Brendan Bracken in the previous year, the terms of the proposal were already well worked out. Indeed Churchill simply recapitulated chunks of the previous correspondence in clarifying his position.

In December 1932 the terms of a contract were agreed. The key stipulation was that Cassells would pay Churchill 'the sum of twenty thousand pounds for the complete copyright'. This complied with Churchill's prior request for 'a net £20,000 as a lump sum, waiving all interest in further royalties'.[41] Here was the important difference from the contract with Harraps and Scribners for *Marlborough*, which had offered a similar sum – but as an advance against future royalties. Cassells, best known at the time as publishers of dictionaries, were well used to buying the copyright of a commissioned work in this way; and it was simply a reversion to the old Victorian way of doing business, before the royalties system had intervened. It meant that Cassells were then free, in due course, to dispose of the North American rights to the highest bdder, not necessarily to Scribners.

The tax advantage of these arrangements for Churchill is obvious. Since Cassells bought the copyright themselves, any payment they made to Churchill would be for the outright sale of a literary property, and thus regarded by the Inland Revenue as a capital sum not liable to taxation as income. This was so even though the contract provided for payments in several tranches, mainly to meet research expenses: £1,000 on signing; £1,000 at the end of December 1933; further advances of up to £3,000, 'should the Author require it'; with the balance to be paid, half on delivery and half six months later.[42]

Churchill had told Flower that the first volume of *Marlborough* would be published in November 1933 and 'the final volume' in March or April 1934. He would then require three years for the *History*. Accordingly, delivery of a work of not less than 400,000 words was specified for 30 April 1937 – but with the possibility that the author could ask for an extension of a further two years. At the time that this second big contract was signed, then, the author's other contract for *Marlborough* was blandly assumed, not least by himself, to be capable of early fulfilment, within a couple of years. Even if that were to prove as optimistic as many of his other plans, there was a built-in escape clause giving two more years. Either way, Churchill expected *Marlborough* to be off his hands well before he faced the task of finishing his other big book by, at latest, 1939. It was a date plucked out of the air, some six or seven years into an uncertain future, and one with a significance in world history that, before Hitler came to power and entrenched the Nazi system, not even the most prescient statesman would have been able to foresee.

The Struggle on Two Fronts, 1933–38

'I have been so hampered in my work by politics that I am behindhand with *Marlborough* . . .'

Churchill to Keith Feiling, 1935

Like many of Churchill's visionary ideas, the strategy was bold and essentially simple. Not easy, admittedly; but it was not unthinkable for a man of his extraordinary energy and determination to complete a contract for a two-volume work and then to turn immediately to another major work conceived as three volumes – no more unthinkable than the idea that a serving cabinet minister could successfully have completed the proliferating volumes of *The World Crisis* and then drafted his early memoirs (and laid a few bricks as well). But, as in any armed struggle, it is a cardinal principle not to open a second front prematurely. As wartime president, Franklin Roosevelt was to hear this principle reiterated persistently by the serving British prime minister. Perhaps, by that time, Churchill had learned his lesson, and had done so in his other career as author.

Cassells must have had a shrewd idea that Churchill would exercise the two options in the contract for the *History*. The first of these stipulated that he would have access to £5,000 in research expenses as required, and since none of this was taxable, he could continue to offset his actual expenses against other literary earnings. Secondly, the contract said that the *History* need not actually be delivered until 1939, by which time he would be in his sixty-fifth year. At that point he would stand to receive, in two instalments, a lump sum for the residual £15,000. The total amount of £20,000, all tax-free, would be worth a million pounds today. 'You will note that the incentive to complete the work – £20,000 – is substantial,' he commented at the time he signed up, adding that 'the time allotted seems ample, that the work could proceed, though rather more slowly even if I were forced to take public office.'[1] His previous big contracts had been short-term expedients, specifying fantastic deadlines for delivery, in return for immediate cash-flow injections in the present, and at the price of incurring tax liabilities for the future, in an unrelenting cycle. By comparison, the 1933 contract with Cassells promised a new model, combining tax efficiency, realism and prudence.

Initially his overall plan seemed to be working. In his own private forecast of income for 1933, there is a key expectation from 'half Marlborough', estimated to bring in £7,000 with the publication of Volume One, with the other half to fall due in the following year. Then there is the usual reliance on journalism to make a big contribution, not only six of his 'Riddells', retelling great stories for the *News of the World* for £2,500, but also no fewer than forty-four articles for Lord Rothermere's *Daily Mail*, expected to bring in £6,600 – thus, from these two sources alone, promising over nine thousand pounds.[2] The Rothermere connection was currently important in a political as well as a financial sense, since the two men had the common objective of contesting Baldwin's leadership of the Conservative Party, making opposition to any concessions to Gandhi's Indian National Congress their main platform.

As it turned out, the Rothermere connection was a boom-and-bust affair, both politically and financially. Not only did Churchill's political challenge falter but the *Daily Mail* never again succoured his finances to this extent, with effects that were soon manifest. Thus in 1932–33 Churchill's assessed income held up well at £13,981, but in the next year his taxable income was halved, producing a total of only £6,572 in 1933–34. This was his lowest figure for the interwar period – wholly insufficient to sustain Chartwell. At first glance this abrupt decline might be thought a deferred effect of the slump, but the real explanation is, as usual, Churchill's fluctuating literary earnings. Not only was the *Daily Mail* now sadly missed but the expectation was dashed that the publication of *Marlborough* could come to the rescue, as projected, with the other half of its expected earnings. The simple reason was that Churchill had not yet actually finished writing it – thus seriously prejudicing his professional standing.

For this author had another career too. He did not consider himself finished in politics, though many people now wrote him off as a wild card, as a politician who had changed his stripes too often, and as a man who would never again be trusted. His remarks about the possibility of being 'forced' to take office attest that he did not envisage long years in the wilderness, in which he would simply be dallying with destiny. Far from renouncing immediate political ambitions, he thought that he could buck the system and beat the party hacks at their own game. In this he was still father's boy.

It should be remembered why Winston Churchill had changed party – twice. In 1904 he had left the Unionists, whose devotion to the imperialist cause he professed to share, because Joseph Chamberlain made tariffs an essential part of the programme that would sustain and unify the British Empire. Churchill did not believe in this, any more than he believed in imperial federation, because his own conception of imperialism was essentially sentimental and rhetorical. Not until the Conservatives dropped their tariff proposals, following their electoral upset in 1923, when they had again challenged Free Trade, did Churchill rejoin them. In short, he had acted for over twenty years as a consistent Free Trader.

The very fact that he went to the Treasury in 1924–29 was itself a guarantee that Free Trade was now safe in Conservative hands. It was one leg of a tripod of 'sound-money' orthodoxy. Free Trade was thus allied with the supposedly automatic workings of the Gold Standard, and with the 'Treasury View' that there was no role for government in tackling unemployment through fiscal intervention. Yet this orthodoxy had not produced a happy record for the Conservative government, which was forced to preside over years of high unemployment that confounded the revered Treasury orthodoxies. This is why the Tories had lost office in 1929, which Churchill appreciated as keenly as anyone. 'We see our race doubtful of its mission and no longer confident about its principles, infirm of purpose, drifting to and fro with the tides of a deeply-disturbed ocean,' he declared in a lecture at Oxford on the economic problem in 1930. 'The compass has been damaged. The charts are out of date.'[3] His own political position was accordingly unsettled and his convictions unusually fluid.

No longer did Churchill really believe in the economic orthodoxies, accepted since his youth. He may have lamented this development, but no longer was he prepared to make a principled stand in defence of Free Trade. Faced with the Great Depression, as unemployment escalated worldwide, he was now prepared to consider tariffs. The Ottawa Agreements of 1932, which introduced imperial preference in trade between Britain and its Empire, were a long-awaited deliverance in the eyes of loyal Tariff Reformers, supposedly the triumph that Joe Chamberlain had anticipated a quarter of a century earlier. The work in 1932 fell to his younger son Neville, as Chancellor of the Exchequer, who told the House of Commons how proud he was to fulfil his father's prophecy; but the Ottawa Agreements were hardly the word made flesh. They were in fact a pragmatic expedient in bad times. A few stubborn Free Traders, mainly Liberals, conscientiously resigned ministerial office; but Churchill, elected as a backbench supporter of the National government, led no wider rebellion. Instead of reproaching the government from a Liberal viewpoint, he chose to attack it from a diehard position. He declared last-ditch resistance against its moves towards self-government in India.

It was not simply that this stance identified Churchill as an imperialist: he now seemed the wrong sort of imperialist. It is worth reflecting upon this point for a moment since it is so central to contemporary perceptions of him. In the perspectives conventional within Anglo-American society by the 1930s – what with the advent of jazz, the flapper, the cocktail, Art Deco – it was all too easy to depict Churchill as a throwback to the Victorian era in which he had precociously made his name. And it was not just younger people who took this view.

Leo Amery was Winston Churchill's contemporary, his rival, his political colleague, his imperialist alter ego. They had been at school together, at Harrow, as each liked to recall anecdotally. The version in *My Early Life* has young Winston pushing the diminutive Leo into the swimming pool and, faced with the discovery that his irate victim is three years older, adroitly propitiating the much more senior boy by saying: 'My father, who is a great man, is also small.'[4] Only the facts have been changed here, since Amery was a mere twelve months the elder; but their rivalry was real enough. It was, in the early 1900s, the Chamberlainite Amery who had made the case that Britain alone could not face the rising power of Germany, the United States or Russia without the British Empire at its back, and that imperial preference alone could deliver this unity.

It was the same Amery who, having served with Churchill in Baldwin's cabinet, accidentally found himself with 'the Churchill Troupe' aboard ship to Canada in 1929. After a long discussion late one night in his cabin, Churchill unselfconsciously undressed, put on his long silk nightshirt with a woollen tummy band on top – and then asked Amery why he was smiling. 'Free Trade, Mid Victorian Statesmanship and the old-fashioned nightshirt, how appropriate a combination,' responded Amery, who wrote in his diary: 'the key to Winston is to realize that he is Mid Victorian, steeped in the politics of his father's period, and unable ever to get the modern point of view'.[5]

Churchill remained a non-believer in the Chamberlainite vision of an Empire of white settlement united by tariffs. But he was now, as his contract for the *History* affirmed, literally signed up as a pledged believer in the mission of the English-speaking peoples. And the pedigree of that notion, as we have seen in Chapter 3, was essentially liberal – this was what legitimated its crucial Anglo-American axis. Consistent with this, a previous historian of 'the history of the great English-speaking fellowship', Ramsay Muir, was himself a Liberal. As

Muir had argued at such length, it was its common institutions, 'the institutions of political freedom, which have mainly determined the character and course of the history of the whole Commonwealth'. A sympathetic American, writing an introduction to Muir's work, affirmed that 'the historian of a future generation will see in the transformation of the British Empire into a commonwealth of free nations the most significant fact of the new century'.[6]

Obviously, the conception of burgeoning self-government within a British Commonwealth of Nations presented no challenge to the formal principles that Americans held dear. Churchill's own words in frequently lauding the American Declaration of Independence spoke in this register. Yet, as much on the American as on the British side, the grandiloquent rhetoric about freedom had a blind spot about race – a sort of inconsistency always easier to identify as hypocrisy in someone else. And in taking an intransigent public stand against the extremely moderate advances towards self-government proposed in the India Bill, Churchill undoubtedly displayed a kind of prejudice against Indians that had a racial tinge. Thereby he was now stoking animosity against himself not only in India, or within liberal circles in Britain, but within the much wider swathe of American opinion that, professing historic truths about liberty and equality to be self-evident, harboured deep suspicions about an atavistic British Empire.

Yet Churchill persisted in his diehard campaign, his activities as a politician daily contradicting the fine words of the prospectus for his *History of the English-Speaking Peoples*. He was still restlessly exploring any way of challenging the Conservative leadership in 1933 and 1934, much as Lord Randolph had done half a century before; and with a similar lack of final success for these eye-catching efforts to mobilise grassroots support within the party. Sir Austen Chamberlain, son of the great Joe and half-brother of Neville, and himself a former leader of the Conservative Party during the Lloyd George coalition, was well placed to understand the situation. After a weekend at Chartwell in October 1933, he reported that Churchill 'anticipates that he and his

Indian Die-Hards will continue to hold about ⅓rd of the Party, that the India Bill will be carried but that the fight will leave such bitter memories that the Govt will have to be reconstructed'.[7] The explicit message may have been that the amenable Austen (rather than the abrasive Neville) should lead this reconstructed administration; but there was no mistaking Churchill's subtext, that the diehard ticket of unreconstructed imperialism was to be his own passport back into the cabinet.

Successive setbacks simply stimulated the family reflexes: no surrender, double or quits! In 1933 Churchill's failure to capture the party organisation through a rank-and-file mutiny was paralleled by a parliamentary failure to win concessions on the India Bill. The House of Commons set up a select committee, before which this hard-pressed man, in giving his own evidence, seemed uncharacteristically lacking in due preparation. Little wonder: Volume One of his *Marlborough* was published in October 1933. Then, in April 1934, Rothermere's *Daily Mail* handed Churchill documents alleging government impropriety in tampering with other evidence before the select committee; and Churchill went for broke in taking this to the House of Commons as a breach of privilege. An unanimous report, dismissing all of his allegations, was debated by the House of Commons in June 1934. Churchill's case hinged on showing that the Secretary of State for India, Sir Samuel Hoare, had misled the House.

For better or worse, this was billed as a great parliamentary occasion. Leo Amery – like Churchill now a backbencher, but unlike him a warm supporter of the India Bill – had briefed himself at the India Office to answer the charges. Churchill, who had this time expended his usual painstaking efforts in preparation, spoke for an hour, 'vigorous and eloquent from sentence to sentence,' as Amery acknowledged, 'but clearly making no great impression on the House'. This provided his own opening to mock his old schoolmate's cataclysmic rhetoric, which Amery characterised with the Latin tag, *fiat justitia ruat coelum*. When Churchill unwisely demanded translation – literally, 'do the just thing though the heavens fall' – Amery was ready with his vernacular version: 'If I can trip up Sam the Government is bust.' The House virtually laughed Churchill out of court. 'I hit him again with a most appropriate quotation from his *Marlborough* about Macaulay's unquestioning glee in jumping at conclusions leading up to a sensational and malicious charge,' Amery recorded, with more than literary satisfaction at having the better of this encounter.[8]

None of this brought Churchill any nearer to regaining government office; none of it did his reputation as a wise elder statesman any good; none of it enhanced his reputation in the United States. But all of it, month after month, stole the time that the author of *Marlborough* desperately needed if he were to complete his task. And until that was done, serious work on the *History* could hardly begin.

The first volume of *Marlborough* was published, to an acclaim that spanned the political spectrum, in October 1933. Stanley Baldwin, his continued leadership of his party currently under direct challenge from the author, nonetheless wrote in warm appreciation of his complimentary copy, expressing his amazement at 'the miracle' of a book that 'would mean years of work even for a man whose sole occupation was writing history'. Baldwin had almost as much difficulty in finding time to read it as the author had in finding time to write it. All things considered, this was a good beginning for a major biographical project, where, as Churchill privately admitted in 1934, he was 'browsing in an only too well-gleaned field'.[9]

The feat could never have been performed without the efforts and expertise of Maurice Ashley. Churchill had taken on Ashley for this project (as his Marlborough man, one might say) for three years in June 1929. In the event Ashley stayed for four, until the summer of 1933, when he joined the *Manchester Guardian*, a left-leaning Liberal newspaper, which suited his own politics. He was never an academic historian with a university appointment, though he was duly awarded the research degree of D.Phil., the Oxford way of saying Ph.D.

Instead, he was happy to become a journalist with a scholarly bent. The post-war years were to see him installed at *The Listener*, then the BBC's literary house journal, ultimately as its editor. He maintained his historical output with a string of books, mainly on seventeenth-century England, and often lauding Oliver Cromwell.

Ashley was thus a Roundhead to Churchill's Cavalier. But, despite ideological and age differences, they got on well. In the preface to Volume One of *Marlborough*, dated August 1933, the author thanks Ashley 'who for the last four years has conducted my researches' and salutes 'his industry, judgment and knowledge'. In this and the subsequent two volumes, no comparable tribute is paid to anyone else's contribution to the biography. Ashley knew more than anyone about the historical research that lay behind it – certainly more than its author – and he knew where the bodies were buried. Yet he remained intensely loyal, declining opportunities to write about the great man until after his death, and then producing a book called *Churchill as Historian* (1968), which is tantalising in its restraint. In it, Ashley admits to regrets that he had not written it as a younger man; but, despite beginning with some irreplaceable personal insights, after ten pages he misguidedly declares his wish not to 'intrude myself too much'.[10] The rest of the book, dutifully trundling through the Churchill oeuvre, is a haystack in which the needles are well concealed – though often with a sharp point when discovered.

Ashley would have been the last person to claim that he was really the author of *Marlborough*. And rightly so, given that Churchill stamped the book with his own distinctive literary imprint. 'Every word of it was originally dictated to his secretary, mostly in the small hours of the morning,' Ashley declared later. 'As his research assistant, I sat by in case he needed any facts supplied or verified, but he had such a marvellous memory that he rarely got them wrong.'[11] There is no reason to challenge this observation; but it needs unpacking.

For Churchill had often been far away while *Marlborough* had taken shape. The author had toured North America twice; he had lain prostrate in hospitals; he had diverted vital energies to other books; he had learned how to fiddle with a 'Riddell'; he had pursued a campaign against Gandhi in terms that revealed ugly, atavistic prejudices, not much to liberal tastes. Meanwhile it had been the unobtrusive Ashley who spent dull, dusty days at Blenheim (with the occupational hazard, as he confessed later to Churchill, that the latter's ducal cousin 'used to frighten me a bit'). It was Ashley who had to locate and choose and quarry and dress the stones from which the master-builder constructed the final edifice. 'A historian, after all, selects for himself from all the evidence that he has collected and even the celebrated "amateur" historians like Voltaire or Gibbon or Grote soaked themselves in their subject before they started to write,' Ashley explains in his own book. 'The essence of historical writing is selection and though some of the preliminary sifting can be done for one, this is never entirely satisfactory.'[12] Ashley goes so far as to doubt whether historical information can be adequately compressed onto 'half a sheet of paper' – notoriously one of Churchill's requirements in transacting government business.

This is not some sort of devastating insider disclosure, exposing Churchill's pretensions to authorship as fraudulent. We are in different territory from the ghostwriting of the 'Riddells', on which Churchill readily admitted 'artistic' qualms. What he was doing in writing *Marlborough*, with full acknowledgement to Ashley, was to apply his own skills in presenting a brief that he made assiduous efforts to master for himself. Churchill assumed unquestioned responsibility for his own decisions on how he used the materials that he had commissioned. To say that every word is his own could never be literally true of any historian; but the prose is as he cast it – and often recast it too. In his own archive there are the successive proofs of his big books, which he would work through, in blue crayon or in red ink, with an attention to detail that itself helped to prolong the process of composition. All this is true; but it consorts with another truth, to which Churchill himself was rather naively obtuse, that the scholarly activity of 'writing history' has rather more to it than the exercises in delegation that can bring an effective statesman mastery of government or give an eloquent orator the better of an argument.

Churchill, then, may have been a professional writer but he was not a professional historian. But George Macaulay Trevelyan now was. In 1927 Trevelyan had been appointed to the most prestigious historical chair at Cambridge University, the Regius Professorship, and had duly devoted himself to his research on a trilogy, *England under Queen Anne*. This was to take up where his great-uncle, Lord Macaulay, had left off, three-quarters of a century previously, in his *History of England*. It promised a piquant confrontation with the rival loyalties of the Churchills.

The first volume of Trevelyan's three volumes, simply called *Blenheim*, was published in 1930. Anne's succession as queen in 1702 marked the moment when Marlborough's career, tainted and stymied by charges of Jacobite disloyalty in the 1690s, was transformed, giving him supreme military command in the war against France and thus enabling him, by 1704, to achieve his dazzling success at the Battle of Blenheim. From the beginning of his research, Trevelyan found himself taking a less hostile view of this undeniably ruthless and ambitious soldier-politician than had his great-uncle Tom, as he told his wife: 'I am getting very fond of Marlborough, for all his faults.'[13]

Sentiment aside, however, there was also, from the moment that Churchill signed his contract for *Marlborough*, a technical conflict of interest between himself, the aristocratic amateur, and Trevelyan, as gentleman turned player. In the preface to the first volume of *England under Queen Anne*, the author declares that 'all roads in it, foreign and domestic, lead to Blenheim'. But he had found his own road barred when Sunny, the current duke, had closed the archive at Blenheim to everyone except his cousin Winston until the latter's biography was finished. Trevelyan, who had to make do with earlier printed copies of some of the relevant correspondence, advised his readers that whether 'the papers in Blenheim have still any important secrets to reveal, we shall shortly know, when the work of family piety, for which the world is so eagerly waiting, sees the light'. This gently barbed remark had appeared in his preface of 1930; but though Trevelyan published his second volume in 1932, the eager world was kept waiting for Churchill's first until October 1933.

A personal line of communication had meanwhile been established. Trevelyan, far from sulking, was in fact proving more helpful to his rival than had been anticipated. Churchill was touched. 'I have wondered whether it would not be kind to open to him the Blenheim archives,' Churchill wrote to Ashley in February 1934. 'I suggested this to the Duke who was good enough to leave it to me.' Ashley, by now beginning his journalistic work in Manchester, responded at once that, though of course he was in favour, there was a rather obvious snag. He tactfully pointed out that Trevelyan's final volume was due out in May, only three months away, thus completing the trilogy on which Trevelyan had been labouring for seven years: 'Will not Professor Trevelyan and the general public find it hard to explain why he is being admitted at this particular time when his work is almost finished?'[14]

Churchill's bizarre suggestion was not pursued. But it demonstrates his lack of appreciation of what was really involved here and his need for guidance on the realities of archival research. Ashley, of course, as an aspiring young scholar, had his own concern not to give gratuitous offence to 'that other great historian of the age, Professor G. M. Trevelyan' (as Ashley referred to him).[15] Trevelyan's own eminence can be judged from the fact that he was given his country's highest honour, the Order of Merit, in 1930, sixteen years before Churchill himself. In fact, an impressive degree of goodwill and mutual respect was fostered between these two keepers of their rival flames, with family piety a phrase that each could level at the other.

The emblematic charge against Marlborough, carried from Macaulay into Trevelyan's pages in 1930, was that of treachery. In particular, there was no escaping 'Camaret Bay'. This was the incident in 1694, under King William III, when an English attack upon the northwestern French port of Brest had been planned; and it was alleged that the secret had been betrayed to the French by Marlborough. The best that anyone had said for Marlborough, in his double-dealing, was that the French probably knew anyway. 'But even so,' Trevelyan's *Blenheim* concluded, 'it was a base thing for an English soldier to do.'[16] The evidence was the 'Camaret Bay letter', preserved in a Jacobite archive held in the Bodleian Library at Oxford University. Macaulay had used it, quoting it directly as a letter from Marlborough to James Edward Stuart, the 'Old Pretender' to the British throne. Trevelyan was naturally aware of this in endorsing the charge of treachery. Churchill's expertise in the scholarly archives, by contrast, was somewhat lacking; but his combative instinct not so.

The salience of this historical dispute is shown by the fact that Churchill had long accepted Macaulay's strictures on his ancestor as a reason not to write the biography at all. He had only changed his mind, under Rosebery's prompting, once he had assimilated the critique of Macaulay's methods in 'Paget's Examen'. (In fact a new edition of this neglected work was to be published in 1934, with an introduction by Churchill, who received 1/6d a copy as a royalty – every ten copies sold would have paid for another bottle of Pol Roger.) Relying on Paget for initial reconnaissance, and on Ashley for the necessary ammunition, Churchill set out to march on Macaulay's position with all the bloody-minded tenacity of the 'scarlet caterpillar', the redcoats with which Duke John had once marched halfway across Europe to do battle at Blenheim. The literary campaign plan is disclosed in the preface to Volume One of *Marlborough*, where the author duly tells the story of Rosebery's tip-off and reveals that he intends to out-Paget Paget in disputing the sources. 'The argument upon this point occupies about four chapters of this volume,' he warns. 'Upon this issue I join battle.'[17]

Hence the extraordinary infighting that dominates – and disfigures – the work. This is no bland, amateur treatment, brushing over

Blenheim Palace, Winston's birthplace, built in rural Oxfordshire at public expense for the first Duke of Marlborough in the early eighteenth century.

Chartwell Manor in Kent, bought by Winston in 1921 (without telling his wife, Clementine): a more modest home than Blenheim, and subsequently much loved by him, much resented by her.

The engagement photograph of Lord Randolph Churchill and Jennie Jerome of New York, taken in Paris before their marriage there in April 1874; a glamorous and improvident couple, they were to become parents of Winston on 30 November of that year.

Lady Randolph Churchill, dressed to kill: Winston's adored mother, ready to exert her charms as an unofficial literary agent.

A spontaneous glimpse in 1909 of the young politician with the old editor
– C. P. Scott of the *Manchester Guardian*, the Liberal newspaper that helped
propagate the idea of 'the English-speaking peoples'.

Winston's word factory: the study on the top floor of Chartwell where he composed his big books in the 1930s, notably his biography *Marlborough* and *A History of the English-Speaking Peoples*.

A room with a view: the Weald of Kent as seen from Winston's window – deep England, this blessed plot.

William Deakin as a young don at Oxford: the most influential of the 'young men' whom Churchill recruited to help him write his big books in the 1930s.

Three English men of letters relax on the Riviera: Somerset Maugham, Winston Churchill and H. G. Wells at the Villa Mauresque, Maugham's home on Cap Ferrat.

Clementine Churchill and her admirer Terence Philip aboard Lord Moyne's yacht, the *Rosaura*, during their exotic five-month cruise in 1934–35, while Winston was at Chartwell writing *Marlborough*.

The Prime Minister at the peak of his powers in 1941, attended as always by his 'honorary man of business', Brendan Bracken (though the photograph can hardly do justice to the latter's startling red hair).

'Some chicken, some neck.' The classic image of the defiant war leader, dubbed 'the Roaring Lion', taken by Yousuf Karsh in Ottawa immediately after Churchill's speech to the Canadian House of Commons in December 1941.

difficulties in the historical sources with evasive dissimulation. Instead, the relevant documents are rigorously enumerated, and each is subjected to textual exegesis. The crucial 'Camaret Bay letter' is even printed in facsimile as well as in translation (from the French). 'Here is the damning piece,' Churchill declares. 'It is upon this document that the pinnacle of Macaulay's libels upon Marlborough has been erected.' Page after page, the familiar line of extenuation for Marlborough – that the famous letter made no difference – is explicated before Churchill, as advocate, moves to mount his own defence. 'We had always supposed', he declares, with an affectation of ingenuousness, that an original version of the letter must have survived in the archives. But no! Yet even the fact that no original can be produced had been used to malign his ancestor (treated almost as his client by now) in a process that had culminated in Macaulay's 'fabric of accusation' on the basis of a letter 'that does not exist; it has never existed.' Hence the final plea before the court of history: 'Such evidence would not hang a dog.'[18]

In this style, a great chunk of Volume One was developed into a full-dress arraignment of the ghost of Macaulay. For once, Evelyn Waugh's inveterate distaste for Winston Churchill and all his works finds some justification, in commenting on *Marlborough* to the author's son thirty years later: 'I was everywhere outraged by his partisanship & naïve assumption of superior virtue. It is a shifty barrister's case not a work of literature.'[19] It was, in fact, all too like the House of Commons Select Committee on the India Bill, which was distracting the author's attention during 1933, just as he was finishing this volume. Indeed *Marlborough* prefigured the style of Churchill's allegations of parliamentary privilege in the following year, as the well-read Amery was shrewd enough to discern. There was the same obsessive quest for a villain; the same self-sustaining inability to let charges drop; the same dogged pursuit of victory at all costs, with Thomas Babington Macaulay cast in the role that Samuel Hoare was subsequently to occupy in Churchill's demonology. If only Winston could trip up Tom, the Whigs would be bust!

Churchill won the battle at the price of prejudicing the campaign. His first volume indeed discredited the Camaret Bay letter. In subsequent editions of Trevelyan's *Blenheim* volume, the verdict of baseness was replaced by the conclusion that 'Mr Winston Churchill's recent researches and arguments have rendered it so doubtful whether Marlborough's alleged warning was not a Jacobite fabrication' that the charge of treachery was not repeated. When Ashley himself wrote a short biography of Marlborough, while not defending him against a general charge of treason, he judged the famous letter 'in all probability a forgery'; and Marlborough's most recent biographer concurs, simply citing Churchill's conclusion with the comment that 'it is hard to disagree'.[20] Thus did Churchill in 1933 score his point against the greatest professional historian of his day, on his own ground, and in a manner endorsed by the latest historical research. This remains an impressive tribute. But it came at a price – literally so, when Churchill's publishers, especially Charlie Scribner in New York, began to count the cost of the vast project that they had unwarily taken on.

Churchill's study at Chartwell is on the top floor. It is a well-proportioned but not grand room, approximately thirty feet by fifteen, lined with bookcases on most of the walls. The sense of space is enhanced by the height, reaching up twenty feet to the oak beams directly under the roof, exposed during the renovations of 1922–24. It must have been a difficult room to heat, with a single fireplace that would have needed help. Though one wall is on the west-facing front – itself the house's least attractive aspect, and all too close to the road – the study is orientated towards the other side, overlooking the garden and grounds. Over the years, Churchill created several ponds, two of them substantial lakes, by damming the stream, expending his own labour, ingenuity and, of course, money in the process. But the view that he wanted to capture from his study window was not this so much as the breathtaking vista given by Chartwell's position, 650 feet high on the North Downs, looking to the south-east far over the Weald of Kent,

with its forested slopes, its distant oasthouses and other ancient build-
ings signifying long settlement. This was, for Churchill, deep England:
this blessed plot, this fortress built by nature against infection and the
hand of war.

The view from Churchill's desk was best captured in the morning.
But he was, of course, never a morning person. After waking around
eight o'clock, he liked to lie in bed, in the small room next door which
also had a share of the view; and he would have his breakfast sent up
along with the morning papers and other pressing political communications. There was, down a couple of stairs next door, a small bathroom,
where, twice a day, he would immerse himself, sometimes while
continuing conversations through the doorway, or even dictating to a
discreetly positioned secretary. If the barrage of words was momentarily interrupted, it was because he was under water, literally as well as
financially.

He was an avid reader, impatient to follow up on leads. His research
assistants wondered when he found the time to read all the materials
that were brought to him; but they knew he did so because so much
of what he perused would stick in his memory, enabling him to pull
out apt quotations that needed checking only for strict verbal accu-
racy. When working on *Marlborough*, he would meet Ashley for an
hour's work before lunch, then, following the daily ritual of the sacred
snooze, meet again for a further hour or two following afternoon tea
(for which Churchill would personally substitute whisky and soda).
Dinner would duly follow, the great occasion of the day, perhaps with
other guests, certainly with much talk, and just as certainly champagne. Likewise there was always port and brandy, circulated round
the table after the ladies had withdrawn. Then Winston, compensat-
ing for any earlier uxorious negligence, would play backgammon with
Clementine. By this time it might well be eleven o'clock – time for
bed, perhaps?

Not for Winston. This was when the day's literary work would
really begin. Ashley would accompany him up to the study and the

materials for the current chapter would be laid out on a long, raised table. Either Violet Pearman or Grace Hamblin would also be present for dictation. But other assistants, notably Colonel R. P. Pakenham-Walsh on the military campaigns and Commander J. H. Owen on naval matters, seldom appeared in person, communicating their expertise by mail. Keith Feiling likewise gave bibliographical advice from a distance, often specifying the actual pages that were relevant – and displaying scholarly horror when Churchill told him just to cut them out of the book in question. Most books survived intact, assembled on the shelves at Chartwell through purchase or borrowing. Churchill's own library contains, for example, his own leather-bound sets of the works of the economist Adam Smith and of the American historian Francis Parkman, as well as the Victorian Histories of England by W. E. H. Lecky and J. A. Froude. We know too that Churchill possessed his own well-thumbed copies of comparable works by J. R. Green and, of course, Macaulay. 'He knew Macaulay almost by heart,' thought Ashley.[21]

Churchill, then, did not go on to the night shift alone. He was fortified by the assistance of skilled helpers, as well as by copious supplies of whisky and soda, freely offered to his research assistants too, though prudently accepted by them only if their concentration were not thereby impaired. They could not afford any lapse of attention when some arcane fact that they had unearthed might suddenly be demanded, as Churchill launched into framing their researches within his own flowing narrative. Once the flow had begun, it was unwise to offer unsolicited comment. That could wait till later, when the author revisited his imaginative utterances of the night before in the cold light of the morrow. For the essential task was to generate the requisite rhetoric in a way that did no violence to the research that had been fed in. 'Give me the facts, Ashley, and I will twist them the way I want to suit my argument,' he said on one occasion, rather shocking his young assistant, as no doubt was intended. Churchill plainly relished his mastery of the process, delighting in his sheer professionalism while on the job. 'Well, we must have done three thousand words,' he would say, to everyone's relief, normally at about 2 a.m., and the duty secretary could be sent home.[22] An hour or two later, the great wordsmith too would retire, his own labours done for the day.

Though he now slept, the work itself continued. For the dictation that he had given to his secretary was immediately typed up – not so that the author could read it in that form but so as to reach the printers at Harraps in London the next day. Churchill had a special contractual provision, allowing for excess printing costs to be met, so that the galley proof of each night's work was, day by day, sent back to Chartwell, for him to mull over. After a bad night, chasing hares up false trails, or developing plausible historical insights that turned out to be fallacious, a draft might be scrapped altogether. After a good night, initial amendments might be minimal before the corrected proof was sent out.

At this stage, then, the proofs would be checked by the experts whom Churchill employed. Their suggestions too would be considered and a further proof demanded. In addition, Churchill's scientifically distinguished friend, Professor Frederick Lindemann, 'the Prof.', was also drawn into the composition of *Marlborough* during frequent visits to Chartwell. In London, Harraps' own meticulous copy-editor, C. C. Wood, would then intervene in the process by mail; indeed it was difficult to restrain Mr Wood, and ultimately he too ended up working for Churchill. Proof after proof was produced, each circulated as appropriate by roster, and always subject to Eddie Marsh's interventions (especially on the author's aversion to hyphens – was 'panicstricken' really acceptable?). So many proofs survive in Churchill's archive that it is sometimes difficult to trace exactly which amended set had priority at any one time, and simply monitoring the flow was a problem in itself. Indeed, Ashley's successor after 1934, another Oxford graduate called John Wheldon, fell foul of Violet Pearman because of his lack of respect for her staff-work in marshalling the whole complex operation.

However good the support team, the ultimate burden fell upon the author. He carried it resiliently, night after night, before finally quitting the study alone for his bedroom next door. Clementine's bedroom was on the floor below: an arrangement not uncommon in their class and era. The pattern of her day (if indeed she was at Chartwell) unfolded on a different schedule. She was living with an author who needed to focus on his work, not only when actually dictating but also while reflecting upon the looming nightly task. The words might come easily but the thoughts needed gestation. She knew that her husband duly husbanded his intellectual resources, often with little left over for a wife who had to settle for the hour at the backgammon table as the only time when she really had his attention. She knew too that, if she needed to persuade her husband on any important matter, it was often better to write a letter to him, even when they were under the same roof. Winston took more notice of the written than of the spoken word, at least of any word not spoken by himself.

Clementine loved Winston. She readily helped promote his political career, with a judgement often better than his own (and with a fairly consistent Liberal bias too). She had mixed feelings about his other career as author, reading proof copies of *Marlborough* with admiration, but intermittently expressing her frustration at the literary overload made necessary under the Chartwell regime. Winston's irresistible temptation to create yet more new ponds in the grounds, with liquidity hazards and financial drains equally instigated by his own gratuitous blunders, exhausted her patience. She saw, all too clearly and all too often, that Winston was taking on commitment after commitment that he simply could not afford, without ever counting the true cost in advance. Just as Winston's solution was to hole up, tending his herd of cash cows, so Clementine's solution was to flee Chartwell, taking long holidays with friends who had more common sense than her husband, and often more money too.

Lord Moyne was high on this list. Born Walter Guinness, he was not only a former government colleague of Churchill's but, as a member of the famous brewing family, endowed with ample resources. The Churchills were welcome guests on Moyne's luxurious yacht the *Rosaura*, and together spent a month in the late summer of 1934 visiting the eastern Mediterranean. With two volumes of the big biography finished, the author allowed himself this break; but he could not contemplate Moyne's invitation for a further, longer voyage that winter, capturing live specimens of rare Asian reptiles for the London Zoo. While Winston remained, somewhat uneasily, at Chartwell with *Marlborough*, Clementine went off for nearly five months on the *Rosaura*. She was nearly fifty, a handsome, elegant and often neglected woman; for weeks at a time one constant shipboard companion was the art dealer Terence Philip, an admirer several years younger than herself, and considerably more attentive than Winston. Then she got home; then the relationship faded; then her old familiar life resumed, with a long marriage to a man continually in the throes of authorship. At the end of her life, Clementine summed up the episode to her daughter Mary with the saying: *C'était une vraie connaissance de ville d'eau.*[23] A literal translation – 'it was really a spa-resort relationship' – hardly does justice to the poignancy of the situation.

Understanding the process of composition explains a lot about the form that *Marlborough* finally took. Though the final consequences were stored up for resolution in the later volumes, the root cause of its undisciplined expansion lay in the methods adopted from Volume One, with a lack of focus and rigour that surely reflected the author's intermittent engagement with the work. Episodically drawn into one tactical skirmish after another in Duke John's career, this busy man failed to emulate his ancestor's ruthless grip on strategic priorities. His own inability to rein in his sheer loquacity was an intractable problem. Once he was striding up and down, late at night, with a whisky and soda at hand, he was unstoppable, unquenchable and, in the end, frankly unreadable by all but a faithful few who were undeterred by the brute length of the whole work.

Marlborough: His Life and Times is the biography's full title, fully merited. It is very full on the life, equally full on the times. Harraps' London edition of Volume One runs to 612 pages, offered to the general public at 25 shillings (say sixty pounds in today's money; the limited edition of 150 copies sold at three guineas). In New York, Scribners – unwisely as it turned out – decided to divide this huge initial instalment, hoping to sweeten the price by issuing their resulting two volumes together as a boxed set for $6. This may have been a fair price at the current exchange rate, but American customers evidently did not think so, as Charlie Scribner kept complaining. His decision to issue boxed sets, for this and the next instalment too, meant that his edition of the entire biography ran to a stupendous six volumes, which in itself further inhibited sales. In his eyes, 'the work has grown to a so much greater size than originally planned that it has lost all semblance of general popularity,' as he was to tell Churchill in 1936.[24]

In all, whether in four or six volumes, the complete biography ran to a total of one million words (about ten times the length of the book you are reading). Churchill periodically tried to pretend otherwise to Harraps but had to bow to Mr Wood's more scientific word-counts. In 1929 the contract had envisaged a work of a quarter that length, as the publishers were aware – persistently aware, ruefully aware, impotently aware.

Many of the problems with *Marlborough* were thus apparent from the first volume. So was its overall perspective, albeit in ways that were to some extent masked by the author's highly personal motivation in writing it. Two notable early readers offered contrasting but revealing comments at the time, each in a long and cogent private communication. Lewis Namier had already established a formidable reputation as an academic historian after publishing two books that revolutionised views of mid-eighteenth-century British politics. Instead of the principled party system that the Whigs had idolised, the Namierite analysis posited a structure based on individual self-interest and careerist manoeuvre. However low Marlborough had stooped in playing the political game, it would not have shocked the hard-nosed, deeply conservative Namier.

Namier absolved the author from the charge of forcing an open door in his lengthy strictures on Macaulay. 'The Whig mind is not an open door; it is a rubber ball which speedily regains its previous shape,' he assured Churchill in February 1934. To this extent, they were agreed in their anti-Whig stance. Yes, Macaulay had to be taken down, but Namier's criticism was that the depiction of Marlborough had suffered in the process. He suggested that, had an appendix of about fifty pages been used for an explicit dissection of Macaulay, 'you would have destroyed him just as effectively, or perhaps even more effectively, without distracting the reader from your own portrait of Marlborough; and you would have avoided giving the book the polemic touch, which is disturbing in a great work of art.'[25]

Three months later, in May 1934, Churchill received a provokingly different, though equally long, critique from George Bernard Shaw. He was like Churchill in being an autodidact who combined strong political views with literary eminence (and had won the Nobel Prize for Literature in 1925). The old Marxist's point was that 'very oddly – since it is so largely a protest against Macaulay – it is badly damaged in places by its Macaulayisms'. To Shaw, what was wrong with Macaulay was more fundamental than any personal bias: it was 'his Whiggery, his idolatry of parliament, of public opinion, of "free" institutions, of an underlying divinity in the British character'. But these were values and assumptions that Churchill himself took for granted and exalted as national, not party virtues. Whereas Namier applauded Churchill as a Tory, Shaw berated him as a covert Whig. 'All this is clear to me because I read Karl Marx 14 years before Lenin did, and therewith got Macaulay out of my blood forever,' Shaw briskly concluded. 'You, having had a class education, swallowed the poison without the antidote. Hence the amazing, and, believe me, hopelessly obsolete passages in an otherwise splendid book which might have been written by Tom himself.'[26]

What Churchill offered was indeed Macaulayism without Macaulay.

He relished Shaw's letter; he showed it with amusement to Ashley; he took no offence; but he also took no notice. Successive volumes of *Marlborough* remained imbued with a (lower-case) whig interpretation that faithfully reflected his own perspectives, not just on the age of Marlborough but on the history of the English-speaking peoples. Churchill's impatience with a Namierite interpretation was eventually to become manifest once he finally got round to writing his own big *History*. In it there is a barbed reference to unnamed 'modern scholars' with their contention 'that there was no such thing as a two-party system in eighteenth-century Britain'. To which Churchill offers the dismissive comment: 'It is not much of a conclusion to come to about a great age of Parliamentary debate.'[27] But in 1934 such methodological differences were masked for the moment by Churchill's common cause with Namier against the Whigs.

Marlborough stands as a monument to its author's historical commitment, insight – and fortitude. Forty years ago, in an era of self-conscious academic professionalism, it was admittedly fashionable for historians to disparage the research behind the biography. One such charge came from Robert Walpole's biographer, obviously well placed to comment since he was like Churchill in undertaking a multi-volume work on a major figure of the early eighteenth century – though unlike Churchill in not finishing it.

At the time of the publication of the final volume of *Marlborough*, however, its scholarly merit had been widely saluted. The biography had received serious appraisal in both the *English Historical Review* and the *American Historical Review*, with some understandable academic disdain for its moralism but no disabling criticisms of its scholarly underpinning. Moreover, at the end of May 1939 its author was approached by Sir Frederic Kenyon, a former Director of the British Museum and currently Secretary of the British Academy, the equivalent in the humanities of the Royal Society. Kenyon, in effect, offered Churchill election as a Fellow, a much-coveted scholarly honour, held by such heroes of his youth as Balfour, Rosebery, Morley and Bryce.

That Churchill declined, pleading that 'in the present circumstances he fears he is too fully occupied to avail himself of your courtesy', is rather puzzling.[28] Since he had recently resigned from the Turf Club as one of his symbolic economies, could he perhaps have regarded the annual subscription to the British Academy in the same light?

These were all judgements by the standards of 1939. But Churchill's biography also remains a work cited by the present generation of scholars. The entry on Marlborough in the *Oxford Dictionary of National Biography* appraises Duke John's stature and role in relation to the conditions of warfare in the nineteenth and twentieth centuries – a point that had not escaped Winston S. Churchill, whose biography is listed as a source. It is neither forgotten, nor only mentioned as a curiosity because of its author's later fame. Instead, the work is still treated respectfully in the twenty-six explicit references made to it in the most recent scholarly biography of Marlborough, even in cases of disagreement with what Churchill wrote over seventy years ago. He was writing as long ago from us as Macaulay was from Churchill himself. How many historical works survive so long?

In general, the historian with whom Churchill most closely agreed was Macaulay's great-nephew. For Trevelyan too the history of this period embodied the triumph of characteristically English virtues, with the growth of liberty as a national achievement, not as the prerogative of any single party. And for Trevelyan too the dominating figure was John, Duke of Marlborough: heroic in his political as well as his military career, if personally flawed through his devious character. Once Trevelyan and Churchill had resolved their initial petty differences over the evidence – the over-inflated matter of the Camaret Bay document – it was their common affinities that stood out. And with his own trilogy on Queen Anne's reign published by 1934, Trevelyan was ready to help Churchill complete his own three volumes of *Marlborough*.

For three volumes it clearly had to be. Harraps, pleased at selling eleven thousand copies of the first volume by the end of 1933, had readily agreed to this amendment of the contract. George Harrap envisaged publication of the modified second volume for early 1934 and stressed that 'it would naturally be highly important that the third volume to complete the whole should also be available to the public by the middle of the year 1935'.[29] The fact that Harrap was ready to pay an additional advance of £3,000 was also material. When Churchill put the equivalent proposal to Scribners in January 1934, however, he did so in the face of disappointing sales in New York, as he acknowledged: 'I am distressed that you have not made money out of my books like all my other publishers have done, and would not wish you to commit yourself to anything which was not sound business.' It was little surprise, then, that Charlie Scribner simply responded by telegram, tersely stating that a third volume might increase the chances of meeting the original advance; and Churchill had to accept that no more dollars would accrue to him.[30]

Volume One had taken Marlborough from his birth in 1650 to the accession of Queen Anne in 1702, thus covering fifty-two years. But Volume Two covered less than four, albeit including the Blenheim campaign of 1704. 'Will you get all the rest done in *one* vol.?' asked Trevelyan, after reading it in proof for the author in August 1934; and he offered the pertinent advice that 'if you intend to keep it to one more vol. you must set about it at once and *ration* yourself from the very beginning'. In particular, Trevelyan seized on the number of documents printed verbatim, in the style of the author's five volumes of *The World Crisis* (or later, the six volumes of *The Second World War*).

The edition of *Marlborough* in general circulation today is the abridged version that Scribners issued in 1968. It benefits in almost every way from the sharp eye and equally sharp scalpel of Henry Steele Commager, running to half the original length and, successful in four paperback volumes, it eventually recouped Scribners' investment. What Commager did, as an experienced historian himself, was to cut out the historiographical controversy, notably Macaulay. Also cut were most of the verbatim documents. Conversely, Churchill's

vigorous exposition of Marlborough's feats in the War of the Spanish
Succession (1701–14) survive, essentially through excising the wordy,
whiggish pieties of the political treatment, which Trevelyan had
done better – as Commager was free to say in 1968, three years after
Churchill's death.

Trevelyan had obviously not recommended quite this in 1931; but
he had said enough to make his point. 'It is my only criticism on this
volume, and it may be a wrong one,' he reiterated to Churchill, 'but *if*
you intend to finish in one more vol. you must adopt another method
hereafter so it is not impertinent of me to mention it.' Coming from
the author of a well-paced trilogy, who clearly wished similar success
for *Marlborough*, despite the impact on his own sales, this was advice
worth heeding. It combined notable magnanimity with good historical judgement, an acute literary sensibility and, not least, simple
common sense in saying that 'four vols. is a very long book for folk to
read in days to come'.[31] Unsurprisingly, Churchill purported to heed
this advice but actually disregarded it. It was already too late to effect
a remedy.

For the three-volume *Marlborough* was a chimera. Given Churchill's entrenched methods, and his other commitments, it was never
feasible to complete the biography in this format. True, Pakenham-
Walsh and Owen remained active in preparing the materials on the
War of the Spanish Succession during 1934; and a further extension
was made in Maurice Ashley's employment, now on a part-time basis,
nominally in cooperation with his successor, John Wheldon. As well
as her son's services, those of Lady Ashley, with her fluent German,
were also enlisted by Churchill for translating documents. No expense
was to be spared; no corners were to be cut.

Again, however, the whole schedule began to slip and slide into
arrears. Churchill confidently assured Feiling in February 1934 that he
had decided to conclude the modified second volume of *Marlborough*
with 'the Ramillies campaign which is a beautifully self-contained
episode making an admirable curtain'.[32] In the event, the battle of

Ramillies (1706) was not to be reached until Chapter 6 of the new Volume Three, which itself, of course, was projected as the final volume. Ashley, now fully launched on his journalistic career in Manchester, was increasingly missed at Chartwell; Wheldon was not working out well and left unlamented in 1936; he was never thanked in any of the prefaces to *Marlborough*. There was nobody to shape the prospective final volume, least of all the author. 'My work has been interrupted during the last fortnight by political matters,' he told Ashley in February 1934, excusing himself with an oblique reference to his continuing diehard campaign over India, in which he could hardly have expected much sympathy from the liberal pieties of the *Manchester Guardian*.[33]

Volume Two was nonetheless delivered. The contract contained the financially important provision for prior serialisation in the *Daily Telegraph*; but its joint proprietor, Lord Camrose, who owned it with his brother (soon to be created Lord Kemsley), decided to transfer the serial rights to the *Sunday Times*, of which he was simultaneously sole proprietor. This made for even more haste over the proofs. By July, determined to pack it all off to the waiting presses, Churchill wrote to Ashley: 'Most of the political and peace material you sent me will have to go into Vol. III. We are now 260,000 words. Too many!' As for abbreviating the volume, Churchill had candidly told Harraps that it would not be until his reading of the final slip-proofs that 'I shall hope to cut 5 or 6,000 words out, perhaps more, and until I have done this I cannot quite see where to end.'[34] The result is that Volume Two stops rather than ends, with the promised land in view but never reached, and with the last paragraph offering only a feeble hint about the coming confrontation at Ramillies.

Nevertheless, on publication in October 1934 it received some glowing reviews. 'Mr Winston Churchill Writes a Masterpiece', claimed the *Manchester Evening News*. The fact that Maurice Ashley's name did not appear among the acknowledgements was just as well, given that he was almost certainly the writer of this encomium in the

Manchester Guardian's sister paper. But even in London, let alone New York, sales did not match those of the first volume, which had reached 13,000 by May 1936 as against only 9,500 for the second. 'It is a disappointing fall away,' Harrap told Churchill at that point, 'but we should, no doubt, have sold many more had it been the concluding volume, that is to say, with the completion of the work it would have been possible to have advertised the book and so on, and this could hardly be done with the second of three books.'[35] Too true. And the vital third volume, so often promised for publication in 1935? Naturally, it had been deferred – and Harraps were now being asked to publish a fourth volume.

The nature but not the extent of Churchill's political commitments had meanwhile changed. The India Act had been passed in May 1935. It had four hundred clauses; all had to go through the committee stage; Churchill had attended for most of them. 'Marlborough lingers on the battlefield of Ramillies,' he admitted to Clementine, away on Lord Moyne's yacht. Churchill had made sixty-eight speeches in the House of Commons, replete with lamentation. When he finally sat down, his nemesis Leo Amery rose and again caught the mood of the House: 'Here endeth the last verse of the last chapter of the Book of Jeremiah.'[36] It was surely time for the old man – he was already looking old at sixty – to stop harrying his own party leaders and return to the more worthwhile task of finishing *Marlborough*.

As leader himself, Baldwin certainly thought so. He had an immensely high opinion of his gifted colleague – so long as he did not actually have to have him back in the cabinet that he now formed in June 1935, after taking over from MacDonald as prime minister. For, with the alleged threat from Gandhi in India a dormant issue, Churchill was now making trouble about the alleged threat from Hitler in Germany. Solid, sensible, middle-of-the-road opinion was unmoved by such displays of inveterate alarmism. In fact Churchill still hoped for office, and accordingly kept relatively quiet while Baldwin, in November 1935, engineered a further election triumph for the increasingly Conservative forces of the National government. But Baldwin, content at being back in 10 Downing Street, was equally content that Churchill should spend his own time at Chartwell.

By the early months of 1936, the spawning of the materials necessitating a fourth volume of *Marlborough* came as a surprise to virtually nobody except the author himself. It was not until he had actually spilled his words, in his normal manner, with his usual delays, with his familiar excuses, that he had been able to do the arithmetic and see that the scale on which he was working now exceeded three volumes as inexorably as it had exceeded two. If Harraps were to have a third volume in the autumn of 1936, which they needed to retain credibility in the work, they would have to agree to a final volume, to be published later. 'Indeed I see no other comparable alternative,' Churchill stated in May, 'having regard to the scope and balance of the work, the shortness of time and my own serious political duties.'[37] Not only did Churchill get his way: he also got yet another additional advance, again of £3,000. But if the three-volume *Marlborough* had been a chimera, the four-volume *Marlborough* was to be an albatross.

Clementine Churchill had taken an instant dislike to Brendan Bracken on meeting him in the 1920s. She was obviously right to mistrust his adventurism, his opportunism and his careerism alike; but she turned out, in the end, to be wrong in doubting the loyalty that he professed towards her husband. 'Mr Bracken has been here once or twice,' Clementine reported from Chartwell in January 1931. 'I am giving up my vendetta against him & shall probably end by quite liking him.'[38] That was going too far – she was to find adequate cause for future concern. But it is true that, without Bracken, there might have been no *History of the English-Speaking Peoples* – and no Chartwell left in which to write it.

The fact that Bracken had been in attendance at Chartwell in the winter of 1930–31 was crucial to launching the *History*. It was then that he took responsibility for picking up the author's bright idea, at the back of Churchill's mind since Scribner had taken him to watch American football a year or so previously. Bracken worked hard to turn an idle fancy into a viable book proposal. Initially Churchill's line was that, since *Marlborough* would be finished in 1933, the three volumes of the *History* could be ready in 1934, in 1935 and in 1936. The contract with Cassells, signed at the beginning of 1933, was still premised on *Marlborough* being finished by April 1934, with three years' work to follow on the *History*.

Churchill remained well aware of the pledges he had given. He was entitled to £1,000 from Cassells on signing the contract, and another £1,000 one year later, specifically for research assistance. Building on the good relationship that they had already established, he therefore lined up Keith Feiling for a central role in preparing the *History*. But since Volume Two of *Marlborough*, on which Feiling was meanwhile fully occupied, was not yet published, his starting date on the new project had to be deferred. The final arrangement with Feiling was that, in each of the two years from October 1934, he would reserve four months for his own academic research, but give the other eight months to the *History*, while continuing to perform his teaching duties at Christ Church. He was paid £500 a year, at a time when a successful Oxford don would earn about a thousand. Colleagues at Oxford thought he was simply being diverted; but since he was already planning to write his own history of England (finally published on his retirement in 1950), Feiling was simultaneously being subsidised in his own research by Churchill.

Feiling relished his role. 'My dear First Lord (if I may coin a term of art to express our relation rather more warmly)' was his new gambit, as a form of address. The archives contain many further letters, sometimes reporting on progress, more often commiserating over the lack of it; but, though plainly seeking a closer relationship, Feiling often seems thwarted at never quite achieving the role of confidant. He was only ten years junior to Churchill. A Conservative in his own politics – and later the biographer of Neville Chamberlain – Feiling was never a real Churchillian, though sympathetic to the conflicting claims on a man whom he admired alike as politician and author. Churchill had assured Feiling in January 1934 that the projected third volume of *Marlborough* would 'in no way conflict with the work we have planned together beginning in October of this year. I hope to have broken the back of volume three by then and anyhow my tasks can go forward together.'[39]

Churchill was never more stretched than in these years. 'I have been very hard-pressed lately in politics, and have hardly had time to touch literature,' he told Feiling in February. Two months later, with Churchill still trapped in the last throes of the India Bill, plus the ongoing demands of his two burgeoning literary projects, the stress seemed unrelenting. 'I have been much burdened by politics which have thrown *Marlborough* Volume III over to the Spring of 1936,' he admitted to Feiling. 'But thereafter we must go ahead with the *History* which I hope to finish by the end of 1937 (D.V.).'[40] This, however, was a hope entertained before the necessity for a fourth volume of *Marlborough* had become apparent.

Lloyds Bank, as usual, also had some insight into Churchill's dilemmas. Their calculations, which showed his taxable income declining to £6,572 in 1933–34, also showed it bouncing back to £13,505 in 1934–35 and touching £16,312 in 1935–36. It would be nice to suppose that *Marlborough* was behind this; but, though it helped that the first two volumes were published in successive years, the main reason is that Churchill had stumbled upon a new source of income – films. He was employed by Alexander Korda's London Film Productions Ltd. at a salary of £4,000 in the fiscal year 1934–35; and though the salary in 1935–36 was £3,000, there was an additional compensatory payment of £4,000.[41]

Churchill's career in the film industry is a subplot that must (rather against his own literary practice) be kept in proportion. But it would itself make a great motion picture, with a scenario of Oscar potential. For while Mr Churchill is busy saving the British Empire, and while the squire of Chartwell is up to his knees in mud creating a new pond, and while the author of *Marlborough* is pleading for extra time and money alike, he is also producing a shooting script for a film about World War I, its dialogue replete with inward touches all his own. Thus the captain of a dreadnought proceeding up the English Channel at the end of July 1914 opines: 'If it were war it could not come at a better moment for the Navy.' (Churchill's great claim as First Lord of the Admiralty had always been that the Navy was ready.) There is also a prescient appeal to the English-speaking peoples, when a lightly wounded American pilot, who had signed up as a Canadian, is told that the USA is now in the war. 'Oh! I'm so glad!' he exclaims. 'I was brought up on George Washington, who never told a lie.' A second film scenario was prepared on the reign of George V. Here, Churchills's further labours – 'which have been most arduous', as he reported to the absent Clementine – proved abortive; neither film was made; hence the compensation paid in 1936.[42]

This too had stolen time, indirectly from the *History* though initially from *Marlborough*. It was a point not lost on another of Volume Two's eager readers, aircraftman T. E. Shaw (better known as Lawrence of Arabia). Obviously aware of the projected film-making at Elstree studios, and making also a well-worn allusion to the site of London's bankruptcy courts, the intrepid airman told Churchill in November 1934: 'It will be very wrong if you allow India or Westminster or Elstree or Carey Street to distract your aim.'[43] As we can see, Churchill's literary career was under threat from all four of these hazards, with the first two intertwined, and with the third as one expedient to avoid the fourth.

If he was at the mercy of events, he was also at the mercy of his own impulsive temperament. This ambitious politician was yet again to inflict a disservice on his own cause when, following the death of George V in January 1936, the abdication of the new King Edward VIII, later Duke of Windsor, in December drew Churchill into prompting a futile agitation on behalf of Edward (rather than, in the fictive realm of *The King's Speech*, offering support to Edward's vulnerable brother in taking over as King George VI). Perhaps some excuse for Churchill's emotionally erratic behaviour might be sought in the recent elopement of his actress daughter Sarah to New York with the American comedian Vic Oliver – 'common as dirt', Winston and Clementine agreed.[44] But they disagreed about Winston's stance on the abdication, all too characteristic of his inability to govern his own restless impulses.

If films proved transient, journalism was more reliable, provided it paid properly. Thus in 1936, Churchill sent a telegram to New York, quickly agreeing to write twelve articles for the Hearst press at $500 a time and reporting that the London *Evening Standard*, owned by his crony Lord Beaverbrook (another of Clementine's bêtes noires), had made him a firm offer for eighteen articles at £100 each. But when *The New York Times*, trailing great prestige but wielding a somewhat thinner chequebook, made an offer later that year, Mrs Pearman was deputed to inform them by ordinary mail that 'the payment has no relation to what is customary'. Churchill personally declined an offer from George Harrap of £500 for a short political book in 1937: 'I often get as much as the figure you mention for an article of 5,000 words.'[45]

The trouble was not that Churchill's income declined in the 1930s. Its peak figure of £16,312 in 1935–36 would be worth over £800,000 at today's prices. At least a quarter of it was generated in the United States. The real problem was that income needed to be maintained at these extraordinary levels in order to meet Churchill's outgoings. Hence his continued vulnerability. He was ill-equipped to face a fall in his income to £12,914 in 1936–37, even though this figure was much in line with his average earnings.

The Chartwell system was simply too heavy a financial burden to be maintained, as he intermittently recognised. Intermittently, then, he had to face the possibility of selling up. 'If I could see £25,000 I should close with it,' he wrote to Clementine on 2 February 1937. 'If we do not get a good price we can quite well carry on for a year or two

more. But no good offer should be refused, having regard to the fact
that our children are almost all flown, and my life is probably in its
closing decade.'[46] And then, on the same day, he flew to Paris, where
he stayed in style at the Ritz with his profligate son Randolph, before
catching the train to Lord Rothermere's hospitable villa on the Riviera,
taking his secretary Mrs Pearman with him so as to dictate a few more
chapters and 'great stories'. A postdated cheque for £5,000 from the
News of the World had recently appeased Lloyds Bank, and more could
be expected.

Chartwell was not sold. It seems to have been saved at this juncture
by the sale instead of the ground rents of the Garron Towers estate, for
which Churchill anticipated getting £12,000. Obviously, this meant
renouncing a source of assured income in favour of a capital sum, to
be applied to immediate needs, but Churchill's need for the money
was urgent. For he also now encountered another problem, maybe
largely of his own making, which prompted his plaintive request to
Lloyds Bank in June 1937 for some explanation of 'why it is that I, who
have paid every year my full tax, have got two years behind'.[47] In fact
he faced arrears of about five thousand pounds, at a point when
current income had declined. He had also recently been caught out by
changes in US tax law for foreigners, leaving liabilities that were
equally unexpected, albeit smaller.

Moreover, for all Churchill's efforts, his literary schedule had lapsed
badly. Politics was an excuse that he was always reluctant to use, since
it simultaneously diminished his professional status as an author who
fulfilled his contracts. But his correspondence shows him alluding to
it in private, within a trusted circle well placed to understand why the
History is stalled. He tells Feiling as the General Election of November
1935 approaches: 'I have been so hampered in my work by politics that
I am behindhand with *Marlborough*, and I want to have a clear week
to put myself in the atmosphere of the new work.' Again, following
the crisis over Hitler's occupation of the Rhineland in March 1936, he
admits to Feiling in May that 'I find it a very great difficulty to finish

Marlborough, with all this political distraction.' To the *History*'s publisher, Newman Flower at Cassells, Churchill writes in August 1936, exercising his option to extend the deadline for the *History* to April 1939: 'I have been so much ridden in upon by politics owing to the need of urging the country to rearm.'[48] *Marlborough* thus remained unfinished and, in consequence, the *History* barely begun, well into 1938.

Whereupon, things went from bad to worse for Churchill. The New Year had opened well, with Churchill's confident assurance to his bank manager that his account was 'in better condition than it has been for a long time'.[49] But, with a sudden recession in the United States, the stocks that he had bought in New York for £18,000 had fallen to less than one third of that value. Chartwell was put on the market, now at a price of only £20,000. A move to a London house was projected, much to Clementine's relief, and negotiations continued for some time, though increasingly subject to some prevarication on Winston's part, for reasons that initially seemed unclear.

At this point Brendan Bracken rode to the rescue – and not entirely out of the blue. He had prepared the ground by making sure that Churchill, while on a recent long visit to Cannes, had purposefully cultivated the better acquaintance of Bracken's wealthy colleague in financial journalism, Sir Henry Strakosch, who had provided useful information on the economics of rearmament. 'He is a lonely old bird,' Bracken had advised, 'so I venture to suggest that you might ask him for lunch one day.'[50]

Never did Churchill's hospitality bear more fruit. In March 1938 Strakosch offered to take over Churchill's holdings on Wall Street, at the price that Churchill had misguidedly paid for them, and to hold them at his own expense for three years, meanwhile paying Churchill £800 a year in interest for the privilege. It seems as extraordinary that Churchill agreed to this arrangement, with a concomitant risk of compromising his political standing, as that Strakosch offered it. The motive for the latter's generosity – attested also by a legacy of £20,000 in his will, revealed on his death in 1943 – appears to have been simply his fervent belief in the importance of his hero's anti-Nazi stand.[51]

Churchill accepted this fortuitous bailout, apparently without many qualms, and certainly without many alternatives. For once, it was not authorship that supported his political commitments but the reverse. Chartwell was saved – again. The study was not put under dust sheets; the Pol Roger lay ready in the cellar. All that remained to be done was to write *The History of the English-Speaking Peoples*.

Churchill was finally able to rid himself of the albatross that he had been carrying, almost like an ancestral curse, when *Marlborough* was finished. In the third massive volume of the biography, published in October 1936, the preface had given special mention to 'the illuminating and impartial work of Professor Trevelyan', who read it for Churchill. As with Volume Two (and later Volume Four), all of them dealing so largely with Marlborough's record in war, the technical advice of Churchill's military advisers is acknowledged. It was an aspect of the work that Churchill relished and performed well, using good maps to back up his lucid descriptions of how manoeuvres were executed amid the messy realities of warfare – just like Malakand or, as his text often pointed out, the Western Front. He had hugely enjoyed his visits, under Pakenham-Walsh's guidance, to the battlefields at Ramillies, Oudenarde and Blenheim. But the revised Volume Three covered only three years, an even shorter period than its predecessor. Its lengthy account of the battle of Ramillies in 1706 (itself left over from the second volume, of course) was now paralleled by an examination of the Oudenarde campaign of 1708 at equal length. The awkward fact remained that the story had still not got beyond that year.

If this clouded Harrap's view of the enterprise, even more did it depress Scribner's in New York. Admittedly Charlie Scribner had little reason to grieve when he had learned from Churchill in January 1934 that the *History* would be 'retarded' by the new third volume for

Marlborough. The bottom line was that Scribners had not signed up for the American rights of the *History* – though Churchill obviously assumed that they would do so. For when Scribner reported on his American edition of *Marlborough* in July 1935 that 'the sales on the 2nd volume (or vols. III and IV with us) has been very disappointing to date', Churchill reiterated his commiseration: 'You are the the only publisher I have ever dealt with who has not prospered by our collaboration.' Then, after saying that he would waive further US advances, he added by way of consolation: 'Here in England my books go well. We must hope the English-speaking People will break the charm.'[52]

The clouds disclosed, as usual, a silver lining. Since the reason put forward for a fourth volume in 1936 was essentially that there was a spillover of excess material from the third, much of the text already existed; and the publication of a final volume in 1937 could confidently be expected. Such reasoning ignored the schoolboy glee with which Churchill, having got himself out of this scrape, instead used this stolen time for another project altogether. The book that he in fact finished in 1937 was *Great Contemporaries*, published by Butterworth in London, while in New York, since Scribners had been too badly burned already, the book was published by Putnams. George Haven Putnam was a notable Anglophile, who had had to explain himself in New York in 1920, at the height of the Anglo-Irish conflict, for sharing a platform with Churchill in London two years previously at the foundation of the English-Speaking Union. This made for an ideologically appropriate connection, to be revived when Churchill subsequently looked for an American publisher for his speeches.

It may seem obvious that, in 1936–37, the author should have behaved more responsibly in honouring his existing contracts, with his loyal publishers, rather than publishing *Great Contemporaries*. Had he done so, however, it would have been a distinct loss to literature. Along with *My Early Life* (*A Roving Commission* in its American edition), Churchill's *Great Contemporaries* is a book that can be read today with lasting enjoyment. This collection of biographical essays had long been planned; it had, in fact, been deferred on Scribner's advice that at least one American subject should be included – a provision now met, to Putnam's benefit, by an appraisal of Franklin D. Roosevelt, albeit one written in rather guarded and unilluminating terms. The author had forgotten ever meeting Roosevelt, though a couple of complimentary copies of *Marlborough* had been collected personally from Chartwell by one of his sons, and the president later claimed to have 'much enjoyed reading them'.[53]

The interest of the book lies elsewhere. The portraits of contemporaries whom Churchill had actually known well, and genuinely thought great, retain their freshness and insight today: Rosebery and Joe Chamberlain, of course, but also Asquith and Balfour, and, perhaps unexpectedly, Gladstone's disciple and biographer, John Morley. All of these men had had a real respect for books. They would certainly not have condoned burning them. By contrast, the portrait of Hitler in *Great Contemporaries*, written in 1935, is almost as guarded and equivocal as that of FDR, albeit with a cool scepticism about the Nazi leader that, by the time of its publication in October 1937 – after the Rhineland crisis – had already frozen into the antipathy and distrust expressed in Churchill's speeches.

Churchill's endemic financial worries would have provided ample excuse for him to withdraw from a leading role in politics in the late 1930s. After all, his long Indian campaign and his brief fuss over the abdication of Edward VIII had each achieved nothing, while serving to discredit him personally. The role of elder statesman may have beckoned; it might have allowed him time to buttress his fortune through well-rewarded and well-respected literary activities – adequate time for 'great stories' and *Great Contemporaries* alike, for *Marlborough* and the *History* too. Instead, of course, Churchill became increasingly consumed in warning about the rise of Nazi Germany. His collected speeches on this theme from these years were to be published by Harraps in 1938, initially under the title, *The Locust Years*, but with a late switch to *Arms and the Covenant*. This title with its allusion to the Covenant of the League of

Nations, showed how, from 1936, Churchill was now reaching out to a swathe of liberal, anti-fascist, pro-League opinion in Britain. Hence too the suggestion that there was 'peculiar interest for us today', as he claimed in his latest volume of *Marlborough*, in the War of the Spanish Succession: 'We see a world war of a League of Nations against a mighty, central military monarchy, hungering for domination not only over the lands but over the politics and religion of its neighbours.'[54]

This language was admittedly less appropriate for deployment in New York. Putnams, in publishing the American edition of the speeches, realised that allusions to the League, of which the United States was not a member, would not work; and they suggested the more catchy American title, *While England Slept*. The volume, identical in contents, was nominally edited by Randolph Churchill. In his preface he stressed that his father suffered 'from the disadvantage of being strangely free from the prejudices and ideologies' of a conventional party politician. This pointed to a significant reorientation of the political spectrum. One straw in the wind is a letter of February 1936 from Ashley, still on the *Manchester Guardian* at the time, and previously content to keep his own counsel on politics. 'I hope that war will not superimpose itself on literary work,' he now writes to Churchill, amid mounting concern about Hitler. 'I find it almost impossible to focuss my mind on the correct attitude to adopt, but broadly I cannot envisage any possible war in which I could conscientiously take a pacifist line.'[55] In the same letter Ashley agrees to read the drafts (as yet unwritten) of the *History of the English-Speaking Peoples* – a project acquiring more resonance with every passing year.

It was by now a team that was used to working together. Feiling's decision in 1936 that he could not continue to give so much of his own time faced Churchill with a gap in the ranks; he manifestly needed another of those 'young men' with First Class Honours from the Oxford history school; and one was soon recruited, on the strength of Feiling's discernment of the sort of qualities needed – 'Great spirit and courage, as I have seen in several fields.' This was William Deakin, twenty-two and recently married when Churchill first met him in May 1936 – 'I like Mr Deakin very much and find him much more lively and sensible than Wheldon.'[56] Churchill's acknowledgement in the preface to Volume Four of *Marlborough* that he had been 'greatly assisted in the necessary researches by Mr F. W. Deakin' was well earned. Ashley too liked him much better than Wheldon and they co-operated readily, with a similar unillusioned affection for their extraordinary boss. By this time, all of them found that their work in steering their own *Marlborough* campaign to victory was interspersed with desperately belated efforts to mount the second front in the shape of the *History*.

Though Churchill naturally kept from them any explicit mention of his financial concerns, these were intrusively obvious. He even toyed with the idea of accepting an offer of commercial employment, or so he told Clementine. 'Then I should be able to do my books more slowly and not have to face the truly stupendous task like *Marlborough* Vol. IV being finished in 4 or 5 months, simply for current expenses,' he explained on 2 February 1937. 'For 1938–9 we have the *History of the English-Speaking Peoples*, worth £16,000, but entailing an immense amount of reading and solitary reflection if justice is to be done to so tremendous a topic.' He specified this particular sum because, out of the £20,000 lump sum, he had meanwhile drawn £4,000 from Cassells, in four instalments since 1933, for research expenses; and this thought evidently prompted him to write that same day to Newman Flower, asking for his final tranche of £1,000. 'I am making good progress with the last volume of *Marlborough*' was the more optimistic tone he instantly adopted for his publisher, 'and hope to begin the Magnum Opus in earnest in the late autumn.' None of these sums were to be declared to the Inland Revenue, Churchill correctly stressed to his bank manager, since 'the contract is explicit that it is a loan'.[57]

The Cassells advance would thus be liable for repayment, should the author default on delivery. This was indeed a central point of the contract, with its outright sale of the copyright, which allowed the entire lump sum to escape taxation. Thus, given the Strakosch bailout in 1938, the way was clear for Churchill to net £15,000 as income in 1939 – provided *Marlborough* were meanwhile published as planned. George Harrap had accordingly told Churchill that he saw the publication of Volume Three in 1936 as 'full of promise for the happy fulfilment of your task next year'.[58]

By June 1937, the promise was dashed. Churchill was well practised in conveying such news to publishers – 'I grieve to reach the conclusion that it is impossible', etcetera – and brazenly told Harrap that Butterworth's publication of *Great Contemporaries* 'will in no way interfere with *Marlborough*', though it was self-evidently the main reason for the delay. 'I am working very hard at *Marlborough* now,' he assured Harrap a fortnight later, 'night and day in fact.'[59] True, Churchill declined an invitation to the Riviera from the former American actress Maxine Elliott, whose Chateau de l'Horizon, near Cannes, was both hospitable and tempting. 'Thinking much of you all and the pool,' he telegraphed her at the beginning of September. 'Alas am tied here by work on Marlborough.'[60] A twenty-seven-chapter outline of the volume had now been produced; Churchill reckoned that the whole volume might run to 520 pages, though the punctilious Mr Wood at Harraps was already doubtful about the arithmetic.

By October 1937 Churchill had his tail up. He was telling Deakin that he had done five thousand words on the death of Queen Anne in 1714 (which became Chapter 37), with only one subsequent chapter allegedly required (though Duke John lived until 1722, which comprised chapters 38 and 39 in the end). But Churchill was deluding himself, if not Deakin, about how near to completion he really was, since the much earlier treatment of Malplaquet (notably the long Chapter 9) was still unwritten. ' "The Battle of Malplaquet" is not begun,' Churchill admitted to Ashley in November, 'though all the material is prepared, and I know what to say.' Ashley likewise knew what to think, from long experience, and must have blenched at the warning: 'You will be surprised at the detail in which the political drama is told.'[61]

Publication, already put off until the spring of 1938, began looking less assured. It was clearly at risk from all the inveterate faults and temptations of Churchill's nocturnal regime. The later at night he worked, the less discipline he exercised, with the slip proofs now sprawling out of control, as in each previous volume, serving as a predictable prelude to the ritual of the final reckoning, with a long letter that Harrap must have half-expected. It was sent on 23 December 1937: it was still optimistic that the work could be printed, still confident that serialisation in *The Sunday Times* could take place in February, but confessing now to a total of 790 printed pages, enough to make Mr Wood's hair stand on end. And the options for publication? Either damaging cuts of two hundred pages – or a double volume. Hence the effrontery of the claim that 'I feel we are in a strong position, for I think the four (or five) volumes as they will be finished have a good chance of superseding for some years to come the existing works on Marlborough.'[62]

George Harrap, now happily in semi-retirement, had once told Churchill that the final volume would represent 'an achievement in which I hope to have pride as long as I live'.[63] As it turned out, he enjoyed that satisfaction all too briefly, since a gallstones operation led to his unexpected death on 29 October 1938, at the end of the month in which the last volume of *Marlborough* was published. His firm had squashed any idea of a fifth volume, instead requiring Churchill to implement drastic cuts to bring the concluding instalment down to a size comparable with the other three volumes. In the process, a spring publication had yielded to the obvious publishing logic of a date in October. This at least gave Churchill the small, symbolic satisfaction of dating his final preface 13 August, the same day and month as those written in 1933, 1934 and 1936: the anniversary of the Battle of Blenheim. Harrap, for his part, had proudly signed up his famous author for another book in June 1938: a history of Europe since the Russian Revolution for the relatively small advance of £1,500, which Churchill, his bargaining position weakened by his Wall Street losses, agreed to accept.

In New York, Scribner enjoyed a longer life than Harrap, though with a more rueful pride. 'There is nothing especially exciting to report on the sale,' he told Churchill at the end of the year. 'Unfortunately Americans do not seem to have the regard for your ancestor that he merits.'[64] But by the time that he received this letter, the author was devoting himself – day and night, in the usual proportions – to working on his next literary assignment. This was not, of course, the newly contracted history of contemporary Europe but the commitment that Churchill had so long promised, and so long evaded: composing his *History of the English-Speaking Peoples*.

The Historian as Prophet, 1938–39

'Thus I condemn tyranny in whatever guise and from whatever quarter it presents itself. All this of course has a current application.'

Churchill to Maurice Ashley, 1939

The cash-strapped literary drudge who turned immediately from one big book to the next nonetheless lived in mouth-watering, eye-popping luxury. Even when faced with the task of making the final cuts to *Marlborough*, he had done it in style. Throughout January 1938 he had retreated to a favourite Riviera villa, this time taking up his standing invitation from the socially well-connected Maxine Elliott to stay at Le Chateau de l'Horizon. He told her that it was 'the first really good rest I have had for a long time'; and he told Clementine that, although 'I have spent all my mornings in bed correcting and recasting the proofs, this is not at all fatiguing.'[1] He even persuaded his wife to join him there briefly. Meanwhile communications with headquarters at Chartwell were maintained by enlisting, in the role of a courier delivering the corrected proofs, the multimillionaire owner of the *Daily Mail*, Lord Rothermere. This arrangement much amused Mrs Pearman, left minding the shop; but her own days at Chartwell were numbered, with a significant changing of the guard upon the completion of *Marlborough* and the beginning of the *History*.

From 1937 Kathleen Hill had served as Churchill's personal secretary, resident at Chartwell. This appointment was all the more necessary since it looks as though Violet Pearman was showing signs of strain. Suffering from high blood pressure, and trapped in a blighted marriage from which she could not escape, her medical problems took a turn for the worse. In November 1938, after consulting her physician, Churchill was to tell her of his decision that 'you need a good long rest, if you are to recover your health. I have therefore decided to offer you a year's leave at a salary of £3 a week.'[2] This was as generous on his part as it was well deserved on hers, though her retirement to part-time employment did not prevent her early death at the age of forty some three years later. Churchill then continued to support one of her young daughters throughout her education.

A work schedule drawn up in the summer of 1938 indicates an ambitious attempt to tackle the secretarial problem. It was assumed that the author's demands could be met by Kathleen Hill, in residence, and two capable stenographers, commuting from London and staying alternate nights in a spare room at Chartwell. One stenographer would be on duty from 10 a.m. to 2 p.m. on Monday morning, then off until Tuesday, meanwhile being whisked back home to London. Her colleague would take over at 2 p.m on Monday until 4.30 p.m. and come on duty again from 7.30 p.m. 'for night work'; she would then finish her stint on Tuesday, 10 a.m. to 2 p.m., and be taken to the station at Westerham, for the train up to London, transported in the same car that would meet the other secretary, now refreshed after her night away, off the train down from London. The two stenographers, on these shifts, would alternate in this pattern. We do not know whether this neat plan was implemented exactly as specified here, but something like it was needed to meet the peculiar needs and peculiar hours of the master of the house in generating the income that maintained it.

These were heroic months of sustained effort. Years later Churchill reminisced to his doctor, Lord Moran, claiming that the four volumes of the published *History* – 'a million words' – had been written in a year and a quarter before the war: 'I worked at them every night till two in the morning, though at the time I was fighting for rearmament. Of course I had a team to help, but I wrote every word myself.'[3] Some of the details here are awry: half a million words altogether; and

not, in the end, all by himself, unlike *Marlborough*; and not, as the
official story subsequently had it, all completed by the time war broke
out in September 1939. But in essentials the *History* is a product of the
years 1938–39. Indeed, in the published work, a number of footnotes
punctiliously indicate that particular passages were written at that
time. Plainly it was later felt necessary to state this because some
remarks or allusions in the published text might otherwise have struck
a post-war reader as smacking of hindsight. It is to Churchill's credit
that they so often smack of foresight, with a prophetic dimension that
cannot be ignored.

Since 1936 he had published a series of fortnightly columns, initially
in Beaverbrook's *Evening Standard*. These ran to about a thousand
words each: a commitment that Churchill managed to fulfil regularly,
come what may, earning him a useful hundred pounds a time (about
five thousand pounds each at today's prices). Focused largely on the
international situation, these columns were not simply puffed up with
empty late-night rhetoric but instead often embodied hard factual
evidence, not easily come by, on such matters as the economics of rearmament (on which Sir Henry Strakosch had been helpful). But
Churchill's trenchant criticisms of the National government's foreign
policy were increasingly at odds with the views of his old sparring
partner, Lord Beaverbrook, the *Standard*'s proprietor. After Neville
Chamberlain, who had succeeded Baldwin as prime minister in 1937,
got rid of his young Foreign Secretary, Anthony Eden, in February
1938, Churchill's outspoken criticism of the government's foreign
policy finally became too much for Beaverbrook. Churchill supported
Eden's view that Roosevelt rather than Hitler was now the man to be
appeased, as the author made clear in his ongoing columns, which
henceforth appeared, thanks to Lord Camrose, in the *Daily Telegraph*.

Churchill collected eighty-four of these columns, published by
Butterworth in June 1939 as *Step by Step*. In this, as in the American
edition, nothing of substance was altered, and little needed to be
altered, then or later. Indeed *Step by Step* could virtually have served as

a draft for the memoirs that Churchill composed after World War II, the first volume of which was to be published as *The Gathering Storm* in 1948. Churchill's column of 30 October 1936 had actually been called 'The Gathering Storm', though everyone seems to have forgotten this, eleven or so years later, when, in finally settling on the right title for the memoirs, the wheel was painfully reinvented, albeit during an otherwise painless escape from post-war austerity at the Mamounia Hotel, Marrakesh, over New Year 1948.

The Gathering Storm instantly became the classic post-war vindication of Churchill's pre-war prophetic stance. It depicted him long intent on mobilising a great international coalition against the Nazis. He had indeed said it all earlier. His column of 12 June 1936 had called for a Grand Alliance; his column of 11 December 1936 had indicted Baldwin for his 'astounding apologia' in allegedly putting party before country in resisting rearmament – a narrative elaborated, with deadly impact, in *The Gathering Storm*. As Churchill's column of 17 November 1938, after Chamberlain's Munich agreement in September, put it, the emerging political division 'does not follow exactly the regular groupings of party, but it cuts very deep, and will sever many ties of friendship'. In 1939 Baldwin did not receive a complimentary copy of *Step by Step*, but Clement Attlee, now the leader of the Labour Party, got one. 'It must be a melancholy satisfaction to see how right you were,' Attlee wrote to Churchill, in warm terms that would have been inconceivable even a few years previously.[4]

'I am very careful not to prophesy,' Churchill had written in his column of 25 June 1937. In so far as he tended to break his own rule, he now had many overt means of doing so. He made well-publicised political speeches, which were collected in published volumes. He wrote polemical newspaper articles, which were now achieving unprecedented worldwide syndication once the astute and energetic literary agent Emery Reves had persuaded Churchill to let him handle the foreign rights. Churchill generally kept his activities as a politician apart from his career as an author. Thus he plainly did not need to smuggle out coded messages about current events within the pages of *Marlborough*, though allusions to Grand Alliances against the dark forces of tyranny are not hard to find, and conversely *Step by Step* contains a couple of references to Duke John.

Yet the *History* turned out to be different and acquired an inescapable ideological dimension. The author had certainly not acted as one of Dr Johnson's blockheads in clinching the agreement with the publishers in 1932; nor had he previously been more than opportunistic in celebrating the Anglo-American connection. As we have seen in Chapter 3, the English-speaking peoples had a history of which young Winston had long seemed oblivious. It was, in fact, only as his sixty-fifth birthday approached in 1939 that the author became seized of the prophetic significance inherent in writing his own *History of the English-Speaking Peoples*.

The *History* owed crucial debts to others and the team showed much continuity from the *Marlborough* campaign. William Deakin was the key figure, with assistance from Maurice Ashley, now working on *The Times* in London, and mainly helping Churchill on the seventeenth century. John Wheldon was similarly called back to write a couple of drafts on the Tudors and also to check this part of the proofs. At the proofreading stage, Eddie Marsh was brought into more formal employment, delighting in each honorarium as a generous gift for services that he would have performed anyway, as hyphenator-in-chief. It was he who introduced Churchill in February 1939 to Marsh's former civil-service colleague, G. M. Young. The initial invitation was simply for Young, who had recently published his own book on the seventeenth century, to look over this part of the proofs; but his services on a far wider front were soon commissioned for six months at £50 a month.

He was an important recruit to the project. Young in name only, and an Oxford scholar through and through, he was a slight, stooped, anaemic-looking figure, called a 'pantomath' by friends who believed that he knew everything. He proved a more fervent Churchill loyalist than Feiling, who was to fulfil his role as authorised biographer of Neville Chamberlain by producing an apologia for Chamberlain in 1946; whereas Baldwin's reputation later took many years to recover from the authorised biography of him that Young published in 1952. Both Feiling and Young were in their late fifties in 1938, and Marsh a decade older: a more senior and authoritative trio, according Churchill esteem but not deference. They were not only of a different generation to Ashley but fully thirty years older than either Deakin or his Oxford friend, Alan Bullock, who had begun postgraduate research at Oxford in 1938–39, working on the sixteenth century, but was soon recruited for assistance on the *History*. In later life, Sir William Deakin and Lord Bullock were both to become distinguished academic figures, each of them the head of a newly founded Oxford college that he moulded in his own image; each of them, in 1939, formidable historians in the making, as Churchill seems to have recognised in the respect he accorded to the opinions that they respectfully offered to the great man.

Had it been finished, as originally promised, by 1937, the *History* would surely have been very different. It was Feiling who had been given charge of the project in October 1934, and he did his best to get it moving until the cessation of his formal employment in the summer of 1936; thereafter he continued only as a consultant on the *History*, with his services purloined for the immediate exigencies of *Marlborough*. His conscientious efforts on the *History*, then, came early rather than late; but the writing of the *History* came late rather than early; and much was lost accordingly.

It had all started so well, with Churchill determined to give the work his personal oversight. Accordingly, he had sketched out the plan to Feiling in September 1934. There were to be 400,000 words, which Churchill imagined would allow for 150,000 on the period up to the Declaration of American Independence. Then 100,000 words each for British and for American history up to 'the common victory of the two nations in the Great War where I draw the curtain'. This would leave about 50,000 words for Canada, Australia, New Zealand and South Africa; so the Dominions, though not excluded, were not to be integrated into an Anglo-American story that Churchill conceived in four sections. The first was to be 'the origin of the English Speaking Peoples'; the second, 'the quarrels of the English Speaking Peoples'; then a third section on 'the rise' in the nineteenth century; and a concluding section that 'covers about the last forty years'.[5]

These proportions bear no relation to the *History* as finally published in 1956–58. In 1934 Churchill had plainly envisaged that most of the coverage would be devoted to the period *after* 1776, the Declaration of American Independence; and that the work would extend well into the twentieth century, certainly up to 1918. But in the four volumes of the published *History*, the War of Independence is not reached until halfway through the third volume, and the final volume barely stretches to the end of the nineteenth century. So the balance of coverage is tipped towards the earlier, not the later period.

Moreover, it was the later period that he himself neglected to cover. Volume Four of the published *History*, like each of its predecessors, is divided into three parts. Churchill was only responsible for writing the second of these, on the American Civil War. He concluded this part of the volume in 1865, wholly fittingly, by quoting some words uttered by John Bright 'to his audience of English working folk'.[6] This is virtually the only hint of the resonance of Lincoln and democracy in shaping the concept of the English-speaking peoples. The other parts of Volume Four are essentially the work of others in the 1950s, assembled in the drive to complete the book before the death of 'the greatest living Englishman'.

The discrepancy between what was promised in 1934 and what was delivered in 1939 was not Feiling's fault. Ample testimony survives in the archive to the shape of a book planned with some thought and care in 1934–36. Here is Feiling, duly preparing his promised dossiers. No fewer than eight chapters reach Churchill by January 1935 – 'I think you will find that these notes are pretty packed and ought to expand very considerably.' Churchill sends his thanks by telegram for 'so much valuable material which am hoping to read soon'. In February more dossiers arrive; but Churchill now simply pleads the pressure of politics; and in April he pleads the pressure of *Marlborough*. 'You must be deep in *Marlborough*, and I see you are in politics,' Feiling writes, understandingly, at the end of September 1935. 'So if I do not hear, I shall go right ahead, planning out the remaining chapters . . .' Churchill responds by saying how anxious he is 'to have some good long talks with you, but before I do so I wish to read thoroughly the whole of the material which you have sent me'.[7] Evidently he has not done so up to that point, a year into Feiling's appointment.

In December 1935 Churchill duly receives Feiling's draft for a three-volume work. The second volume is to begin with the Industrial Revolution and to cover the conflict in the American colonies, the Napoleonic wars, the War of 1812 (as a separate chapter, on Churchill's insistence), British North America up to 1837 and British India. That leaves the third and final volume to cover the Victorian Age and the American Civil War, to include parallel chapters on 'American Democracy' and 'British Democracy', to bring in the history of the Dominions, and to lead up to a final chapter: 'The Relations of the English Speaking Races before the Great War'.[8] All this is consistent with the conception of a work weighted towards a full treatment of the more recent period, albeit with a terminal date now set at 1914.

Feiling's emphasis on a comparative treatment of British and American democratic culture was, of course, in line with the historical provenance of the concept of 'English-Speaking Peoples'. There was nothing particularly original in what he proposed; it was much what any competent and well-read historian aiming to write on this theme would have done, as is attested by the closely similar contents page of the *History of the English-Speaking Peoples* that R. B. Mowat and Preston Slosson were to publish in 1943.

Why, then, did Churchill depart from the agreed plan? Feiling had shown industry in making a solid start but by the time his two-year appointment was due to end in May 1936, Churchill had barely begun to engage with the project in any serious way. His own input had been minimal. As he confessed to Feiling in April 1936: 'Events have taken some hold of me, and I have not been able to think about the *English Speaking Peoples*. All that is for the future.' Feiling signed off graciously, having done what was possible in the circumstances: 'As to these latter-day chapters for your book, – things like British democracy from 1881 or America in the same age – you know much more than I do and I feel rather a fraud.'[9] These promised chapters never materialised; it was Churchill who proved fraudulent in pretending that they had not been promised in the first place. The plans of 1934–36 were thus for a book that was never written – at least, never written by Churchill, though Feiling salvaged some of his own discarded research when he ultimately published his *History of England* (1950).

The empty façade of the projected *History* remained as an impressive monument to Feiling's doomed efforts. Churchill proudly showed it off, like a Potemkin village, to Newman Flower of Cassells in February 1937. 'For each of these chapters I have now gathered together a very substantial mass of material, and also lists of the authorities to be consulted,' he adroitly explained, with his 'to be' doing a lot of work in purporting mastery of the pile of unread dossiers left by Feiling. Bluffing Flower along in this style, Churchill concluded that he had 'every hope and resolve to finish this task before the end of 1939'. But the Cassells contract, of course, had originally specified a deadline of April 1937, only recently extended, at Churchill's request, by two years, which thus meant April 1939. Bowled over by his recent glimpse of the Potemkin village, Flower proved ready to vary the terms of the contract, to allow the *History* to be serialised in part form by Amalgamated Press, a division of the publishing empire of Lord Camrose. In June 1937 Flower agreed to this further extension of the deadline for the book itself until 31 December 1939, 'but not beyond it'.[10]

Churchill had again bought time, but at some loss to his credibility.

For Cassells could not help but see that, whatever they had been led to believe earlier, the final volume of *Marlborough* was not published in the autumn of 1937, nor indeed in the spring of 1938, but only in October 1938. Thus when Churchill sent Cassells the first actual instalment of the *History*, Newman Flower exploded with pent-up frustration in a curt letter on 2 September. He declined to set up any of this in print until the delivery of the manuscript for the whole book, and he continued: 'So far you have only delivered 30,000 words out of 400,000, and we fail to see how you are going to complete the other 370,000 words by the 31st December 1939, on which date the agreement falls in.' For the avoidance of doubt, he added that 'we are not going to extend the agreement beyond that date by a single day'.

Churchill was not accustomed to receiving letters like this. Young Desmond Flower had been far more emollient, ready to welcome 'the real beginning of the book, as distinct from the false dawn of preliminary research', but his recently knighted father, the head of the firm and only five years younger than Churchill himself, was a more august figure, who had to be humoured. For Churchill simply could not afford to let this contract lapse, in which case he would not only lose his long-awaited £15,000 but also have to repay the £5,000 already advanced (and spent). With Chartwell yet again at risk, the stakes were high and an emollient reply, much redrafted, the prudent option. In it Churchill had the delicate task of vindicating his ability to deliver the *History*, but could do so only by revealing just how disingenuous he had previously been in his claims to have long since finished his work on *Marlborough*. He now said that, since its final volume, which ran to a quarter of a million words, had been written in barely more than a year, he did not see why he could not write 370,000 words of the *History* in the remaining sixteen months of his contract.[11]

And he was right. If he could write a thousand words a day, six days a week, the sums would add up nicely. This is what he set out to do from 1 August 1938. He subsequently claimed at various points to have done 18,000 words by mid-August, 50,000 by September, 90,000 by

October, and 136,000 by 30 November, his sixty-fourth birthday. On this reckoning, in four months he averaged 1,115 words for every single day. Far from the flow abating, he then enhanced his strike rate. By 6 June 1939, Churchill was able to tell Eddie Marsh that 450,000 words were in print. In ten months, then, the author could claim to have done an average of about 1,500 words each day.

This seems to be the most reliable figure. But there is room for confusion here, for two connected reasons. First, Churchill incorrigibly boasted of even more to Cassells, knowing that they had no means of checking. They could be kept in the dark about exactly how much was done because, when they had refused to set up the work in type, Churchill had gone back to Harraps and privately agreed with their printing house that he could have proofs as needed, just like the composition of *Marlborough*. So the punctilious Mr C. C. Wood remained in charge here – a third pedant to join Marsh and Young in constant efforts to restrain the over-exuberant author. Secondly, the word-count is only what it says – Mr Wood's calculation of how many words were set up in print on a first proof that everyone knew would have to undergo a long process of revision before it had the status of a publishable book. Thus, even though the words might be done, the book might remain unfinished.

Churchill deserves credit for over-fulfilling his own target, at least so far as quantity is concerned. It must be remembered that these were the same months that saw the intensification of the crisis over the Sudetenland, the dramatic three airflights by Neville Chamberlain to meet Hitler, the Munich Agreement for the partition of Czechoslovakia and the emotional parliamentary debates that followed in October 1938, the response after Kristallnacht to the Nazi campaign of anti-Semitism, the moves leading to Hitler's annexation of the rest of Czechoslovakia in March 1939 and the ensuing Anglo-French guarantees to Poland. All of these were matters on which Churchill's views were reported worldwide, demanding his immediate attention and close study. He wrote his regular fortnightly column and also gave ten major speeches, about one a month, running to over a hundred pages when they were subsequently published in book form. They cover such matters as the detailed case for a Ministry of Supply (of war munitions) and a dissection of the Navy estimates. And on top of all this, he had also intended to visit the United States for a lecture tour in the autumn of 1938.

It is hardly surprising that the author met his word-count target for the *History* at a price – ultimately by sacrificing quality, in this respect unlike *Marlborough*. In another respect, though, the *History* was all too like *Marlborough*, in betraying the manner of its composition, night after night, with only a loose thread of narrative to determine direction and relevance alike. Churchill faced two great threats at this time: from Hitler and from Sir Newman Flower. The former occupied him during crowded, critical days. The latter consumed his attention on every night he could spare, as he dictated the *History*, proving the chairman of Cassells wrong by flinging the words in his face. Caught in his own trap, Churchill abandoned the tight, disciplined structure that Feiling had long since prepared. There was simply no time to make the *History* shorter; and the more the first part grew, the less space and time were left to develop the later part of the work in line with the original prospectus.

Churchill had established authentic historical credentials over the years. He certainly understood modern warfare, extrapolating from much first-hand involvement. Malakand had taught him about the elusiveness of political control of hostile territory, the Nile campaign about the decisive impact of differential technologies, South Africa about the discrepancies between formal and guerrilla operations, the Admiralty about the changing techniques of naval mastery, the Western Front about the horrendous carnage of trench warfare. General Sir James Edmonds, as the chief British official military historian, had helped Churchill with relevant advice since the composition of *The World Crisis* and was ready still to advise, especially on the American

Civil War. Churchill had himself surveyed the major battlefields in Virginia and Pennsylvania in 1929, just as he inspected those of Marlborough's campaigns, and had done so with a practised eye as well as amateur enthusiasm. And of course he understood politics, with some professional insights that both Ashley and Deakin acknowledged as timelessly relevant to the era of his great ancestor.

In earlier periods, however, Churchill was frankly an amateur: indeed incorrigibly amateurish. He badly needed guidance, as he realised; he both sought it and ignored it. William Deakin, always at his elbow, was a versatile young historian but became a specialist on modern Italian history, not on Great Britain in the first millennium. Feiling's strategic target had been to get to the Normans, along with the Vikings, in the fourth chapter of a volume that would stretch ahead into the eighteenth century. But in the published *History*, the first eight chapters struggle to reach 1066, with the Norman invasion deferred as the beginning of the ninth; and the last of Volume One's four hundred pages (or five hundred in the North American editions) take the reader no further than the death of Richard III at the Battle of Bosworth in 1485.

The reason is that the author had indulged himself too freely in the late summer of 1938. He revelled in the discovery that there was so much more to the story than his schoolboy history lessons had imparted or than he had subsequently picked up from the pages of J. R. Green's *Short History of England*. Green, as a good Anglo-Saxonist, had begun in 449, with the coming of the 'English race', and minimised the significance of 1066, which was buried in the midst of his fourth chapter out of fifty, that together covered the whole period up to 1815. Churchill was proposing to finish later, of course; but also to start earlier, requiring ruthless discipline in sketching some salient aspects of the early history of Britain without exceeding the space allotted.

Plunging into the work with all too little preparation, Churchill could not restrain his innocent appetite to learn more. One delight lay in making the acquaintance of the archaeologist Mortimer Wheeler. With a charm in projecting his subject that was to captivate a later generation of BBC television viewers, Wheeler found that he had an eager pupil when he happened to meet Churchill, who followed up purposefully on their encounter, seeking instruction on 'these early chapters where the spade is mightier than the pen'. There was an immediate proposal for Wheeler to accept an honorarium and to give three informal lectures during a weekend at Chartwell in July 1938 – 'Your audience would be attentive and select, – Mr Deakin and me!' Though this had to be postponed, Churchill's appetite, once stimulated, made him greedy for more and he confessed to Feiling that he was 'now rollicking with the "Piltdown Man", Cassivalanus [sic], Julius Caesar, the Scribe Gildas, the Venerable Bede and other hoary figures'.[12]

Nobody knew better than Feiling that this was not the agreed plan. Churchill's expectation, as recently as 4 July 1938, that 25–30,000 words would carry him to the Norman Conquest, was steadily eroded as the work of long summer nights rollicked away. 'I had expected to get to the Norman Conquest with about 40,000 words,' he wrote to Wheeler on Monday, 19 September, 'but it seems that 65,000 or 70,000 will be required.' If any excuse were needed, it is worth noting that this letter was dictated on the same day that Churchill had to go up to London for a personal briefing from the Foreign Secretary about the British response to Hitler's territorial demands on the Czechs; and it was the day before Churchill then flew to Paris, in a personal mission to stiffen resistance within the French cabinet. Hence the inwardness of the author's concluding comment to Wheeler: 'It has been a comfort to me in these anxious days to put a thousand years between my thoughts and the twentieth century.'[13]

A month later, after the Munich agreement had averted an immediate European war at the expense of dismembering Czechoslovakia, the author took stock of progress on the *History*. Anxious to mend relations with Cassells, he found it easier to bypass the irascible Sir

Newman Flower by dealing with his son Desmond, whom Churchill now sent another of his emollient letters. 'The early part has been most laborious on account of the vast period covered and the fact that I myself knew nothing about it until I began my studies,' Churchill confessed on 18 October. 'I now approach the period after Henry VIII, with some of which I am most fully acquainted and upon all of which I have accumulated a large store of thought.'[14] He thus implies that the 90,000 words now in print would get as far as the Reformation in the sixteenth century; but in the published Volume One, 90,000 words takes the reader little more than halfway through – say, to the chapter on 'The Mother of Parliaments', dealing with the thirteenth century. Churchill's impressive tally of words may indeed have been sent to Harraps for printing, as he claimed, but the author was still celebrating Simon de Montfort's triumph at the Battle of Lewes in 1264 rather than mourning the death of Henry VIII in 1546.

And so it continued. But the problem was not simply scale: it was bound up with style. For example, in the treatment prepared by Feiling in 1934–36, we can see how he had envisaged the task of integrating Scotland and Ireland into an historical overview, which went as far as the eighteenth century in the projected first volume, though largely confined to English history up to that point. 'The bearing of Scotland and Ireland upon British fortunes,' Feiling had suggested, 'might be traced backwards; from the Ulster emigrants who fought for America in 1774, or the Scots who ruled India, to the fatal influence of the Scottish Stuarts and all the share of Ireland in Elizabeth's duel with Spain.'[15] Through the use of a flashback technique, it would thus be possible to bring out the significance of such matters as the ethnic balance within the British Isles, as far back as the eleventh century. Moreover, Feiling's dossiers do not simply invoke some airy concept of the English-speaking peoples: they also offer, chapter by chapter, the necessary historical support by providing the relevant pages copied in typescript – or literally cut – from the latest scholarly publications, field by field. But all of this implied an ambitious thematic approach that perhaps demanded more of Churchill than he was intellectually capable of giving, certainly under his current constraints. Feiling's dossiers rest in the archive, painstakingly compiled in the 1930s, largely ignored, now as then.

Churchill was hardly unintelligent, nor idle. He did not resort to getting Eddie Marsh to provide him with 'great stories of the Ancient Britons retold' and was, in fact, proud to tell Marsh that, in 'Britannia', as his first chapter was now called, 'every word of this apart from quotations was mine, and some good judges, Wheeler for instance, a great archaeological expert, declared himself "thrilled" by the presentation of the story'. True, the authentic Churchill note is struck early, in the description of the gruesome archaeological evidence for the beginning of the Iron Age: 'A biped capable of slaying another with iron is evidently to modern eyes a man and a brother.'[16] Churchill popularised scholarship while respecting it. In the 1939 proofs of the *History*, the warrior queen of the East Anglian Iceni is scrupulously introduced as 'Boudicca (known to history through an early clerical error as Boadicea)'. It was not until the later textual revisions of the 1950s that the octogenarian Churchill insisted on reverting to the forms of his schooldays by printing 'Boadicea (relished by the learned as Boudicca) . . .'[17]

In 1938–39 he was still ready to learn, and thereby was forced to reflect about history itself. In Chapter 4 of Volume One, 'The Lost Island', there is a discursive opening passage, cautioning against the temptation to telescope our view of long periods of history as compared with 'the experience of our own short lives'.[18] Evidently this was the fruit of an unusually pensive late night at Chartwell some time in August 1938, for the proofs expatiated further in this vein. 'In order to make history intelligible,' Churchill suggests, 'storytellers divide it into sharply defined epochs.' Simplification and signposting made for the sort of 'agreeable generalizations' that he had himself once been taught. Then came professional scholars and archaeologists, bringing to light their 'many facts and objects which cannot be disputed', with the result that the old certainties of the nineteenth century could no longer be sustained. But then, impatient with too much scholarship, there comes the amateur's rebellion: 'From knowing little, much of it wrong, but having a fine tale, we pass at length to a plethora of obstinate facts and irreconcilable conclusions with no tale at all worth the telling.' He now held it 'remarkable how the old legends keep on soaking through the mass of modern criticism which have been laid upon them', giving ground for a defiant flourish: 'The old story is often found to be the best.'[19]

Beneath his reluctant deference to academic scholarship, Churchill still asserted a visceral commitment to the sort of history on which he had been brought up. He insisted on telling a story. His account is cast throughout in narrative form, with a chronological rather than an analytical discipline. In this he was applying the method of his biography of Marlborough. In an early, undated draft of a preface for the *History* he explicitly invokes the model of 'the life of some famous man', with a need to reflect in turn on 'his several achievements in statesmanship or war or literature or science', on his 'character or personality' and on 'what imprint he left, what difference he made, what the world would have been like without him' – all of them considerations relevant to a man like John Churchill, or indeed Winston himself, who confidently concludes: 'It is the same with the history of a nation.' And he claims that, in tracing 'the unifying thread in the history of the English people', he will explain 'how our distinguishing institutions came to be what they are, and what this significance is, for human history as a whole'. This passage, later cut, immediately preceded the second section of the preface as published, beginning: 'Our story centres in an island . . .'[20] The first part of Volume One is called 'The Island Race'.

Not only was Churchill intent on framing the *History* as a story: he was intent on retaining particular stories that modern scholarship had questioned. The earliest proofs of what became Volume One, circulated during 1939, show a series of skirmishes between Churchill and, in particular, the austere 'pantomath' G. M. Young, who may not have known literally everything but certainly knew infinitely more than the author about the revisionist work done by professional historians in recent decades, challenging comforting old myths with inconvenient new facts. There is a unique reference to Young in the published text as 'a modern writer of remarkable insight'.[21] He and Marsh carried the authority to correct and to chide the eminent author – and needed to exercise it. In dictating these early chapters, Churchill was all too ready to enlighten everyone on his own opinions, for example on spelling: 'There is a strange fashion among the learned of spelling all these ancient names in the forms likely to be the most repulsive to the modern generation of readers', and so on over a paragraph. When Young and Marsh read the proofs, they quickly agreed. 'I wonder if this is necessary.' 'So do I.' The paragraph was cut.[22]

Young scored other direct hits. In dealing with the Anglo-Saxon system of 'wergild', or putting a money price on injury, Churchill cited 'vivid examples of the working of these sordid laws'. Young wrote: 'Really, you are flogging a dead horse here.' The passage was cut. In a further paragraph in the same section, Churchill had let himself go about the Dark Ages, an expression that he seems to have taken rather literally – 'Two hundred years of fighting and suppression in the dark!' He could vividly imagine these centuries of murky, dusky, shadowy, internecine warfare – 'They fought among themselves. But they left no records of their conflicts.' Young's unanswerable marginal comment – 'Then how do you know?' – led to a further omission.[23]

Some of Young's victories, however, proved short-lived. When Churchill had described the revolt in 633 against Edwin, King of Northumbria, he not only enthused that 'for the first time noticed in history British and English fought side by side', but went on to pronounce: 'We see again the spirit of Boudicca.' Young advised omission on the grounds that the source, Geoffrey of Monmouth, 'is not a good authority'. But in the published version of 1956 Churchill reasserted himself, in spirit and name alike: 'We might almost be seeing again the spirit of Boadicea.'[24] Likewise Churchill's account of the death-song of the Viking Ragnar in 845, where Young had written dismissively in the margin of the pre-war proofs: 'As a matter of fact, this death-song is a subsequent invention, it is not authentic.' But in Volume One as published in 1956, after Ragnar has been cast into the snake-pit: 'Amid the coiling mass of loathsome adders he sang to the end his death-song.'[25]

In most cases, Churchill retreated under protest. 'I parted rather ruefully with some of my titbits,' he told Young in June 1939 after reading his comments on the first volume, 'but I bow to knowledge.'[26] He knew better than to contest Young's exact scholarship. Instead Churchill often sought escape by cloaking his original contention with inexact rhetoric. In his prose, when he is not quite sure of the facts, he often reaches for some characteristic, elevating metaphors; for example, commendable events or persons are said to be 'gleaming' or 'glittering' or 'glowing', and often doing so 'through the ages'. This sort of vacuously inspiring vocabulary was deployed to salvage some extravagant claims made on behalf of Alfred the Great. King of Wessex from 871 to 899, he emerges from the pages of the *History* as a time-lessly heroic figure, 'one of the great figures of history', with a 'sublime power to rise above the whole force of circumstances' that took him, through victory and disaster alike, 'to his pinnacle of deathless glory'.[27]

There is here, for the first but not the last time in the *History*, fairly obvious self-identification. Indeed the former First Lord of the Admiralty, with his own apologia that 'the fleet was ready' in 1914, had initially gone further in early drafts, claiming that Alfred's fame 'rests largely upon the creation of the British fleet. He saw too the vision of English sea-power.' This occasioned a sharp demurral in the proofs, recorded in Deakin's writing: 'No, says G.M.' And Young's veto was sufficient to scale down the claim that appears in the published *History* to a rather lame concluding line: 'Still, the beginning of the English Navy must always be linked with King Alfred.' Similarly, the 'celebrated story of Alfred and the Cakes' was allowed to survive, prefaced with the distancing comment: 'This is the moment when those gleaming toys of history were fashioned for the children of every age.'[28] Later, when in 1478 the Duke of Clarence meets his end in the Tower of London, Shakespeare's version that he was drowned in a butt of Malmsey wine is blessed with the demand: 'Why should it not be true?'[29]

It was not always possible, then, to dispose of favourite historical anecdotes with which the boy Winston had grown up. Still less was it easy to get rid of myths to which Churchill had an emotional or patriotic attachment. It is not just that the author does not conceal his admiration of the recorded deeds of the historical Boudicca; he also makes the significant claim that the statue we know as Boadicea, on the Thames Embankment near Big Ben, 'reminds us of the harsh cry of liberty or death which has echoed down the ages'.[30] There is an obvious patriotic resonance here – not least for American readers who would remember Patrick Henry's similar cry in late eighteenth-century Virginia. But, back in the first century of the Christian era, whose side was the author on? The Britons for whom Boudicca fought against the Romans? Yet Churchill plainly empathised with the Romans too. 'The Roman world, like an aged man, wished to dwell in peace and tranquility and to enjoy in philosophic detachment the good gifts which life has to bestow upon the more fortunate classes.'[31] He makes it sound as though he often had a few Romans over for a cosy dinner in his habitation at Chartwell.

The departure of the Romans by the fifth century is certainly not celebrated in the rhetoric of liberation. In the first proof of the *History*, the account of the last battles fought by the Britons, struggling to retain their territory after the Roman withdrawal, is duly sonorous: 'Among these clouds there looms large, uncertain, dim but glittering, the legend of King Arthur and the Knights of the Round Table.' When Young read this, he immediately pencilled it for omission, and even in a redrafted version, where Churchill restates his version of Arthur with only tactical amendments, Young comments in the margin: 'The trouble is that except for 2 or 3 mentions of the *name*, there is absolutely *nothing* about A. till the 12th century, when he floods all Europe. It was an age of fiction.'[32] Draft after draft, proof after proof, Churchill insisted on affirming what 'we prefer to believe' about a residual Arthurian myth, despite the alleged pusillanimity of sceptical modern historians who cravenly lived in fear of contradiction. 'It is all true, or ought to be; and more and better besides,' the *History* affirms. 'And wherever men are fighting against barbarism, tyranny, and massacre, for freedom, law, and honour, let them remember that the fame of their deeds, even though they themselves be exterminated, may perhaps be celebrated as long as the world rolls round.'[33] All of this was written before 1940.

The first surviving proof is dated 9 September 1938, just before the Munich agreement. In it there is a passage imagining what a citizen of Roman Britain in the third century, if he 'could wake up to-day', would find around him. The moral was how similar he would find most things – law, religion, an Empire past its prime. 'He would still fear the Huns,' Churchill had baldly claimed, though later proofs from 1939 show this already changed to 'fear the people across the North Sea,' as in the published *History*.[34] As we have seen in Chapter 3, attitudes towards Germany were freighted with both political and historiographical significance. J. R. Green had written feelingly of 'the fatherland of the English race' and had begun his *Short History of the English People* with a chapter on 'The English Conquest of Britain, 449–577'. This standard work of his youth became Churchill's explicit target in several paragraphs of the first proof, with an affectation of sorrow that the great Victorian historians had been 'roughly maltreated by later criticism'.[35]

This professed sentiment was partly feigned, partly real. Churchill had never been an ideological Anglo-Saxonist, neither radical nor racialist in this respect. His own racial prejudices, triggered over India, had no ideological root in Aryanism, of the kind that a Victorian like

Freeman cultivated with naive reverence. In October 1934 Churchill had received a letter from Rudyard Kipling about *Marlborough*, flattering the author by commenting on its style, 'as craftsman to craftsman'. Kipling's reservation was that 'you use that infamous non-Aryan, cinema-caption-epithet "vibrant", which is as base as "glimpse", "sense", "grip", "urge", "glamourous" [sic], and the rest of the thieves-kitchen dictionary that Judaea has decanted upon us'.[36] Churchill had no truck with this kind of appeal to a supposed Aryan heritage, its anti-Semitic overtones made all the more jarring by current developments in Germany.

Churchill was now unusually receptive to historical revisionism – at least if it meant diminishing Teutonic influence. In this he was plainly reinforced by his scorn for the Nazi and Fascist propaganda line (as he put it sarcastically in a radio broadcast to the United States on 8 August 1939) 'that these German and Italian armies may have another work of Liberation to perform'. The hollow Nazi claim to be spreading freedom with every territorial annexation and the hollow historical myth of self-government 'arriving behind the swords of the Saxons' evoked the same sceptical response. 'To read Mr Green,' Churchill wrote in the 1938–39 proofs, 'we might suppose that the Teutonic invaders and the settlers who followed in the wake of their massacres brought with them a dignified order of society, many of whose institutions and habits corresponded with the ideals of modern self-government and democracy.' These principles are indeed admirable, the *History* suggests, and 'have formed a recognizable part of the message which the English-speaking peoples have given to the world'; but this benign process owed little to the practices under the German occupation of England. Churchill's original conclusion (omitted on Young's advice) was more strident: 'No Englishman need think of himself therefore as the mere product of Teutonic invasion.'[37]

If Churchill had been somewhat ambivalent about the merits of the Roman occupation, he was thus even more torn about later invasions. Rejecting the Anglo-Saxons as the bearers of democratic values,

Churchill nonetheless discerned a proto-nationalist mission in Alfred the Great's defeat of the next wave of Danish invaders at the Battle of Ashdown (871): 'If the West Saxons had been beaten all England would have sunk into heathen anarchy.' Yet a few pages later, these fearsome Vikings have suddenly become model Scandinavian colonists who 'mingled henceforward into the Island race'.[38] Indeed in an early draft, adopting a prophetic mode of which the great American historian J. L. Motley would have been proud, the author had gone further in saluting the qualities that these immigrants brought to the country in which they settled: 'All through English history this strain continues to play its part, and to this day the peculiar esteem in which law and freedom are held by the English-speaking peoples in every quarter of the globe may be shrewdly and justly referred to a Viking source.' To which Young responded: 'I doubt it.' The claims were duly diluted and drained of specific content in the published conclusion: 'All through English history this strain continues to play a gleaming part.'[39]

In 1874, the year of Winston's birth, J. R. Green had included one chapter on the earlier 'English Conquest' but not one devoted to the 'Norman Invasion'. In 1938 Churchill did the opposite. True, in the account of the Battle of Hastings (1066), there is a sonorous sentence declaiming that 'ever must the name of Harold be honoured in the island for which he and his famous house-carls fought indomitably to the end'.[40] Abruptly, with the defeat and death of Harold, a chapter ends (literally). 'The day's battle at Hastings,' so the early proofs tell us, 'linked England with France and made her once again a partner in the life of Western Europe – dynastic, chivalrous, and ecclesiastical.'[41] As published, the *History* offers a cursory assurance about the new invaders that 'very soon in true Norman fashion they intermarried with the free population and identified themselves with their English past'.[42] In a book that contains virtually nothing about either demography or language, this is certainly a quick way to dispose of 'the English question'. But plainly it neither enlisted Churchill's romantic sentiments, in nostalgia for Anglo-Saxon England, nor stimulated his

interest in a cultural interpretation of the processes of colonisation
and assimilation.

Churchill's writing was simply true to his own instincts, not the
product of any historiographical school. True, there are some grounds
for arguing that the first volume of the *History* was not written by a
radical, populist Anglo-Saxonist but by a Conservative, hierarchical
Normaniser. Thus in one preliminary outline Churchill stated that, in
the period from 1066 to 1485, 'the race was formed into a nation under
the guidance of the feudal system introduced by the Normans, and
maintained by the great Plantagenets'. So far, so hierarchical. Yet this
process had another dimension, which he presciently discerned and
persistently admired. This was the all-embracing vision of an ordered
national progress that protected the growth of liberty by codifying it
in constitutional forms, duly documented. The familiar landmarks
ahead could thus be glimpsed: the rule of law, Magna Carta and the
Mother of Parliaments. 'The structure of these early Parliaments,'
Churchill declared, 'was the definite forerunner of the institutions
which have now spread over the most wealthy, powerful and liberal
states of the modern world.'[43] The stages by which the final destina-
tion, Anglo-American democracy, would ultimately be reached were
already in view.

Winston's letters to Clementine are both candid and reliable about the
process of composition of the *History*. They are candid because he had
no reason to conceal from her those awkward facts that he constantly
needed to massage for his publishers; and they are reliable because the
information is based, not on any back-of-the envelope scrawls at
Chartwell, but on what Mr Wood at Harraps had told the author
about the exact number of words actually in print. Hence Winston
could tell Clementine on 19 December 1938 that 'our score tonight is
180,000, or 30,000 above the tally of 1,000 a day from Aug. 1', and ten
days later that 192,000 words were in print. Winston reported again,
on 8 January 1939, that his 'unbroken routine at Chartwell' had

resulted in putting 221,000 words into print, which suggests two thousand words a day in the three weeks' interval (including Christmas at Blenheim). Hence his expectation that he might 'cover the whole ground by May, wh wd leave 7 months for polishing'. All this adds up provided it is kept in mind that he was contracted to deliver a three-volume work of 400,000 words.

These private communications between Winston and his wife remind us, despite his public brave face, of the onerous and unrelenting drudgery of this task. 'It is vy laborious: & I resent it, & the pressure,' he had admitted to her on 19 December, sending a letter because Clementine was currently aboard the *Rosaura* again, on a Caribbean cruise, though not enjoying it much without Winston. A cable on 4 January informed her that Winston was about to fly to the Chateau de l'Horizon for a fortnight's break as the guest of Maxine Elliott, on the model of his visit twelve months previously. This year Clementine obviously could not join her overworked husband in indulging one of the temptations of the Riviera that they both enjoyed: gambling at the roulette tables. BEWARE CASINO. TENDER LOVE, she cabled. At l'Horizon, Winston stayed in bed in the mornings, and in the evenings dined, to and fro, with the Duke and Duchess of Windsor, themselves now installed in luxurious exile, next door to Lord Rothermere's nearby villa. For this social set, life was one long holiday. But not for Winston, who daily dictated fifteen hundred words of the *History*. 'Just as at Chartwell I divided my days between building and dictating,' Winston reported, 'so now it is between dictating and gambling.'[44] Again, the fruits of decadence and the fruits of his labour stood juxtaposed.

His words continued to flow, whether at home or abroad. But it should already have been apparent that Churchill's steady drift into composing more than planned on the early period now implied a book different from that commissioned. Volume One, of the four that Cassells eventually published in 1956–58, is about 160,000 words, and virtually all of it was in first proof before the end of 1938. Indeed,

Volume Two was also in proof by April 1939, when Young and Bullock started work on revision. The scrutiny of the proofs by Young and Marsh then proceeded alongside the dictation of further sections, with the drafts from Wheldon and Ashley coordinated by Deakin. 'It has been a most educative ride for me,' Churchill told Marsh in June. 'Though I have frequently had to dismount and talk politics to the wayfarers.'[45] His political stock was steadily rising as the international situation deteriorated, bringing war nearer daily, in a way that further concentrated the author's mind on his nightly task.

The published Volume Two begins auspiciously with the accession of the Tudor dynasty in 1485. Then, through the sixteenth and seventeenth centuries, the volume sees England's destiny unfold, simultaneously Protestant and parliamentary – forces duly reconciled through the Glorious Revolution, which installs on the throne the 'gleaming figure' of William of Orange.[46] Thus the *published* second volume (out of four) ends with the accession of King William III in 1688; but the *planned* second volume (out of three) was supposed to end with the accession of Queen Victoria in 1837. The published volumes are similar in length to those planned, but only because four were ultimately to be published instead of three. The good news was that the target of 400,000 words would be reached in the summer of 1939, earlier than anticipated. The bad news was the now inevitable consequence, that this would not be the end, nor even the beginning of the end, but only the end of the beginning.

There was no obvious solution. Churchill simply concentrated on maintaining the momentum of his dictation. 'At this stage,' he told Ashley on 12 April, 'working against time, and with so many distractions, my aim has been to get the narrative through from the beginning to the end, leaving behind many omissions and many general questions.'[47] In such an intractable situation, as the war leader's intimates later came to appreciate, his motto was simple: KBO – Keep Buggering On.

There is, of course, nothing intrinsically wrong with writing history as a story. Indeed the English language is unusual in using different words for the two things. It is a strenuous challenge, and a correspondingly fine achievement, for any historian to sustain a narrative drive while instilling it with analytical power. Churchill recognised his problem, responding defensively in April 1939 to Alan Bullock's annotation of some of the medieval proofs: 'It is quite true that in the first instance going over this long story I do dwell on battles and kings, but I am most anxious that the other side should be represented so far as it lends itself to narration.' And he had, again rather defensively in writing to these young historians, made the valid point to Ashley a few days earlier: 'As you know, an enormous amount of changes are made by me after the first proof is printed.'[48] But the trouble with that particular line, at this particular point, was that the circumstances under which Churchill was currently working foreclosed the possibilities of thorough revision.

In an important sense, the work remains unfinished. Only the first two volumes of the published *History* are wholly Churchill's. Jumping ahead and working episodically rather then chronologically on what became the fourth volume, his own drafts were never to progress beyond the American Civil War. He had expected to cover it in 10,000 words, an estimate exceeded fivefold. 'It is quite true the scale is rather outside that of the rest of the volume,' he admitted to Young in September, 'but this book is intended to appeal to the United States and it is necessary to emphasise their dramatic struggle.'[49] He clearly enjoyed reliving the Virginia and Pennsylvania campaigns, and the fact that they were fought over ground that he personally inspected shows in the treatment of such set-piece episodes as the 'superb effort' of Pickett's doomed charge in the Battle of Gettysburg in 1863.[50] In a wartime speech to the US Congress (19 May 1943) Churchill made a well-justified reference to 'the field of Gettysburg, which I know well, like most of your battlefields.' In the *History* this sort of intimate soldierly appreciation surely helps to evoke the encomium on the 'agile, flexible grasp' of Robert E. Lee's generalship, showing 'how great commanders seem to move their armies from place to place as if they were doing no more than riding their own horses'.[51]

Churchill's lucid account of the military campaigns showed his genuine interest and received his close attention, amid distractions that became increasingly blatant. On 24 March 1939, as Hitler moved on Prague, Churchill had written to Ashley: 'It is very hard to transport oneself into the past when the future opens its jaws upon us.' Yet, on the very same day, Churchill sent another letter to his adviser, Sir James Edmonds, who held a largely honorific position as head of the historical branch of the Committee of Imperial Defence: 'Have you read *Gone with the Wind*? It is a terrific book, but I expect you are too pressed with your work to read.'[52]

The revised proofs in the Churchill archive show us the *History* as he actually wrote it. Ashley, who only read part of the 1939 proofs, later came to think of it as 'a manufactured book'; but though his judgement carries some weight, it is flawed by his (understandable) error in supposing that 'most of the book was, in fact, rewritten long afterwards'.[53] This is true only of Volumes Three and Four, which Ashley personally preferred to the two earlier volumes. In fact, virtually all of what survived the critical scrutiny of Deakin, Bullock, Edmonds, Young and Marsh in 1939 – not to mention the vigilant eye of Mr Wood at Harraps – survives also in the published *History*, certainly in Volumes One and Two. Subsequent publications under Churchill's name admittedly became much more of a team effort, from first to last.

In one sense, what he managed to get done in 1939 is ragged in structure and uneven in quality. If the early parts of the *History* were flawed, the later parts were chronically disabled by the constraints of its composition, lapsing into an increasingly formless second-hand narrative. Yet its interest is enhanced, even if its quality was impaired, by the context. It may not be judged the best work that ever came from Churchill as an author; but perhaps he deserves also to be judged as a prophet.

Here, for example, is a *History of the English-Speaking Peoples* that is very hospitable to the French-speaking peoples who conquered the English homeland in 1066. It was, of course, written by a Francophile whose mother and wife had each become fluently Francophone through youthful residence in France. 'I have just finished writing about Joan of Arc,' Winston tells Clementine at the end of 1938. 'I think she is the winner in the whole of French history.'[54] Moreover, the reason that the great English patriot expresses such fervent admiration for 'the peasant Maid' surely lies in her charismatic appeal to the 'rough soldiery' over the heads of the appeasers at Court, thus inspiring a nation that currently needs such reminders of its own military prowess.

This is not a history with the politics left out. At exactly the time when the medieval part was written, its author was far from hostile to French military pretensions, whether in the fifteenth or twentieth centuries. He preferred the anti-fascist Popular Front, led by the socialist Leon Blum, to the current crop of French conservatives; and Churchill would meet Blum privately in Paris, their bond being a determination to defend their countries from Hitler. 'The reasons why France does not present herself in her full strength at the present time are not to be found among the working masses, who are also the soldiers of France,' Churchill wrote in his *Daily Telegraph* column of 1 December 1938, only four weeks before he confessed his love affair with the Maid to his wife. The published text of the *History* does not recant any of his passion for 'the ever-shining, ever glorious Joan of Arc', saying that 'she finds no equal in a thousand years'. Churchill's own countrymen of 1431 receive no commendation, nor even extenuation, for conniving at the Maid's death. 'She embodied the natural goodness and valour of the human race in unexampled perfection,' he claims.[55] No comparable magnanimity is extended to any German, throughout a book intended for publication in 1940-41.

There is, too, a broader, ideological aspect. With the sharpening of the conflict between the Western democracies and the rising power of the dictators as Hitler got into his stride, the project had come to acquire more immediate resonance than its harassed author could initially have anticipated. 'In the main, the theme is emerging of the growth of freedom and law, of the rights of the individual, of the subordination of the State to the fundamental and moral conceptions of an ever-comprehending community,' Churchill wrote to Ashley in April 1939. 'Of these ideas the English-speaking peoples were the authors, then the trustees, and must now become the armed champions. Thus I condemn tyranny in whatever guise and from whatever quarter it presents itself. All this of course has a current application.'[56]

The 1939 text survives as Churchill's testament. It shows that the *History* takes more from the Victorian historians than he fully acknowledged (or fully realised). Thus it gaily endorses claims about the long flowering of liberty while cutting off the Teutonic roots alleged in the classic works of Stubbs or Motley or Freeman or, most explicitly, Green. 'What men found themselves fighting for at Edgehill and Marston Moor was government by the will of the nation for government by the will of the king,' was how Green's *Short History* had once put it, with the sort of fudging of intention and effect characteristic of whig history.[57] But just as Churchill's *Marlborough* could be called Macaulayism without Macaulay, so his *History* can be called Greenery without Green.

The *History* bears the marks of a whig interpretation because the reader is continually made aware of the destiny that it is celebrating. It is patently judgemental. 'Justice quite suddenly gathered up her trappings and quitted one cause for the other,' Churchill writes of Europe in 1709 (in a passage lifted from his *Marlborough*).[58] More than that, its judgements are those of the present, that of 1939. For all its well-researched period detail, often supplied by others, the project remained essentially Churchill's, informed by his own vision. Though he made commendable efforts to incorporate the latest scholarship, this seldom fundamentally affected the way that he understood the story as a whole. Only in minor matters was he a revisionist, sometimes under duress, sometimes drawing on new publications simply to settle old scores over matters on which his own opinions had never really changed anyway. He drew on the past for encouragement, solace, warning and inspiration in the present.

The *History* often nudges the reader into accepting the author's own vision of the past. This can be seen as clearly in the earlier as in the later volumes. 'We are watching the birth of a nation,' Churchill tells us in his account of Alfred the Great. Under Edward I, eleven chapters and four centuries later, nation-building is still in progress, with a new twist, since 'the foundations of a strong national monarchy for a United Kingdom and of a Parliamentary Constitution had been laid'.[59] The intervening constitutional landmarks, of course, were the result of the epic struggles of the thirteenth century, leading to Magna Carta in 1215 and to a Parliament.

Churchill showed himself well aware that the academic historians had yet again been demythologising his preferred story. 'Anyone who has heard from childhood of Magna Carta, who has read with what interest and reverence one copy of it was lately received in New York, and takes it up for the first time, will be strangely disappointed,' the published preface to Volume One runs, in words taken verbatim (even 'lately') from the 1939 text, which acknowledges that the Charter might be interpreted as a defence of the 'privileges of the nobility at the expense of the State'. This is, of course, only preparatory to the author's quest for some gleam or glow to point the way forward. 'The leaders of the barons in 1215 groped in the dim light towards a fundamental principle,' Churchill assures his readers. This was the idea, 'perhaps only half-understood', that the king's power was limited by law.[60]

The regressive methodology is obvious here. It relies on the foreknowledge of the historian in detecting premonitions of a final outcome that nobody quite got round to voicing at the time.

Churchill's rehabilitation of Simon de Montfort as the founder of the parliamentary system is achieved in much this fashion – 'Certainly he builded better than he knew.' In besting King Henry III, and his heir the future Edward I, in battle at Lewes in 1264, de Montfort proved able to 'create the far broader and better political system which, whether he aimed at it or not, must have automatically followed from his success'. With this sleight of hand, the 'fierce battle' at Lewes is projected straight into the struggles between King and Parliament of the seventeenth-century civil war – 'In some ways it was a forerunner of Edgehill.' The baronial party of the late thirteenth century, in their continuing struggle against Edward I, are thus credited with extraordinary insight about future political developments; indeed 'they spoke no longer as the representatives of the feudal aristocracy, but as the leaders of a national opposition'. In the British edition, the term appears capitalised as 'Opposition', thus emphasising Churchill's point: 'Here was a real constitutional advance.'[61]

Churchill thus always has one eye on what comes next. He is accordingly impatient when historical actors seem to stumble over their lines and need a prompt. 'We reach here, amid much confusion, the main foundation of English freedom' is his comment on the House of Commons' passage of the Petition of Right in 1628. It is the same technique that has already alerted the reader to the significance of the rise of the gentry after 1066: 'Out of this in the process of time the Pyms and Hampdens arose.' But it was to be half a millennium, of course, before John Pym and John Hampden made their mark on English history, and did so in a very different context. Churchill's account of the divisions in the English Civil War likewise says of the Royalists: 'They preferred the ancient light of divinely blessed authority to the distant glimmer of democracy.'[62] G. M. Young failed to demand: how do you know they could see this glimmer?

As befits its title, the *History* is particularly alert to premonitions that bear on the destiny of the English-speaking peoples. None of this was attributed to divine will or intervention, as the proofs indicate

with wry scepticism, for example a comment on the Black Death of
the fourteenth century: 'But when at length the Almighty, in his inef-
fable mercy, had used the process of harrowing and purging upon His
creatures sufficiently to further His sublime purposes, the plague
abated its force.' Churchill's sense of history was strongly providential,
but in a secular sense. He had prepared a stirring encomium on the
England of Edward the Confessor: 'This whole body of moral, social,
and political usages constitutes the root inheritance of the English-
speaking peoples, and is exemplified through all the recurring crises of
history, and find their most resolute and definite expression at the
present day.'[63] Unfortunately, in the absence of any plausible supporting evidence, this fine claim, like that about the Almighty, had to be
deleted in proof.

Churchill remained unabashed in pursuing his prophetic theme.
The *History* assures its readers that in New England, 'the tiny colony
of Plymouth pointed a path to freedom'. And precedents common to
the English-speaking countries are sonorously saluted. Thus in 1679
Parliament 'passed a Habeas Corpus Act which confirmed and
strengthened the freedom of the individual against arbitrary arrest by
the executive Government'. The beneficent effect was that 'wherever
the English language is spoken in any part of the world, wherever the
authority of the British Imperial Crown or of the Government of the
United States prevails, all law-abiding men breathe freely'.[64]

In the same spirit, there is a salute to Lord Chatham (Pitt the Elder)
for his successes in the Seven Years War (1756–63). It was not just
another defeat for the French but a providential achievement: 'North
America was thus made safe for the English-speaking peoples.' But
surely this safety paved the way, all too quickly, for separation by the
ungrateful colonists? Any such taint of British chauvinism is airbrushed
out of Churchill's benign interpretation of the American revolt. The
pedigree of the Declaration of Independence, with its 'familiar and
immortal' opening, is comfortingly claimed as 'a restatement of the
principles which had animated the Whig struggle against the later

Stuarts and the English Revolution of 1688'.[65] The title deeds of liberty, going back to Magna Carta, were timelessly self-evident in their internal consistency, if sometimes temporarily misunderstood by the two rival nations who disputed them. Though the story has heroes and villains, the British do not monopolise the former roles nor the Americans the latter.

The gleaming heroes of the *History* are, unsurprisingly, great leaders of their peoples in just wars. Some of this is foreshadowed in the efforts to burnish the image of Alfred the Great, or even reconstruct the credentials of Boadicea and King Arthur as proto-nationalists and freedom fighters. With Edward III's victory at Crécy in 1346, during the Hundred Years War, a distinctively modern perspective is applied: 'This astounding victory of Crécy ranks with Blenheim, Waterloo, and the final advance in the last summer of the Great War as one of the four supreme achievements of the British Army.'[66] Yet neither Edward III nor his grandfather Edward I ('a master-builder of British life, character and fame') figure prominently in the *History*'s pantheon.

Nor, for that matter, does the Duke of Wellington. Perhaps this is simply because he has the bad luck to appear in Volume Four, to which Churchill gave relatively little personal attention apart from his lengthy account of the American Civil War. Though his background reading extended beyond *Gone with the Wind*, there is a pervasive, romantic air of elegy for the South in its defeat. The treatment of Lincoln, by comparison, as dictated in June 1939, seems slightly forced and the extended tribute to his fortitude as war leader was subsequently spliced in to the published Volume Four. Earlier in the 1939 text, George Washington receives more fulsome recognition: 'Almost alone his staunchness in the War of Independence held the American colonies to their united purpose.'[67]

This staunchness against the English, of course, was a good thing, just like that of Joan of Arc. Washington's role as Father of his Nation, Churchill asserts in the same passage, is 'one of the proudest titles that history can bestow'. His own *History* ungrudgingly bestows it.

Conversely, the greatest villain in Churchill's eyes was a fellow Briton. Perhaps surprisingly, given the virulence of the censure, this villain was an acknowledged English patriot with a providential sense of his country's destiny and of his own unique ability to guide it. Indeed some of this sense of affinity survives in Churchill's ultimately negative account of Oliver Cromwell: 'We feel his passion for England, as fervent as Chatham's, and in some ways more intimate and emotional.' There is also a wonderfully sly tribute to Cromwell's sheer military prowess, in accounting for his victory over the Scots: 'Both sides confidently appealed to Jehovah: and the Most High, finding so little to choose between them in faith and zeal, must have allowed purely military factors to prevail.' Churchill could genuinely see both sides of the ancient arguments about a uniquely gifted statesman, with an 'imperial eye' fixed on advancing his country's interests, who nonetheless left 'the curse of Cromwell' in Ireland as 'a potent obstacle to the harmony of the English-speaking peoples throughout the world'.[68]

Ashley, with his Roundhead sympathies, had been commissioned to write a draft essay on Oliver Cromwell. But hardly more than a phrase or two survives in the *History*, which, for once, advises due methodological caution against the sort of whiggery elsewhere rampant: 'We must not be led by Victorian writers into regarding the triumph of the Ironsides and of Cromwell as a kind of victory for democracy and the Parliamentary system over Divine Right and Old World dreams.' Oliver Cromwell is duly rebuked for abandoning 'all the constitutional safeguards and processes built and treasured across the centuries, from Simon de Montfort to the Petition of Right'. Most of this is fairly unremarkable; but the account is also infused with an undercurrent of passion. As Churchill had told Young in revising the proof, 'I remain hostile to him, and consider that he should be condemned as a representative of the dictatorships against which all the whole movement of English history has been continuous.'[69]

It is a sort of class action against dictatorship. Cromwell was thus the unlucky defendant against an indictment neither entirely generated by nor faithful to a purely seventeenth-century context. Thus the so-called Parliamentarians' temporary triumph is seen as the work of 'resolute, ruthless, disciplined, military fanatics', under the autocratic leadership of a 'harsh, terrific, lightning-charged being, whose erratic, opportunist, self-centred course is laid bare upon the annals . . .'[70] At any rate, this sort of iniquity is laid bare in the sort of annals that Churchill himself composed, as one kind of dictator about another, whether his target was Oliver Cromwell or Adolf Hitler.

Unsurprisingly, Marlborough is a hero who gets the full treatment. Or rather, he had already got so full a treatment in the million-word biography that Churchill simply decided to repeat himself more concisely. In March 1939 he persuaded Harraps to let Cassells publish material from *Marlborough* in an abridged form, an exercise that can hardly be described as plagiarism but rather as a nifty, thrifty dodge to popularise his own scholarly work. In the published Volume Two of the *History*, the last two chapters have been transmogrified in this way, and the first six of the next volume too. This conserved the author's own time and energy by drawing a total of about 50,000 words from *Marlborough*. In Volume Three of the *History* the early chapter headings alone give sufficient indication of the provenance: 'The Spanish Succession', 'Marlborough: Blenheim and Ramillies', 'Marlborough: Oudenarde and Malplaquet', 'The Treaty of Utrecht'. What J. R. Green once disparaged as the 'drum-and-trumpet' school of history was on parade with a second-hand drum, a renovated trumpet.

Marlborough's claims, then, need not be rehearsed again here. In the *History* they become the benchmark for others. Hence the status claimed for Pitt the Elder, later Lord Chatham. 'William Pitt ranks with Marlborough as the greatest Englishman in the century between 1689 and 1789,' the *History* tells us; and claims that 'he is the first great figure of British Imperialism' – suffusing it (as the first proof put it) 'with the glitter of his imagination'.[71] This comes in a chapter provocatively entitled 'The First World War', meaning that of 1756–63 against the French, in which Clive secured India and Wolfe won Canada for the British Empire. James Wolfe was a local boy, from Westerham, and always a hero to Churchill.

It was Chatham, however, for whom Churchill reserved an adulation verging on self-promotion. The fact that 'he had used the House of Commons as a platform from which to address the country', and that his 'studied orations in severe classical syle were intended for a wider audience', spoke to the power of his example. In the revision of the proofs, in Churchill's first week back at the Admiralty in September 1939, he enjoined Young to bring out 'the rugged grandeur of Chatham's rise: a man who from a private station compelled a sluggish, all-powerful Government to capitulate, and thereafter in four brilliant years gained the Seven Years' War, and completed the building of "The first British Empire" '.[72]

There is a fairly obvious double standard at work here. Many of the qualities denounced as dictatorial in Cromwell become admirable features of Chatham's unique personal command of the whole situation. 'Now, as at all times, his policy was a projection on to a vast screen of his own aggressive, dominating personality,' the *History* tells us. 'In the teeth of disfavour and obstruction he had made his way to the foremost place in Parliament, and now at last fortune, courage, and the confidence of his countrymen had given him a stage on which his gifts could be displayed and his foibles indulged.'[73] All of this is in the 1939 text, dictated when war was clearly imminent, and revised in proof when Churchill had already re-entered government. In a transatlantic radio broadcast on 8 August 1939, he ruminated to American listeners about the efficacy of British and American institutions in preventing the rise of a Hitler: 'It is curious how the English-speaking peoples have always had this horror of one-man power.' A lot depended, of course, upon which man was being judged by these elastic historical standards.

The Author of Victory, 1940–45

'I hold a latchkey to American hearts.'

Churchill in a broadcast to the United States, 1941

On 3 September 1939, two days after Hitler's invasion of Poland, the United Kingdom declared war on Germany. Neville Chamberlain, his hopes of peace finally dashed, remained prime minister of a predominantly Conservative government. Winston Churchill, his warnings of war finally confirmed, now became First Lord of the Admiralty (again). He thus resumed his career in government office: a career that many people supposed had finished ten years previously after he left the Treasury. The date simultaneously marked the end of his career as an author – or so his tax lawyers were successfully able to argue. Their story was that he had ceased to exercise his 'professional vocation' as a writer and that, unless or until he returned to writing, his literary income would be treated accordingly, escaping income taxes.[1]

There was always an element of unreality in this scenario. Although it was of the essence that the retirement should suddenly come into force on 3 September 1939, at that moment everyone had more immediate problems on their minds. True, since the 'retirement' option had been hypothetically explored in 1925 when Churchill had gone to the Treasury, the idea was not wholly novel. But, as the various sets of legal opinions in Churchill's archive show, it was essentially a fiscal fiction, retrospectively constructed. The key provision was that any literary receipts that accrued would be treated as windfalls, provided that Churchill totally abstained from writing for publication while in office. Thus, although the outright sale of the copyright of the *History* to Cassells would in any case exempt the proceeds from income tax, any literary work that Churchill continued to perform – even on the *History* – might subject all his other literary receipts to taxation. The annual salary of the First Lord was £5,000, taxed at source. In wartime the standard rate of income tax soon reached 50 per cent; the top rate of surtax reached 47.5 per cent – together making a maximum levy of nineteen shillings and sixpence in the pound. Churchill would not immediately have been liable at this marginal rate; but, with an increasingly valuable backlist as his fame grew, he had a lot at stake.

Little wonder, then, that the official version insisted that the *History* was laid aside on the outbreak of war. To admit otherwise would have been to compromise Churchill's favourable tax status as well as to raise questions over his single-mindedness about the vitally important tasks that faced him at the Admiralty. There is no reason to doubt his commitment to the war effort. He manifestly revelled in his new naval responsibilities and immediately became a key figure in the war cabinet of eleven ministers. And he welcomed the opportunity to deal directly with President Roosevelt, who now decided to open a private correspondence with him. But when FDR wrote, in his first missive on 11 September, that 'I am glad you did the Marlboro volumes before this thing started', the president little imagined that the First Lord of the Admiralty was even then engaged in finishing yet another big book, *A History of the English-Speaking Peoples*.[2]

On the previous day Churchill had composed a long letter to G. M. Young, addressing the task in hand. It forms our best guide to where things really stood, cutting through various claims bandied around that about half a million words were already in proof. The author regarded his *History* as finished only up to the death of Queen Anne (1714) in Book VII, which later formed the first of three parts of the published Volume Three; and since virtually the whole of Book VII was an abridgement of the relevant parts of *Marlborough*, it is easy to see why it was already in good shape. From that point on, however, with the exception of the subject of the American Civil War, Churchill realised that the proofs still needed a lot of attention. 'There are words a-plenty,' he admitted to Young, 'but what is needed is the clamping together and the adornment.' He had no illusions about his coverage of the origin of the conflict with the American colonies – 'this is in some disarray' – and the War of Independence was 'capable of improvement'. He made the significant admission: 'I have not attempted yet the chapterisation of this book.'[3]

There was no false modesty here. On the contrary, the surviving proofs show that even in Volume Two, there was still much work to be done, not only by Young but by Churchill himself, who made detailed corrections in red ink, his efforts stretching into October 1939, amending much of what he had previously dictated on the late seventeenth century. The 1939 text really falls apart in the middle of what became Volume Three, where the surviving proofs unravel into a tangle of improvisation. The tone of the original opening to Book IX – 'The year 1783 was one of the most confused in the political history of the eighteenth century' – is not auspicious. An initial draft on the increasingly contentious American situation lacks even a clear chronological sequence and omits events as important as the Declaration of Independence. This is, in short, unformed, unfinished, unpublishable work by any standards. Above all, the lack of any satisfactory integration of the American issue into the history of Britain in this period – this was only attempted subsequently – is the most disappointing feature of these proofs. In writing to Young, Churchill spoke of his strong instinct that the conflict should be 'a climax in the whole book', yet he proved incapable of seizing this opportunity.[4]

The reason is not hard to find. 'I am staggering along to the end of the job,' he had told Eddie Marsh on 20 July 1939, 'and am glad to have found the strength to have accomplished it.'[5] But the result was one of his less accomplished accomplishments, though his excuses are valid enough. Attendance in the House of Commons in early August had been taxing; an invitation to inspect the French Maginot Line had been accepted in mid-August, with a well-merited short holiday with his family in Normandy to follow. In the limited time left for dictating the *History*, Churchill had abandoned the discipline of chapters in favour of an unimpeded flow of words that could be cudgelled into shape later. 'I have tried to fit these Galleys together,' Churchill told Deakin on 29 August. 'The present result is quite impossible.' He could see all too clearly some of the things that were lacking. 'What we want is a coherent account of the Seven Years War, featuring the rise of Chatham,' he wrote, asking Deakin to see what he could do to salvage the situation.[6]

With the clock ticking in the countdown to a now predictable war, how was the delivery deadline to be met? Newman Flower had made it plain that it could not be deferred beyond 31 December. It was simply not an option for Churchill to default on the contract at this stage. His financial imperative was as sharp as ever. His government salary went partway to meeting his current expenditure; and the government covered the costs of his official accommodation on the top two floors of Admiralty House, allowing him to pocket the proceeds of the sale of his lease on his Morpeth Mansions flat. Nonetheless, unless Churchill could keep the £5,000 that Cassells had already advanced to him, and then net the further tax-free £15,000 due on delivery, there would – yet again – be no alternative to a forced sale of Chartwell.

So everything still depended on the *History*. But the part of it that was actually finished by the end of August, up to the death of Anne, totalled only 320,000 words. This is what Young was candidly told, despite the fact that Churchill had boasted to Cassells fully six months previously that he already had 330,000 words in print, and had also, as recently as 13 July, confidently advised them to expect 480,000 words. About 160,000 words of publishable text were thus unaccounted for – Churchill's literary credibility gap. Not for the first time, Cassells were now told what they wanted to hear. 'I am, as you know, concentrating every minute of my spare life and strength upon completing our contract,' Churchill assured them on 31 August, with evident sincerity; but, trying to keep up appearances, he disingenuously added: 'However 530,000 words are now in print and there is only cutting and proof reading, together with a few special points, now to be done.'⁷ On the following day Hitler invaded Poland.

Far from 3 September 1939 marking the author's retirement, it saw his final desperate struggle to fulfil his contract for the *History*. If the December deadline was to be met, the work had to continue in every minute that could be snatched. This was facilitated by new arrangements in the Admiralty, where Churchill arranged for a bedroom to be created for him above the Upper War Room. And the First Lord had meanwhile imposed his own schedule on admirals and civil servants alike. 'I regretted having to send myself to bed like a child every afternoon,' he later wrote in *The Gathering Storm*, 'but I was rewarded by being able to work through the night until two or even later – sometimes much later – in the morning, and begin the new day between eight and nine o'clock.'⁸ What he presents as an innovation in the service of the state was actually a continuation of his practice in his career as an author: a career that was still pursued in the long watches of the night.

Churchill became more dependent than ever upon his trusted literary team. He already addressed Deakin as 'My dear Bill', which is one indication of the growing friendship that developed between them. But though Deakin's departure for military service with the 63rd Oxford Yeomanry obviously met with his master's warm approval, it was equally obviously a further handicap in finishing the *History*. Alan Bullock, unfit for active service because of asthma, was drawn more closely into the final stages of composition. He had originally been commissioned in late 1938, through Deakin, to write on Australia, where he dwelt too much on the convict presence for Churchill's taste, and also on New Zealand, where he met with warmer appreciation. The fact that Churchill had never visited either Dominion had not inhibited him, in more peaceful days, from suggesting to Bullock that 'here again a little about the beauty of the country, the climate, the flora and fauna, the Yellowstone Terraces, etc., would be welcome'.⁹

That manifestly unsoldierly scholar, G. M. Young, was in any case well beyond the age of military service. His role in salvaging the *History* became more important in Deakin's absence. Churchill delegated to Young a wide discretion over the later proofs: 'Here again I must rely on you to clamp it all together, and also to bring out the salient points in the proper light.' It was Young who was made primarily responsible for pulling the inchoate proofs into a shape that could, within a matter of weeks, be sent back to the printers. 'We shall then have a final text of about 530,000 words to which I hope to be able to give a final reading,' Churchill told him 10 September.[10] In this way, the promise to Flower, like a postdated cheque, would be validated retrospectively. Likewise, two days later, Churchill took steps to satisfy the provision in the contract specifying a terminal date of 1914. He summoned Bullock to the Admiralty, where, in the course of a long monologue, Bullock was asked, without success, to cover a period that he thought Churchill himself uniquely qualified to write about.

Apart from the current hostilities, Churchill's attention was simultaneously claimed by that earlier world war of 1756–63. The immediate need, in knocking the first proofs into shape, was for a proper 'chapterisation' of the eighteenth century. He wrote to Deakin on 6 October: 'I do hope you will be able to get on with this during the week, as the matter is so important and the stress here is very great.' But Deakin, now with the 63rd Yeomanry, was facing his own stress. His regiment had been relocated; as adjutant, he was therefore busy enough; but then there were Marsh's proof corrections of Bullock's text on New Zealand to deal with; and the sections on Waterloo and Trafalgar were still only in note form. 'I cannot get a secretary here or any privacy in which to write,' Deakin reported in November. 'We are sleeping four Officers in a room (which is unheated), and there is one mess.'[11]

There were frantic efforts to collate the diverse proofs, sometimes even to locate them. 'I am afraid I cannot find Australia, but will have another search,' Kathleen Hill told Deakin in November. 'I remember Mr Bullock writing about this, but forget if and when it went to print.'[12] It turned up, just in time. Then there was Churchill's commitment to write a 20,000-word introduction for the serialisation in parts, for which Lord Camrose's Amalgamated Press was now waiting. It had been a promise lightly given in early 1937, as Desmond Flower had to remind Churchill, though its fulfilment in late 1939 now weighed heavily. Having first got Flower to scale this requirement down to 10,000 words at the beginning of November, Churchill then got Young to start work on drafting it for him, knowing that the task was now beyond him.

Criticism of the quality of the *History*, as revealed in the proofs of late 1939, seems rather churlish. Given the conditions of the time and the other responsibilities of those most closely concerned, it is remarkable how much was achieved. Churchill asked Deakin to reserve the weekend of 25–27 November 'for the final piecing together'. Marsh had duly corrected the chapters he had been sent, including Australia (a lost continent no longer), which complemented his earlier dutiful attention to other Dominions – 'I can never get worked up about the history of Canada!'[13] Young's draft introduction was promised for the end of the month, so a submission date was now within sight, despite dislocation and relocation, after toil and stress, and amid the crises facing the Royal Navy.

The original target date for delivery was 7 December. But on that day Churchill decided on the spur of the moment to travel north to investigate the heavy damage inflicted on the battleship HMS *Nelson*. The problem was German magnetic mines, which were causing a series of British shipping losses, serious in themselves and also such a political embarrassment that the news was kept secret. On 16 December the First Lord reported to the war cabinet on the day-and-night efforts that, it might be supposed, now consumed all attention in the Admiralty.

Not literally all, however, even now. For on the same day Churchill sent the final text of the *History* to Desmond Flower at Cassells: 'It has been a work of great interest, but also of great labour to me to

accomplish this task, and I am very glad to be able to deliver it to you.'
It had been printed, under Harraps' direction, by Sherratt and Hughes
in Manchester, at a cost of £1,065, which Churchill expected Cassells
to defray (though he also remonstrated with Harraps that the bill was
too high). 'I regard the delivery of this copy in full readiness for press
as the fulfilment of my contract with you,' he wrote to Desmond
Flower, with a sense of pride but, above all, of relief.[14] It was almost
exactly seven years since the author had settled the terms of the
contract with Flower's father, now retired from active participation in
the firm.

What happened next, then, cannot be blamed on the notoriously
short fuse of Sir Newman Flower. Desmond Flower had immediately
sent Churchill a gracious acknowledgement of the submission of 'your
great book'. But then he read it. On 27 December he told Churchill
that 'we are alarmed by the abrupt manner in which the work finishes'.
Churchill tried offering to send a 10,000-word epilogue. Flower, after
consideration, conveyed a more serious view of the situation on
4 January 1940: 'We cannot feel that your MS., ending as it does with
the close of the American Civil War, fulfils your contract with us to
write a History of the English Speaking Peoples.' A possible epilogue
could not atone for the omission of the further fifty years of history
that had been promised in the contract. Indeed the 1937 plan (Feiling's, of
course) was quoted back to Churchill, and there was explicit complaint
about the the absence of an adequate history of the Dominions, the
projected chapters on American and British democracy, and the
promised survey of the English-speaking peoples on the eve of the
Great War. One example of the sort of blatant inadequacy apparent to
Flower is a brazen claim in the proofs that 'it is not inappropriate that
we end our survey of Australian history here in 1860' – a survey that
had only properly begun in about 1850.[15]

No publisher could have reached any other conclusion. There was
only one thing to be done to avert financial disaster: send in Brendan
Bracken. His official title was now Parliamentary Private Secretary to

the First Lord of the Admiralty; his unofficial designation, as he reminded Desmond Flower, was 'Mr Churchill's honorary man of business', and as such he played the weak cards in his hand with skill, and with determination, and without scruple. He did the business on the telephone, in an age when such dealings left no trace. It is a reasonable conjecture that he played the patriotic card, as he was to do in later dealings with publishers on Churchill's behalf, browbeating them with the prospect of adverse publicity should they enforce their rights against a man now perceived as indispensable to the war effort. Within twenty-four hours of sending his letter holding that Churchill was in breach of contract, Flower sent another letter, this one enclosing a cheque for £7,500, the contracted sum on delivery. The deal was that, before the second instalment, for the same amount, was due six months later, Churchill would supply the missing chapters.

Churchill thus survived his ordeal. With this tax-free sum added to his net salary, his income in 1939–40 was sustained at pre-war levels. He sent a cheque for £700 to Deakin, with warm recognition of how much he had done: 'Please always count on me as a friend.' (Four years later, he was likewise to refer in the House of Commons to 'a young friend of mine', Lt. Col. Deakin.)[16] In 1940 Churchill renewed his efforts to get Bullock to write on the most recent period; Bullock later remembered discussing one draft chapter at the Admiralty in February, and other drafts were produced as late as March and April 1940; but the work was then put aside. The printing bill remained unpaid until Bracken brusquely engineered a settlement for half of it in January 1941, provoking Walter Harrap's lament: 'You break a man's heart.'[17] Likewise, Bracken secured successive payments from Cassells over the next year, despite the lack of concluding chapters, thus making up the full lump sum except for a balance of £1,000, withheld pending the delivery of the promised coverage up to 1914.[18]

Cassells' copies of the 1939 proofs were destroyed when the company's premises were bombed later in the war. Churchill's own copies remained in Kathleen Hill's custody: a verbose but truncated work, totalling 499,800 words, not looked at again in any serious way until the last months of the war. But the author, of course, with his prodigious memory, did not need to look again at what was in print in order to recall echoes of what he had himself declaimed, night after night, through many anxious months in 1938 and 1939.

On 10 May 1940 Churchill became prime minister and Brendan Bracken too secured a new job. He was to become Parliamentary Private Secretary to the prime minister. This marked the partial repayment of a double debt owed by Churchill: not only as the newly appointed prime minister to his most loyal political supporter, but also as a profitably retired author to his indispensable man of business. King George VI raised objections to Bracken being made a Privy Counsellor, with access to confidential information, but Churchill insisted. He needed Bracken at his side, all the more so since many of the officials whom the incoming prime minister inherited when he displaced Neville Chamberlain were initially unreconciled to the change at the top.

John Colville is the most interesting example, not least because he kept a detailed diary. An upper-class graduate of Trinity College, Cambridge, Colville had become, at twenty-four, one of the Assistant Private Secretaries to the prime minister in October 1939. He fitted in nicely; on Chamberlain's fall from power on 10 May, Colville joined like-minded colleagues in toasting the 'King over the Water' in champagne, sharing their profound sense of regret that 'the good clean tradition of English politics, that of Pitt as opposed to Fox, had been sold to the greatest adventurer of modern political history'. He knew what to expect as this dubious new leader moved in with his opportunist cronies. 'Bracken is a cad,' Colville wrote in his diary eight days later, closeted willy-nilly with these deplorable hangers-on (Frederick Lindemann, 'the Prof.', was another now in the back room).[19]

'Jock' Colville's diary provides us with a case-study in changing perceptions of Churchill in 1940. Still learning the ropes, and strongly impressed by Chamberlain's executive discipline, he was all too aware of Churchill's adventurist reputation. On 17 April, with the First Lord of the Admiralty now pressing for action against the Nazis in Norway, Colville records worries among insiders that it was all too reminiscent of the Dardanelles (in 1915). On 25 April his diary gets to the root of the problem: that 'the country believes that Winston is the man of action who is winning the war and little realise how ineffective, and indeed harmful, much of his energy is proving itself to be'. Two days later, with the Norwegian campaign in trouble, Churchill's undeserved popularity continues to rankle: 'One of Hitler's cleverest moves has been to make Winston Public Enemy Number One, because this fact has helped to make him Public Hero Number One at home and in the U.S.A.' And, in the post-mortem on Norway, after the three-day debate in the House of Commons unwarrantably turned not against the Admiralty but against Chamberlain personally, Colville's despair on 10 May – 'I am afraid it *must* be Winston' – is palpable. Hence the rueful, bitter, nostalgic glass of champagne at the end of this dismal day.

The outlook was grim. Not only were the German armies sweeping across the Low Countries into France but, as Colville saw, the new prime minister's 'inconsequential' habits of work now infected his new staff with a malaise; and 'the prospect of constant late nights – 2.00 a.m. or later – is depressing'. (14 May) For the moment, the Chamberlains retained 10 Downing Street, though the Churchills began to use Chequers, the official country house of the prime minister. Crucially for Colville and his colleagues, the lower floors of Admiralty House, below the living quarters, were meanwhile commandeered to accommodate Churchill's eccentric hours. 'He has fitted up the ground floor for this purpose,' Colville's diary notes on 14 May: 'the dining-room in which the private secretary and one of Winston's specially trained night-women-typists sit; the lovely drawing-room with its curious ugly dolphin furniture, which is used as a kind of promenade; and an inner room in which the Great Man himself sits. At the side of his desk stands a table laden with bottles of whisky etc.'

Maurice Ashley and Bill Deakin had seen it all before – and heard some of it too.

Churchill's habits were now long set. It was thirty-two years since he had first entered Asquith's cabinet, at a time when Neville Chamberlain, now serving in the new Coalition government under Churchill, had been virtually unknown outside his native Birmingham. The other members of the war cabinet of five – the Foreign Secretary Lord Halifax, the Labour leader Clement Attlee and his deputy Arthur Greenwood – had been equally obscure back in 1908. Leo Amery was one of Churchill's few contemporaries in the new government with a political career of comparable length. Amery was now beginning a long stint as the Secretary of State for India, there as elsewhere in intermittent despair about Churchill's failure to understand the modern point of view. Amery's ticket to office, however, had been well earned by his intervention in the Norway debate, when he had memorably told Chamberlain: 'Depart, I say, and let us have done with you. In the name of God, go.' These potent words, of course, were originally those of the dictatorial Cromwell, dismissing his parliament. But Churchill was not so fastidious as to repudiate such sentiments in May 1940, now that he was walking with destiny, shaped for office by long years of preparation.

Just as the routine of Churchill's ministerial career had left a mark on his subsequent style of authorship, so his vocation as author left a mark on his peculiar style of government in World War II. Now that he was back in office, as Colville had reason to observe, Churchill sometimes overestimated the value of his own sonority, of his own loquacity, and of his own verbal inventiveness. He was, for example, inordinately pleased with his proposed action about some supplies of food abandoned on the Channel Islands – to evaluate it and evacuate it – which was little more than a weak epigram masquerading as a policy. If Colville himself was sometimes left frustrated in this way, some of those who went on pining for Chamberlain's terse efficiency and administrative grip were even less impressed by the change of style. On 16 May a meeting of the cabinet in Downing Street received a 'terrifying' telegram from Churchill, engaged in emergency talks with the French government in Paris, in which he spoke of 'the mortal gravity of the hour'. Colville notes the dry comment of Chamberlain's trusted private secretary: 'He is still thinking of his books.'

We can see that it took Colville himself, a Chamberlainite on 10 May, days rather than weeks to revise his opinion of his new master. When, on 13 May, the new prime minister tells the House of Commons that he has 'nothing to offer but blood, toil, tears and sweat,' Colville thinks it 'a brilliant little speech'; yet all Churchill actually offers by way of policy is simply the declaration 'to wage war' and to do so 'with all our might'; and all he offers by way of aim is 'victory at all costs'. The lack of executive substance here now seems to be no problem for Colville, who faults neither such Churchillian orations nor the amount of time that is devoted to their composition. 'It is refreshing to work with somebody who refuses to be depressed even by the most formidable danger that has ever threatened this country,' Colville writes on 19 May, already indulgent of the way that Churchill has absconded from London to sit in the sunshine, on one of his last wartime visits to Chartwell, devoting his hours there to dictating his first broadcast speech. Colville's diary now repents of the harsh judgements of only a few weeks earlier: 'In any case, whatever Winston's shortcomings, he seems to be the man for the occasion.'

The crisis of 1940 was an occasion to which the man rose in some style. Was it a desperate situation? Was this a threat to hearth and home? Were slender resources already over-committed? Was there no obvious way out of an appalling predicament? Was the outcome a gigantic gamble? Yet was there any alternative to a visceral refusal to accept defeat? The scale was admittedly hugely different; but the challenges and crises of the author's career had always evoked a characteristic response. He never said in public, 'keep buggering on', but, in his private office, the expression KBO became familiar.

The policy enunciated on 13 May was to wage an all-out war 'against a monstrous tyranny, never surpassed in the dark, lamentable catalogue of human crime'. This hardly seems compatible with simultaneously seeking terms for a negotiated peace with these criminal tyrants. Yet Halifax, supported by Chamberlain, wished to explore this rational, diplomatic option; and it took long days of close discussion before Churchill, backed by the two Labour members of the war cabinet, prevailed with the argument that, despite everything, the right thing was to fight on regardless.

Churchill's maxim that governing meant talking had never served him better. Crucially, the prime minister cut the ground from under his prudent Conservative colleagues by talking also to the wider group of cabinet-rank ministers who were outside the war cabinet, in an address on 28 May. Amery was one of those who loudly applauded Churchill's resolution: 'He is a real war leader and one whom it is worth while serving under.' Hugh Dalton, an equally combative Labour minister who also kept a diary, recorded Churchill as saying: 'If this long island story of ours is to end at last, let it end only when each of us lies choking in his own blood upon the ground.'[20] Here, if not for his publishers, the author was prepared to bring the *History* right up to date, with sentiments redolent of Boadicea, King Arthur, Alfred the Great, Marlborough and – above all – Chatham.

Six days later, on 4 June, this perspective was developed. In the meantime, with the evacuation of the British army from Dunkirk, the picture had become even more sombre, as the prime minister did not attempt to conceal from the House of Commons. They now had to reckon with a chance of invasion – as there had been in the days of Napoleon 'when the same wind which would have carried his transports across the Channel might have driven away the blockading fleet'. Colville was in attendance at the Commons, listening to 'a magnificent oration which obviously moved the House', and he copied out the concluding passage, with punctuation that nicely indicates its origin in dictation. 'We shall defend our Island, whatever the cost may be. We shall fight on the beaches. We shall fight on the landing grounds. We shall fight in the fields and streets. We shall fight in the hills. We shall never surrender.' And Plan B? That the British Empire, supported by the Royal Navy, 'will carry on the struggle until in God's good time the New World with all its power and might sets forth to the rescue and liberation of the old'.

It had not altogether escaped young Colville's attention that the old stager Churchill had some histrionic talent. 'He is indeed an orator – perhaps the only one in the country today,' Colville had reluctantly conceded a few months previously, about a belligerent speech from the First Lord of the Admiralty. Yet, unlike Lloyd George, the essence of Churchill's oratory was not spontaneity but prior composition. Colville observed how the new prime minister would walk around Admiralty House, talking half-aloud to himself or to others or to the cat alike, with phrases already in rehearsal for later use. 'It is curious to see how, as it were, he fertilises a phrase or a line of poetry for weeks and then gives birth to it in a speech,' he reflected later in his diary. For example, alerted by his master's recent predilection for Andrew Marvell's lines on Charles I ('He nothing common did or mean/Upon that memorable scene'), Colville records being in the House of Commons to hear the quotation duly pop out.[21]

This speech of 18 June 1940 had entailed special preparation. A rather acerbic comment in the diary of Sir Alexander Cadogan, Permanent Secretary at the Foreign Office, captures the official view: 'Cabinet 12.30. Winston not there – writing his speech.'[22] This was simply not how Mr Chamberlain had conducted himself. Listening in the Commons once more, Colville thought that Churchill 'spoke less well than on the last occasion, and referred more often to his notes; but he ended magnificently'. To achieve this effect, with the whole world listening, was perhaps worth skipping a cabinet meeting.

His oration of 18 June is classic Churchill. Evelyn Waugh's deprecating phrase in his novel *Men at Arms* (1952), 'sham-Augustan', may identify the style but perversely fails to capture the resonance in 1940.

Churchill spoke under the shadow that France would be overrun in a 'colossal military disaster'. He sought to indicate the 'solid, practical grounds' for supposing the defence of Britain still possible. He revealed his efforts in consulting all the Dominions, 'these great communities far beyond the oceans who have been built up on our laws and on our civilization, and who are absolutely free to choose their course, but are absolutely devoted to the ancient Motherland, and who feel themselves inspired by the same emotions which lead me to stake our all upon duty and honour'. The sentimental basis of Churchill's conception of Empire could hardly have been stated more clearly. Moreover, he was able to cite messages from each of the Dominion leaders 'in which they endorse our decision to fight on, and declare themselves ready to share our fortunes and to persevere to the end'. Hence the significant strengthening of his declaration, one that he had already made two weeks previously with reference to 'our Island home', but now extended to cover the whole British Empire: a resolve to fight on, 'if necessary alone'.

Little wonder that this speech on 18 June needed its hours of composition, methodically paving the way for the well-known phrases of its peroration. As Churchill put it, if the Battle of France was over, what he dubbed 'the Battle of Britain' would now begin. 'Upon it depends our own British life, and the long continuity of our institutions and our Empire.' He invoked the prospect of 'broad, sunlit uplands', if Hitler could only be stopped. And if not, he claimed that the whole world, 'including the United States', would 'sink into the abyss of a new Dark Age'. Churchill's rhetorical task was thus to stake the future of the British Empire – essentially the self-governing Commonwealth – on the outcome of the war while simultaneously appealing to the common values of the English-speaking peoples in terms that avoided rebarbative and atavistic conceptions of imperialism. He projected himself far into the future, into the shoes of a future historian perhaps, in his final plea: 'Let us therefore brace ourselves to our duties, and so bear ourselves that, if the British Empire and its

Commonwealth last for a thousand years, men will still say, "This was their finest hour".'

Privately, Churchill deployed his verbal skills in the diplomatic arena. 'If words counted, we should win this war,' Churchill had commented after dictating long telegrams to Roosevelt and to the Dominions on 15 June. Colville recorded this at the time; and much later in the war, by then used to supplying his master's needs in the private office, reflected: 'Looking at the messages and letters that go out from this office under the P.M.'s signature, I often think how diffi-cult it will be for future historians to know what is "genuine Churchill" and what is "school of".'[23] Ashley, Deakin and Young could all have said the same in their time.

Publicly, Churchill used his tongue in establishing an empathy with the public. Here he was served well by his rhetorical trick of a sudden descent into the vernacular. For example, in his speech to the Canadian House of Commons on 30 December 1941, he solemnly built up his story about how the French military had written off Britain's chances of survival in the summer of 1940. He quoted their generals as saying, 'In three weeks England will have her neck wrung like a chicken.' Churchill's simple punchline – 'Some chicken; some neck' – brought the house down.

Popular impersonations of Churchill's distinctive tones established apocryphal anecdotes and sayings that were also 'school of'. Churchill was appealing over the heads of the British political establishment, which he felt had excluded him, and which he saw entrenched in the war cabinet, on the Conservative benches in the House of Commons, and also in the BBC, which had previously denied him airtime. In the early months of the war, the broadcasts of the First Lord of the Admir-alty had not gone down well with either the Foreign Office or BBC officials; and even the 'Finest Hour' speech, when repeated on radio, seemed less effective in delivery than it had been in the electric atmos-phere of the House itself. Public rhetoric and private persuasion differed only in register. Churchill's broadcast of 18 June was followed by a special radio talk on 14 July, which BBC audience research found was heard by 64 per cent of the adult population. Moreover, radio reached the world in a new sort of diplomacy. 'But really he has got guts, that man,' commented his junior minister at the Ministry of Information, Harold Nicolson, after listening to Churchill's words. 'Imagine the effect of his speech in the Empire and the U.S.A.'[24]

Churchill's next broadcast, also specially prepared for radio, did not come until two months later. He did not speak as often on the BBC as folk memory would suggest (though it is a canard that he did not actually deliver the words himself). When he spoke on 11 September, then, it was after the critical struggle for control of the skies had turned in Britain's favour. This was now being called the 'Battle of Britain', a coinage initially applied in a more general sense by Churchill. It was indelibly linked with his famous tribute of 20 August (in the Commons, not on the BBC): 'Never in the field of human conflict was so much owed by so many to so few.' This quickly became a popular catchphrase, much adapted. When the author, a year or so previously, had dictated his account of Henry V before the battle of Agincourt (1415) in the *History*, he had himself adapted Shakespeare in saying: 'He and the "humble few" lay for the night . . .' In the published volume in 1956, in a rare example of contrived prescience, this wording was retrospectively amended simply to 'the few'.[25]

The moment was historic. Churchill sensed this, and said so at the time to Colville, when he heard the total of enemy planes destroyed on 15 August: 'this is one of the greatest days in history'. It exemplifies, in a particular instance, the comment made later about Churchill by Isaiah Berlin, that 'the single, central, organizing principle of his moral and intellectual universe' was 'an historical imagination so strong, so comprehensive, as to encase the whole of the present and the whole of the future in a framework of a rich and multi-coloured past'.[26] This mentality was sentimental, but not often triumphalist: more often reflective. Colville records that the prime minister kept musing in 1940 on the apparent puzzle of his own popularity, since 'everything had gone wrong' since he came into power: 'It was curious but in this war he had had no success but had received nothing but praise, whereas in the last war he had done several things which he thought were good and had got nothing but abuse for them.'[27]

These were the early days of public opinion polling, which was often disparaged at the time. But the Gallup Poll's standard question, asking whether people were satisfied or dissatisfied with the prime minister of the day (to which those answering 'satisfied' had plummeted to 33 per cent in Chamberlain's last month), showed satisfaction with Churchill at either 88 or 89 per cent in July, in October and in November 1940. Nor was this effect temporary. The only month during his wartime premiership in which his personal support was to flicker below 80 per cent was in July 1942, though the proportion satisfied with the government's conduct of the war dipped as low as 35 per cent early that year.

Churchill's popularity thus survived all setbacks in the course of the hostilities. At his weakest moment, in early 1942, popular discontent focused on the faltering British war effort in contrast with current Russian resistance to Hitler's invasion; and this led to the left-wing minister Sir Stafford Cripps, in the reflected glory of his return from the Moscow embassy, being talked up as a potential challenger. In his diary, Harold Nicolson had at one low moment in April 1941 bemoaned the fact that 'the old enthusiasm is dead for ever. How foul is public life and popular ingratitude!'[28] This was an insider view, from the perspective of a parliamentary supporter whose personal loyalty had survived his own demotion to the backbenches. Yet, outside Westminster too, the opinion-poll evidence clearly suggests that Churchill's hold on public support barely faltered, allowing him to manage the crisis by bringing his supposed rival into the war cabinet. 'I have my niche in history, nothing can displace me,' he had genially assured Cripps in January 1942, after a long lunch at Chequers. 'I am England.'[29]

*   *   *

Churchill knew how to tease the House of Commons. Surely few of its Members took him literally when he asked them (12 November 1941) to 'remember that no sensible person in wartime makes speeches because he wants to' and added: 'He makes them because he has to, and to no one does this apply more than to the Prime Minister.' His public rhetoric was an extension of his own insatiable appetite for his own words and of his doctrine that the British way of governing was by talking. He had come to power as an orator whose words as much as his executive actions identified him with the war effort, and in this role he did not abandon the perspective of author. 'I never admire the habit which some people follow of always skipping the pages of a book and looking to see how it ends,' he admonished a too-eager press conference in Cairo on 1 February 1943. 'The authors must be permitted to tell their tale in their own way, and to unfold the story chapter by chapter.'

That Churchill would eventually write a big book about World War II was obvious from the moment when it also became obvious that the Nazis would not be controlling the printing presses. As early as 12 December 1940 Colville records table talk in this vein: 'He would retire to Chartwell and write a book on the war, which he already had mapped out in his mind chapter by chapter.' This might seem another implausible, tongue-in-cheek claim; yet it has some substance in drawing attention to the uncanny way that he responded to some key developments in the course of the war.

The important broadcast that Churchill made on 22 June 1941, following Hitler's invasion of Russia, began with the statement: 'I have taken occasion to speak to you tonight because we have reached one of the climacterics of the war.' Giving his listeners little time to stumble to their dictionaries to look up this arcane word, Churchill went on to explain that this turning point followed those seen in the fall of France in June 1940, in the Battle of Britain that summer, and in the recent implementation of lend-lease supplies to Britain from the United States. 'Those were the three climacterics,' said Churchill. 'The fourth is now upon us.' This immediate perception of the wider significance of the day's hot news distinguishes Churchill's peculiar frame of mind, at once passionate and dispassionate; just as on a slow news day he might loftily assure Colville that 'what we are going through now is of importance only on the stage of history' (22 October 1940).

There were six volumes of Churchill's war speeches, each quickly published (plus a later volume of five of his speeches to secret sessions of the House of Commons). These volumes sold well, published in London by Cassells as some compensation for the failure of the *History* to appear. Not only did royalties on the volumes of speeches, edited for Churchill initially by his son Randolph and later by the journalist Charles Eade, escape liability to British income tax: their high sales in the United States also made them valuable as British war propaganda. Cassells understandably wished to call the first volume *Their Finest Hour* but, faced with Winston's refusal, had to settle for Randolph's suggestion, *Into Battle*. In North America this volume achieved a huge success under the title *Blood, Sweat and Tears*, being selected by the Book of the Month Club, and producing £12,000 for Churchill in untaxed royalties by 1942.[30]

The speeches collected in this first volume have the highest content of pure ore. They cover the period from May 1938, the long prelude to the Munich agreement, to February 1941, when Britain had survived the immediate Nazi onslaught. There are some early indications of the author's multiple preoccupations. 'I was reading the other day a letter from the great Duke of Marlborough,' he confided to the House of Commons on 25 May 1938, making a pointed parallel with current events while still finalising the proofs for his fourth biographical volume. Likewise, in the Munich debate on 5 October 1938, some of his literary fans among the Honourable Members must have got their first indication that the *History* was now under way: 'In my holiday I thought it was a chance to study the reign of King Ethelred the Unready.' And he duly quoted the passage from *The Anglo-Saxon Chronicle* that appears in Chapter 8 of Volume One, 'The Saxon Dusk'.

Such parallels, of course, can often be supplied by historians who have their own agenda. When Churchill looked back on the war in his world broadcast on 13 May 1945, he could duly expatiate on Britain's wonderful historical record in holding out – 'from time to time all alone', of course – 'against a Continental tyrant or dictator', whether in the era of the Spanish Armada or of Louis XIV, whether under Marlborough or against Napoleon. In retrospect, this paradigm is so obvious as to seem rather trite. Rather more impressive, perhaps, is what Churchill said at the time of the climacterics that he perceived, indicating a remarkable degree of self-consciousness about the historical significance of the role that he called upon his people to play.

On 11 September 1940 the prime minister used a BBC broadcast to put the moment into context. Because it would mark the closing of the window for a possible German invasion, 'we must regard the next week or so as a very important period in our history'. He invoked Drake; he invoked Nelson. 'We have read all about this in the history books,' he continued; 'but what is happening now is on a far greater scale and of far more consequence to the life and future of the world and its civilization than these brave old days of the past.' This was not nostalgic or backward-looking in its appeal to the past, but instead projected a sense of history into the present. 'These are not dark days: these are great days – the greatest days our country has ever lived,' he later told the boys at Harrow School on 29 October 1941, still with precious little to celebrate beyond survival.

When Churchill implored others to keep the faith, it was because he himself had faith. It was an appeal couched less in religious terms, beyond a few conventional platitudes, than in terms of secular judgementalism, with his own countrymen cast in a privileged role that can be called virtually Miltonian. Thus on 7 November 1941 he offered 'that crown of honour to those who have endured and never failed which history will accord to them for having set an example to the whole human race'. Even retrospectively, Churchill rarely admitted to his own doubts in public – perhaps never more than in the broadcast of 10 May

1942, commemorating the anniversary of his appointment as prime minister two years previously. 'He would have been a bold man, however, who in those days would have put down in black and white exactly how we were going to win,' he now confessed. 'But, as has happened before in our island history, by remaining steadfast and unyielding – stubborn, if you will – against a Continental tyrant, we reached the moment when that tyrant made a fatal blunder.' He meant that Hitler had invaded Russia – an adventitious stroke of luck, perhaps.

Or more than luck? For the dice were loaded in this great contest, with a sense of patriotism that imported too some of Milton's providentialism. 'We have much to be thankful for,' Churchill reflected in a speech to the Commons on 31 October 1942. 'I sometimes have a feeling, in fact, I have it very strongly, a feeling of interference. I want to stress that. I have a feeling sometimes that some guiding hand has interfered. I have the feeling that we have a guardian because we serve a great cause, and that we shall have that guardian so long as we serve that cause faithfully.'

Churchill was often at his best, not in fulsomely celebrating victory, but in frankly acknowledging setbacks. 'It is a British and Imperial defeat,' he starkly admitted in his broadcast on 15 February 1942, after the fall of Singapore. 'But I am sure even in this dark hour that "criminal madness" will be the verdict which history will pronounce upon the authors of Japanese aggression, after the events of 1942 and 1943 have been inscribed upon its sombre pages.' This, then, was the final court of judgement, which Churchill often sought to anticipate. In his parliamentary tribute on 12 November 1940, marking Neville Chamberlain's death, the prime minister chose to display magnanimity about a man from whom he had so sharply differed in the past. He speculated on the verdict of some 'future generation of English-speaking folks – for that is the tribunal to which we appeal'. In a sense, this was always Churchill's higher tribunal, with the House of Commons as its antechamber. He enumerated examples of military progress to the Commons on 9 September 1941, with the words: 'I cannot help feeling that these are achievements which, whatever the future may contain, will earn the respect of history and deserve the approval of the House.'

This was partly a politician's resort to inflated rhetoric. It was also the perspective of a whiggish historian who was not afraid to judge one era by subsequent standards or to raid the historical locker for timeless examples. In the House of Commons on 27 February 1941, the issue was precedents for Members to retain their seats while serving in state office, and Churchill's view was accordingly clear: 'it was so in the Marlborough wars, it was so under Lord Chatham, it was so in the wars against Napoleon'. Case closed. Similarly in the House on 21 October 1941: 'These high-sounding familiar phrases like "Habeas Corpus", "petitioners' right", "charges made which are known to the law", and "trial by jury" – all these are part of what we are fighting to preserve.'

He knew, of course, that such talk had an appeal that might go well beyond Westminster precedent-hunting, and cross the Atlantic. In a pre-war speech, on 9 May 1938, just as the author was finally turning his attention to his long-promised *History*, he said: 'Have we not an ideology – if we must use this ugly word – of our own in freedom, in a liberal constitution, in democratic and Parliamentary government, in Magna Charta and the Petition of Right?' And he was already talking of ideals that 'stir the pulses of the English-speaking peoples in every quarter of the globe'. He pitched the same message directly to an American radio audience on 16 October 1938: 'If ever there was a time when men and women who cherish the ideals of the founders of the British and American Constitutions should take earnest counsel with one another, this time is now.'

These pre-war speeches were reprinted in 1941 in *Blood, Sweat and Tears*, the American edition of the speeches. The preface, issued over Randolph Churchill's name, said that 'I have not altered even a phrase on the grounds of political expediency.' Although there had been excisions, little of substance needed alteration. 'We are confronted with another theme,' Churchill had intoned in this same radio broadcast on 16 October 1938. 'It is not a new theme; it leaps out upon us from the Dark Ages – racial persecution, religious intolerance, deprivation of free speech, the conception of the citizen as a mere soulless fraction of the state.' The section of his *History* that he was currently dictating dealt with this early period, reinforced in its scepticism about the Anglo-Saxons as bringers of freedom by current examples of Nazi propaganda. 'We are left in no doubt where American conviction and sympathies lie: but will you wait until British freedom and independence have succumbed, and then take up the cause when it is three-quarters ruined, yourselves alone?' asked the author, in a passionate entreaty, sketching a nightmare scenario if the Nazi system triumphed. 'Let that not be the epitaph of the English-speaking peoples,' he had said in 1938; and in essentials, his message was still apt enough to be worthy of reiteration in 1941.

What were Churchill's war aims? And were these aims articulated in terms that he could reasonably expect Americans to accept? Both in private and in public he was often ready to give a short answer to the first question, as he did in Glasgow on 17 January 1941: 'My one aim is to extirpate Hitlerism from Europe. The question is such a simple one.' Here is a patriotic imperative to defend the sceptred isle, of course; but not to stand alone by choice, rather by representing a wider cause. In 1940 he exhorted his countrymen to see their noble task accordingly. 'Two or three years are not a long time, even in our short, precarious lives,' he told the House of Commons on 20 August. 'They are nothing in the history of the nation, and when we are doing the finest thing in the world, and have the honour to be the sole champion of the liberties of all Europe, we must not grudge these years or weary as we toil and struggle through them.'

Those European countries threatened by Hitler had good reasons to unite against German aggression. For many of them, of course, this was for the second time within thirty years. Churchill often claimed not to talk about hating the Germans but about fighting the Nazis. It was certainly a prudent way to talk, given that he remembered the problems posed during World War I by the presence of a large ethnic-German element among American citizens. But he did not always remember.

Churchill's vocabulary during this war contained more than a trace residue from the invective of the previous war. Thus in his public speeches there are persistent references to 'the might and fury of the Huns' in Greece (9 April 1941); to 'the ruthless and highly mechanized Hun' in the Balkans and to 'seventy million malignant Huns – some of whom are curable and others killable' (27 April 1941). It could be said that the ferocity of this language simply identified and matched the deeds of the Nazi invaders; and Churchill, as 'the one whose head should be cut off if we do not win the war', warned Parliament accordingly to expect 'an even more unpleasant fate at the hands of the triumphant Hun' (7 May 1941). Conversely, when Russia too suffered invasion, he recalled that 'the Royal Air Force beat the Hun raiders out of the daylight air' and spoke contemptuously of 'the dull, drilled, docile, brutish masses of the Hun soldiery' (22 June 1941). In a Bastille Day message to the Free French Churchill talked of 'the intrigues and infiltrations of the Huns' (14 July 1941), in an echo of language that both these Allies had long used against the common foe.

None of this, it is safe to say, would have shocked the European peoples concerned, common victims of German aggression. But it would be a mistake to suppose that the entry of the United States into the war after the attack on Pearl Harbor on 7 December 1941 led Churchill to clean up his Old World vocabulary. Indeed it was in the Canadian House of Commons on 30 December 1941 that he now claimed: 'The tide has turned against the Hun.' Most striking of all, it was in an address to the United States Congress on 19 May 1943 that Churchill snarled that the German surrender in North Africa 'once again proved the truth of the saying, "The Hun is always either at your throat or your feet" . . .'

From the moment when Britain declared war, Churchill can be found stating the issues at stake in their broadest terms. On 3 September 1939 he told the House of Commons: 'We are fighting to save the whole world from the pestilence of Nazi tyranny and in defence of all that is most sacred to man.' On 12 October he warned his listeners on the BBC: 'If we are conquered, all will be enslaved, and the United States will be left single-handed to guard the rights of man.' In the meantime, however, it was the British Empire that was fighting – fighting alone by the summer of 1940 – and that very fact stood as one obstacle to participation by the United States. It was not only 'isolationists' (let alone Marxists) who harboured deep suspicions of fighting, for a second time, in an imperialist war, to perpetuate an institution to which good Americans had both principled and practical objections. The British Empire did not measure up to their ideals of self-government; and its system of imperial preference offended American economic ideas and interests alike.

Churchill, as we have seen, had never believed in imperial preference. But in October 1940 he became leader of the Conservative Party after Neville Chamberlain's resignation through mortal illness. Not only was it a party that still professed a commitment to the old Chamberlainite cause but, in May 1940, some of Churchill's personal ministerial appointments had reinforced the ranks of the economic imperialists. For Leo Amery at the India Office or Lord Beaverbrook at the Ministry of Aircraft Production, imperial preference remained a political cause to which they were fervently committed. In the Dominions too, in varying degrees, there was support for the Ottawa Agreements of 1932, which had helped the Commonwealth weather the world economic crisis. As prime minister, then, Churchill was politically bound to maintain imperial preference – and honour-bound, as a patriot, to defend it against American dictation.

On being elected as Conservative leader, he gave his credo on 9 October 1940. In effect, he had been foisted on the party by the fact that he had become prime minister of a coalition government that remained reliant on Conservative support. He could hardly claim to have been a party loyalist, having spent half of his long political career outside its ranks; but he had some grounds for claiming consistency over the course of forty years: 'I have always faithfully served two public causes which I think stand supreme – the maintenance of the enduring greatness of Britain and her Empire and the historical continuity of our Island life.' At that time, especially with airmen from the Commonwealth among those who had recently won the Battle of Britain, this otherwise rather thin political credo passed muster.

In Churchill's conception of the grand strategy of the war, Britain depended crucially on two successive measures of reinforcement. In 1940 it was the support of the Empire that was indispensable to survival; and from 1941 it was the support of the United States that made victory possible. Hitler's own decision to go to war with Stalin was also hugely important in its consequences, but in ways that Churchill himself could not seriously influence. His own task was to reconcile the imperialist dimension with the American dimension, as best he could. It was a political problem peculiarly susceptible to his own gifts and his own experience, not least as the author of his (unpublished) *History of the English-Speaking Peoples*.

Churchill now spoke on this theme with a new consistency. 'Some foreigners mock at the British Empire because there are no parchment bonds or hard steel shackles which compel its united action,' he had told the Canada Club on 20 April 1939. The advocates of imperial federation had, of course, long said as much, just as the true believers in imperial preference had insisted on the necessity of economic incentives to hold the Empire together. Two years later, on 12 April 1941, speaking in honour of Robert Menzies, Australian prime minister at the outbreak of war, Churchill drew attention to the 'marvellous fact' of the aid given to Britain by Australia and New Zealand: 'No law, no constitution, no bond or treaty pledges them to spend a shilling or pledge a man.' On 2 June 1941, with special reference to Canadian financial assistance, Churchill commented: 'To Nazi tyrants and gangsters it must seem strange that Canada, free from all compulsion and pressure, so many thousands of miles away, should hasten forward into the van of the battle against the evil forces of the world.'

There were other allusions in the same timbre. It was a sort of idealistic appeal to shared sentiments that had often infused the terminology of a 'commonwealth of nations', from W. E. Forster to Ramsay Muir. Yet Churchill showed little cognisance of this tradition. Instead, he duly marvelled at free consent, nobly given by self-governing communities, implicitly referring only to the Dominions, while himself obdurately opting for the term 'Empire', conceding on this usage only when under pressure. Thus in a world broadcast on 29 November 1942, he retold the epic story of 1940: 'That wonderful association of States and races spread all over the globe called the British Empire – or British Commonwealth if you will; I do not quarrel about it – and above all, our small Island, stood in the gap alone in the deadly hour.'

Churchill repeatedly called this a 'miracle'. But it was not one that came to him as a surprise: rather as a vindication of what he had always taken for granted about the Empire. In a speech to the Commons on 8 June 1943, the moral was again drawn from the experience of 1940. 'Then, surely, was the moment for the Empire to break up,' he claimed rhetorically, only to emphasise that the opposite proved to be true, and that 'the bonds which unite us, though supple as elastic, are stronger than the tensest steel'. And just a few weeks later, on 30 June 1943, he put his point with a more complacent sense of self-congratulation: 'Alone in history, the British people, taught by the lessons they had learned in the past, have found the means to attach to the Motherland vast self-governing Dominions upon whom there rests no obligation, other than that of sentiment and tradition, to plunge into war at the side of the Motherland.'

This Empire, then, had no institutional structure, neither steel nor parchment to bind it. It apparently relied neither on treaties nor ties of material interest – no mention of preferential tariffs on this elevated plane. This sort of Churchillian rhetoric was the despair of those true believers who thought themselves the real imperialists. They suspected him of selling the pass in 1941 when he signed up too eagerly to the conditions that the United States imposed in offering lend-lease, essentially to dismantle preferential tariffs. True, Churchill had insisted on qualifications in the small print, but his heart was not in this fight, so long as the Americans were not seen to be telling the Empire what to do. But, as Amery drily commented when Churchill effusively thanked him for fulsome greetings on his seventieth birthday in November 1944: 'Naturally I did not emphasise the fundamental differences between our two conceptions of Empire and its consequential economics, which have divided us all our lives.'[31]

Churchill's was an Empire of the imagination. His insistence on using the term 'British Empire' was no passing foible. It was historic, which naturally appealed to him, as politician and author alike. It was nostalgic, which reflected the fact that the prime minister was a man in his late sixties who had himself fought in distant imperial wars. It was atavistic, as seen in his campaign against Indian self-government ten years previously, reflexes spasmodically reasserted in wartime (again to Amery's exasperation). Forced to swallow the bitter compromises forced upon him by Britain's weakness in the early years of the war, Churchill notoriously responded to the Allied victories in North Africa with his declaration at the Mansion House in London on 9 November 1942: 'I have not become the King's First Minister in order to preside over the liquidation of the British Empire.'

This was the part of the speech that affronted American opinion. Yet, within the same paragraph, Churchill had gone on to declare that he was 'proud to be a member of that vast commonwealth and society of nations and communities' and to conclude by saying that victory would be 'a new bond between the English-speaking peoples and a new hope for the whole world'. Though on this occasion its flourishes had given offence, Churchill's rhetoric was equally adapted to conciliating the English-speaking peoples – or so he believed. Its essentially emotional register was the common theme. And this can surely be heard in perhaps his most fervent and self-conscious affirmation of the 'Spirit of the Empire' in a parliamentary debate on 21 April 1944. 'You must look very deep into the heart of man, and then you will not find the answer unless you look with the eye of the spirit,' he enjoined. 'Then it is that you learn that human beings are not dominated by material things, but by ideas for which they are willing to give their lives or their life's work.'

Churchill was initially disappointed in his anticipations of American support. Looking with the eye of the spirit, he naively expected another 'miracle', for which he had all the suitable rhetoric ready and waiting. 'During the last year we have gained by our bearing and conduct a potent hold over the sentiments of the people of the United States,' he assured listeners to the BBC on 27 April 1941, as though the exemplary effect would, as with the Dominions, be sufficient to turn the situation. Moreover, with an air that can be called patriarchal or patronising, he added that 'in the long run – believe me, for I know – the action of the United States will be dictated, not by methodical calculations of profit and loss, but by moral sentiment, and by that gleaming flash of resolve which lifts the hearts of men and nations, and springs from the spiritual foundations of human life itself'.

Readers of his *History* would recognise such insubstantial gleams. Churchill unwarily claimed in a broadcast to the United States on 16 June 1941, invoking his ancestry, that 'I hold a latchkey to American hearts.' But it would not turn in the lock. For eighteen months he was left waiting for an American commitment that, time and again, he hailed prematurely. His agreement with Roosevelt, swapping decrepit American warships for bases on British territories, was portentously saluted in the Commons on 20 August 1940: 'Undoubtedly this process means that these two great organizations of the English-speaking democracies, the British Empire and the United States, will have to be somewhat mixed up together in some of their affairs for mutual and general advantage.' Persistently talking up this process left many people mixed up.

In the winter of 1940–41, the inception of lend-lease was indeed a boon. Churchill naturally made the most of it in his first broadcast for five months, on 9 February 1941. 'And all the time,' he warned Hitler as well as his listeners, 'masters of the sea and air, the British Empire – nay, in a certain sense, the whole English-speaking world – will be on his track, bearing with them the swords of justice.' On 12 March, with lend-lease now a reality, it was duly hailed as 'a new Magna Carta'. And on 7 May the prime minister told the House of Commons that 'we are no longer a small island lost in the Northern mists, but around us gather in proud array all the free nations of the British Empire, and this time from across the Atlantic Ocean the mighty Republic of the United States proclaims itself on our side, or at our side, or, at any rate, near our side'.

But exactly how near? Churchill's hopes that his first wartime meeting with Roosevelt in Placentia Bay, Newfoundland, would be the prelude to an American declaration of war were to be disappointed, and he had to make do with a common declaration of peace aims. Again, in hailing the resulting 'Atlantic Charter' in a broadcast on 24 August 1941, Churchill stretched the envelope as far as he decently could in speaking of 'these two major groupings of the human family: the British Empire and the United States, who, fortunately for the progress of mankind, happen to speak the same language, and very largely think the same thoughts, or anyhow think a lot of the same thoughts.' It was a moment for 'the pages of history', and one marked by self-conscious historical resonance, at least for the author of his own *History*. 'We sang the hymn founded on the psalm which John Hampden's soldiers sang when they bore his body to the grave,' Churchill revealed, and in his peroration painted an evocative picture of his sea journey home: 'We overtook one of the convoys which carry the munitions and supplies of the New World to sustain the champions of freedom in the Old.'

The Atlantic Charter certainly signalled a closer Anglo-American relationship. It was difficult to see how the United States could plan for a victorious peace without further participation in a victorious war. It was a formal document and, as such, contained commitments that could not subsequently be repudiated (though Churchill tried to do so). Liberal critics in the United States assumed that the reactionary old man had difficulty in swallowing the Charter's social commitments, as a sort of international New Deal. In fact, throughout the war, Churchill was quite happy to rediscover and rehabilitate his own record in social reform.

Where the Charter gave real trouble was, as usual, over the British Empire. And even here, Churchill faced down as best he could domestic criticisms, voiced by the likes of Amery and Beaverbrook, that imperial preference had (again, as usual) been surrendered. Instead, it was the Charter's assertion of 'the right of all peoples to choose the form of government under which they will live' that provided most embarrassment, over India and also Africa. Churchill's argument, that the aspiration to see 'self-government restored' could not apply to subject peoples who had never had such a right, did more to undermine his own reputation than it did to blunt the impact of the document that he had unwarily signed.[32] There was thus some bluster in his later remarks, at the London Guildhall on 30 June 1943, about the relationship between the Empire and the United States: 'If they walk, or if need be march, together in harmony and in accordance with the moral and political conceptions to which the English-speaking peoples have given birth, and which are frequently referred to in the Atlantic Charter, all will be well.'

This was the theme of many of Churchill's paeans to the Anglo-American alliance. A few days after Pearl Harbor had finally done the trick, Churchill spoke on 11 December 1941, in the Commons: 'Our foes are bound by the consequences of their ambitions and of their crimes to seek implacably the destruction of the English-speaking world and all it stands for, which is the supreme barrier against their designs.' A month later, after his warm reception in both the United States Congress and the Canadian House of Commons, he spoke in Bermuda on 15 January 1942, reaffirming that the English-speaking peoples were fighting for 'the strong principles inculcated in the birth of the English parliamentary system and by the American revolutionary war, by Hampden and by Washington . . .' The great Whig relay race of liberty was obviously in his mind. 'We in this Island for a long time were alone, holding aloft the torch,' he claimed, back at Westminster, on 27 January 1942. 'We are no longer alone now.'

In 1940 there had been an austerity in Churchill's rhetoric. His people were fighting alone, as he kept telling them; they were living through great days; but he offered them nothing but blood and toil and tears and sweat – an offer that apparently went down so well with the public that he kept repeating it, his personal popularity undented. The British reverses of 1942, especially the fall of Singapore in February and of Tobruk in June, were less easy to extenuate: less easy for him to bear and less easy, after two years, for his fellow citizens to forgive. The victory at El Alamein between 23 October and 4 November 1942 was thus a personal turning point, and again he caught the mood, in his speech on 10 November, in deliberately not claiming that this was the end for the Germans: 'It is not even the beginning of the end. But perhaps it is the end of the beginning.' With further Anglo-American victories in North Africa, however, a note of triumphalism crept in, almost hubristic in its heady expectations.

It was on his visit to the United States in May 1943 that Churchill began investing the Anglo-American theme with overtly political content. Privately, he broached an extraordinary proposal for common citizenship, without evoking much response from wary American officials. In public he spoke in bland and general terms in his speech to a joint session of Congress on 19 May 1943: 'The experiences of a long life and the promptings of my blood have wrought in me the conviction that there is nothing more important for the future of the world than the fraternal association of our two peoples in righteous work both in war and peace.' There was the usual applause for the usual platitudes.

But Churchill went further in his public plea for closer links on his next transatlantic visit later in the same year. In accepting an honorary degree at Harvard on 6 September 1943, he said that 'you will find in the British Commonwealth and Empire good comrades to whom you are united by other ties besides those of State policy and public need. To a large extent, they are the ties of blood and history.' As usual, it was tempting to allude to his own family ancestry at this point, but his emphasis remained cultural and institutional rather than racial. 'Law, language, literature – these are considerable facts,' he maintained, and suggested building upon them. He claimed, in similar terms to those he had already used in the House of Commons a few months previously (11 February 1943), that Bismarck had identified their common language as 'the most potent factor in human society at the end of the nineteenth century'. At Harvard he deliberately went further: 'The gift of a common tongue is a priceless inheritance, and it may well some day become the foundation of a common citizenship.'

Here Churchill overplayed his hand. Not only was the Roosevelt administration not interested but the press across the United States reflected public opinion in scorning a suggestion more likely to stir up old suspicions of British motives than to sustain the wartime Alliance. The incident exposed alike the tight constraints on British policy, the limitations on Churchill's powers of persuasion and, yet again, his own exaggeration of the potency of sentimental appeals to the English-speaking peoples. This was a world conflict, won in the end by both Russian and American might on the battlefield. Both of these super-powers were driven by their own imperatives, not least the United States in reaching out for a new post-war role.

Churchill entertained his own expectations, his own hopes, his own illusions. On 14 May 1943, when making a broadcast to Britain during his visit to the United States, he had sounded a confident note: 'These are great days,' he reiterated, now in a context of rejoicing; 'they are like the days in Lord Chatham's time, of which it was said you had to get up early in the morning not to miss some news of victory.' As in the *History*, Chatham was his personal benchmark as war leader.

But victory came tinged with tragedy as well as triumph for

Churchill. As he privately said more than once, it was at the Big Three conference in Teheran at the end of 1943 that he suddenly realised what a small country Britain was, alongside the American elephant or the Russian bear. And when he attended the next Big Three summit at Yalta in February 1945, he was awkwardly aware of his diminished status in the eyes of Roosevelt, who seemed to have become bored with this inveterate British imperialist, now aged seventy. In one session, when a frustrated Churchill misunderstood the course of a discussion of international trusteeship, and imagined the British Empire threatened, there was an extraordinary incident. The notes made by the US State Department official, charged with taking the official minutes, record the old man's response, as he sat mumbling in his chair: 'Never, Never, Never.' None of those present, so puzzled at the time, would have had the opportunity of reading the thirteenth chapter in Volume Three of the *History of the English-Speaking Peoples*, published in 1957 but written in 1939. Its highlight was a quotation from Chatham's last speech in the House of Lords in 1778, declaiming that, if he were an American, 'I never would lay down my arms – never, never, never.'[33]

The Author as Celebrity, 1945–65

'I can't write like that now.'

Churchill to his doctor, 1955

At the end of World War II, Winston Churchill was probably the most famous person in the world. Not only had his name alone achieved unusually wide recognition, his image had become as iconic as that of Mohandas Gandhi or Charlie Chaplin. Churchill had a reputation for wearing funny hats and for dressing up in the many uniforms to which he had some claim, going back to that of a lieutenant in the 4th Hussars (which was now rather a tight fit). His liking for cigars had become his trademark and a gift for the cartoonists, as he knew well; and he would rarely show himself in public without one. His fondness for champagne and brandy became legendary. He viewed wartime restrictions on consumption with distaste – but from a privileged distance. 'Personally I prefer to make my number by increased effort rather than by self-denial,' he once told Jock Colville.[1] Unlike other Britons, he had the choice and was spared the rigours of rationing; yet it is remarkable how little criticism his lifestyle attracted. The Indian joke was that it cost a fortune to keep Gandhi in poverty; the British seem to have winked at the cost of keeping Winston in luxury.

Among world political leaders, Churchill now had a lonely eminence, rivalled only by Stalin. The date 12 April 1945 had seen the death of President Roosevelt at sixty-two, already ailing at Yalta two months previously. Churchill paid a rather laboured tribute in the House of Commons on 17 April, too obviously striving for effect in saluting their wartime comradeship, and concluding that 'in Franklin

Roosevelt there died the greatest American friend we have ever known, and the greatest champion of freedom who has ever brought help and comfort from the new world to the old'. Before the end of the month, the humiliating end of Benito Mussolini at the age of sixty-one and then the suicide of Adolf Hitler, ten days after his fifty-sixth birthday in his bunker in devastated Berlin, signalled the end of the war in Europe. Churchill had celebrated his seventieth birthday on 30 November 1944, in style and in office; he did not see why he should not seek to follow victory in war with his own electoral victory, just as Lloyd George had done in 1918; and again like Lloyd George, he wanted to perpetuate a wartime Coalition government into the peace. But there the parallels suddenly failed. The Labour Party decided to leave Churchill's coalition after VE-Day and to seek power themselves, under Attlee's leadership, in the General Election of July 1945.

Around the world, it was taken for granted that the great Churchill would nonetheless remain prime minister. Even in Britain, many people misread the signs, although they were clearly there to be read by those who gave credence to opinion polls, which had shown the Conservative Party consistently behind Labour in a projected postwar election. In Gallup's standard questions in February 1945, 85 per cent said they were satisfied with Churchill as prime minister – but Labour was 20 per cent ahead of the Conservatives in voting intentions. In April no fewer than 91 per cent claimed to be satisfied with Churchill, but Labour's lead was hardly dented. And in May, when the coalition broke up, Churchill's final satisfaction-rating as prime minister was an impressive 83 per cent. But there was still a big Labour lead over the Conservatives of 12 per cent, and although this was narrowed to 8 per cent in the General Election in July, this was enough to give Labour a landslide victory. Churchill was rejected along with the tired and discredited Conservative Party, which he had so often denounced before 1940, but which he now led himself. Moreover, he intended to go on leading it, at least in his spare time, through the five years of the forthcoming parliament.

If he had remained prime minister in 1945, Churchill's retirement from his profession as an author might have been final. In that case, his *History of the English-Speaking Peoples* might have become his final published book. After all, the text had long since been submitted to Cassells, and, in the agreement brokered by Bracken in 1940, accepted by them subject to the provision of adequate coverage up to 1914. Much had changed meanwhile. At the end of 1939 the firm had been given a manuscript that it regarded as unpublishable from an established author whose work now seemed past its best. By the end of the war, however, Cassells found themselves in a wonderful position to capitalise upon becoming the famous war leader's British publisher. They came to realise that their ownership of the copyright of the *History* had not only become hugely more valuable in itself but could also be played as a trump card in negotiations about Churchill's war memoirs.

Whatever its intrinsic flaws, the value of the unpublished *History* grew along with its author's fame. Already in July 1940, G. M. Young, who knew the manuscript better than anyone, suggested raiding it for passages that might now be published with telling effect. 'It would be your counterblast to *Mein Kampf*, and honestly I believe it would sweep the world,' he wrote to the prime minister.[2] The plan died, if only because the total copyright had been granted to the publishers. Indeed in November 1939, under a tripartite agreement, Cassells had sold the North American rights for the *History* to Dodd, Mead and Company in New York, and to McClelland and Stewart in Toronto, firms with whom Churchill had had no previous dealings. In New York, Frank Dodd became increasingly restive about the restraints on his right to publish the *History* – 'a very fine piece of work, in our opinion', so he assured the British Embassy in Washington in July 1941, adding: 'this would seem to be the psychological moment to publish this work'.[3] The problem was that Dodd could not publish until after Lord Camrose's Amalgamated Press, which had long held the serialisation rights, had brought out their weekly parts in Britain;

and this was prevented by the wartime paper shortage. Dodd also tried to enlist the help of the Ministry of Information; but the new minister, appointed in July 1941, was Brendan Bracken, who had his own advice for his master. Cassells and the prime minister's office accordingly closed ranks in preventing publication in New York ahead of London.

All the while, the market was rising. Every time that the British prime minister talked about the English-speaking peoples in his speeches, the value of Cassells' proofs appreciated. This was no longer a question of literary judgement but of celebrity publishing. It was now worth simply paying the going rate for the right to use Churchill's name. In 1943 Bracken secured an offer from the film producer Alexander Korda, with whom Churchill had been profitably associated in the mid-1930s, of £20,000 for the film rights of *Marlborough*; and although Korda was bested in bidding that eventually reached £50,000, he came back early in 1944 with another offer at that level, this time for the film rights of the *History*. These two large sums, both of them windfalls that escaped income taxes, helped transform Churchill's finances and prospects. The combined total at today's values would be over three million pounds.

The problem with this deal, however, was that Cassells still owned the entire copyright of the *History*. True, they could not sell film rights to Korda without Churchill's consent; but they could block any sale. In asking Cassells to release the film rights in 1944, Churchill had his own bargaining counter: the right to publish any war memoirs that he chose to write, on which he now offered Cassells first refusal. But this raised another problem. For such memoirs, of course, would constitute a new book; and Churchill had, during his personal 1938 financial crisis, already signed up for his next book not with Cassells but with Harraps, for a history of Europe since the Russian Revolution. Worse still, when Churchill's backlist with Thornton Butterworth, whose firm had gone into liquidation in 1941, had been acquired by Macmillans, they too had acquired rights to the author's future works. In manoeuvres executed at arm's length, in the interstices of such developments as the D-Day landings and the preparations for the second Quebec conference in 1944, the prime minister's reputation was a further card to play. Macmillans were squared first; the presence of Harold Macmillan in the government would have made public conflict unthinkable. Harraps finally capitulated, saying in September 1944 that 'it is distasteful to us, whether we are in the right or not, to litigate the matter with a man to whom every one of us is so much indebted'.[4]

No other author, it is safe to say, could have exacted the terms that the author of victory was now granted. In a manner that affronted the concept of a contract as a binding two-sided agreement, Churchill was able to walk away from commitments that he had previously given while pocketing all the proceeds himself, tax-free. Cassells thus became Churchill's post-war publishers, whether for the *History* or for possible war memoirs (if he chose to write them). In an exchange of letters in late November 1944, they backed down on requiring further chapters to bring the *History* down to 1914 and instead settled for the old promise of an epilogue of up to 10,000 words. As well as their option on the memoirs, they secured an agreement that the *History* could in any case be published six months after Churchill ceased to serve as prime minister. As it turned out, since Churchill left office at the end of July 1945, that meant publication was envisaged for some date in 1946, subject to continuing paper shortages. Throughout 1945, this was the agreed plan. The old proofs were exhumed accordingly. 'I am making slow progress,' Churchill confided to his friend Lord Camrose on 17 October 1945.[5]

Camrose had an interest since, as owner of the Amalgamated Press, he possessed the serialisation rights of the *History*. Moreover, through the *Daily Telegraph*, of which he had been sole proprietor since 1937, he had an even greater interest in acquiring serialisation rights on possible war memoirs. But Churchill could not start work on such a book (as distinct from tidying up the *History*) without emerging from his tax-free retirement as an author. The current level of personal taxation, with a top marginal rate still at 97.5 per cent, was thus one reason for Churchill's reluctance to embark on any new project. 'I'm not going to work when they take nineteen and six out of every pound I earn,' he grumbled to his doctor, Lord Moran, in August 1945.[6]

Camrose's friendly assistance to Churchill was now to prove important in two respects. One was in finding a way of enhancing his net income, if he resumed authorship, by minimising his tax liability. This was ultimately achieved through the creation of a nominally independent Literary Trust to hold Churchill's war papers, rights to which were (after complex transatlantic negotiations) sold for a large capital sum, which escaped taxation. This allowed for relatively modest payments to be made from the Trust to the author, as taxable income, for his work in composing the volumes that were published as *The Second World War*, based chiefly on his extensive papers as prime minister (as he was careful to state in the preface).

Camrose's other initiative eased Churchill's finances by removing the major source of strain upon them. It was the maintenance of Chartwell that had driven the author's schedule during the interwar years, prompting his relentless quest for a succession of literary projects. Fulfilling these contracts had weighed all too onerously on a backbench MP in his sixties; a reversion to this punishing regime could hardly have been contemplated by a man in his seventies who was Leader of His Majesty's Opposition and still aspired to serve as prime minister again. When Chartwell was reoccupied by the Churchills in August 1945, its dilapidated state was depressing. Yet it seemed shocking that a man hailed as the saviour of his country should now contemplate selling his beloved home, and the notion of acquiring Chartwell for the nation took root in Camrose's mind.

By 1946 Camrose accordingly put together a consortium of benefactors, in effect to buy Chartwell. They confidentially subscribed £50,000 to fund the acquisition of the estate and £35,000 to endow its maintenance. On this basis, Chartwell was sold by Churchill to the independent charity, the National Trust, giving him not only the immediate proceeds of the sale but also the prospect of residence, free of basic upkeep, during his lifetime. Churchill was thus enabled to acquire much adjacent land and to expand the farming activities at Chartwell, managed for several years by his new son-in-law, Christopher Soames. The net result was that Chartwell became no longer a perpetual headache but a joy, which Clementine too came round to appreciating once it ceased to threaten their finances. Moreover, it remained Winston's word factory.

What, then, of his *History of the English-Speaking Peoples*? For Cassells, this was their bird in the hand, while their option on any possible memoirs was one of many birds in this author's bush. Until the Flowers, father and son, knew that they would definitely have the projected volumes of *The Second World War* to publish, their focus was on publishing the book that they already had in proof. Likewise, until Churchill knew that it would be profitable for him to resume his profession as author, the only form of writing in which he could meanwhile engage was the revision of the *History*.

It was a project now trapped in a fiscal timewarp. Everyone agreed that Cassells had acquired the total copyright under the 1933 contract. Conversely, it had always been the plan that their payment of £20,000 to the author, as a capital transaction, should not incur liability to income tax. Churchill therefore owed nothing to the Inland Revenue for the amounts paid in 1940–41, and although some documents in his archive loosely suggest that tax had been paid, the real point was that none had been due. There seems to have been a tacit understanding with the Inland Revenue by 1944 that, even though £1,000 had been withheld by Cassells, this final payment too would escape income tax since the work in completing the contract was deemed residual. This was evidently a delicate matter and, in late November 1945, Kathleen Hill was to remind her employer that the manager at Lloyds Bank, long responsible for paying Churchill's income taxes, 'particularly does not want to re-open the matter with the Revenue authorities'.[7] So long as some discretion was observed, then, the entire proceeds from Cassells would escape income taxes. Guarded by the legal advice that he received in 1944–45, but still preoccupied with affairs of state, Churchill examined the practicalities of publishing the *History*.

As usual, Brendan Bracken was at hand. Just after Churchill's return from the Big Three meeting at Yalta in February 1945, the prewar proofs had been retrieved and Bracken (still the Minister of Information) sent them to Denis Brogan, Professor of Political Science at Cambridge. 'He certainly knows more about American history than any other Englishman and he has written a number of very impressive books,' Bracken reported to Churchill on 9 March. 'I don't think we could have found a better man.' This judgement rings true (though it was Brogan's mixed Scots and Irish background that was surely one of the reasons for his empathy with American political culture). When he later met Churchill, they got on well: raconteurs who both enjoyed a drink, thought history should be painted with a broad brush, but equally relished its adornment with personal detail and quirky snippets of incidental information. Bracken had secured Brogan's services for £1,000 – 'I can pay more,' Churchill commented – and in the end, Cassells paid it direct to Brogan. The fee was equal to the amount withheld by the publishers under the contract; it was accordingly tax-free and thus worth as much as the professor's annual salary. He happily took on this unusual commission, which he thought would take a year.[8]

Brogan began work revising the proofs at a time when the general assumption was that Churchill would win the post-war election. Thus the *History* would become the prime minister's swansong as an author, with publication to be achieved under Brogan's supervision. Such assumptions, of course, did not outlast the summer of 1945. By October, Brogan found himself discussing the proofs in detail with the new Leader of the Opposition, who explained that, 'after a six years' interval', he was now perusing them himself 'and the story comes back to me'. Not only did the author enjoy re-reading himself: he started asking for advice on which other historians he might read. Churchill wanted Cassells to publish the work in three volumes and was relieved to hear that Brogan thought that the first two, going up to the accession of George III in 1760, were 'practically fit for issue'.[9] It was in its coverage of the subsequent period that the 1939 text of the *History* was manifestly deficient, as Brogan quickly realised.

At the end of October, Churchill had good news to report. He had met Sir Newman Flower; Cassells would not begin publication before the end of 1946, even in serial form; there was thus more time to play with (or work against); and a terminal date of 1874 – Churchill's birth date – would now be acceptable. Brogan was meanwhile working through the earlier period, aided by his wife, herself an archaeologist, and also by the medieval historian, V. H. Galbraith. Here minor amendments were gracefully accepted by Churchill, who thought that the narrative read well up to the end of the fourteenth century and was also pleased with his treatment of the Tudors and Stuarts. It was the eighteenth century that continued to present the unresolved problem. 'I have taken a great dislike to the English political and public life under the first three Georges,' Churchill told Brogan in December. 'We must mark it with deep aversion and censure, – corruption, complacency, iron class rule, Tory follies and Whig caste prejudices and intrigues.'[10] This judgemental exercise was hardly the task for which an academic historian like Brogan had signed up; but he knew better than to demur, confident that it was all capable of resolution over another long lunch at Chartwell.

Brogan worked hard for his fee. One section of his detailed comments, eighteen typed pages on the eighteenth century, shows his attentiveness to incorrect details, like dates of birth or of wars, the legal status of New York, the spelling of Pittsburgh or the name of the Governor of Canada. But the unsatisfactory nature of the text went far beyond this, showing serious structural flaws. 'The account of the

Coalition is far too brief,' Brogan suggested, and again: 'The Regency question ought to be discussed.' Indeed, he latterly resorted simply to volunteering his services for rewrites, especially on the American side. Aaron Burr? 'This whole paragraph needs to be redone. I will send that with my other notes.' The Louisiana Purchase? 'I will supply paragraph,' Brogan offered, as the quickest expedient. 'The whole account of the framing of the Constitution should be redone. I will do it within the next ten days,' Brogan wrote, but then crossed out this last sentence, evidently thinking better of how much he was taking on.[11] All this was sent by Brogan on 27 December 1945, showing that the revision of the *History* was well under way, with publication expected within a year.

This did not happen. Churchill undertook his first post-war visit to the United States in January 1946 and was away for two months. The notable event was his speech at Fulton, Missouri, on 5 March 1946. It was his reference to an 'iron curtain' in Europe that attracted most subsequent publicity, and Churchill's reputation as an early cold warrior became misleadingly inflated as a result. His own intention at Fulton had been to emphasise his plea for what he now termed a 'special relationship' between the English-speaking peoples, which, as with his Harvard speech in 1943, provoked at least as much suspicion as approbation among Americans. Churchill returned home with renewed international prestige and a higher profile than ever in the United States. Although, on the voyage out on the *Queen Elizabeth*, he had still been working through Brogan's suggestions on the *History*, by the time he got home at the end of March, his thoughts were elsewhere. The tax advice he had received cleared the way for the Literary Trust to be set up and Churchill contacted Bill Deakin, now back at Oxford as a don, to enlist his assistance in writing the war memoirs.

The writing and publication of *The Second World War* makes a fine story which has been told with great effect by Professor David Reynolds and does not need retelling here. But its impact on the *History*'s publication was as crucial as the impact of *Marlborough* on the *History*'s composition. Once Churchill had finally decided to write his memoirs, this task consumed all the time and energy that he could spare while serving as Leader of the Opposition (and latterly as prime minister from October 1951). Moreover, since Cassells were to be the British publishers of both books, their interests coincided. Publishers and author alike seized the main chance, with the result that the *History* was cast into limbo for a second time.

The deal on the memoirs was put together by Lord Camrose, latterly in uneasy cooperation with Emery Reves, Churchill's agent for foreign rights. The guiding principle, as ever, was that Churchill wanted a large sum of money up front; so he settled for less than he would have got in the long term from royalties. But the sum he got for the projected five volumes far exceeded any previous contract. That Cassells paid £40,000, double what they had for the *History*, was almost a detail compared with the huge amounts for the overseas rights, whether in book or serial form. The Boston publishers, Houghton Mifflin, acquired the American rights relatively cheaply, for $250,000 (at a time when the exchange rate was four dollars to the pound). Serialisation rights for the Murdoch newspapers in Australia, for Camrose's *Daily Telegraph*, for Henry Luce's *Life* magazine and, rather belatedly, for *The New York Times*, swelled the package. The 1947 deal thus gave Churchill, either as a capital sum for publication of his papers (through the Literary Trust) or as personal income for his work as author, a total of £550,000. This would be worth at least £17 million today; and the author's income instalments alone, at £35,000 a year for five years, would be well over a million pounds a year today.[12]

The author as celebrity, with his international fame, could now command such sums. There was, in keeping with this new status, a new professional edge in making arrangements that maximised his net income. Churchill had long reckoned on offsetting copious literary expenses against tax, and this practice resumed alongside the resumption of new literary earnings, with expenses claims that ratcheted up to twenty thousand pounds a year. The American deal for his memoirs also provided sixty thousand dollars from Luce and *The New York Times* for the 'working vacations' that Churchill took, at such places as the Mamounia Hotel in Marrakesh. The effect was simultaneously an escape from British weather, from British income taxes and from British exchange-control restrictions.

Even so, Churchill was still liable for appreciable personal income taxes. During the war he had drawn a salary of £10,000 as prime minister, taxed at source, with the perquisite of official government residences in London and at Chequers, and no tax liability on his literary income, which, boosted by his war speeches, reached six thousand pounds a year. During the fiscal year 1945–46, Churchill left office and accordingly lost his government housing, though his royalties still escaped tax that year. His assessable income amounted to £10,692, most of it subject to deduction of income tax at source, and generating a subsequent surtax payment of £2,292 (payable in the following year). But Churchill's large literary income from 1947 onward removed him from his tax shelter and exposed him to much higher levels of taxation. Thus his bank manager estimated that his net income for 1948–49 might be the same as in 1947–48, so about £21,500, on which £9,700 would be payable immediately in standard income tax, given a rate of 45 per cent; and in addition a surtax liability of £7,800 would also be due, assessed one year in arrears.[13] It meant that tax would take about 80 per cent of his net income. At this time his salary as Leader of the Opposition was £2,000 a year, taxed at source; but it was once more his literary earnings that subsidised a political career that he insisted was far from over.

The Second World War was produced with businesslike efficiency, tempered by the author's whims. Bill Deakin, despite new teaching responsibilities at Oxford, was brought back in a close working relationship with the author, already tested on *Marlborough* and the *History*. Deakin was the key figure in the 'Syndicate' that was established to organise the research, working alongside military and naval experts (General Sir Hastings Ismay, General Sir Henry Pownall and

Commodore Gordon Allen) who fulfilled a role that went beyond what Owen and Pakenham-Walsh had done on *Marlborough*. From May 1947 the impecunious barrister, Denis Kelly, was recruited and soon graduated from devilling in the muniments room of Chartwell to full participation in the Syndicate. To this team, in the more focused capacity of proofreader, Mr C. C. Wood, late of Harraps, was subsequently recruited; and the interventions of Sir Edward Marsh, in his own subsequent reading of the proofs, made it almost like old times.

The Second World War has to be regarded as essentially a collaborative effort. In this it was different from *Marlborough* or from the large parts of the *History* that went up to 1714. What was not different was that the scale of the work expanded in the writing, from the five volumes of the contract to the six that were clearly in view by 1948. When Churchill eventually became prime minister again, in October 1951, four volumes had been published and the fifth was already in the press.

The work had already achieved a staggering success, both literary and commercial. *The Gathering Storm*, published in 1948, set the tone for the reception and was the volume of which Churchill was most fully and manifestly the author. Cassells sold over 200,000 copies and, as the attentive Mr Wood calculated, probably netted £100,000 for this volume alone, more than double what they had paid for five. The first five volumes sold 1.75 million copies in Britain, 1.76 million in the United States and 77,000 in Canada. This was the known position when the sixth volume, *Triumph and Tragedy*, was published in the United States on 30 November 1953 (to be followed by publication in London in April 1954). It was an agreeable fiction that this final volume had been finished before Churchill became prime minister again in 1951. Jock Colville, now serving as Churchill's Principal Private Secretary, knew all about the subterfuges that could readily pass as 'school of' – among which the successful completion by the Syndicate of *The Second World War* occupies an esteemed position.

*   *   *

On the day that *Triumph and Tragedy* was published in North America, the author entered his eightieth year. At the end of June 1953 he had suffered a stroke, not his first but certainly his most severe, leaving him in no fit condition to act as a modern prime minister. Between them, Colville and Christopher Soames, now a Member of Parliament and serving as his father-in-law's Parliamentary Private Secretary, managed an awkward situation that, in a later era, would not have survived media exposure. The fact that Anthony Eden, the designated successor, was simultaneously critically ill allowed Churchill time to make an outwardly impressive if still shaky recovery. While Colville and Soames kept business ticking over, the prime minister enjoyed an unwontedly idle summer of convalescence. On 3 July his doctor, Lord Moran, reported in his diary: 'Winston has discovered Trollope.' On 27 July Colville reported in his own diary: 'Gave Winston *Candide* to read. He has had a surfeit of Trollope's political novels.' What other reading matter might be found to divert the old man?

Denis Kelly was sent to the Chartwell cellars to retrieve the proofs of the *History*. This idea may have come from Brendan Bracken, now elevated to the peerage as Viscount Bracken, having declined office under Churchill, but still his crony. Bracken, who had founded the monthly magazine, *History Today*, certainly suggested that its editor, Alan Hodge, might be able to help with the work of revision. 'I've been living on the *Second World War*,' Churchill told Moran on 19 August. 'Now I shall live on this history. I shall lay an egg a year – a volume every twelve months should not mean much work.' That same day, the introduction over lunch to Hodge, a professional writer in his late thirties, went well when and together they looked through the proofs of the early part of the *History*. 'I wish I could write as I did ten years ago,' said Churchill afterwards.[14]

Cassells too had been living on *The Second World War*. Indeed the extent of their profits made it both possible and profitable for Desmond Flower to recast the contract for the *History*. Bracken fully realised, even if Churchill sometimes forgot, that any golden eggs from the *History* would belong to Cassells alone. But by the end of 1953 Bracken had got Flower to agree that, as the contract stood, the author would have no financial inducement to return to the book. Cassells thus offered to regard their original payment of £20,000 simply as an advance upon future royalties, with the copyright on the book (though not British serialisation rights) reverting to the author. In this way, Churchill again got the best of both worlds: as a cash-strapped author before the war he had secured a lump sum worth a million pounds at today's values, and now, on the strength of his post-war fame, he was likely to net a similar sum – all for rights that, in law, he had already signed away. He eagerly anticipated his returns, misguidedly assuring his Minister of Pensions in August 1954 that he was already getting $50,000 a year from this source. On 26 October he told Moran: 'The four volumes of my *History of the English-Speaking Peoples* will bring me a great income, but the Treasury will take it all.'

This worry was somewhat notional. It is true that, even under a Conservative government, the top rate of surtax remained at 50 per cent on incomes above £15,000, levied on top of a standard rate of income tax set at 45 per cent. But Churchill, who had been faced with a similarly dreadful scenario in 1945–46, turned again to his tried and trusted advisers: his accountant J. Wood, his solicitor Anthony Moir and the barrister L. C. Graham-Dixon.

Again they proved successful in mitigating fiscal rigours. The farms of the Chartwell estate, previously managed by Soames with Churchill's enthusiastic participation, had incurred growing annual losses. Moir and Wood spotted that these could be played off against literary income. The effect was dramatic. For the year 1951–52, in round terms, Churchill's literary earnings of £35,000 were first offset by literary expenses of £20,000 and then set against a farm loss of £11,000. The effect was to reduce tax liability to under one thousand pounds, and for the following year it was projected that no income tax or surtax at all would be due. As Wood later commented privately, 'I believe Sir

Winston, like many others, finds it more pleasant to pay for the pleasure of farming than he would to pay the Inland Revenue.'[15]

For the moment, the prime minister's income was sheltered in this way. Work on the *History* began while he was still in Downing Street, with Hodge assembling a team of outside experts. But for Churchill himself it was essentially a retirement project: an 'occupation' or a 'standby', as he kept telling his doctor on his increasingly frequent visits, requiring little work on the author's part, with his own role limited to polishing and rearrangement. The chapters on 'The Saxon Dusk' and 'William the Conqueror', from the middle of Volume One, were shown to Moran on 3 June 1955, evidently with mixed feelings. 'I think you may like them,' Churchill said. 'I can't write like that now.' Deakin sadly agreed, as he confided to Moran in August when paying his own first visit for several months; and he thought Churchill was labouring under an illusion in supposing that his minor interventions were of value. Looking at the evidence of the surviving proofs, such as the reversion from 'Boudicca' to 'Boadicea', or at Churchill's wearisome quest to rehabilitate Richard III over the death of the princes in the Tower, it is difficult to disagree.

Belatedly, in April 1955, Churchill had indeed retired as prime minister. Was it also time for him to retire from his profession as author? From a tax point of view, of course, this seemed the obvious option, remembering the profitable example of 1939–46. From an emotional perspective, it was a less easy decision. Churchill's own morale had become dependent on the *History*, as Moran repeatedly records in his patient's remarks throughout 1955. 'I'm interested in my book, that's all I care about now.' (17 June) 'Any fun I get now is from my book.' (20 June) 'I find the fifteenth century more interesting than the twentieth.' (21 November)

As therapy, coping with a withdrawal from half a century of active politics, the revision of the *History* seemed ideal. Maxine Elliott, Churchill's pre-war hostess at Le Chateau de l'Horizon, had died there in 1940. Two other Riviera villas were now put at Churchill's disposal, with the effect of evading exchange controls on sterling, which would otherwise have precluded him from taking long holidays in the winter sunshine. He already knew the house built for Lord Beaverbrook, La Capponcina, near Monte Carlo, where Churchill now stayed for a couple of months in the autumn of 1955, latterly with hospitable accommodation for Hodge and the proofs too. But then Emery Reves made his own bid for Churchill's presence, offering even more extensive hospitality at La Pausa, a villa only a few miles away.

The acquisition of this luxurious villa undoubtedly reflected the boom in Churchill's foreign rights sales, on which Reves made sure that he retained an exclusive option. He and his new wife now went to immense lengths to accommodate their eminent author's every comfort, during long visits from himself (but not usually Clementine) over the three years 1956–58. Indeed Churchill may have stayed at La Pausa for as many as four hundred days in all until, like a hothouse plant forced too fast, this purposefully developed friendship collapsed with equal suddenness, with perfunctory regrets from Winston and some evident relief on Clementine's part.[16] The relationship with Emery Reves, so important in boosting Churchill's worldwide earnings during his years of fame, thus barely outlasted the literary career that had sustained it.

Churchill had for a while clung to his metaphor of laying one egg each year. He envisaged doing so in a leisurely style that he had never previously enjoyed. But this clashed with the fiscal imperative of making a clean break with authorship as soon as possible. Graham-Dixon's advice was that delivery of successive volumes would in itself constitute a continuance of his profession, meaning that the royalties would be taxable as income, whereas, on retirement from his profession, such royalties could be commuted into a lump sum that would be treated as a capital transaction (still untaxed in Britain).

This issue was not resolved until the summer of 1956. Meanwhile the revision of the *History* continued under Hodge's direction, with

Kelly chiefly responsible for retrieving and collating the various sets of proofs. It was difficult to establish, after more than fifteen years, which set had priority; Brogan's cogent revisions of 1945 seem to have been disregarded; Kelly busily circulated new drafts and what he termed 'Returned Empties' or, ominously, 'Debris' (in which much of Alan Bullock's pre-war work ended up). Kelly had labelled one set of proofs 'New Discovery', made in the summer of 1954, but as late as December 1955 he came across drafts that had been commissioned from G. M. Young and then forgotten, telling Churchill: 'I have discovered among your pre-war papers an outline of the Industrial Revolution'.[17]

As a result, much unnecessary originality was displayed. A whole new set of post-war professional historians were deputed by Hodge to work through the pre-war proofs. For Volume One it was just A. R. Myers, author of the late-medieval volume in the newly published *Pelican History of England* (to which Maurice Ashley contributed on the seventeenth century and J. H. Plumb on the eighteenth). For Volume Two, the Tudor historians, Joel Hurstfield and A. L. Rowse, and the seventeenth-century specialist D. H. Pennington, were brought in. For Volume Three, where the eighteenth century had needed more fundamental revision, the services of other reputable academic historians were enlisted: Plumb from Cambridge, J. Steven Watson from Oxford, Asa Briggs, currently at Leeds, and Frank Freidel of Stanford University. Briggs also helped on Volume Four, along with the Americanist Maldwyn Jones, then at Manchester University, and the Oxford historian Maurice Shock.

Nobody but Alan Hodge knew exactly who had done what. He later took steps, so Kelly disclosed, to destroy many of his drafts lest their discovery impugn Churchill's originality. The pre-war work of Bill Deakin and G. M. Young was formally acknowledged in each volume, but that of Keith Feiling only in Volume Two, and that of Ashley and Bullock not at all. Neither was Brogan's work acknowledged (though he was sent complimentary copies), nor that of the imperial historian A. P. Thornton. Yet all had contributed at some stage. Hodge's recruits, many of whom never met Churchill, took on the challenge of restructuring Volume Three and were responsible for composing virtually all of Volume Four except the American Civil War. These parts of the *History* can politely be termed 'school of' or, more crudely, a hodgepodge.

Churchill was increasingly excluded from the process. The parts of the *History* that were his own in the first place – essentially the coverage up to 1714 – were those to which he returned with most enthusiasm, much of it misguided. The parts with which he had not engaged closely in 1939, when he had had the intellectual capacity but not the time to do so, were those to which he had little to contribute in revision. In part, as he himself recognised, this was because he was now too old in his eighties to begin again; one of the books by his bedside, kept for reference, was J. R. Green's *Short History*, an authority of exactly the same age as himself, and not much cited by scholars in the 1950s. But another reason why Churchill's part diminished was because he was abruptly left with less time than anticipated for revision of the later volumes. The schedule of publication, long envisaged as a volume a year, was speeded up. The preface of Volume One is dated 15 January 1956; of Volume Two, 4 September 1956, nearly eight months later; of Volume Three, 24 December 1956, less than four months later; and of Volume Four, significantly, 10 February 1957.

The explanation for the last date lies in the circumstances of Churchill's retirement from his profession. 'I do not think,' Anthony Moir advised in January 1957, 'after the 15th February, anything should be published over Sir Winston's signature in connection with any of his Works, although such may have been written on a purely honorary basis.' The point was that he 'should not perform any act which would normally be carried out by an Author while continuing his profession'. It was an injunction that Churchill took to heart; and he gathered some satisfaction in rehearsing, for the benefit of friends and publishers alike, the line that he had ceased to carry on the profession that had financed his whole career. 'I have now retired from literature,' he wrote to the American financier Bernard Baruch in August 1957, 'and am endeavouring to find ways of spending pleasantly the remaining years of my life.'[18]

The retirement plan had been finalised over many months in 1956. It was partly a response to the huge commercial success of the publication of Volume One of the *History*, especially in the United States, where Dodd, Mead and Company found their patience in waiting for fifteen years well rewarded. In July 1956 they reported that, in addition to their own edition of 50,000, the Book of the Month Club had printed 224,000 copies and that a further 15,000 had already been sold by McClelland and Stewart in Canada, with net royalties estimated at $90,000. Cassells had initially printed 130,000 copies, with nearly £25,000 already due in royalties.

These net royalties, moreover, excluded all the advances. For Cassells, this had simply meant the money already advanced in 1940. For Dodd and McClelland, however, abruptly told by Cassells that the copyright had now reverted to Churchill, it had meant negotiating new advances with Moir, who had demanded ('cynically', as Dodd thought) that the North Americans also make good the effects of the post-war devaluation of the pound, from $4 to $2.80.[19] Moir's steely vigilance thus extracted every advantage for his client in amassing the proceeds on both sides of the Atlantic. If taxed as income in Britain, a formidable surtax liability loomed, pointing to the desirability of retirement, if possible. Yet this was not a simple matter, given that the Inland Revenue had its own tight rules about taxpayers opportunely ceasing to practise a profession in such circumstances.

For technical reasons, as Moir explained to Churchill, his retirement needed to be accelerated so as to maximise the prospective returns. By October 1956 it was clear that Churchill could expect to receive a further £75,000 from Cassells and £100,000 from Dodd, Mead and McClelland and Stewart in future royalties. On the assumption that the various publishers would commute these expected payments, Moir was able to advise that 'it seems probable that, owing to retirement, you should receive, as capital, a sum in excess of £100,000'.[20] This would be worth about two million pounds today – all tax-free. It was the author's retirement bonus.

If Churchill did well, Cassells did even better. Never did the firm make such a good long-term investment as its bold decision in 1932 to stake £20,000 on this project. They had printed 130,000 copies of Volume One for publication in April 1956; a second edition of 30,000 followed in May; and a further 75,000 by the time of Churchill's death in 1965. Other volumes had an initial print run of 150,000 each. There were to be numerous other versions: through serialisation, in illustrated parts, as textbooks and abridgements. The critical reception at the time was, in a word, uncritical. Churchill was broadly right when he responded to his doctor, who had been trying to cheer him up by citing the American reviews of his first volume: 'Yes, pages of unending flattery.' (19 June 1956)

One of the most interesting contemporary reviews of the *History* was by Geoffrey Barraclough. He was an academic historian with an unusual eminence both in medieval and contemporary history; and he wrote successively as each volume appeared, for the Liberal newspaper the *Manchester Guardian*. On the first volume, which he saw as celebrating a 'way of life' common to the English-speaking peoples, he commented: 'This is an old story, particularly dear to the Whig historians of the nineteenth century, writing when the Empire was at its height.' And he detected a dualism in the book: 'the historian telling us what happened and the moralist distilling the lessons'. This cool but not disrespectful view would be shared by most historians today. What evidently surprised Barraclough about the volume, as he subsequently remarked, was the way that 'our professional historians, with rare exceptions, tumbled over themselves in a hyperbole of praise and self-abasement.'[21]

This is certainly true, both in print and, more understandably, in the private correspondence that Churchill received. Joel Hurstfield, for example, was not only effusive in expressing his admiration in

April 1956 but added: 'From what I hear from my colleagues, this is an opinion very generally held.'[22] Plumb was another who, at the time of publication, wrote in this extravagant tenor, whatever his subsequent misgivings. Barraclough's more sceptical contemporary comments, notably on Volume Three, reflect an unwillingness to be co-opted by either Churchill's reputation or his rhetoric into a commendation of the spirit of Chatham and a robust defence of Empire, as though such values remained self-evidently relevant.

What was the *History*'s message, then, for the post-war world? When it came to reviewing the final volume, even Barraclough softened his reproaches, with a salute to the work's political inclusiveness, as liberal history. But it was liberal history infused with little liberal optimism about progress, and Barraclough called it 'a rounding-off of the past rather than an overture to the future'.[23] This was, by the time that the *History* was published, broadly the outlook of Churchill himself, an old man far removed from the context in which he had projected a work initially intended to bring an inspiriting message to a contemporary situation. 'I could not write about the woe and ruin of the terrible twentieth century,' he sadly told Moran on 19 June 1956. 'We answered all the tests. But it was useless.'

Epilogue

Hundreds of books have been published about Churchill. Few of them critically evaluate his literary interests. Even those that do so – and do so with a general measure of sympathy – are largely of one mind about the merits of his *History of the English-Speaking Peoples*. 'By no stretch of the imagination was it the best of Churchill's books,' writes Roy Jenkins, while to Paul Addison it is 'outwardly impressive but inwardly the least successful of his histories'. In Geoffrey Best's judgement, 'his sources were old-fashioned and by scholarly criteria out of date, and he sought verification only of what would improve the story he enjoyed telling'. In David Cannadine's words, 'it was essentially a brightly lit cavalcade of the great public figures who had made up the nation's story', and Norman Rose goes so far as to say that the *History* 'reads as a kind of pastiche'.[1]

Over forty years ago, J. H. Plumb offered one necessary caveat: 'Yet it was a remarkable book and its publication a remarkable event, remarkable, very largely, because Churchill had written it.' This seems undeniable, though Churchill himself manfully sought to deny that his *History* depended upon this personal aspect for any success it might achieve. 'I hope and believe,' he had crisply reprimanded Emery Reves in 1955, 'that it has some merits of its own.'[2] Such merits rest chiefly on the way that the narrative drive is sustained. It passes the test of telling its story with admirable lucidity and unforced brio. In particular, there is the lively treatment of episodes in military history that enlisted Churchill's attention: not only his recapitulation of Marlborough's campaigns but his cogent exposition of the Wars of the Roses, with which he had grappled in 1938–39, and also his account of the American Civil War, despite the disproportionate length of its treatment. And there remain other incidental felicities and engaging passages.

But this did not, of course, amount to the book that had been promised in 1932. Maurice Ashley, who had been well placed to appreciate this point, wrote later: 'One does not know whether to feel pleased or sorry that Churchill did not actually produce the book that he set out to write, a book that might conceivably have helped by its arguments to strengthen Anglo-American understanding.'[3] A missionary endeavour of this kind, however, implied three requirements: a polemical focus that Churchill had not yet acquired in 1932, a single-mindedness that the author was unable to bring to his task until his *Marlborough* was finished, and – quite simply – sufficient time when he belatedly came to fulfil his task in 1938–39. Instead, the words poured out to meet an overdue professional commitment, with ideological strategy subservient to financial imperatives.

The text of 1939, unfinished and in some respects incoherent, was a product of all these pressures. It was a work in progress – but one, as it turned out, on which the author could happily draw in his wartime oratory. The published *History* finally appeared in a different form and in a substantially different context, long years later, as Victor Feske's well-considered judgement on the publication of the four volumes suggests: 'When they finally appeared beginning in 1956, they sold in vast numbers, yet their moment had already passed.'[4]

Churchill's profession was, in an important sense, in literature. His vocation, however, was in politics. The vision that informs his writings is essentially political, as the *History of the English-Speaking Peoples* makes clear enough. By the time it was published in the 1950s, the term 'special relationship' had come into common parlance, applied in the sense of Churchill's Fulton, Missouri speech of March, 1946. Yet this was never envisaged by him as an exclusive commitment, certainly not on the part of Great Britain. For he orated also about a European dimension in British policy, and has sometimes been hailed (somewhat indiscriminately) as one of the fathers of the post-war movement for European unity. Nor was he ready to abandon the imperialist rhetoric of a lifetime to suit American sensibilities. He was still unrepentant, right up to the final words recorded in the official minutes of his last cabinet meeting in 1955, in affirming the importance of 'the threads which bound together the countries of the Commonwealth, or, as he still preferred to call it, the Empire'.[5]

This was not some senile lapse. The three options facing Britain had never been exclusive choices for Churchill. In an unpublished article of the early 1930s on 'The United States of Europe', drafted at the time that Churchill agreed to write the *History*, he is transparent in his views. 'Great Britain herself has for centuries been the proved and accepted champion of European freedom,' he declared. 'She is the centre and head of the British commonwealth of nations. She is an equal partner in the English-speaking world.'[6] If Churchill later aspired to promote a 'special relationship' between Great Britain and the United States, then, it was still on this rather promiscuous basis.

In American eyes, of course, such Churchillian pretensions did not look like real politics. The disparity in physical size and resources, population and production, wealth and power, between Great Britain and the United States vitiated any notion of an equal partnership. Even to theorists of 'soft power', hard economic, military and political realities could hardly be dismissed or ignored in policymaking. Moreover, the rhetoric of the English-speaking peoples, with its fine liberal pedigree from the late nineteenth century, came to be regarded as tainted by modern American liberals, for whom it signalled little more than the Anglo-Saxon core in the acronym WASP. It remained true, as ever, that many Britons unthinkingly talked up the extent to which a common ancestry was actually the experience of a large proportion of American citizens. Winston Churchill certainly did so.

Many Americans formed an exaggerated impression of Churchill as an unreconstructed imperialist. So far as India was concerned, he laid himself open to this charge, by trying (ineffectually) to maintain the imperial structure of the Raj much as he had seen it in his own youth.

The main reason for Churchill's imperialist reputation, however, was not a matter of policies but simply that he talked so much about the British Empire. Of course he did; it was a staple of his rhetoric, as a politician who ultimately relied on the politics of emotion as much as Gladstone had done in his prime.

Churchill thus clung to his essentially sentimental vision of Empire. It was often derided by the tough-minded materialists in the Chamberlainite tradition. But Churchill's alternative view was one that he could claim was vindicated in 1940, when the self-governing Dominions were thus motivated in making their momentous decision to join in resisting Hitler. The British Empire, as Churchill claimed, exerted a decisive influence on the course of world history; but it did so for the last time, as he was more reluctant to recognise.

Churchill, as we have seen, was far from alone in entertaining his similarly sentimental vision of the unity of the English-speaking peoples. From the time of the American Civil War onward, this tradition was already well established, even though Churchill himself was remarkably slow to pick up a theme with which, from the late 1930s, he became identified. It naturally informed the *History of the English-Speaking Peoples*, as drafted by the author in 1938–39, though as a statesman from 1940 onward, Churchill surely asked too much of sentiment. American policy towards Britain, whether under Roosevelt or his successors, was based on more substantial considerations. Churchill's consolation was that, as the author of the *History*, he found that he was still able to turn his soft words into hard cash, dollars and pounds alike.

The sales of the *History* tell their own story about the author as celebrity. In 1957, the wife of this recently retired member of the literary profession, moved by the fact that the whole audience would rise when her husband entered a theatre, remarked on his extraordinary fame to his attentive doctor (who wrote down every word as usual in his diary for 10 April 1957). 'You know Winston has become a legend,' Clementine mused. 'I wonder why? I think that the speeches in 1940 had a lot to do with it.' Churchill's phrases from that epochal moment had shown the power of words – spoken words that were delivered from a text that had itself been dictated. It was a highly literary form of rhetoric that nonetheless acquired a demotic force. In this sense, imitation flattered the orator and parody enhanced appreciation of the distinctiveness of his style. Behind each speech lay long hours of preparation – in a sense, long years of preparation.

When Churchill was given US citizenship in 1963, he was being honoured as a statesman. But in saying on that occasion that 'he mobilized the English language and sent it into battle', President Kennedy was lifting an aphorism (often attributed to Edward R. Murrow) from the citation of Churchill's Nobel Prize for Literature, awarded ten years previously. At that time, in 1953, Ernest Hemingway had commented, rather ungraciously coming from a disappointed rival for the award, that Churchill was 'the greatest master of the *spoken* word'. In awarding the Prize, moreover, specific mention had been made of his wartime speeches, while nothing was said about *The Second World War*, his most recent publication at the time. In his presentation oration, the Swedish author Sigfrid Siwertz concluded: 'With his great speeches he has, perhaps, himself erected his most enduring monument.'[7] Still in Downing Street when he received news of this impending honour, the author accepted it in a pragmatic and cheerful spirit. 'It is all settled about the Nobel Prize,' Winston wrote to Clementine. '£12,100 free of tax. Not so bad!'[8]

Churchill's great days, as he then knew, lay behind him. And even in 1940, his claim about the finest hour of the British Empire was phrased in a way that implied elegy. In confronting Hitler, Churchill played his part on a number of levels, not simply as an orator. Yet, though monstrous tyranny may not simply yield to rhetoric, his inspirational role can hardly be discounted. The morale of his compatriots was indeed crucial in holding the line against the seemingly irresistible Nazi advance in 1940. Churchill's oratory, and the sheer tenacity it projected, played a crucial role in sustaining the will to resist, identifying it as the national will and the fulfilment of an historic destiny. Before World War II, his parliamentary style had often been dismissed as simply old-fashioned, as Winston had recognised in an ironical remark on his performance to Clémentine in 1935: 'There is apparently nothing in the literary effect I have sought for forty years!'[9]

Yet everything changed with the coming of the hour that his carefully prepared utterances had prophesied with orotund sententiousness. It was this that the award of the Nobel Prize recognised. 'Behind Churchill the writer is Churchill the orator' was the claim that Siwertz understandably made on that occasion. Yet the opposite would be more accurate, especially once we fully understand that his *History of the English-Speaking Peoples*, though published much later, was written in 1938–39. It has often been judged as a late, luxuriant efflorescence of Churchill's rhetoric; but it was in fact the seedbed of much of his memorable wartime oratory. For, in finding appropriate language to meet his historic challenge, the author drew on his professional expertise. As he was to say in his speech to both Houses of Parliament, assembled to celebrate his eightieth birthday in 1954: 'if I found the right words you must remember that I have always earned my living by my pen and by my tongue'.[10]

Appendix: Churchill and the British Tax System

The Board of Inland Revenue, responsible for collecting taxes, was responsible to the Chancellor of the Exchequer. It was a matter of pride that, ever since Robert Peel's reintroduction of income tax in 1842, the Inland Revenue had administered it under five different schedules. Of these, salaries and pensions from an office or permanent position formed Schedule E, paid net of tax, as in Churchill's case while he was Chancellor. The same principle of deduction at source also applied to Schedule A, rents of real estate; so Churchill's income from the Garron Towers estate was likewise paid to him net of tax. Income under Schedule C, profits from government stock and dividends, of which Churchill had some holdings, was also subject to deduction at source. Schedule B covered profits from farming, which in their nature could not be taxed at source; this did not affect Churchill significantly until after World War II, when he purposefully developed the farming activities of his Chartwell estate, not least with an eye to minimising his taxes. Schedule D was his real problem. This covered profits from trade, commerce and the professions, which were in their nature not only unpredictable but also complex in origin, and therefore could not be taxed at source.

A document that was prepared for him, probably early in 1923, clearly demonstrates how the system worked. It set out the future pattern of tax liabilities incurred by his literary receipts from *The World Crisis*.[1] This was based on the British fiscal year, running from 6 April to 5 April, and made calculations of the payments that would fall due on the full £27,000 over the next seven years. It assumed that a first tranche of the advance (£18,000) would be received in the year 1922–23; a second tranche of £6,000 in 1923–24; and a final tranche of

£3,000 in 1924–25. This assumption was too simple to be wholly realistic but it clarified the principles of tax liability in relation to cash flow.

Thus in Churchill's case, though the first cheque for *The World Crisis* might come in 1921–22, nothing would become liable for tax until he made his tax return for 1923–24; and even then, because of the three-year averaging provision, only one-third of the first tranche of the advance (thus £6,000) would then be assessable. On this he would be liable for standard-rate income tax, to be paid in January 1925. The rest of the advance, year upon year, averaged out on the same method, would successively enter into future annual tax assessments, with a cumulatively delayed effect.

Capital gains escaped liability to taxation. Schedule D defined annual profits or gains, which were liable, as meaning annually recurring or ongoing, thus excluding 'casual profits' and one-off sums, which were exempt. Here was the loophole that Churchill explored in 1925 if it could be argued that, on becoming Chancellor, he had retired as an author. On that line of argument, Churchill's past literary advances might be treated not as the deferred taxable earnings of a professional author but as financial windfalls that would escape tax altogether. Churchill was shown two different assessments of his literary earnings, calculated on alternative assumptions: either the deferred averages of past years incurring an income-tax liability of about two thousand pounds or – 'if ceased', as the alternative assessment put it – no tax liability whatsoever on this substantial part of his income.

For several months, Churchill toyed with these enticing possibilities. Hence the significance of the inquiry that he received from His Majesty's Inspector of Taxes in November 1925, noting that Churchill's tax return for 1925–26 included nothing 'in respect of literary profits' and asking for an assurance that all such profits had ceased before 6 April 1925.[2] This was the 'retirement option' that he was to adopt from 1939 to 1946 and after 1957. Instead of adopting it in 1925, the Chancellor declared himself still an author and his literary receipts continued to be taxed as previously under Schedule D, on the deferred basis, while his salary was taxed at source under Schedule E.

The standard rate of income tax had been 5 or 6 per cent until 1914; but in wartime it was raised to much higher levels, reaching 25 per cent by 1917 and 30 per cent during the post-war years 1919–22. This was the marginal rate of tax; what was actually paid depended also on tax allowances, rebates and allowable deductions. Churchill tried to charge the interest payments on his overdrafts against tax in 1913 but was told by his bankers that, for this to be allowed, 'a banking account must not have been in credit for a single day in any one year'. That was a condition all too easily met by this particular client. From 1913 he negotiated a loan of £9,000 from his bank, rolled over annually on many occasions, with interest payments of £360 a year subsequently offset against tax.[3] This became part of his standard arrangements, again reinforcing alike his ability to raise cash in the present and his eventual liability for payment.

When 'super-tax' had first been introduced by Lloyd George, with Churchill's vocal support, in the 1909 'People's Budget', it had a threshold set at £5,000 a year (which nicely exempted both of their ministerial salaries, of course). But the threshold for super-tax liability was reduced to £3,000 in Lloyd George's last peacetime budget in May 1914; and Edward Marsh, who handled Churchill's tax returns at the time, had to allow for a payment of £76 13s 6d on Churchill's assessed income of £4,478. This was a first fleabite; but wartime exigency bit deeper. The liability to super-tax was further reduced to £2,000 a year by 1920, while the rate at which it was levied was simultaneously increased.

These factors combined to put the squeeze on Churchill by the late 1920s. For his bumper year 1923–24, he notes actual literary receipts of nearly £14,000, swelling his total income to £18,300. Out of this he records paying income tax of only £236 plus super-tax of £1,000 – both of these sums generated by the deferred method of assessment going back three or four years, when his literary income had been low.

In subsequent years, Churchill was actually paying more income tax as Chancellor than his own figures suggest, since his salary was also taxed at source; but, since he never saw that money, it was evidently invisible to him and did not enter into his peculiar calculations.

What Churchill usually recorded was his own cash flow. This was highly satisfactory in 1923–24 but, because it was partly a function of deferred tax liability, too good to last. For in 1924–25, when his actual literary receipts dropped to £11,200, the tax bill that he faced at the end of the year increased slightly to £1,483. Worse still, in the next two years, although his literary receipts declined to around £10,000 in each year, Churchill was faced with sharply rising tax bills. He records having to pay £3,174 in 1925–26 and no less than £4,585 in 1926–27. This is why his disposable income came under such pressure at this time.

Notes

Prologue

1   Kimball, *Forged in War*, p. 15.
2   Churchill, *SWW*, vol. 1, p. 345 (UK), p. 440 (US).
3   Gunther, *Roosevelt in Retrospect*, p. 14.
4   Foster, *Lord Randolph Churchill*, p. 400.
5   Churchill, *My Early Life*, p. 223.
6   Pilpel, *Churchill in America*, pp. 45–50.
7   *WSC*, vol. 1, p. 353.
8   CHAR 8/484/110.
9   Churchill, *SWW*, vol. 1, pp. 526–7 (UK), p. 667 (US), which capitalises 'Destiny'.
10 Pound, *Strand Magazine*, p. 3.
11 Reynolds, *In Command of History*, p. 5.
12 Colville, *Fringes of Power*, vol. 2, p. 138 (6 September 1944).
13 Gilbert, *Churchill and America*, p. 448.
14 Text in Ziegler, *Legacy*, p. 339.
15 DEKE 2, ch. 6 (Denis Kelly memoirs).

Chapter 1: Father's Boy: Heritage, 1874–97

1   Churchill, *Lord Randolph*, vol. 1, p. 12.
2   Churchill, *Lord Randolph*, vol. 1, pp. 10, 13, 15.
3   *WSC*, vol. 1, pp. 49, 82–3.
4   Churchill, *Lord Randolph*, vol. 2, p. 183; Pelling, *Winston Churchill*, p. 298.

5   Churchill, *HESP*, vol. 2, p. 381 (US); p. 302 (UK) (written after 1939).

6   Churchill, *Marlborough*, vol. 1, pp. 28, 35 (UK); pp. 6, 9 (US).

7   *WSC*, vol. 1, p. 318.

8   Churchill, *Lord Randolph*, vol. 1, p. 123.

9   *WSC*, vol. 1, p. 268.

10   Churchill, *Lord Randolph*, vol. 1, p. 72.

11   Foster, *Lord Randolph Churchill*, pp. 349, 373–4, 395.

12   Churchill, *Lord Randolph*, vol. 2, pp. 248–9.

13   Churchill, *Lord Randolph*, vol. 1, pp. 106–8.

14   Churchill, *Lord Randolph*, vol. 1, p. 18.

15   Churchill, *Lord Randolph*, vol. 1, p. 52.

16   Churchill, *Lord Randolph*, vol. 1, pp. 53, 54.

17   Lady Oxford, *Off the Record*, p. 82.

18   Churchill, *My Early Life*, p. 27.

19   Churchill, *Lord Randolph*, vol. 1, p. 35.

20   Rosebery, *Lord Randolph Churchill*, p. 136.

21   Churchill, *Lord Randolph*, vol. 1, pp. 33, 50.

22   *WSC*, vol. 1, pp. 319, 261.

23   Churchill, *Lord Randolph*, vol. 1, p. 69.

24   Churchill, *Lord Randolph*, vol. 1, p. 72.

25   Churchill, *Lord Randolph*, vol. 1, p. 78.

26   Churchill, *Lord Randolph*, vol. 1, pp. 74, 83.

27   Churchill, *Lord Randolph*, vol. 1, p. 253.

28   Arnstein, *The Bradlaugh Case*, p. 89.

29   Churchill, *Lord Randolph*, vol. 1, p. 416.

30   Churchill, *Lord Randolph*, vol. 1, opp. p. 232.

31   Churchill, *Lord Randolph*, vol. 1, p. 282.

32   Churchill, *Lord Randolph*, vol. 2, p. 65.

33   Churchill, *Lord Randolph*, vol. 1, p. 294.

34   Churchill, *Lord Randolph*, vol. 1, p. 295.

35   Churchill, *Lord Randolph*, vol. 1, p. 296.

36   Churchill, *Lord Randolph*, vol. 2, pp. 239, 244.

37   Churchill, *Lord Randolph*, vol. 2, pp. 223–4.

38   Churchill, *Lord Randolph*, vol. 2, p. 127; Rosebery, *Lord Randolph Churchill*, p. 7.

39   Churchill, *Lord Randolph*, vol. 2, p. 301; vol. 1, p. 210; vol. 2. p. 464.

40   Foster, *Lord Randolph Churchill*, pp. 218–19, 270.

41   Churchill, *Lord Randolph*, vol. 2, p. 484; *WSC*, Comp. to vol. 1, part 1, p. 544.

42   *WSC*, vol. 1, pp. 235, 237.

43   *WSC*, Comp. to vol. 1, part 1, p. 545.

44   Rosebery, *Lord Randolph Churchill*, p. 72.

45   *WSC*, vol. 1, p. 198.

46   *WSC*, vol. 1, p. 211.

47   *WSC*, vol. 1, p. 318.

48   Churchill, *Lord Randolph*, vol. 2, pp. 116–17.

49   Ibid.

50   CHAR 8/594/2.

51   Rosebery, *Lord Randolph Churchill*, pp. 142, 175.

52   Rosebery, *Lord Randolph Churchill*, pp. 82–3.

Chapter 2: Mother's Boy: The Author of his Fortune, 1898–1921

1   *WSC*, vol. 1, p. 364.

2   *WSC*, vol. 1, pp. 371–2.

3   *WSC*, vol. 1, p. 320.

4   Churchill, *My Early Life*, p. 111.

5   *WSC*, vol. 1, p. 288.

6   *WSC*, vol. 1, pp. 341–2; Churchill, *My Early Life*, p. 127.

7   *WSC*, vol. 1, pp. 355–6.

8   *WSC*, vol. 1, p. 359.

9   Toye, *Churchill's Empire*, pp. 42–5.

10   *WSC*, vol. 1, pp. 380–1.

11   Churchill, *My Early Life*, p. 161.

12   *WSC*, vol. 1, p. 383.

13   *WSC*, vol. 1, pp. 365, 382, 384.

14   *WSC*, vol. 1, pp. 384, 390.

15   Churchill, *My Early Life*, p. 170; *WSC*, vol. 1, p. 393.

16   *WSC*, vol. 1, p. 396.

17   *WSC*, vol. 1, p. 437.

18   CHAR 1/78/27/8; Churchill, *My Early Life*, p. 161.

19   CHAR 8/657/53.

20   Martin, *Lady Randolph Churchill*, vol. 2, p. 152.

21   *WSC*, vol. 1, p. 432.

22   Martin, *Lady Randolph Churchill*, vol. 2, p. 171.

23   *WSC*, vol. 1, p. 434.

24   Martin, *Lady Randolph Churchill*, vol. 2, p. 176.

25   *WSC*, vol. 1, p. 427.

26   This is in chapter 13 (out of 20) in the original edition; ch. 12 in the
      reissued version, Churchill, *Frontiers and Wars*.

27   *WSC*, vol. 1, p. 442.

28   Clarke, *Lancashire and the New Liberalism*, p. 44.

29   Churchill, *London to Ladysmith*, preface.

30   *WSC*, vol. 1, pp. 540, 545; Comp. to vol. 2, part 1, pp. 27, 102, for
      quotations in both these paragraphs.

31   CHAR 8/815/13–15.

32   Delany, *Literature, Money and the Market*, pp. 107–15.

33   *WSC*, Comp. to vol 2, part 1, p. 479.

34   CHAR 1/78/27–8.

35   Churchill, *Lord Randolph*, vol. 1, pp. vii, 394; *WSC*, Comp. to vol. 2,
      part 1, p. 436.

36   Churchill, *Great Contemporaries*, p. 63; *WSC*, Comp. to vol. 2, part 1,
      p. 456.

37   Churchill, *Lord Randolph*, vol. 2, p. 339.

38   Amery, *Joseph Chamberlain*, p. 192.

39   Toye, *Churchill's Empire*, p. 93.

40   *WSC*, vol. 1, p. 406; Churchill, *Lord Randolph*, vol. 1, p. 266.

41 Churchill, *Lord Randolph*, vol. 2, p. 452.

42 Churchill, *Lord Randolph*, vol. 1, p. 74.

43 Churchill, *Lord Randolph*, vol. 2, p. 59.

44 Churchill, *Lord Randolph*, vol. 2, pp. 488–9.

45 CHAR 1/78/27–8.

46 Martin, *Lady Randolph Churchill*, vol. 2, pp. 364, 399.

Entr'acte

1 Churchill, *SWW*, vol. 1, p. 62 (UK); p. 79 (US).

2 CHAR 8/624/83–4.

3 Prior, *Churchill's 'World Crisis' as History*, p. 281.

4 *WSC*, vol. 4, pp. 751–4.

5 Soames (ed.), *Speaking*, p. 238.

6 CHAR 1/303/11–12.

7 Soames (ed.), *Speaking*, p. 273.

8 Keynes, *Essays in Biography*, p. 53.

Chapter 3: The English-Speaking Peoples Before Churchill

1 Churchill, *Lord Randolph*, vol. 1, p. 277.

2 Reid, *Forster*, vol. 2, pp. 14, 79.

3 Foreman, *A World on Fire*, p. 213; Mill, *Autobiography*, p. 159.

4 Blackett, *Divided Hearts*, p. 67.

5 Bright, *Selected Speeches*, p. 84.

6 Biagini, *Liberty, Retrenchment and Reform*, pp. 69–81.

7 Young, *Around the World with General Grant*, p. 36.

8 Mill, *Autobiography*, p. 161.

9 *The New York Times*, 2 July 1871; *The Critic*, 26 July 1871; Parry, *Politics of Patriotism*, pp. 359, 363–4, 395.

10 Churchill, *Lord Randolph*, vol. 1, p. 63.

11 Seeley, *Expansion of England*, p. 10.

12 House of Commons Debates (*Hansard*), 16 March 1876, cols.

146–7; Forster, 'Imperial federation', p. 201; Bell, *Idea of Greater Britain*, p. 118.

13   Forster, 'Imperial federation', p. 205; Foster, *Lord Randolph Churchill*, p. 407.

14   Harvie, *Lights of Liberalism*, p. 108.

15   See Bell, *Greater Britain*, ch. 7; quotations both at p. 197.

16   Pelling, *America and the British Left*, p. 53.

17   *Globe and Mail*, 21 September 1940.

18   Young, *Around the World with General Grant*, p. 39.

19   *Manchester Guardian*, 30 September 1882; Kaplan, *Lincoln*, pp. 61–80, 279–80.

20   *WSC*, vol. 1, p. 233.

21   Ziegler, *Legacy*, p. 13.

22   *Manchester Guardian*, 7 November 1904; 18 October 1917.

23   Brundage and Cosgrove, *Great Tradition*, p. 43.

24   Burrow, *Memories Migrating*, p 164.

25   Burrow, *Liberal Descent*, p. 195.

26   Moran, *Struggle for Survival*, p. 690; Moran, *Churchill* (US), p. 700.

27   Roosevelt, *Winning of the West*, p. 15; Bailey, *Diplomatic History*, p. 486.

28   Mahan, 'Possibilities of an Anglo-American Reunion', p. 551.

29   *Manchester Guardian*, 22 April 1896.

30   Roberts, *Salisbury*, p. 748; Hofstadter, *Social Darwinism*, p. 180.

31   Burrow, *Liberal Descent*, pp. 165, 208.

32   Burrow, *Liberal Descent*, p. 189.

33   Brundage and Cosgrove, *Great Tradition*, p. 33.

34   Mandler, *English National Character*, pp. 90–1.

35   Brundage and Cosgrove, *Great Tradition*, p. 42.

36   Birkenhead, *America Revisited*, p. 36; Cohen, *Churchill Bibliography*, p. 921.

37   Anderson, *Race and Rapprochement*, p. 178.

38   Brundage and Cosgrove, *Great Tradition*, p. 160.

39 Beer, *English-Speaking Peoples*, p. 190 and preface; Louis, *Ends of British Imperialism*, p. 249.

40 *Manchester Guardian*, 29 May 1917.

41 *Manchester Guardian*, 8 January and 9 February 1912.

42 Wilson, *Downfall of the Liberal Party*, p. 215.

43 *Manchester Guardian*, 5 April 1919.

44 *New York Times*, 19 January 1921.

Chapter 4: One Author, Two Contracts, 1922–32

1   Churchill, *Thoughts and Adventures*, p. 172 (Romanes Lecture, 19 June 1930).

2   Soames (ed.), *Speaking*, pp. 320–1.

3   Daunton, *Just Taxes*, pp. 109–12, 121; and readers thirsty for more detail can find it in my appendix, 'Churchill and the British Tax System'.

4   Williamson, 'Doctrinal Politics of Stanley Baldwin', pp. 193, 199.

5   *WSC*, vol. 5, pp. 301, 308; Soames (ed.), *Speaking*, p. 332.

6   See Macaulay, *History of England*, ch. 9, on Marlborough's desertion of James II.

7   *WSC*, vol. 1, p. 381.

8   Churchill, *Marlborough*, vol. 1, p. 18; original US edn (1933), vol. 1, pp. 6–7.

9   Soames (ed.), *Speaking*, p. 285; *WSC*, vol. 5, p. 319.

10 Soames (ed.), *Speaking*, p. 336.

11 Gilbert, *Churchill and America*, pp. 115–16.

12 Soames (ed.), *Speaking*, p. 345.

13 Gilbert, *Churchill and America*, p. 120.

14 CHAR 1/212/12.

15 Jenkins, *Churchill*, p. 421; Soames (ed.), *Speaking*, p. 326.

16 Soames (ed.), *Speaking*, p. 310.

17 Churchill, *SWW*, vol. 1, p. 62 (UK); p. 79 (US).

18 Soames, introduction to Cohen, *Churchill Bibliography*, p. xi.

19 CHAR 8/277/52–4.

20 Nicolson, *Diaries*, vol. 1, p. 51 (6 July 1930).

21 *WSC*, vol. 5, p. 364; CHAR 8/297 and CHAR 8/335/55.

22 Ashley, *Churchill as Historian*, p. 29.

23 CHAR 1/304/61–9.

24 Calculated from the table in Burk, *Taylor*, pp. 418–19.

25 Hastings, *Maugham*, p. 271 and ch. 11; photograph at p. 438.

26 WCHL 1/16/13 (Churchill Archives).

27 Soames (ed.), *Speaking*, p. 405.

28 Cohen, *Churchill Bibliography*, pp. 404–5.

29 Wells, *Autobiography*, p. 719.

30 CHAR 8/296/20.

31 Gilbert, *Churchill and America*, p. 129.

32 CHAR 8/296/17–19.

33 CHAR 8/296/20–2.

34 CHAR 8/312/150, 151–4, 159–61.

35 *WSC*, vol. 5, p. 423.

36 Gilbert, *Churchill and America*, p. 140.

37 CHAR 1/239/78b.

38 *WSC*, vol. 5, p. 439.

39 CHAR 1/229/10; CHAR 8/335/44.

40 CHAR 8/335/44.

41 CHAR 8/308/1–5, 12.

42 CHAR 8/327/16ff.

Chapter 5: The Struggle on Two Fronts, 1933–38

1 CHAR 8/308/14–15.

2 CHAR 1/229/10.

3 Churchill, *Thoughts and Adventures*, p. 183.

4 Churchill, *My Early Life*, p. 26.

5 Amery, *Diaries*, vol. 2, p. 49 (4 August 1929).

6 Muir, *British Commonwealth*, vol. 1, p. xxii; vol. 2, p. 4; vol. 1, intro. by David Saville Muzzey.

7   Stewart, *Burying Caesar*, p. 161.

8   Amery, *Diaries*, vol. 2, pp. 382–3 (13 June 1934).

9   *WSC*, vol. 5, p. 496; Churchill to Trevelyan, 1 August 1934, CHAR 8/486/2.

10 Ashley, *Churchill as Historian*, p. 11.

11 Cohen, *Churchill Bibliography*, p. 408.

12 CHAR 8/485/104; Ashley, *Churchill as Historian*, p. 230.

13 Cannadine, *Trevelyan*, p. 117.

14 CHAR 8/484/1–2,10.

15 *Manchester Evening News* review of vol. 2, CHAR 8/486/13.

16 Trevelyan, *Blenheim* (1st edn, 1930), p. 181.

17 Churchill, *Marlborough*, vol. 1, p. 18 (UK); original US edn (1933), vol. 1, p. 7.

18 Churchill, *Marlborough*, vol. 1, pp. 373, 380 (UK).

19 Waugh, *Letters*, p. 627.

20 Trevelyan, *Blenheim* (1936 edn), p. 181; Ashley, *Marlborough*, pp. 30–1; Holmes, *Marlborough*, p. 184.

21 Ashley, *Churchill as Historian*, p. 23.

22 Ashley, *Churchill as Historian*, pp. 18, 10, 25.

23 Soames (ed.), *Speaking*, p. 390.

24 CHAR 8/529/142.

25 CHAR 8/484/19–23.

26 CHAR 8/484/140–44.

27 Churchill, *HESP*, vol. 4, p. 23 (US); p. 19 (UK).

28 CHAR 8/624/124.

29 CHAR 8/483/14–15.

30 CHAR 8/483/46–7, 144–5, 147.

31 CHAR 8/486/26–30.

32 CHAR 8/484/3–4.

33 CHAR 8/484/16.

34 CHAR 8/485/196–7 and 61.

35 CHAR 8/529/122–3.

36 Soames (ed.), *Speaking*, p. 397; Jenkins, *Churchill*, p. 463.

37 CHAR 8/529/115–17.

38 Soames (ed.), *Speaking*, p. 330.

39 CHAR 8/483/113–15.

40 CHAR 8/506/6, 10.

41 CHAR 8/528/140.

42 CHAR 8/526/58; CHAR 8/527/76; Soames (ed.), *Speaking*, p. 376.

43 CHAR 8/486/220.

44 Soames (ed.), *Speaking*, 412–13.

45 CHAR 8/528/43, 175; CHAR 8/547/26.

46 Soames (ed.), *Speaking*, p. 426.

47 CHAR 1/304/47, 64.

48 CHAR 8/506/11; CHAR 8/532/10; CHAR 8/532/16.

49 CHAR 1/329/9.

50 CHAR 1/323/10.

51 Jenkins, *Churchill*, pp. 516–18.

52 CHAR 8/483/46; CHAR 8/517/12, 17.

53 *WSC*, vol. 6, p. 52.

54 Churchill, *Marlborough*, vol. 3, p. 22 (UK); this is the preface for Volume Three, thus Volume 5 of the original US edn, p. 9; and for the similar blurb, see CHAR 8/529/223.

55 CHAR 8/529/44–5.

56 CHAR 8/502/23; 8/532/10.

57 Soames (ed.), *Speaking*, 426–7; CHAR 8/550/1; CHAR 1/329/44.

58 CHAR 8/530/194.

59 CHAR 8/547/44, 65.

60 CHAR 1/300/3.

61 CHAR 8/547/167–8.

62 CHAR 8/547/219–20.

63 CHAR 8/529/123.

64 CHAR 8/596/52.

Chapter 6: The Historian as Prophet, 1938–39

1   CHAR 1/323/12; Soames, *Speaking*, p. 434.

2   CHAR 8/594/174.

3   Moran, *Struggle for Survival*, p. 681, also p. 482; *Churchill* (US), p. 691, also p. 486.

4   *WSC*, vol. 5, p. 1,078.

5   CHAR 8/486/148–50.

6   Churchill, *HESP*, vol. 4, p. 263 (US); p. 207 (UK).

7   CHAR 8/506/3–12.

8   CHAR 8/506/17–19.

9   CHAR 8/532/6, 7.

10 CHAR 8/550/4, 11.

11 CHAR 8/597/28–39.

12 CHAR 8/597/6–7, 16.

13 CHAR 8/597/2–3.

14 CHAR 8/597/29–30.

15 CHUR 4/442/187.

16 CHAR 8/626/61; Churchill, *HESP*, vol. 1, p. 10 (US), p. 9 (UK).

17 CHUR 4/402A/55; Churchill, *HESP*, vol. 1, p. 23 (US), p. 19 (UK).

18 Churchill, *HESP*, vol. 1, p. 47 (US), p. 37 (UK).

19 CHUR 4/413A/38.

20 CHUR 4/402A, draft; Churchill, *HESP*, vol. 1, p. viii (US and UK).

21 Churchill, *HESP*, vol. 2, p. 262 (US), p. 210 (UK).

22 CHUR 4/402A/28.

23 CHUR 4/402C/402; compare Churchill, *HESP*, vol. 1, p. 67 (US), pp. 52–3 (UK).

24 CHUR 4/402C/411; Churchill, *HESP*, vol. 1, p. 78 (US), p. 61 (UK).

25 CHUR 4/402C/425; Churchill, *HESP*, vol. 1, p. 99 (US), p. 78 (UK).

26 CHAR 8/626/207.

27   Churchill, *HESP*, vol. 1, pp. 103, 117 (US), pp. 81, 92 (UK).

28   CHUR 4/402A/118; Churchill, *HESP*, vol. 1, pp. 119, 114 (US), pp. 94, 90 (UK).

29   Churchill, *HESP*, vol. 1, p. 477 (US), p. 377 (UK).

30   Churchill, *HESP*, vol. 1, p. 24 (US), p. 19 (UK).

31   Churchill, *HESP*, vol. 1, p. 44 (US), p. 35 (UK).

32   CHUR 4/402B//351–2; 402C/397–8.

33   Churchill, *HESP*, vol. 1, p. 60 (US), p. 47 (UK).

34   CHUR 4/402A and B/66; Churchill, *HESP*, vol. 1, p. 43 (US), p. 34 (UK).

35   CHUR 4/402B/271.

36   CHAR 8/487/78.

37   CHUR 4/402B/271–2, 276; Churchill, *HESP*, vol. 1, p. 66 (US), pp. 51–2 (UK).

38   Churchill, *HESP*, vol. 1, pp. 106, 110 (US), pp. 84, 86 (UK).

39   CHUR 4/402C432; Churchill, *HESP*, vol. 1, p. 111 (US), p. 86 (UK).

40   Churchill, *HESP*, vol. 1, p. 165 (US), p. 130 (UK).

41   CHUR 4/413A/112; compare Churchill, *HESP*, vol. 1, p. 176 (US), p. 139 (UK).

42   Churchill, *HESP*, vol. 1, p. 169 (US), p. 133 (UK).

43   CHUR 4/413A/2.

44   Soames (ed.), *Speaking*, 442–9; *WSC*, Comp. to vol. 5, part 3, p. 1,328.

45   CHAR 8/626/61–2.

46   Churchill, *HESP*, vol. 2, p. 359 (US), p. 285 (UK).

47   CHAR 8/626/147.

48   CHAR 8/626/241, 147.

49   CHAR 8/626/192.

50   Churchill, *HESP*, vol. 4, pp. 239–40 (US); pp. 188–9 (UK).

51   Churchill, *HESP*, vol. 4, pp. 195–6 (US), p. 155 (UK).

52   CHAR 8/626, 150, 23.

53   Ashley, *Churchill as Historian*, pp. 212, 37; but also p. 216.

54 Soames (ed.), *Speaking*, pp. 443–4.

55 Churchill, *HESP*, vol. 1, pp. 417, 422 (US), pp. 328, 332 (UK).

56 *WSC* – Ashley, 12 April 1939, CHAR 8/626, 147.

57 Green, *Short History*, par. 1,131.

58 Churchill, *HESP*, vol. 3, p. 80 (US), p. 66 (UK); *Marlborough*, vol. 2, p. 558 (UK); Commager edn, p. 706 (US).

59 Churchill, *HESP*, vol. 1, pp. 122, 309 (US), pp. 96, 243 (UK).

60 Churchill, *HESP*, vol. 1, pp. xvi, 253 (US), pp. xiv, 199 (UK).

61 Churchill, *HESP*, vol. 1, pp. 277–9, 297 (US), pp. 218–19, 233 (UK).

62 Churchill, *HESP*, vol. 2, p. 185 (US), p. 148 (UK); vol. 1, p. 176 (US), p. 138 (UK); vol. 2, p. 232 (US), p. 186 (UK).

63 CHUR 4/416A/212, 104.

64 Churchill, *HESP*, vol. 2, pp. 170, 365–6 (US); pp. 137, 290–1 (UK).

65 Churchill, *HESP*, vol. 3, pp. 156, 188–9 (US), pp. 129, 154 (UK).

66 Churchill, *HESP*, vol. 1, p. 348 (US, but omitting the last four words), p. 276 (UK).

67 Churchill, *HESP*, vol. 3, p. 347 (US), p. 281 (UK).

68 Churchill, *HESP*, vol. 2, pp. 313–14, 296, 292 (US), pp. 249, 235–6, 232 (UK).

69 Churchill, *HESP*, vol. 2, pp. 275, 302 (US), pp. 219, 241 (UK); CHAR 8/626/199.

70 Churchill, *HESP*, vol. 2, p. 275 (US), pp. 219–20 (UK).

71 Churchill, *HESP*, vol. 3, pp. 159–60 (US), p. 132 (UK); CHUR 4/427A/93.

72 Churchill, *HESP*, vol. 3, p. 157 (US), p. 130 (UK); CHAR 8/626/190.

73 Churchill, *HESP*, vol. 3, p. 149 (US), p. 124 (UK).

Chapter 7: The Author of Victory, 1940–45

1 Reynolds, *In Command of History*, pp. 6–7, 21; CHAR 8/718/4ff.

2 *WSC*, vol. 6, p. 52.

3 CHAR 8/626/190–3.

4   CHUR 4/427A/104; CHAR 8/626/190–3.

5   CHAR 8/626/58.

6   CHAR 8/626/101–2.

7   CHAR 8/624/205.

8   Churchill, *SWW*, vol. 1, p. 329 (UK), p. 421 (US).

9   CHAR 8/626/279.

10   CHAR 8/626/190–3; and CHUR 4/443/81.

11   CHAR 8/626/97, 73.

12   CHAR 8/626/87.

13   CHAR 8/626/83–4, 54.

14   CHAR 8/626/297.

15   CHAR 8/626/245–6, 55; CHUR 4/427B/262.

16   CHAR 8/658/1; and speech of 22 February 1944.

17   CHAR 8/681/11.

18   CHAR 8/713/107.

19   Colville, *Fringes of Power*, pp. 141–2, 156.

20   Amery, *Diaries*, vol. 2, p. 619; Dalton, *War Diary*, p. 28n.

21   Colville, *Fringes of Power*, pp. 85, 266, 192.

22   Cadogan, *Diary*, p. 304.

23   Colville, *Fringes of Power*, vol. 1, p. 183; vol. 2, pp. 190–1.

24   Nicolson, *Diaries*, vol. 2, p. 102; Asa Briggs, *War of Words*, p. 205.

25   CHUR 4/416/242; Churchill, *HESP*, vol. 1, p. 404 (US), p. 318 (UK); *Henry V*, Act IV, scene 3.

26   Berlin, *Mr Churchill in 1940*, p. 12.

27   Colville, *Fringes of Power*, pp. 255, 276.

28   Nicolson, *Diaries*, vol. 2, p. 223 (22 April 1941).

29   Clarke, *Cripps Version*, p. 259.

30   Reynolds, *In Command of History*, pp. 15–16.

31   Amery, *Diaries*, vol. 2, p. 1,021 (30 Nov. 1944).

32   Toye, *Churchill's Empire*, pp. 212–16.

33   Churchill, *HESP*, vol. 3, p. 198 (US), p. 163 (UK); Clarke, *Last Thousand Days*, pp. 212, 219. The US official was Alger Hiss, later famously identified as a Soviet agent.

Chapter 8: The Author as Celebrity, 1945–65

1   Colville, *Fringes of Power*, vol. 1, p. 309.

2   CHAR 8/658/58.

3   CHAR 8/681/21.

4   Reynolds, *In Command of History*, p. 18.

5   CHAR 8/718/4.

6   Moran, *Struggle for Survival*, p. 313 (UK); *Churchill*, p. 309 (US).

7   CHAR 8/719/25.

8   CHAR 8/719/4–5.

9   CHAR 8/719/11.

10   CHAR 8/719/33–4.

11   CHAR 8/719/39–57.

12   Reynolds, *In Command of History*, pp. 59–63, 533–4.

13   CHUR 1/7/57, 97–102, 106, 112–15.

14   Moran, *Struggle for Survival*, pp. 482, 484 (UK); *Churchill*, pp. 484, 486 (US).

15   CHUR 1/7/198–200, 229, 313; Buczacki, *Churchill and Chartwell*, pp. 240–1.

16   Gilbert, *Churchill–Reves Correspondence*, pp. 19, 347, 385.

17   CHUR 4/443/4.

18   CHUR 1/7/43–4; *WSC*, vol. 8, p. 1,250.

19   Cohen, *Churchill Bibliography*, pp. 943–5.

20   CHUR 1/7/17–19, 32–3.

21   *Manchester Guardian*, 23 April 1956 (vol. 1), 26 November 1956 (vol. 2).

22   CHUR 4/67/88.

23   *Manchester Guardian*, 21 March 1958 (vol. 4); see also 14 October 1957 (vol. 3).

Epilogue

1   Jenkins, *Churchill*, p. 900; Addison, *Churchill*, p. 240; Best, *Churchill*, p. 319; Cannadine, *Churchill's Shadow*, p. 48; Rose, *Churchill*, p. 211.

2   Plumb, 'The Historian', p. 137; Gilbert, *Reves–Churchill Correspondence*, 347.

3   Ashley, *Churchill as Historian*, p. 221.

4   Feske, *From Belloc to Churchill*, p. 227.

5   *WSC*, vol. 8, pp. 1,122–3.

6   CHAR 8/593/136.

7   Ramsden, *Man of the Century*, pp. 129, 272, 357; Reynolds, *In Command of History*, pp. 487–8; *Nobelprize.org*.2 Aug 2011.

8   Soames (ed.), *Speaking*, p. 575.

9   Soames (ed.), *Speaking*, p. 399.

10 Siwertz, *Nobelprize.org*.2 Aug 2011; *WSC*, vol. 8, p. 1,075.

Appendix: Churchill and the British Tax System

1   CHAR 1/185/30.

2   CHAR 1/185/23; and 185/24–5, 31–2.

3   CHAR 1/121/35–41.

Bibliography

My general principle is to give enough information for ordinary readers to identify the source of every direct quotation. For published works, I cite the most accessible editions available today on either side of the Atlantic, not necessarily the original editions, as held in academic libraries. Where any source is self-evident in my text, I avoid also adding a specific endnote. One effect of this minimalist policy is that more general acknowledgement of my scholarly debts appears in my bibliography and in the notes below on sources, chapter by chapter.

The chapter notes give particular attention to the holdings of the Churchill Archives at Churchill College, Cambridge, with the CHAR series broadly up to 1945 and the CHUR series subsequently. The call mark DEKE refers to the papers of Devis Kelly. In endnotes these sources are indicated simply by the internal reference numbers, which allow any specific reference to be located, given that the nature and date of the document should be evident from my text.

ABBREVIATIONS

ODNB   *Oxford Dictionary of National Biography.*

WSC   *Winston S. Churchill*, 8 vols. (London, 1966–88), first two volumes by Randolph S. Churchill; Volumes 3–8, the associated Companion Volumes, and the Churchill War Papers, 1939–41, all the work of Martin Gilbert.

SELECTED WORKS BY WINSTON S. CHURCHILL, as cited in endnotes

Frontiers and Wars (New York, 1962) containing most of *Malakand, River War, London to Ladysmith* and *Ian Hamilton's March*, as listed below.

Great Contemporaries (London, 1937; Fontana edn of 1939 text, 1962).

HESP – A History of the English-Speaking Peoples, 4 vols. (US edn, New York, 1956–58; Canadian edn identical, Toronto, 1956–58); (UK edn, London, 1956–58).

Ian Hamilton's March (London, 1900; Toronto edn).

London to Ladysmith: Via Pretoria (London, 1900).

Lord Randolph Churchill, 2 vols. (London, 1906).

The Story of the Malakand Field Force (London, 1898).

Marlborough: His Life and Times (London, 1933–38; London, 1947 edn, 2 vols.), Commager abridgement (New York, 1968; paperback 4 vols., continuous pagination).

My Early Life: A Roving Commission (London, 1930; Fontana edn, 1965 edn).

The River War: An Historical Account of the Reconquest of the Sudan, 2 vols. (London, 1899) 2 vols.

Savrola (London, 1899; Random House edn 1956).

Step by Step (London, 1939; Odhams edn 1947).

SWW – The Second World War, 6 vols. (UK edn, London, 1948–54); (US edn, Boston, MA, 1948–53).

Thoughts and Adventures (London, 1932; 1947 Odhams edn).

The World Crisis, 1911–1918 (5 vols., 1923–29; 2 vols., Odhams edn, 1938).

OTHER WORKS, cited by short titles in endnotes

Addison, Paul, 'Destiny, History and Providence: The Religion of Winston Churchill' in Michael Bentley (ed.), *Public and Private Doctrine* (Cambridge U.P., 1993) pp. 236–50.

—, 'Winston Churchill's Concept of "the English-speaking peoples"', in Attila Pok (ed.), *The Fabric of Modern Europe* (Nottingham, 1999), pp. 103–17.

—, *Churchill: The Unexpected Hero* (Oxford U.P., 2005).

Amery, Julian, *Joseph Chamberlain and the Tariff Reform Campaign*, 2 vols., continuous pagination (London, 1969).

Amery, Leo, *The Leo Amery Diaries*, ed. John Barnes and David Nicholson, 2 vols. (London, 1980–88).

Anderson, Stuart T., *Race and Rapprochement: Anglo-Saxonism and Anglo-American Relations, 1895–1904* (Farleigh Dickinson U.P., 1981).

Arnstein, Walter L., *The Bradlaugh Case: A Study in Late Victorian Opinion and Politics* (Oxford U.P., 1965).

Ashley, Maurice, *Churchill as Historian* (London, 1968).

—, *Marlborough* (London, 1939).

Bailey, Thomas A., *A Diplomatic History of the American People* (New York, 1955).

Beer, George Louis, *The English-Speaking Peoples: Their Future Relations and Joint International Obligations* (New York, 1917).

Bell, Duncan, *The Idea of Greater Britain: Empire and the Future of World Order, 1860–1900* (Princeton U.P., 2007).

Berlin, Isaiah, *Mr Churchill in 1940* (London, 1964).

Best, Geoffrey, *Churchill: A Study in Greatness* (London and New York, 2001).

Biagini, Eugenio, *Liberty, Retrenchment and Reform: Popular Liberalism in the Age of Gladstone* (Cambridge U.P, 1992).

Birkenhead, Lord (F. E. Smith), *America Revisited* (Boston, MA, 1924).

Blackett, R. J. M., *Divided Hearts: Britain and the American Civil War* (Louisiana State U.P., 2001).

Briggs, Asa, *The War of Words* (Oxford U.P., 1970).

Bright, *Selected Speeches of the Rt Hon. John Bright*, Everyman Edition (London, 1907).

Brundage, Anthony and Richard A. Cosgrove, *The Great Tradition: Constitutional History and National Identity in Britain and the United States, 1870–1960* (Stanford U.P., 2007).

Buczacki, Stefan, *Churchill and Chartwell: The Untold Story of Churchill's Houses and Gardens* (London, 2007).

Burk, Kathleen, *Troublemaker: The Life and History of A. J. P. Taylor* (Yale U.P., 2000).

Burrow, John, *A Liberal Descent: Victorian Historians and the English Past* (Cambridge U.P., 1981).

Burrow, John, *Memories Migrating* (Oxford, privately published, 2009).

Cadogan, Alexander, *Diaries, 1938–45*, ed. David Dilks (London, 1971).

Cannadine, David, *G. M. Trevelyan: A Life in History* (London, 1992).

—, *In Churchill's Shadow* (London, 2002; Penguin edn, 2003).

Charmley, John, *Churchill's Grand Alliance: The Anglo-American Special Relationship, 1940–57* (London and New York, 1995).

Clarke, Peter, *Lancashire and the New Liberalism* (Cambridge U.P., 1971).

—, *The Cripps Version: The Life of Sir Stafford Cripps* (London, 2002).

—, *The Last Thousand Days of the British Empire: The Demise of a Superpower, 1944–47* (London, 2007); US edn: *The Last Thousand Days of the British Empire: Churchill, Roosevelt and the Birth of the Pax Americana* (New York, 2008).

—, 'The English-Speaking Peoples before Churchill', *Britain and the World*, vol. 4:2 (2011), pp. 199–231.

Cohen, Ronald I., *Bibliography of the Writings of Sir Winston Churchill*, 3 vols. (London and New York, 2006).

Collini, Stefan, 'Believing in History: Herbert Butterfield, Christian and Whig', *Common Reading: Critics, Historians, Publics* (Oxford U.P., 2008), pp. 120–37.

Colville, John, *The Churchillians* (London, 1981; Weidenfeld paperback edn, 1986).

—, *The Fringes of Power: Downing Street Diaries*, 2 vols. (London, 1985; Sceptre edn, 1987)

—, 'Memoir', in John Wheeler-Bennett (ed.), *Action This Day: Working with Churchill* (London and New York, 1969), p. 138.

Dalton, Hugh, *The Second World War Diary, 1940–45*, ed. Ben Pimlott (London, 1986).

Daunton, Martin, *Trusting Leviathan: The Politics of Taxation in Britain, 1799–1914*; and *Just Taxes: The Politics of Taxation in Britain, 1914–1979* (Cambridge U.P., 2001–02).

Delany, Paul, 'The New Literary Marketplace, 1870–1914' in *Literature, Money and the Market: From Trollope to Amis* (Basingstoke and New York, 2002).

Edgerton, David, *Britain's War Machine: Weapons, Resources and Experts in the Second World War* (London, 2011).

Feske, Victor, *From Belloc to Churchill: Private Scholars, Public Culture, and the Crisis of British Liberalism, 1900–1939* (U. of North Carolina Press, 1996).

Flower, Desmond, *Fellows in Foolscap: Memoirs of a Publisher* (London, 1991).

Foremen, Amanda, *A World on Fire: An Epic History of Two Nations Divided* (London, 2010).

Forster, W. E., 'Imperial Federation', *Nineteenth Century*, xvii (1885), pp. 201–18.

Foster, Roy, *Lord Randolph Churchill: A political life* (Oxford U.P., 1981).

Gilbert, Martin (ed.), *Winston Churchill and Emery Reves: Correspondence, 1937–1964* (U. of Texas Press, 1997).

Gilbert, Martin, *Churchill and America* (New York and Toronto, 2005).

—, *In Search of Churchill* (London, 1994: Penguin edn, 1995).

Green, J. R., *History of the English People*, American Publishers Corporation popular edn, 5 vols., continuous paragraph numbers (New York, 1899).

Gunther, John, *Roosevelt in Retrospect* (London, 1950).

Harvie, Christopher, *The Lights of Liberalism: University Liberals and the Challenge of Democracy, 1860–86* (London, 1976).

Hastings, Max, *Finest Years: Churchill as Warlord* (London, 2009).

Hastings, Selina, *The Secret Lives of Somerset Maugham* (New York, 2010).

Hofstadter, Richard, *Social Darwinism in American Thought* (revised paperback edn, Boston, MA, 1955).

Holmes, Richard, *Marlborough: England's Fragile Genius* (London, 2008).

Jenkins, Roy, *Churchill* (London, 2001).

Kaplan, Fred, *Lincoln: The Biography of a Writer* (New York, 2008).

Keynes, John Maynard, *Essays in Biography* (London, 1933; Royal Economic Society edn, 1972).

Kimball, Warren F., *Forged in War: Roosevelt, Churchill and the Second World War* (New York, 1997).

King, Anthony and Wybrow, Robert J., *British Political Opinion, 1937–2000: The Gallup Polls* (London, 2001).

Lee, Celia and John, *The Churchills: A Family Portrait* (London, 2010).

Louis, Wm Roger, *Ends of British Imperialism: Collected Essays* (2nd edn, London and New York, 2006).

—, *In the Name of God, Go!: Leo Amery and the British Empire in the Age of Churchill* (London and New York, 1992).

Lovell, Mary S., *The Churchills: In Love and War* (London and New York, 2011).

Lukacs, John, *Churchill: Visionary, Statesman, Historian* (Yale U.P., 2002).

Macaulay, Lord, *History of England from the Accession of James II*, Everyman edn, 3 vols. (London and New York, 1906).

Mahan, Alfred T., 'Possibilities of an Anglo-American Reunion', *North American Review*, vol. 44 (1894), pp. 551–73.

Mandler, Peter, *The English National Character: The History of an Idea from Edmund Burke to Tony Blair* (Yale U.P., 2006).

Martin, Ralph G., *Jennie: The Life of Lady Randolph Churchill*, 2 vols. (Englewood Cliffs, NJ, 1969–71).

Mill, John Stuart, *Autobiography*, ed. Jack Stillinger (Oxford U.P., 1969).

Moran, Lord, *Winston Churchill: The Struggle for Survival, 1945–65* (London, 1966; Sphere Books edn, 1968); US edn, *Churchill: Taken from the Diaries of Lord Moran* (Boston, MA, 1966).

Mowat R. B. and Preston Slosson, *History of the English-Speaking Peoples* (Oxford U.P., 1943).

Muir, Ramsay, *A Short History of the British Commonwealth*, 2 vols. (London and New York, 1922–23).

Nicolson, Harold, *Diaries and Letters*, ed. Nigel Nicolson, 3 vols. (London, 1966–68).

Oxford, Countess of Oxford and Asquith, *Off the Record* (London, 1943).

Parry, Jonathan, *The Politics of Patriotism: English Liberalism, National Identity and Europe, 1830–86* (Oxford U.P., 2006).

Pelling, Henry, *America and the British Left: From Bright to Bevan* (London, 1956).

—, *Winston Churchill* (London, 1974).

Perkins, Bradford, *The Great Rapprochement: England and the United States, 1895–1914* (New York, 1968).

Pilpel, Robert H., *Churchill in America, 1895–1961* (New York and London, 1976).

Plumb, J. H., 'The Historian' in *Churchill: Four Faces and the Man* (London, 1969), which also includes essays by A. J. P. Taylor, Robert Rhodes James, Basil Liddell Hart and Anthony Storr.

Pound, Reginald, *The Strand Magazine, 1891–1950* (London, 1966).

Prior, Robin, *Churchill's 'World Crisis' as History* (London and Canberra, 1983).

Ramsden, John, *Man of the Century: Winston Churchill and his Legend since 1945* (London, 2002).

Reid, T. Wemyss, *Life of the Rt Hon. William Edward Forster*, 2 vols. (London, 1888).

Reynolds, David, *In Command of History: Churchill Fighting and Writing the Second World War* (London, 2004).

Roberts, Andrew, *A History of the English-Speaking Peoples since 1900* (London, 2006).

—, *Eminent Churchillians* (London, 1994; Phoenix edn, 1995).

—, *Salisbury: Victorian Titan* (London, 1999).

Roosevelt, Theodore, *The Winning of the West* (New York, 1910).

Rose, Norman, *Churchill: An Unruly Life* (London and New York, 1994).

Rosebery, Lord, *Lord Randolph Churchill* (London, 1906).

Ryan, Henry Butterfield, *The Vision of Anglo-America: The US-UK Alliance and the Emerging Cold War, 1943–46* (Cambridge U.P., 1987).

Seeley, J. R., *The Expansion of England* (London, 1883; 1904 edn).

Siwertz, Sigfrid, 'Winston Churchill, Award Ceremony Speech', *Nobel-prize.org.*2 Aug 2011.

Soames, Mary, *Clementine Churchill: The Biography of a Marriage* (Boston, MA, 1979).

Soames, Mary (ed.), *Speaking for Themselves: The Personal Letters of Winston and Clementine Churchill* (London and Toronto, 1998).

Stewart, Graham, *Burying Caesar: Churchill, Chamberlain and the Battle for the Tory Party* (London, 1999).

Toye, Richard, *Churchill's Empire: The World that Made him and the World he Made* (London and New York, 2010).

—, 'Phrases Make History Here: Churchill, Ireland and the Rhetoric of Empire', *Journal of Imperial and Commonwealth History*, vol. 38, (2010), pp. 549–70.

Trevelyan, G. M., *England under Queen Anne: Blenheim*, vol. 1 of 3 (London, 1st edn, 1930; 2nd edn, 1936).

Waugh, Evelyn, *The Letters of Evelyn Waugh*, ed. Mark Amory (London, 1980; Penguin edn, 1982).

Wells, H. G., *Experiment in Autobiography*, 2 vols., continuous pagination (London, 1934).

Wenden, D. J., 'Churchill, Radio, and Cinema', in Robert Blake and Wm Roger Louis (eds.), *Churchill* (Oxford U.P., 1993).

Williamson, Philip, 'The Doctrinal Politics of Stanley Baldwin' in Michael Bentley (ed.), *Public and Private Doctrine* (Cambridge U.P., 1993), pp. 181–208.

Wilson, Trevor, *The Downfall of the Liberal Party, 1914–35* (London, 1966).

Woods, Frederick, *A Bibliography of the Works of Sir Winston Churchill*, rev. edn (London, 1969).

Young, John Russell, *Around the World with General Grant* (1879), ed. Michael Fellman (Johns Hopkins U.P., 2002).

Ziegler, Philip, *Legacy: Cecil Rhodes, the Rhodes Trust and Rhodes Scholarships* (Yale U.P., 2007).

Prologue and Epilogue

Roy Jenkins's *Churchill* is the most accessible biography, with ch. 23 especially worth reading for its insights on the statesman as writer. Robin Prior, *Churchill's 'World Crisis' as History*, made a good start in examining Churchill's version of World War I. More ambitious in scope, David Reynolds, *In Command of History*, offers the best account to date of Churchill's methods of authorship and of his fiscal stratagems. Maurice Ashley, *Churchill as Historian*, has unique authority as a first-hand source, as I suggest in ch. 5. Apart from these books, and J. H. Plumb's very uneven essay, 'The Historian', written over forty years ago, there is little on Churchill as author apart from specialist academic comment; and the fine scholarly chapter on Churchill by Victor Feske in *From Belloc to Churchill* remains the most searching study to date. So I think it is justifiable to point to some neglect of Mr Churchill's profession as author.

All speeches by Churchill are cited simply by their date. Robert Rhodes James's edition of *Churchill's Complete Speeches* is the fullest compilation and is my source for the 1918 speech inaugurating the English-Speaking Union. There is useful organisational detail on comparable contemporary bodies in 'Anglo-American Societies', *The Times*, 4 July 1919. Apart from the prominent 1918 speech, Rhodes James gives six other speeches mentioning the English-speaking peoples, 1919–23, then virtually nothing until 1929 when Churchill revisited the United States; and, as will be seen in ch. 4, this became the origin of the book proposal. The quotation from Denis Kelly is taken from his unpublished memoir of his literary work for Churchill, deposited in the Churchill Archives.

Chapter 1: Father's Boy

The excellent biography of Lord Randolph by Roy Foster was a constant guide (and corrective) in my own interpretation of Lord Randolph's career, on which the *ODNB* gives us not only Roland

Quinault's useful entry on Lord Randolph but also on his father, the 7th Duke. There are entries on the earlier Dukes of Marlborough, and also on Henrietta Godolphin who would have been 2nd Duke but for her gender. There are two recent books, both titled *The Churchills*. Mary Lovell gives a lively account of the family, mainly in the nineteenth century; whereas Celia and John Lee, drawing on close cooperation from Peregrine Churchill (1913–2002), Winston's nephew, seek to defend the family honour on such matters as the cause of Lord Randolph's death, on which others have recently written. My point, broadly following Foster, is less about modern diagnosis than about contemporary reactions, especially by Winston and his mother.

Chapter 2: Mother's Boy

There are numerous biographies of Jennie but the most useful remains Ralph Martin's two-volume *Lady Randolph Churchill*. Richard Toye, *Churchill's Empire*, has recently opened up a searching line of research on Churchill's early books, exploring their viewpoint and demonstrating their relation to his original newspaper articles. Paul Delany's chapter, 'The New Literary Marketplace, 1870–1914', is highly germane on the economics of authorship and publishing. The Churchill Archives contain much material in CHAR 1, throwing light on Churchill's financial affairs in this period, for example CHAR 1/78–9; 1/85–6; and 1/121–2. For much pertinent information, from dates of ministerial appointments to surtax rates, I naturally turn to David and Gareth Butler's invaluable compilation, *Twentieth-Century British Political Facts* (8th edn, London, 2000).

Chapter 3: The English-Speaking Peoples Before Churchill

The scholarly foundation for this chapter can be found in the Frank Turner Memorial Lecture that I gave, under the same title, at the University of Texas at Austin in March 2011, published in the journal

Britain and the World, making clear many debts. Duncan Bell, *Greater Britain*, is excellent in defining the terms of these late-Victorian debates about Britain's place in the world. On the great Victorian historians John Burrow, *A Liberal Descent*, remains essential reading. Compared with my own sketch of what we can understand as 'Whig' or 'whig' or 'whiggish' history, Anthony Brundage and Richard Cosgrove, *The Great Tradition*, pp. 106–11, offer further refinement, and Stefan Collini, *Common Reading*, pp. 138–43, brings more subtlety to the scholarly discussion. The *ODNB* has useful entries on W. E. Forster (by Allen Warren); W. T. Stead (by Joseph O. Baylen); Julian Pauncefote (by Peter Calvert); Evelyn Wrench (by Alex May); and R. B. Mowat (by Derek Drinkwater). The degree of oblivion into which the work of Ramsay Muir has fallen can be checked in the volume on historiography in the *Oxford History of the British Empire* (1999), which, in over seven hundred pages, still gives Seeley over a dozen citations but Muir's name no mention.

Chapter 4: One Author, Two Contracts

In this chapter and my appendix below, I have turned frequently to the great authority on British fiscal policy, Martin Daunton, whose volume *Trusting Leviathan* illuminates the nineteenth-century origins of the system, while his second volume, *Just Taxes*, provides an invaluable analysis of how the system worked in Churchill's era. Churchill's own tax affairs can be reconstructed from abundant materials (seldom previously consulted) in the Churchill Archives, especially for the 1920s, CHAR 1/121, 185; 1/211–12; and see also the Lloyds Bank files, CHAR 1/229, 241, 292–3, 297, 304, 321, 329. The consolidated wine bills for 1935–36, as supplied to Churchill in 1937 by Randolph Payne, are in CHAR 1/318. On Chartwell, Mary Soames's biography of her mother, *Clementine Churchill*, rings true on many domestic matters; and Stefan Buczacki, *Churchill and Chartwell*, supplies further useful detail, not only on Chartwell itself but the Churchills' other houses.

On such matters as comparative wages and exchange rates B. R. Mitchell, *British Historical Statistics* (Cambridge U.P. 1988) is a treasure trove; and in all conversions of money values I have relied on the website *MeasuringWorth.com*, converting to 2008 retail prices – the best rough guide to purchasing power.

On Churchill's publishers, see the *ODNB* for George Godfrey Harrap (1868–1938) and also Flower, *Fellows in Foolscap*, esp. pp. 147–8. For Charles Scribner (1890–1952), known as 'Charlie', there is an austere entry in the *Dictionary of American Biography* by Maxwell Bloomfield and a much fuller one by Robert L. Gale in the successor series, *American National Biography*. There are some insights on Churchill's American finances in his files for the Bank of New York, CHAR 1/238–9, 293.

Chapter 5: The Struggle on Two Fronts

My understanding of Churchill writing *Marlborough* benefited enormously from reading David Cannadine's *G. M. Trevelyan* with its perceptive account of the links between the two men's literary and political concerns. Maurice Ashley's *Churchill as Historian* is best regarded as a source in its own right, and as such is indispensable. Gilbert, *In Search of Churchill*, is likewise helpful, especially in drawing on first-hand testimony about secretarial support, pp. 156–61. The Churchill Archives holdings listed for ch. 4, especially the Lloyds Bank files, can be counterpointed with the general correspondence in CHAR 1/300, 303, 323–7 and the literary series, especially CHAR 8/277, 296–7, 308, 311–12, 327, 337. Then *Marlborough* and *HESP* become intertwined, notably in CHAR 8/483–9, 528–31, 546–7, 550, 594–7, 624–5, 657.

The original London edition of *Marlborough* was published by Harraps in four volumes, 1933–38; the standard reprint of this text is the Harraps edition of 1947, Book One containing the original Volumes 1 and 2, and Book Two the original Volumes 3 and 4. This is the text that I normally cite. The New York edition was published by Scribners, vols. 1 and 2 together in 1933, vols. 3 and 4 together in 1935, vol. 5 in 1937 and vol. 6 in 1938. My references to the prefaces give parallel citations to this US edition, since these were not subsequently included in Scribners' post-war edition, abridged by Henry Steele Commager, issued in a single volume in 1968 and in four paperback volumes, with continuous pagination. I supply parallel citations to this abridged US text wherever possible. By this time, Commager had already prepared an abridgement of *HESP*. Harraps decided not to use the Commager abridgement but instead toyed with the idea of getting Maurice Ashley to prepare a separate British version. The story is well documented in Cohen, *Churchill Bibliography*, pp. 446–9, which is in general a painstaking guide to the writing as well as the publication of *Marlborough*.

Chapter 6: The Historian as Prophet

Mary Soames's helpfully annotated edition of her parents' correspondence, *Speaking for Themselves*, is particularly useful on the actual composition of *HESP*. This had long been conducted under a smokescreen, so as to render the progress (or lack of it) invisible to the publishers; and many earlier accounts have thereby been misled. The spine of the *HESP* correspondence really begins with Bracken in CHAR 8/815, followed chronologically by the series CHAR 8/308, 327, 506, 532, 550, 597, 626, 658, 681. The surviving proofs are vast, and not always easy to date since there were post-war raids on what survived from 1939. I have worked closely through the whole of the 'main pre-war revise', contained in CHUR 4/416 (*HESP*, vol. 1); 4/422 (vol. 2); 4/427A and B (vols. 3 and 4), and have checked this, page by page, against the text of the published volumes. Other pertinent pre-war proofs are in CHUR 4/413, 428, 430, 433.

My quotations from *Step by Step* are not endnoted but given simply by the date of original newspaper publication, as identified in the volume. Martin Gilbert's extensive work in editing the third part of the *Companion* to *WSC*, vol. 5, and the first part of the *War Papers*, helpfully prints much relevant correspondence, though I relied on the originals, which are even fuller. On Alan Bullock, there is a good memoir by Peter Dickson and Jose Harris, *Proceedings of the British Academy*, Biographical Memoirs of Fellows, vol. 7 (2008) pp. 125–46.

Chapter 7: The Author of Victory

All Gallup polls are from Anthony King and Robert Wybrow's useful compilation, *British Political Opinion, 1937–2000*. I have usually cited entries from Jock Colville's very revealing diary simply by dates in my text, with my quotations taken from the published version in his *Fringes of Power*. Likewise all Churchill's speeches of this period are identified by date only. The text which I quote is that given in the contemporary published collections, the first edited by Randolph Churchill, the rest by Charles Eade; and I used the various British, American and Canadian versions that happen to be on my own shelves – its own tribute to the theme of the English-speaking peoples: *Blood, Sweat, and Tears*, speeches 1938–41 (New York, 1941); *The Unrelenting Struggle*, speeches 1940–41 (Toronto, 1942); *The End of the Beginning*, speeches 1942 (Boston, MA, 1943); *Onwards to Victory*, speeches 1943 (London, 1944); *The Dawn of Liberation*, speeches 1944 (Toronto, 1945); *Victory*, speeches 1945 (Toronto, 1946); *Secret Session Speeches*, 1940–42 (London, 1946).

Chapter 8: The Author as Celebrity

There are many insights on Churchill's celebrity status in John Ramsden's well-documented book, *Man of the Century*. The diary published by Lord Moran in 1966, all too close to Churchill's death and all too revealing of his patient's foibles, gave great offence at the time. For historians, though, it has an irresistible allure, tempered by questions over the strictly contemporary nature of the entries. I have borne this in mind in making my own selections, which are given in my text by date alone wherever possible. David Reynolds's *In Command of History* is indispensable, not only on the composition and the reception of the *Second World War* volumes but also on financial aspects. The notion that the saviour of his nation was himself a victim of wartime taxation from which he emerged almost penniless is no longer tenable, as is made clear by the contents of files like CHUR 1/7 in the Churchill Archive. On negotiations concerning *HESP* during the war years, see CHAR 8/713, 718; and 8/719 on Denis Brogan's abortive efforts. The post-war revises of *HESP* are in CHUR 4/419–21, 428–39. On the Hodges era in the 1950s, Denis Kelly is pertinent in DEKE 2/ch. 6, and for the reception of the book see CHUR 4/67, 442–3.

Acknowledgements

After forty years as a writer myself, the first thing I have to acknowledge – with some puzzlement and even reluctance – is how often I have written about Winston Churchill. There he is, as the young Liberal statesman, on the cover of my first book, *Lancashire and the New Liberalism* (1971), and, twenty-five years later, back on the cover of my history of twentieth-century Britain, *Hope and Glory* (1996 and 2004). Here we go again, with evidently unavailing efforts on my part to avoid this particular walk with destiny; but I will leave it to my readers to assess how adequately my own past life has been but a preparation for this hour and for this trial.

I was prompted to envisage this subject after reading two other books by writers whom I admire. When I read the late Roy Jenkins's biography, *Churchill*, in 2001, I found an unusual degree of attention focused on the great war leader's literary career and said in my review that 'we are shown the supreme example of the politician as man of letters – by an author uniquely placed to know what he is talking about.' And when I was asked by David Reynolds to read part of what became *In Command of History: Churchill Fighting and Writing the Second World War* (2004), I was further prompted to wonder about Churchill's earlier big books, written before the war.

I would like to thank David Reynolds for his friendly interest throughout my own project. I have received much shrewd advice from the omnicompetent Director of the Churchill Archives Centre, Allen Packwood, not only indicating what was available in the archives but easing my path in consulting the collections during the years when my work took its final shape. *Mr Churchill's Profession* was first commissioned – albeit under a different title – in New York by Peter Ginna, whose support throughout has been constant; and the able assistance of Pete Beatty throughout is also much appreciated. Especially in the later stages, my editors in London, Michael Fishwick and Anna Simpson, have likewise creatively shaped the book's published form and have actively protected its author's interests.

In Cambridge, the staff at the Churchill Archives Centre have assisted my research, which has been agreeably eased by my continuing connection with St John's College and by my Honorary Fellowship at Trinity Hall. The University Library at Cambridge remains a wonderful resource for scholars. In British Columbia, I have likewise been fortunate to be able to draw on the extensive holdings of the McPherson Library, University of Victoria. During the early part of 2009 I spent a short but productive period at the Institute of Advanced Study in Princeton, New Jersey, and, since my position was that of Director's Visitor, I would like to give Peter Goddard, who was then Director, my personal thanks for this opportunity. I gave a version of what became chapter 3 of this book as the Frank Turner Memorial Lecture at the British Scholar conference at the University of Texas at Austin, an invitation that I felt honoured to fulfil in March 2011.

During research in Cambridge, I benefited from discussions of Marlborough in the Churchill Archives with Charles-Edouard Levillain, whose own forthcoming work will remedy gaps in mine. And my old friend Kenneth Edwards, with the keen eye of a geneticist, ran his eye over my chapter 1. Likewise what became chapter 3 was scrutinised in an earlier draft by Duncan Bell and Eugenio Biagini, both of whom have written perceptively on cognate topics.

As with my two preceding books, *Mr Churchill's Profession* was not actually written in Cambridge, but on Pender Island, British Columbia, in the writers' studio that Maria Tippett and I have created. Its bibliographical resources were enhanced when our neighbours Stuart and Wendy Scholefield made a long-term loan of the works of Lord Macaulay and J. R. Green, which Stuart's historian grandfather had acquired in British Columbia in the late nineteenth century, itself surely corroborating the extraordinary hold of the idea of the English-speaking peoples. Not only Maria but also that acute literary scholar, Paul Delany, read early drafts as they emerged from the Pender Island Research Institute – and it was he who ultimately came up with the title, to general acclamation. Then I turned yet again to trusty readers further afield: to Richard Toye, himself author of a perceptive study *Churchill's Empire*, now generously agreeing to read one of my own drafts on the fourth occasion; to Stefan Collini, who has acted in this capacity for nine of my books; and to John Thompson, who has read all ten before publication. To all of them – for all of them, and for their friendship – I humbly give thanks. (And the remaining stubborn errors are mine alone).

Peter Clarke, February 2012

*　　*　　*

The publication of this book in hardback was very warmly received, so much so that no reviewers pointed out any substantive errors for me to correct. But on a subsequent trawl of the library catalogues I discovered my appalling ignorance of the fine book by Professor Manfred Weidhorn, *Sword and Pen: A survey of the writings of Sir Winston Churchill* (University of New Mexico Press, 1974). I had also omitted to list in my bibliograpy the book by my friend Reba Soffer, *History, Historians, and Conservatism in Britain and America* (Oxford U.P., 2009) which is particularly useful on Keith Feiling. Another subsequent discovery came from the archives of the British Academy, which had been unavoidably closed during my own researches; see 'Winston Churchill and the British Academy, *British Academy Review*, 20 (Summer 2012), pp. 45–7. The new aspect is that an abortive attempt to elect Churchill as a Fellow, mounted in 1938 by the historians in the Academy, notably H.A.L Fisher, had probably soured the context in which the offer of election was belatedly made (and brusquely declined) in 1939. But the main point is still that, in the eyes of his fellow historians in the universities, the quality of output from the Chartwell word factory merited this golden stamp of approval. And for giving me a private tour of the factory in 2011 I remain grateful to Alice Martin of the National Trust.

Peter Clarke, February 2013

Index

Adams, Charles Francis, 83–4, 87
Adams, George Burton, 106
Addison, Paul, 290
Afghanistan, 49
Africa, 264
Agincourt, battle of, 249
Alabama, 84, 86–8
Alaska, 101
Alexandra, Princess of Wales, 17–18
Alfred the Great, 213–14, 217, 225, 228, 245
Allen, Commodore Gordon, 280
Amalgamated Press, 203, 238, 270, 272
American Civil War, 42, 201–2, 206–7
  battlefields, 128, 207, 221
  and English-speaking peoples, 82–8,
    90–1, 94, 293
  and *History*, 228, 233, 239, 286, 290
American Declaration of Independence,
  xv, 85, 110–11, 157, 200–1, 227, 234
American Historical Review, 106, 174
American War of Independence, 201–2,
  228, 234, 265
Amery, Leo, 156, 158–9, 165, 179, 243, 245,
  258, 261, 264
*Amid These Storms, see Thoughts and
  Adventures*
Anglo-Irish Treaty, 113, 124
Anglo Saxon Chronicle, 252
Anglo-Saxon Review, 46–8, 102
Anglo-Saxonism, 96–106, 109, 215
Anglo-Saxons, 103, 216–17, 256
Anne, Queen, 162, 175–6, 192, 233
Annual Register, 48, 57
Arminius, 103
*Arms and the Covenant (While England
  Slept)*, 189–90
Arthur, King, 214–15, 228, 245
Ashdown, battle of, 217
Ashley, Lady, 177

Ashley, Maurice, 133, 174, 190, 200, 243,
  248, 285
  and *History*, 199, 207, 220–2, 224, 229,
    285, 291
  and *Manchester Guardian*, 159, 178–9,
    190
  and *Marlborough*, 127, 132, 138, 159–61,
    163–4, 166–7, 177, 191–2
Asquith, Herbert Henry, 65–6, 189, 243
Asquith, Margot, 14
Atlantic Charter, 263–4
Attlee, Clement, 198, 243, 269
Australia, 89, 92, 201, 236–9, 259, 278
Aylesford scandal, 18, 45, 62

backgammon, 167, 170
Bahamas, 147
Baldwin, Stanley, 116, 122–3, 130, 145, 156,
  197–8, 200
  and Conservative leadership, 153, 159,
    179–80
Balfour, Arthur, xiv, 58–9, 61–3, 65, 101,
  108–10, 124, 174, 189
Balfour Definition, 112
Balkans, 257
Ballot Act, 14
Bangalore, 38
Bank of England, 78
Barnett, Mr, MP, 13–14
Barraclough, Geoffrey, 288–9
Baruch, Bernard, 287
Bastille Day, 257
Battle of Britain, 247, 249, 251, 259
Battle of France, 247
Bavaria, 149
BBC, 248–9, 253, 258, 262
Beaverbrook, Lord, 184, 197, 258, 264, 284
Beer, George Louis, 106–7
Belfast, 31, 110

Belloc, Hilaire, 140
Bering Sea, 100
Berlin, Isaiah, 249
Bermuda, 264
Berne Convention, 93
Best, Geoffrey, 290
Beveridge, Albert J., 101
Birmingham, 11–12, 24–5, 53, 243
Bismarck, Otto von, 266
Black Death, 227
Blackpool, 23–4
Blair, Tony, xix
Blake, William, 14
Blandford, Marquises of, 7
Blenheim, battle of, 5, 162, 164, 176, 187, 193, 228
Blenheim Harriers, 15–16
Blenheim Palace, 5–6, 9, 12, 62, 66, 219
    archives, 57, 125, 127, 138, 161–3
Blood, General Sir Bindon, 39
Blood, Sweat and Tears, see Into Battle
Blum, Leon, 223
Bodleian Library, 164
Boston, xii, 53
Boudicca, 210, 212–14, 228, 245, 283
Bracken, Brendan, 143, 145, 150, 180–1, 186, 241
    and Chartwell, 141, 180, 186
    and *History*, 239–40, 270–1, 275, 281–2
Bradford, 44, 50
Bradlaugh, Charles, 20–1, 23, 61
Briggs, Asa, 285
Bright, John, 84–6, 201
British Academy, 174–5
British Commonwealth, 112–13, 143, 157, 247–8, 259–60, 266, 292
British Empire, xvii, 25, 33, 38, 49, 108, 113, 141, 292–3
    and 'commonwealth of nations', 89–90, 92, 112, 157
    and *History*, 288–9
    and imperial federalism, 89–90, 109
    and imperial preference, 59–60, 92, 156, 258, 264
    and Irish Home Rule, 31–2
    and Second World War, 246–7, 258–64, 266–7, 294
British Guiana, 100
Brogan, Denis, 275–7, 285

Bryce, James, 91, 97, 108–9, 174
Buckle, G. E., 39
Bulgarian atrocities, 94, 97
Bullock, Alan, 200, 220–2, 236–7, 240, 285
Burke, Edmund, 36, 48
Burma, 11, 25
Burns, Robert, 93
Bush, George W., xix
Buzzard, Dr Thomas, 28
Byron, Lord, 93

Cadogan, Sir Alexander, 246
Campbell-Bannerman, Sir Henry, 65
Camrose, Lord, 178, 197, 203, 238, 272–3, 278
Canada, 54, 87, 90–2, 99–100, 108, 127, 156, 201, 230, 238, 259–60
Canadian House of Commons, 248, 257, 264
Cannadine, David, 290
Cape Town, 52
Carlton Club, 28
Carlyle, Thomas, 97
Celts, 104–5, 109
Chamberlain, Sir Austen, 157–8
Chamberlain, Joseph, 12, 22, 24, 31, 53, 59–61, 66, 189
    and English-speaking peoples, 90, 92, 96, 101
    and imperial preference, 59–60, 92, 154–5, 258
    and South African War, 59, 101
Chamberlain, Neville, 66, 145, 155, 158, 181, 197, 200, 254
    and Munich agreement, 198, 205
    and outbreak of war, 232, 241–6, 250, 258
Channel Islands, 243
Chaplin, Charlie, 268
Charles I, King, 246
Chartwell Manor
    acquisition for nation, 131, 273–4
    Churchill's library, 168
    Churchill's study, 131–2, 166–7
    costs, 78–9, 130–1, 134–7, 147, 153
    farm income, 282–3, 297
    improvements, 129–30, 183
    purchase, 77–80, 118

sale threat, 141, 184–7, 204, 235
workforce, 130–1
and writing of *History*, 195–6, 208, 210,
  218–19, 276
and writing of *Marlborough*, 167–71
and writing of *Second World War*, 251,
  280–1
Chatham, Lord (Pitt the Elder), 228–31,
  235, 241, 245, 255, 266–7, 289
Chequers, 242, 250, 279
Chesterton, G. K., 140
Chicago, 95
Chicago Tribune, 82, 149
Church of England, 16, 51
Churchill, Clementine (née Hozier)
  and Beaverbrook, 184
  and Bracken, 180
  and Chartwell, 130–1, 186, 274
  and Churchill's celebrity, 293–5
  and finances, 77–9, 128, 130
  marriage, 67–8
  relationship with Terence Philip, 171
  and Reves, 284
  and writing of *History*, 218–19, 223
  and writing of *Marlborough*, 167, 170–1,
    179
Churchill, Diana, 75, 130
Churchill, Jack, 8–9, 28, 36, 52, 65, 68, 127
Churchill, Johnny, 127
Churchill, Marigold, 75
Churchill, Mary, 75, 130–1, 171
Churchill, Lady Randolph (Jennie
    Jerome)
  affairs, 28–9, 34, 67
  and *Anglo-Saxon Review*, 46 8, 102
  death, 5, 69
  marriage, 8–10, 14, 17
  and money, 35–7, 54
  and Randolph's Chancellorship, 5, 25
  and Randolph's death, 28–30
  second marriage, 34–6
  third marriage, 69
  and Winston's education, 16
  and Winston's literary career, 37–41, 46,
    51
Churchill, Lord Randolph
  and Aylesford scandal, 17–19, 62
  death, x, 5
  education, 15–16

extravagance, 10–11
and Fourth Party, 20–2
gift for publicity, 22–4
illness and death, 27–30, 61
and imperial federation, 89–90, 92
and Irish politics, 19–20, 30–2, 62–3,
  109
marriage, 8–10, 14, 17
political career, 4, 11–17, 20–6, 64, 157
religious belief, 61
resignation, 25–6
sex life, 27–8
speeches, 22–3, 33
and Tory Democracy, 11–12, 24–6, 30–3,
  86
his will, 11, 35–6, 57, 78
and Winston's education, 15–16, 41
Churchill, Randolph, 28, 75, 126–7, 185,
  190, 252, 255
Churchill, Sarah, 75, 184
Churchill, Sir Winston, 5–6
Churchill, Winston S.
  and abdication crisis, 183–4, 189
  alcohol consumption, 135–7, 167–8
  American connections, 8–9
  army career, 15, 30, 34–7, 43–4, 49–51,
    53, 154–5
  breach of privilege allegations, 158–9,
    165
  and brick-laying, 130
  Chancellorship, 5, 36–7, 79, 116, 118–23,
    148, 300
  changes of political allegiance, 59–61,
    64, 114, 154
  and cigars, 268
  currency speculation, 147–8
  depression, 129
  education, 4, 14–16
  and English-speaking peoples, 109–10,
    113–14, 123, 128, 142–3, 147, 156, 271,
    277, 292–3
  and father's death, 27–30
  and film industry, 182–3
  finances, 75–9, 116–22, 128–37, 147–9,
    153, 182, 184–5, 191–2, 240, 271–3
  Fulton speech xix, 277, 291
  honorary US citizenship, xv, 294
  and imperialism, 32–3, 47, 90, 92,
    154–5, 158, 258–67, 293

and Indian self-government, 145, 153,
    155, 157–8, 178–9, 189, 261, 292
and Irish politics, 109
journalism, 37–42, 44–5, 51–2, 149–50,
    184, 197–8
lecture tours, 53–4, 142, 146–7
literary earnings, xvii, 41–2, 117–22,
    125–6, 132–5, 153–4, 191–2, 232–3,
    274–5, 278–9, 282–3, 297–300
literary style, 48–9
marriage, 67–8
and money, 35–7
New York traffic accident, 147, 149
and painting, xvii, 77
parliamentary salary, xvii, 8, 56, 65, 67,
    79, 116, 120, 135, 233, 235, 279
political career, 40, 43–4, 50, 65–7,
    145–6, 179–80
post-war electoral defeat, 269
post-war publishing agreements, 271–3
and race, 157, 161, 215–16
reading, 167–8, 281
religious belief, 61
retirement as author, 283–4, 286–8
and social reform, 264
speeches, 23, 33, 44, 198, 206, 244–9,
    251–66, 293–5
taste for champagne, 33, 136–7, 268
views on Americans, 123
war aims, 256–67
war leadership, 241–67
war service, 69
wartime work habits, 242–3
Churchill, Winston (US author), x–xii, 53
Churchill family pedigree, 6–7
'Churchill Troupe', 127, 156
Citizen Kane, 127
Clarence, Duke of, 214
Cleveland, Grover, 100
Clive, Robert, 230
Cobden, Richard, 84
Colville, John, 241–4, 249, 251–2, 268,
    280–1
Commager, Henry Steele, 176–7
'commonwealth of nations', 89–90, 92,
    112, 157, 260–1
copyright, 55, 93
Cornwallis-West, George, 34–6, 69

Cowen, Joseph, 92–3
Cowes Royal Regatta, 8, 14
Crécy, battle of, 228
Creighton, Mandell, 15
Cripps, Sir Stafford, 250
Cromwell, Oliver, 160, 229–31, 243
Cuba, xvi, 9, 37–8, 100
Curtis Brown, 76, 117, 126, 150
Czechoslovakia, 205, 208

Daily Graphic, 37
Daily Mail, 142, 147, 153, 158, 195
Daily Telegraph, 39, 41, 126, 178, 197, 223,
    272, 278
Dalton, Hugh, 245
Dardanelles, 68, 75, 242
Dark Ages, 212, 256
D-Day landings, 272
de la Mare, Walter, 73
de Montfort, Simon, 209, 226, 229
Deakin, William
    and History, 199–200, 207–8, 213, 220,
        222, 235–8, 240, 243, 248, 283, 285
        and Marlborough, 190–2
    and Second World War, 277, 279
Dervishes, 44
Diana, Princess of Wales, 6
Dickens, Charles, 93, 140
Dieppe, 68
Dilke, Sir Charles, 12, 89–90, 92, 94
Disraeli, Benjamin, 9, 16, 18, 23, 48, 64,
    89, 97
Dodd, Frank, 270–1, 287
Drake, Sir Francis, 253
Dublin, 19, 45
Dunkirk evacuation, 245
Dutch Republic, 104

Eade, Charles, 252
Economist, The, 141
Eden, Anthony, 197, 281
Edgehill, battle of, 224, 226
Edinburgh, 53
Edmonds, General Sir James, 206, 222
Education Act, 83
Edward the Confessor, 227
Edward I, King, 225–6, 228
Edward III, King, 228

Edward VII, King, 17–18, 28, 34, 41, 44–5, 62
Edward VIII, King, 183–4, 189, 219
Edward, Prince of Wales, *see* Edward VII, King
Edwin, King of Northumbria, 212
Egypt, 24, 42–4
Eisenhower, Dwight D., xix
El Alamein, battle of, 265
Elizabeth I, Queen, 209
Elliott, Maxine, 192, 195, 219, 283
English Bill of Rights, xv, 111
English Civil War, 226
English Historical Review, 174
English Navy, 213
English-speaking peoples, xv–xvii, xix, 81–115, 199, 293
    Churchill and, 109–10, 113–14, 123, 128, 142–3, 147, 156, 271, 277, 292–3
    and race, 101–2, 104–6, 108
    and Second World War, 261, 264–6
    stepping-stone theory, 108, 112–13
English-Speaking Union, xv, 81, 108, 113, 188
Epping, 146
Ethelred the Unready, King, 252
Eton College, 3–4, 57, 75
European unity, 291–2
Evening Standard, 184, 197
Everest, Mrs, 4

Farrar, Canon F. W., 55
Feiling, Keith
    and *History*, 200–3, 206–10, 239, 285
    and *Marlborough*, 126 7, 168, 177, 181–2, 185, 190
Feske, Victor, 291
Fitzgerald, Scott, 126
FitzGibbon, Gerald, 63
Flower, Desmond, 204, 209, 238–40, 274, 281–2
Flower, Sir Newman, 150–1, 186, 191, 203–4, 206, 208–9, 235, 237, 239, 274, 276
Forster, William Edward, 83–4, 86–90, 92, 112, 260
Fourth Party, 20–2, 58
Fox, Charles James, 241
Free Trade, 59–60, 154–6

Freeman, Edward Augustus, 15, 94, 96–9, 101, 103–4, 216, 224
Freidel, Frank, 285
Frontiers and Wars, 49
Froude, J. A., 97, 99, 168
Fulton, Missouri, xix, 277, 291

Galbraith, V. H., 276
Gallipoli expedition, 68, 74–5, 79
Galton, Francis, 6
Gandhi, Mohandas K., 153, 161, 179, 268
Garibaldi, Giuseppe, 42
Garron Towers, 76–9, 118, 185, 297
General Strike, 145
Geneva, 87
Geoffrey of Monmouth, 212
George III, King, 111, 276
George V, King, 183
George VI, King, 184, 241
Germany, 99, 103–4, 179, 189, 215
Gettysburg Address, 85
Gettysburg, battle of, 221
Gibbon, Edward, 16, 33, 36, 48–9, 161
Gladstone, William Ewart, 4, 14, 16, 21, 23, 48, 98, 103, 293
    and Irish Home Rule, 22–4, 31, 59, 109
    and United States, 83–4, 87–8, 94
Glasgow, 256
Glorious Revolution, 220, 228
Godolphin, Henrietta, Lady, 6
Gold Standard, 116, 122, 126, 145–7, 154
Gone with the Wind, 222, 228
Gordon, General, 48
Graham-Dixon, L. C., 282, 284
Grand Alliance, 198–9
Grant, Ulysses S., 86–7, 92
Great Contemporaries, 59, 144, 188–9, 192
Great Depression, 144, 155
Greater Britain, 89, 92, 108
Greece, 38, 257
Green, J. R., 97–9, 139–50, 168, 207, 215–17, 224, 230, 286
Greenwood, Arthur, 243
Grey, Sir Edward, 105
Grote, George, 161

habeas corpus, 227, 255
Halifax, Lord, 245
Hamblin, Grace, 131, 168

Hamilton, General Ian, 42–3, 52, 75, 77
Hampden, John, 103, 105, 226, 263, 265
Harding, Warren, 113
Harold, King, 103, 217
Harrap, George, 125–6, 139, 176, 179, 184, 192–4
Harrap, Walter, 240
Harris, Frank, 27, 55–6, 61, 74
Harrow School, 15, 36, 156, 253
Harvard University, 266, 277
health insurance, 66
Hearst, William Randolph, 127
Hemingway, Ernest, 294
Henry III, King, 226
Henry V, King, 249
Henry, Patrick, 214
Hill, Kathleen, 195–6, 237, 240, 274
history, Whig interpretation of, 97–8, 103, 174, 224
History of the English-Speaking Peoples, A
  abrupt ending, 239–40
  critical reception, 288–90
  and democracy, 201–3, 218, 226, 239
  and dictatorship, 229–31
  and the Dominions, 201–2, 236–9
  film rights, 271
  and foresight, 197, 222
  historical stance, 174, 224–31
  post-war publication, 281–9, 291
  printing of proofs, 205
  sales and earnings, 141, 146, 150–3, 181, 191, 204, 232–3, 235, 240, 287–8, 293
  and *Second World War*, 277–8
  serialisation, 238, 270, 272, 288
  and Sir Winston Churchill, 5–6
  style and scholarship, 209–18, 224–5
  unfinished nature, 221–2, 291
  and war leadership, 262–3, 266–7
  writing and publication, 139–43, 145–6, 150–3, 156–7, 159, 180–3, 185, 187, 189–91, 194–241, 270–2, 274–8, 279–89
History Today, 281
Hitler, Adolf, xiii, 151, 179, 185, 190, 242, 247, 256, 263, 269, 294
  and *Great Contemporaries*, 189
  invasion of Poland, 232, 236
  invasion of Russia, 250–1, 254, 259
Mein Kampf, 270

and writing of *History*, 197, 205–6, 208, 222–4, 230–1
HMS *Nelson*, 238
Hoare, Sir Samuel, 158–9, 165
Hodge, Alan, 281, 283–6
Hope, Anthony, 45
Hozier, Henry, 67
Hundred Years War, 228
Hurstfield, Joel, 285, 288

Ian Hamilton's March, 52–3
imperial federalism, 89–90, 109
imperial preference, 59–60, 154–6, 258, 264
imperialism, 32–3, 47, 60, 92, 154–5, 158, 258–67
Inayat Kila, 40
India, 18, 25, 202, 209, 230, 264
  Churchill and, 16, 30, 35–6, 38, 42, 48, 97, 122, 138, 215, 292
  and English-speaking peoples, 89, 111
  self-government, 145, 153, 155, 157–8, 178–9, 261, 292
India Bill, 157–8, 165, 179, 182
Indian National Congress, 153
Industrial Revolution, 202, 285
Into Battle (*Blood, Sweat and Tears*), 252, 255
Ireland, 209, 229
  and English-speaking peoples, 103–4, 109–11
Irish Home Rule, 19, 22–5, 30–2, 59, 62–4, 109
Ismay, General Sir Hastings, 279
Italy, 38

James II, King, 138
James, Henry, 29
Jenkins, Roy, 290
Jerome, Jennie, *see* Churchill, Lady Randolph
Jerome, Leonard, 8, 10
Jerome, Leonie, 29
Joan of Arc, 223, 228
Johnson, Samuel, 36, 42, 47–8, 199
Jones, Maldwyn, 285

Kelly, Denis, 280–1, 285
Kennedy, John F., xv, 294

Kenyon, Sir Frederic, 174
Keynes, John Maynard, 79, 119
Khaki Election, 53
Khartoum, 44
King James Bible, 93, 123, 131
Kinsky, Count, 28–9, 34
Kipling, Rudyard, 29, 49, 99, 122, 140, 216
Kitchener, Sir Herbert, 43–5
Korda, Alexander, 102, 171
Kristallnacht, 205

Ladysmith, relief of, 52
Lawrence of Arabia, 183
League of Nations, 107–8, 112–13, 189–90
Lecky, W. E. H., 168
Lee, Robert E., 221
lend-lease, 251, 261, 263
Lenin, V. I., 173
Lewes, battle of, 209, 226
Liberal Summer Schools, 112
Liberalism and the Social Problem, xii, 66
Life magazine, 278
Lincoln, Abraham, 24, 85–6, 93–4, 103, 111, 201, 228
Lindemann, Professor Frederick, 169, 241
Listener, The, 160
literary agents, 55
Literary Trust, 273, 277–8
Lloyd George, David, xiii, 65–6, 74, 80, 96, 108, 114, 136, 145, 157, 246, 269, 299
London to Ladysmith, 51–2
London Zoo, 171
Londonderry, Marquis, 76
Longfellow, Henry Wadsworth, 93
Lord Randolph Churchill
    and Balfour, 61–2
    cartoons, 23
    FitzGibbon letter, 63
    and Forster, 88
    and Irish politics, 19–20, 31
    political context, 61–4
    and resignation issue, 26
    sales and earnings, 56, 67, 74, 76, 117
    and syphilis, 27, 61
    view of politics, 64–5
    and Woodstock system, 13–14
    writing and publication, 3–33, 55–65
Los Angeles Times, 82

Louis XIV, 253
Luce, Henry, 278–9

Macaulay, Thomas Babington, 16, 33, 36, 48, 97–8, 111, 139, 168
    and *Marlborough*, 124–5, 138, 159, 162–5, 173, 175–6, 224
MacDonald, Ramsay, 122, 145, 179
Macmillan, Harold, xix, 74, 272
Macmillan's Magazine, xi, 45
Mafeking, relief of, 52
Maginot Line, 234
Magna Carta, xv, 106, 111, 218, 225, 228, 255, 263
magnetic mines, 238
Mahan, Captain Alfred Thayer, 100, 106
Maine, 52
Majuba Hill, battle of, 42–3
Malakand campaign, 39–40, 45, 187, 206
Malakand Field Force, The, 39–43, 124
Malplaquet, battle of, 5, 192
Manchester, 85, 163, 178, 239
Manchester Evening News, 178
Manchester Guardian, 82, 107, 111–12, 159, 178–9, 190, 288
Marlborough, Consuelo (Vanderbilt), Duchess of, 9
Marlborough, Frances ('Fanny'), Duchess of, 10, 29, 45, 50, 62, 76
Marlborough, Lily, Duchess of, 9
Marlborough, Sarah, Duchess of, 6
Marlborough, John Churchill, 1st Duke of, xv, 5–6, 12, 42, 207, 211, 245
    and Camaret Bay letter, 163–6, 175
    and Churchill's war speeches, 252–3, 255
    and *History*, 230, 290
    Macaulay and, 124–5, 162–5
Marlborough, George, 6th Duke of, 13
Marlborough, John Spencer-Churchill, 7th Duke of, 5, 9–11, 13, 19–20
Marlborough, George Spencer-Churchill, 8th Duke of, 9
    and Aylesford affair, 17–19, 62
Marlborough, Charles Spencer-Churchill ('Sunny'), 9th Duke of, 9, 51–2, 55, 62, 66
    and Blenheim archives, 125, 127, 161–3
Marlborough, John Spencer-Churchill, 10th Duke of, 9

Marlborough: His Life and Times
  abridged edition, 176–7
  Ashley's contribution, 159–61
  and Camaret Bay letter, 163–6, 175
  critical reception, 172–5
  film rights, 271
  and *History*, 197, 199–200, 202, 204,
    206, 211, 224, 230, 233, 277–8, 291
  and Macaulay, 124–5, 162–5, 173, 175–6,
    224
  price, 172
  proofs, 169, 193, 195, 205
  Roosevelt and, 189
  sales and earnings, 125–6, 128, 146, 150,
    153–4, 175–6, 180, 188
  serialisation, 126, 178, 193
  and Trevelyan, 162–4, 166, 175–7, 187
  and War of the Spanish Succession, 177,
    190
  work schedule, 167–71
  writing and publication, 124–9, 132–3,
    138–9, 141–4, 149–95, 279–80
Marlborough House set, 17–18
Marrakesh, 131, 136, 198, 279
Marsh, Edward, 73, 122, 149, 169, 280, 299
  and *History*, 199–200, 205, 210, 212,
    220, 222, 234, 237–8
Marvell, Andrew, 246
Marx, Karl, 173
Maugham, Somerset, 62, 73, 134–5, 140
Mee, Arthur, 96
Melbourne *Argus*, 92
Menzies, Robert, 259
Mill, John Stuart, 84, 87
Milne, A. A., 73
Milner, Lord, xvi, 107, 109
Milton, John, 107, 254
Moir, Anthony, 282, 286–7
Monroe Doctrine, 100
Moran, Lord, 196, 273, 281, 283
Morley, John, 174, 189
Morning Post, 44–5, 51–2, 82
Motley, J. L., 87, 104, 217, 224
Mowat, R. B., 114–15, 202
Moyne, Lord, 170–1, 179
MPs' salaries, 7–8
Muir, Ramsay, 112, 114–15, 139, 156–7, 260
Munich agreement, 198, 205, 208, 215, 252
Murrow, Edward R., 294

Mussolini, Benito, 269
My African Journey, 67
My Early Life (*A Roving Commission*), 41,
  79, 122–3, 130, 132–3, 141–2, 144, 188
  education, 14–15
  financial affairs, 36–7
  Greece–Turkey war, 38
  interview with Lord Salisbury, 43
  Leo Amery, 156
Myers, A. R., 285

Namier, Lewis, 172–4
Napoleonic Wars, 202, 245, 253, 255
National government, 145, 155, 180, 197
National Insurance Act, 66
National Trust, 131, 274
Nelson, Admiral Horatio, 253
New York Times, xv, 88, 92, 184, 278–9
  and English-speaking peoples, 81–2
New York *World*, 47
New Zealand, 89, 201, 236–7, 259
Newcastle-upon-Tyne, 86, 92
News of the World, 149, 153, 185
Nicolson, Harold, 132–3, 249–50
Nile campaign, 43, 45, 206
Nobel Prize for Literature, ix, 173, 294–5
Norman Conquest, 207–8, 217–18, 223
Normandy, 234
North Africa, 257, 261, 265
Northcote, Sir Stafford, 20–1, 25
Northern Echo, 94
Norway campaign, 241–2

old-age pensions, 66
Oldham, 11–12, 50–1, 53
Oliver, Vic, 184
Omdurman, battle of, 44, 48
opinion polls, 250, 269
Ottawa Agreements, 155, 258
Oudenarde, battle of, 5, 187
Over-Seas Club, 108
Owen, Commander J. H., 168, 177, 280
Oxford University, 15, 57, 76, 181, 277, 279

Paget, John, 124, 164
Paine, Tom, 85
Pakenham-Walsh, Colonel R. P., 168, 177,
  187, 280
Pall Mall Gazette, 94

Palmerston, Lord, 84
Panama, 101
Parkman, Francis, 168
Parliament Act, 109
Parnell, Charles Stewart, 19–20, 22
Pauncefote, Sir Julian, 100–1, 114
Payne, Raymond, 135
Pearl Harbor, 8, 257, 264
Pearman, Violet, 131, 168–9, 184–5, 195–6
Peel, Robert, 297
Pennington, D. H., 285
Pennsylvania, 207, 221
People's Rights, The, 66
perpetual pensions, 5–7, 21, 61
Peshawar, 42
Petition of Right, 226, 229, 255
Philip, Terence, 171
Philippines, 101
Pilgrims Society, xvi
Placentia Bay, 263
Plumb, J. H., 285, 289–90
Plymouth colony, 227
Poland, 205, 232, 236
Porch, Montagu, 69
Pownall, General Sir Henry, 279
Prague, 222
Pretoria, 52
Prohibition, 96
prostitution, 95
Punch, 23
Putnam, George Haven, 188–9
Pym, John, 226

Quebec conferences, 272
Queen Elizabeth, 277

racehorses, 10–11
Ramillies, battle of, 5, 177–9, 187
rationing, 268
Reagan, Ronald, xix
Reform Act, 12–13, 86
Reves, Emery, 198, 278, 284, 290
Reynolds, Professor David, 277
Rhineland crisis, 185, 189
Rhodes, Cecil, xvi, 95, 108
Richard III, King, 207, 283
Riddell, Lord, 149
River War, The, 44, 46, 48, 57
Roman Empire, decline of, 49

Romans, 214–16
Roose, Dr Robson, 28–9
Roosevelt, Franklin D., ix–x, xv, 113, 152,
    189, 197, 233, 248, 262–3, 266–9, 293
Roosevelt, Theodore, x–xi, 99–100, 105
Rosaura, 171, 219
Rose, Norman, 290
Rosebery, Lord, xvi, 16, 27, 29, 33–4, 53,
    57–8, 62, 171, 189
  and 'commonwealth of nations', 89–90,
    92
  and Marlborough, 124, 164
Rothermere, Lord, 136, 147, 153, 158, 185,
    195, 219
Rothschild, Lord, 11, 38
Round Table group, 109, 112
Roving Commission, A, see My Early Life
Rowse, A. L., 285
Royal Air Force, 257
Royal Albert Hall, xv, 81, 108
Royal Navy, xiii, 183, 238, 246
Royal Titles Act, 89
royalties, 55, 151
Russell, Lord, 85
Russia, 250–1, 254, 257, 266
Russian pogroms, 96

Sackville-West, Vita, 132–3
Salisbury, Lord, 25–6, 31, 43, 50, 58, 101
Sandhurst, 30
Savrola, xi, 45–6, 49, 67
Sayers, Dorothy L., 73
Schenk, General R. C., 87–8
Scotland, 209
Scott, C. P., 111
Scott, Walter, 129
Scribner, Charles, xiv, 105, 125–6, 132,
    140–4, 150, 172, 181, 187–8, 194
Second World War, The
  The Gathering Storm, x, xiii, 131, 198,
    236
  sales and earnings, 278–80, 282
  and the 'Syndicate', 279–80
  Triumph and Tragedy, 280–1
  writing and publication, 251, 273–4,
    277–81, 294
Seeley, J. R., 89–90, 92, 97, 99
Seven Years War, 228, 231, 235, 237
Shakespeare, William, 93, 100, 214, 249

Shaw, Bernard, 110, 173–4
Sherman, General William, 83–4
Shock, Maurice, 285
Singapore, fall of, 254, 265
Siwertz, Sigfrid, 294–5
Slosson, Preston, 114, 202
Smith, Adam, 168
Smith, F. E., 105
Smith, Goldwin, 90–2
Soames, Christopher, 274, 281–2
Social Darwinism, 99, 102, 104
South Africa, 11, 52–3, 65, 89, 201
South African War, xvi, 50–2, 59, 95, 101,
	206
Spanish Armada, 253
Spanish-American War, xvi
'special relationship', xix, 82, 277, 291–2
Stalin, Josef, ix, 259, 268
Statute of Westminster, 112
Stead, W. T., 94–5
Step by Step, 197–9
Stevenson, Robert Louis, 14
Stowe, Harriet Beecher, 93
Strakosch, Sir Henry, 141, 186–7, 197
Stuart, James Edward (the 'Old
	Pretender'), 164
Stubbs, William, 97, 99, 224
Sudan, 43–4, 48
Sudetenland, 205
Sumner, Senator Charles, 87
Sunday Times, 178, 193
Sunderland, Earls of, 6–7
Surtees, R. S., 16
Swat Valley, 39, 43
syphilis, 27–30

Tariff Reform, 60, 92, 154–5
taxation, 116–22, 148–9, 233, 273, 297–300
Taylor, A. J. P., 134
Teheran conference, 267
Tennyson, Lord, 93
Thatcher, Margaret, xix
Thornton, A. P., 285
Thoughts and Adventures (Amid These
	Storms), 144
Times, The, 22, 25, 39, 76, 92, 199
	and English-speaking peoples, 81–2
Titanic, 95
Tobruk, 265

Toronto, 91–2
Tory Democracy, 11–12, 24–6, 30–3, 40,
	50, 62, 86
Trafalgar, battle of, 237
Treaty of Ghent, 107
Treaty of Washington, 88
Trevelyan, G. M., 140, 162–4, 166, 175–7,
	187
Trollope, Anthony, 281
Truman, Harry S., 102
Turf Club, 175
Turkey, 38, 68, 75
Twain, Mark, 53, 93

unemployment insurance, 66
unemployment, 154–5
United States of America
	and annexation of Canada, 87, 91–2,
		99–100
	battlefields, 128, 207, 221
	Churchill's lecture tours, 53–4, 142,
		146–7
	and English-speaking peoples, 83–115,
		293
	entry into war, 257–9, 261–6
	and Greater Britain, 89
	isolationism, 112–13, 258
	and literature, 93
	and manifest destiny, 99–100
	and 'special relationship', xix, 82, 277,
		291–2
US Congress, 8, 221, 264–5

Van Antwerp, William, 127–8
Venezuela, 100
Venice, 130
Victoria, Queen, 89, 220
Vikings, 207, 213, 217
Villa Mauresque, 135, 140
Virginia, 207, 214, 221
Voltaire, 161
	Candide, 281

Wall Street Crash, 128–9, 131, 144
Walpole, Robert, 174
war cabinet, 233, 238, 243, 245, 248, 250
War of 1812, 202
War of the Spanish Succession, 177, 190
Wars of the Roses, 290

Washington, George, 103, 105, 183, 228, 265
Washington Post, 82, 147
Waterloo, battle of, 13, 228, 237
Watson, J. Steven, 285
Waugh, Evelyn, 165, 246
Welles, Orson, 127
Wellington, Duke of, 228
Wells, H. G., 135, 140
wergild, 212
Westminster Abbey, 27
Wharncliffe, Lord, 84
Wheeler, Mortimer, 208, 210
Wheldon, John, 169, 177–8, 191, 199, 220
While England Slept, see Arms and the Covenant
Whitman, Walt, 66, 93
Wilde, Oscar, 110
William III, King, 138, 164, 220
William, Prince, Duke of Cambridge, 6–7
Wilson, Woodrow, ix, 94, 111, 113
Windsor, Duke of, *see* Edward VIII, King
Wolfe, General James, 230–1

Wood, C. C., 169, 172, 192–3, 205, 218, 222, 280
Wood, J., 282
Woodstock, 11–14, 24, 85
World Crisis, The
  abridged edition, 142, 144
  The Aftermath, 120
  critical reception, 79, 119–20
  The Eastern Front (The Unknown War), 132–3, 139, 141–3, 145, 149
  sales and earnings, 76, 79, 117–20, 144, 297–8
  selective deletions, 75
  serialisation, 76
  writing and publication, 74–6, 114, 123–6, 132–3, 141–5, 152
Wrench, John Evelyn, 108, 110

Yalta conference, 267, 268, 275
Young, G. M., 199–200, 205, 212–17, 220–2, 226, 229, 231, 233–4, 237–8, 248, 270, 285